The Geography of the World-Economy

Paul Knox
Professor, Urban Affairs Program
Virginia Polytechnic Institute and State University

AND

John Agnew
Professor, Social Science Program, Syracuse University

Edward Arnold
A division of Hodder & Stoughton
LONDON NEW YORK MELBOURNE AUCKLAND

For Anne-Lise, Katie and Christine

© 1989 Paul L Knox and John Agnew

First published in Great Britain 1989
Reprinted 1990 (twice)

Distributed in the USA by Routledge, Chapman and Hall, Inc.
29 West 35th Street, New York, NY 10001

British Library Cataloguing in Publication Data

Knox, Paul L. (Paul Leslie), *1947 –*
   The geography of the world –
   economy
   1. Economic conditions. Geographical aspects
   I. Title
   330.9′048

   ISBN 0–7131–6517–0

Typeset in 10/12 point California by Colset Private Limited,
Singapore
Printed and bound in Great Britain for Edward Arnold, a division
of Hodder and Stoughton Limited, Mill Road, Dunton Green,
Sevenoaks, Kent TN13 2YA by Bookcraft, Avon

Contents

Acknowledgements

The publishers would like to thank the following for permission to include copyright material:

Addison-Wesley Publishers Ltd for figure 10.2 adapted from *Industry and Underdevelopment* by R B Sutcliffe, published by Addison-Wesley Publishing Company 1971; The American Geographical Society for figure 2.12 from 'Regional inequalities in well-being in Costa Rica' by Hall published in *Geographical Review* 74:1984 and figures 5.4 and 5.5 from 'The urban and industrial transformation of Japan' by Harris published in *Geographical Review* 72:1982 and figure 8.8 from 'Transport Expansion in undeveloped countries' by Taaffe, Morrill and Gould published in *Geographical Review* 1963; Edward Arnold for figure 2.11 from *Changing Places: Britain's Demographic Economic and Social Complexion* by Champion, Green, Owen, Ellin and Coombes and for figure 4.1 from *An Introduction to Urban Historical Geography* by H Carter; Basil Blackwell for figure 8.12 from *A World in Crisis* by R J Johnston and P J Taylor; Cambridge University Press for figure 3.4 from *The United States in the World-Economy: A Regional Geography* by Agnew and figure 8.3 from *The United States and Africa: A History* by Duignan and Gann and figure 9.2 from *Farm Labour* by Swindell and figure 10.7 from 'The semi-conductor industry in South-East Asia: organization, location, and the international division of labour' by Scott published in *Regional Studies* 21 (1987) p 150; The University of Chicago Press for figure 2.16 based on fig. 1 from 'Some indicators of stability in the growth of cities in the US' by Madden published in *Economic Development and Cultural Change* 4 (1956); The Economist for figure 8.13 from *The Economist* 24 September 1983; Gower Publishing Group for figure 5.7 from *International Economic Restructuring and the Regional Community* by H Muegge and W B Stohr; Harper & Row and Paul Chapman Publishing Ltd for figure 6.5 and figure 3.5 from *Global*

Shift by Peter Dicken; The Johns Hopkins University Press for figure 2.14 from *China* by World Bank 1985 and figure 9.3 from *State and Countryside: Development Policy and Agrarian Politics in Latin America* by Grindle; Longman Group UK for figure 5.3 from *The US: A Contemporary Human Geography* by Knox *et al.* and figures 8.1 and 8.2 from *Political Geography: World Economy, Nation, State and Locality* by Taylor; Macmillan Publishers Ltd for figures 6.2 and 12.1 from *The Geography of De-Industrialisation* (eds) Martin and Rowthorn and figures 4.2 and 4.4 from *The European Past: Social Evolution and Spatial Order* by Dodgshon; Macmillan Publishers and St Martin's Press for figure 5.9 from *Long Waves Regional Development* by M Marshall; McGraw-Hill Publishing Company for figures 3.1 and 3.2 from *Man's Economic Environment* by Conkling and Yeates; Methuen & Co for figures 8.10, 8.11, 10.1 and 11.1 from *The Fragmented World: Competing Perspectives on Trade, Money and Crisis* by Edwards and figure 8.9 from 'The River Plate Countries' by Crossley published in *Latin America: Geographical Perspectives* 2nd edition by Blakemoor and Smith and figure 9.1 from *The Politics of Hunger* by Warnock; W W Norton for figure 4.3 from *Before the Industrial Revolution: European Society and Economy, 1000–1700*, Second Edition by Carlo M Cipolla by permission of W W Norton & Company, Inc Copyright © 1980, 1976 by W W Norton & Company Inc; Open University Press for figures 10.5 and 10.6 from *The Third World Atlas* Open University Press 1983; Oxford University Press for figure 5.1 from *Peaceful Conquest: The Industrialization of Europe* by S Pollard published by Oxford University Press 1981; Penguin Books Ltd for figure 8.4 from *Industry and Empire* by E J Hobsbawm (Penguin Books, 1969) copyright © E J Hobsbawm, 1968, 1969; Pergamon Press for figures 6.1 and 6.6 from 'Industrial restructuring: an international problem' by Hamilton published in *Geoforum* 15 (1984); Simon and Schuster Ltd for figure 5.2 from *Underdeveloped Europe* by Seers, Schafer and Kilijunen; Unwin Hyman for figure 1.2 from *The World Economy in Transition* by Beenstock; Van Gorcum & Company for figure 10.9 from *The Third World in Perspective* by Reitsma and Kleinpenning; Westview Press for figure 10.8 from *Urbanization and Urban Politics in Pacific Asia* by Fuchs and Pernia.

Every effort has been made to trace copyright holders of material reproduced in this book. Any rights not acknowledged here will be acknowledged in subsequent printings if notice is given to the publisher.

We are indebted to many of our colleagues for their advice and encouragement at various stages in the conception and preparation of this book. We would particularly like to recognize Stuart Corbridge, Raymundo Cota, Bob Dyck, Larry Grossman, Soo-Seong Lee, Ragnhild Lund, Sallie Marston, Ezzedinne Moudoud, Pritti Ramamurthy, Bon Richardson, Freddy Robles, and David Short for their contributions. Todd Logan and Michael Kirkhoff of the Syracuse University Cartographic Laboratory drafted many of the figures.

Part One

Economic Patterns and the Search for Explanation

In this first part of the book, we introduce the scope and complexity of our subject matter, establish the salient patterns in the world's economic landscapes, and review alternative theoretical approaches to understanding the development of these patterns. Chapter 1 provides an orientation for the whole book by outlining the relationships between economic organization and spatial change. In Chapter 2, the major dimensions of the world's contemporary economic landscapes are described at various scales: international, regional and inter-urban. The objective here is to identify dominant and recurring patterns and to note the major exceptions to these patterns. Both the patterns and the exceptions raise a number of critical questions about process and theory in economic geography. What are the locational principles that govern patterns of economic activity? How should the development process be conceptualized? What are the processes that initiate and sustain spatial inequalities? These are pursued in Chapter 3. First, a critical review of ideas relating to the principles of distance and movement that are central to location theory is provided. Second, two major approaches to regional economic change – neo-classical economic/liberal models and structuralist models – are discussed. Finally, an historical–global context is presented. It is this context which provides the framework and orientation for the rest of the book.

1

Economic Organization and Spatial Change

As its title suggests, the perspective of this book is global. The reasons for this are twofold. First, the rapidly increasing interdependence of the world-economy means that the economic and social well-being of nations, regions and cities everywhere depends more and more on complex and volatile inter-actions that are framed at the global scale. Although local, regional and national circumstances remain very important, what happens to the economies of Australia, India, Nigeria and the United Kingdom; of Lombardy, New England, the Pampas and the Sahel; and of cities from Auckland, Bogotà and Cologne to Xi'an, Youngstown and Zagreb is deter-mined increasingly by their changing role in systems of production, trade and consumption which have become global in scope and complex in structure. We need a global perspective, therefore, not only to understand the world-economy but also to help interpret what might otherwise appear to be purely local or regional issues.

The second reason for pursuing a global perspective as an introduction to economic geography is that it enables us to merge what have hitherto been taught and researched a separate elements of human geography. In particu-lar, it enables us to bring together ideas from the geography of economic development – which has been dominated by a focus on the experience of less-developed countries (LDCs) – with ideas from the systematic study of resources, economic activity and economic behaviour – which have been dominated by the analysis of economic phenomena in western, industrialized countries and which constitute the subject matter of 'traditional' approaches to economic geography. Merging elements of both economic development and traditional economic geography allows us to develop a framework which, we argue, is not only sensitive to the increasing interdependence of the world economy but also to the shifts that have occurred within academic human geography. What we are alluding to here is the decreasing emphasis on quan-titative modelling, systems analysis and behavioural analysis and the increas-ing concern for a deeper understanding of the *processes* which create both the general context of spatial differentiation and local variability within this context.

The job of the student of economic geography is to make sense of the world – the real world – and the ways in which its economic landscapes are changing. How, then, can we cope, intellectually, with the local, regional and national implications of a succession of what are literally headline-making events? Acute unemployment in Detroit, Liverpool and Bochum. A rapidly escalating budget deficit in the United States. Debt repayments that are not only a crippling handicap to the economic development of many debtor LDCs but also a threat to the economic and political stability of creditor nations. Bitter trade disputes between developed and underdeveloped countries, between the United States and Europe, and between Japan and nearly every other trading nation. Three-digit inflation in parts of Africa and Latin America. Violent labour disputes in South Korea and Taiwan. Famine in Ethiopia. Switchback stock markets; and so on. Furthermore, how should we approach the local, regional and national implications of less newsworthy but equally profound changes in the world-economy: such as the remarkable developments that have taken place in international finance and banking; and the quiet but substantial increase that has taken place in East–West economic interaction? Most of all, how should we interpret the significance of specific changes that have been occurring in the world's economic landscapes: the deindustrialization of traditional manufacturing regions (e.g. northern England, the Ruhr), the economic revival of 'lagging' regions (e.g. New England, Bavaria), the spread of branch factories in the countryside of industrialized nations (e.g. East Anglia, Jutland) and in the towns and cities of some newly-industrializing nations (e.g. Taipei, Seoul), the emergence of high-technology complexes (e.g. Silicon Valley in California, Research Triangle in North Carolina), and the consolidation of global financial and corporate control functions in a few cities (London, New York, Tokyo)?

In attempting to answer such questions, many of the methods, models and theories of 'traditional' economic geography seem to fall short. The traditional approach to 'economic regions' has been undermined as the very constitution of 'urban' and 'regional' scales have been radically redefined through advances in telecommunications and the speed and volatility of economic restructuring. Moreover, studying 'economic regions' invites the danger of confusing appearance with explanation and, at best, tends to abstract regions from their context. On the other hand, traditional approaches to systematic economic geography (locational analysis, etc.), because they rest so heavily on the assumptions of neo-classical economics (and in particular the assumption of rational behaviour on the part of firms and individuals), have become less convincing as the power and significance of monopolistic and oligopolistic elements and of national and regional governments have become more apparent in shaping economic landscapes. Moreover, the normative approaches of neo-classical economic models tend to make for an unfortunate bias towards the general and away from the variability that characterizes the 'real world'.

Nevertheless, it would be imprudent to throw out the baby with the bathwater. Traditional approaches may fall short but they are by no means without merit. We can gain useful insights from traditional approaches to economic geography if we can set them within a broader, more flexible and more dynamic perspective. That perspective can be provided by the political economy approach inherent in economic development theory. Political economy can properly claim to deal with economic and social relations rather than hypothetical actors, with the spheres of production and consumption as well as the arena of exchange, with tensions, conflict and crisis rather than equilibrium, and with an historical dimension rather than without one. The task, as Johnston (1984) has pointed out, is to develop an understanding both of the general economic forces and socio-economic relationships within the world-economy *and* of the unique features that represent local and historical variability. Following Johnston, we should clarify here the use of 'general' and 'unique'. By 'general' we mean something that is universally applicable within the domain to which it refers. By 'unique' we mean something which is distinctive, because there is no other instance of it, but whose distinctiveness *can be accounted for* by a particular combination of general processes and individual responses. For those phenomena that are distinctive but entirely remarkable because no general statements can be made in reference to them, we can use the term 'singular'. With this perspective, as Johnston observes, 'the world is our oyster':

> There is but one world-economy, to which all places are linked, to a greater or lesser degree. That economy and the ways in which it operates – almost independently now of the human societies that created it – provide the framework within which regional differences have evolved and are evolving. What is done, where and how, reflect human interpretations of how land should be used. These interpretations are shaped through cultural lenses (which may be locally created, or may be imported); they reflect reactions to both the local physical environment and the international economic situation; they are mediated by local institutional structures; they are influenced by the historical context; and they change that context, hence the environment for future interpretations. Unique they certainly are. Singular they are not. (Johnston, 1984, p. 446)

Furthermore, Johnston notes, such a perspective, while placing the world-economy in a central role, is not to be equated with economic determinism. 'Economic, political, social and cultural activities are all inter-related in a world-system whose trajectory is guided through decisions made by knowing individuals, constrained but not determined by their context, and enabled by their knowledge to make decisions that will restructure that context' (Johnston,1984, p. 444).

From such a perspective we can begin to establish some of the central inter-relationships surrounding economic organization and spatial change (Fig. 1.1). At this level of abstraction, the idea of 'economic organization' approximates to the concept of 'mode of production': the way in which human societies organize their productive activities and thereby reproduce their socio-economic life. The theoretical and historical identification of different modes of production is a difficult and controversial matter, but there are five

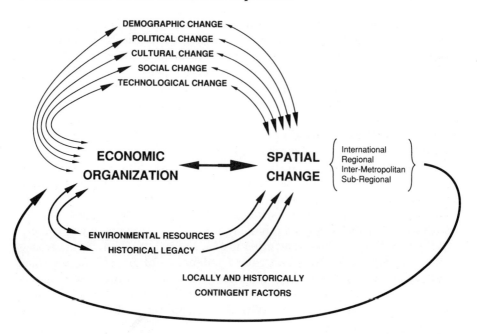

Fig 1.1   The inter-relationships surrounding economic organization and spatial change

major modes of production, or forms of economic organization, that are commonly recognized: subsistence, slavery, feudalism (or rank-redistribution), capitalism and socialism. These are all broad categories, however, and each can be broken down into more specific forms of economic organization. It is often useful, for example, to differentiate between merchant capitalism (or mercantilism), industrial capitalism (or competitive capitalism), and advanced capitalism; and it is sometimes useful, as we shall see in Chapter 5, to subdivide each of these still further. What distinguishes one mode of production from another most are differences in the relations between the *factors of production* (land, resources, labour, capital, enterprise). With the slave mode of production, for example, the labourer is bought and sold, along with other instruments of production, by the slave owner. Under feudalism, the peasant labourer may own some of the instruments of production, but the land and a certain amount of the product is the property of the feudal lord and the peasant is legally tied to a specific tract of land. Under capitalism, the labourer owns no instruments of production but is free to sell his or her labour power. It should be noted, however, that different modes of production are also characterized by different forces of production (technology, machinery, means of transportation) and by different social formations (made up of specific proportions of different social classes).

Economic Change and Economic Landscapes

The significance of all this to spatial change is that the economic 'logic' of different modes of production requires substantially different forms of spatial organization. Thus, for example, whereas feudalism brings a patchwork of self-sufficient domains with little trade and, therefore, few market centres, merchant capitalism requires a highly developed system of market towns and brings a built-in tendency for the colonization of new territories (in order to furnish new resources and bigger markets). Industrial capitalism requires spatial restructuring in order to exploit new energy sources, new production techniques and new forms of corporate organization. New mining and manu-facturing towns appear, and whole regions become specialized in production. It is, of course, much more complicated than this, as we show in subsequent chapters. In addition, there are no definitive forms of spatial organization that can be associated with particular modes of production. Just as each mode of production is a dynamic, evolving set of relationships, so economic land-scapes are restructured and reorganized to reflect, articulate, and, sometimes, constrain the evolution of the economic dynamo.

It should also be stressed that there is no set sequence of transformation from one mode of production to another, although the 'classic' sequence, as experi-enced in much of western Europe, runs from subsistence economies through slavery, feudalism, merchant capitalism and industrial capitalism to advanced capitalism. Largely because capitalism first developed in Europe and because the 'logic' of capitalism requires ever-expanding markets, the sequence elsewhere has been different. In North America, capitalism was imposed directly on subsistence (i.e. native American) economies. In Japan, feudalism was displaced very suddenly by state-sponsored industrial capital-ism. In the Soviet Union, an embryonic industrial capitalism was displaced by a socialism which soon gave way to state capitalism; and so on. As a result, regional variations have come about within the world-economy because par-ticular modes of production – and their economic landscapes – are super-imposed on a variety of pre-existing forms, some of whose characteristics become obliterated but many of which persist as legacies which add to, and often modify, the new order.

More spatial change, and further regional differentiation, occurs with the evolution of a particular mode of production. Take, for example, industrial capitalism. As Massey (1984) has shown, each phase of capital accumulation, or 'round of investment' under industrial capitalism involves the allocation of different functions within the relations of production (e.g. headquarters offices, branch factories) to different regions within the national and inter-national space-economy. Gregory (1987) has attempted to clarify this by way of an analogy with a game of cards (Fig. 1.2). In the first round, a single suit is dealt (representing a phase of capital accumulation), and each player (region) receives a different card (representing a different economic function: head office, regional office or branch plant). In the second and third rounds, other single suits are dealt. As one phase of capital accumulation is succeeded by

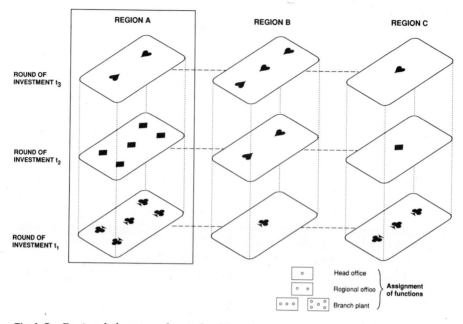

Fig 1.2   Regional change and rounds of investment
Source: Gregory (1987) Fig. 2, p. 8.

another, so the structure of local economies can be seen as the product of the combination of layers; of the successive imposition over the years of new rounds of investment and new forms of activity.

> Similarly, at the end of three rounds of our game, each player has a different hand: but in each case this is connected 'horizontally' to the hands held by other players and 'vertically' to the cards dealt in the previous rounds. In much the same way a local economy may, through the mix of its activities, be embedded in a multitude of 'horizontal' spatial structures, each of which entails different relations of domination and subordination put into place during previous rounds of investment (Gregory, 1987, p. 9).

It follows that the same round of investment can produce very different effects in different regions as a result of its combination with different pre-existing structures.

At a still more detailed level of resolution, further regional differences develop as different social, cultural and political contexts – themselves a product, in large part, of particular sequences and stages of economic organization – affect the ways in which people react to the economic imperatives of particular modes of production. Thus, for example, different forms of land tenure (e.g. corporate-owned, family-owned, rented) can develop within the capitalist mode of production, with very different outcomes in terms of patterns of land use. In addition, different socio-cultural contexts make for different interpretations of environmental possibilities, desirable products and marketable opportunities; so that a particular regional agricultural landscape must be seen as just one of a number of possible realizations. It cannot be seen as a simple reflection of a particular mode of production. Rather, it should be interpreted as the product of the combination of broad economic forces inter-acting with local social, cultural, political and environmental factors: a pro-duct of both the 'general' and the 'unique'.

While this example is drawn at the regional scale, the same argument applies to other spatial scales, as Figure 1.1 suggests. Questions of spatial scale and the interactions between economic organization and spatial change are, however, only part of the complexity that must be addressed by the student of economic geography. Figure 1.1 also shows that economic organization, while critical to spatial change, is itself implicated with demographic, politi-cal, cultural, social and technological change, as both cause and effect. For the moment, it must be sufficient to give brief examples of each. In relation to *demographic* change, for instance, it has long been recognized that the par-ticular form of economic organization represented by industrial capitalism brought with it certain demands on the organization of people's daily lives, demands which eventually affected patterns of family organization, house-hold size, and patterns of residential mobility. Meanwhile, we must also recognize that demographic change can directly affect economic or-ganization. Rapidly decreasing death rates in underdeveloped countries, for example, have created massive excesses of labour which have induced eco-nomic 'involution' (the creation of 'survival' occupations in an 'informal' sec-tor of the economy).

As an example of the effects of economic organization on *political* change, we can draw on the macro-scale example of the dramatic change in the world political framework as colonies were imposed on Latin America, Africa and Asia with the evolution and extension of merchant capitalism. As for an example of political change affecting economic organization, there is the recent experience of the rise of the 'new conservatism' in the United States and the United Kingdom, where conservative administrations were elected at the beginning of the 1980s with a mandate to privatize public industry, 'deregulate' private industry, cut back on welfare-related expenditures, and expand defence budgets. This same example provides us with examples of more direct effects of political change on spatial change. Defence expendi-tures have had significant effects on local economies within the American 'sunbelt', while welfare cutbacks have been very uneven in their impact, affecting most of all the concentrations of low-income and service-dependent households in the inner-city neighbourhoods of industrial regions.

One of the most celebrated examples of the effects of economic organization on *cultural* change is the penetration by advanced capitalism of the tradi-tional cultures of underdeveloped countries. Along with the western colas, fast foods and consumer products that come with participation in the modern world-economy have come changes in attitudes, values and life-styles. Mean-while, the 'counterculture' associated with western 'baby boomers' during their college years (the late 1960s) has evolved into an important component of the emergent 'postmodern' culture that is beginning to affect economic organization as changed life-styles and consumer preferences carry over into the market place and changed attitudes to work carry over into labour markets.

As an example of *social* change brought about by economic change, the best example is also the most important. This is the way that changes in economic organization necessarily recast the structure of social classes. Thus the onset of industrial capitalism brought with it a fundamental change in class structure, with a new blue-collar class of factory workers, a much-expanded middle class of white-collar workers, a new upper middle-class of professional workers, and a new élite of factory owners. In comparison, examples of economic organization being affected by social change seem less significant. They are, nevertheless, important to the dynamics of economic change and to the detail of economic landscapes. The social changes that have occurred in the United States in terms of people's perceptions of, and behaviour towards, racial minorities, for example, have clearly carried over to affect labour markets, occupational composition, and the racial composition of particular regions and neighbourhoods.

There are many different examples of the relationships between economic organization and *technological* change; though it is often difficult to disentangle cause and effect. Many technological changes, while not causing or being caused by changes in economic organization, are *preconditions* for change: the improved textile manufacturing technologies of the late eighteenth century, for example. Sometimes, however, there are direct relationships. Changes in birth control technology (the introduction of contraceptive pills) in the 1960s, for example, have had a profound effect in many western countries, not only in demographic terms but also in terms of women's participation in the workforce and the consequent changes in patterns of trade union membership, corporate hiring policies, and wages.

It will be appreciated, of course, that all of these examples have been presented briefly and, therefore, rather simplistically, in an attempt to illustrate the diversity of inter-relationships that surround the central dynamic between economic organization and spatial change. It will also be appreciated that we have said nothing about the many interactions between, for example, political change and cultural change, or between locally contingent factors and spatial change. The point to emphasize at the moment is that all these direct, indirect and interaction effects are important to an understanding of spatial change. They are all implicated, in other words, in accounting for both the general and the unique. The task of the economic geographer is to unravel these relationships within a coherent and comprehensive framework. The remainder of this book represents an attempt to provide such a framework. We begin, in Chapter 2, by establishing the major dimensions of the contemporary economic landscapes within the world-economy. In Chapter 3 we review the ideas and theories that address these outcomes, drawing on both traditional economic geography and economic development theory before setting out a more comprehensive global-historical framework which serves as the context for the rest of the book. In Part II, we trace the emergence of the world's core economies – Europe, North America and Japan – following their different paths towards increasing scale and complexity. Part III deals with the world outside the core of the world-economy, paying special attention to the spatial transformations that have occurred as a consequence of the colonialism and global capitalism emanating from the core economies, and to the role of agriculture and manufacturing industry in economic development and spatial change. Finally, in Part IV, we examine some of the reactions to the emergence of ever-larger and more powerful economic forces that have come to characterize the world-economy, describing the spatial consequences of transnational political and economic integration and of decentralist reactions: nationalism, regionalism and grassroots movements towards economic democracy.

2

Patterns in the Economic Landscape

Geography is about local variability within a general context.

R.J.Johnston (1984, p. 444)

In this chapter, we describe the major dimensions of the contemporary economic landscape at various scales: international, regional, and inter-urban. Space does not permit anything like a full coverage of patterns of economic activity or of the quilt of economic development, let alone a systematic review, resource by resource, industry by industry, flow by flow of commodities, services and capital. Such a catalogue, in any case, is not our purpose. Rather, our objective is to identify dominant and recurring patterns and to note the major exceptions to these patterns. We are, in other words, concerned primarily with characterizing the *general context* referred to by Johnston in the quote above. To the extent that we identify exceptions and contradictions, we are also concerned to some degree with *local variability*. In subsequent chapters our objective will be to uncover the processes that have contributed to these patterns – both the general and the locally distinctive or unique. As we shall see, it is the interaction of the unique with the general that produces distinctive regions – economic regions or other kinds – at whatever scale.

International Patterns

It has been widely recognized for several decades that the dominant components of economic geography at the global scale are cast in terms of core–periphery differences. Meier and Baldwin (1957) were perhaps the earliest writers to attempt a conceptual description of this core–periphery structure on a global scale. According to them, a country is at the centre of the world economy if it plays a dominant, active role in world trade. Usually such a country is a rich, market-type economy of the primarily industrial or agricultural-industrial variety. Foreign trade revolves around it: it is a large exporter and importer, and the international movement of capital normally occurs from it to other countries.

In contrast, they argued, a country could be considered peripheral

if it plays a secondary or passive role in world trade. In terms of their domestic characteristics, peripheral countries may be market-type economies or subsistence-type economies. The common feature of a peripheral economy is its external dependence on the centre as the source of a large proportion of imports, as the destination for a large proportion of exports, and as a lender of capital. (Meier and Baldwin, 1957, p. 147)

This cleavage of the economic world into two interdependent but highly unequal camps was echoed more recently by the Brandt Report (Independent Commission on International Development Issues, 1980, 1983), where core–periphery contrasts were cast in terms of 'North' and 'South'. The North includes the industrialized countries of North America, Europe (East and West), the Soviet Union, Japan, Australia and New Zealand; the South includes China and all of the countries of Latin America, Africa, the Middle East, South Asia and South-East Asia. By this definition the South has over 3.75 billion people – three-quarters of the world's population – living on one-fifth of the world's income. But, as the Report notes,

It is not just that the North is so much richer than the South. Over 90 per cent of the world's manufacturing industry is in the North. Most patents and new technology are the property of multinational corporations of the North, which conduct a large share of world investment and world trade in raw materials and manufactures. Because of this economic power Northern countries dominate the international economic system – its rules and regulations, and its international institutions of trade, money and finance (p. 32).

Figure 2.1 shows the North-South divide of the 'Brandt line' superimposed on a map of Gross National Product (GNP) per capita: one of the most widely used international economic indicators. The core–periphery contrast is very clear. A glance at the map shows that the burden of poverty lies heavily across the peripheral regions of Asia, Africa and Latin America. The extreme cases include countries such as Bangladesh, Chad and Ethiopia, where, in 1984, per capita GNP was around US$110. Altogether, some 2,400 million people live in countries where per capita GNP was less than US$400 in 1984. Yet not all of the South exhibits low levels of national economic output. Oil-rich countries like Saudi Arabia, Iran, Libya and Venezuela, together with one or two small export-processing countries like Hong Kong and Singapore, are comparable, in terms of GNP per capita, with some of the advanced industrial nations of the North. And countries like Brazil, Chile, Malaysia, Uruguay and South Africa, with favourable resource endowments, vigorous export industries and a degree of economic diversification, generate a GNP per capita that is around ten times that of their regional neighbours. Meanwhile, it should be

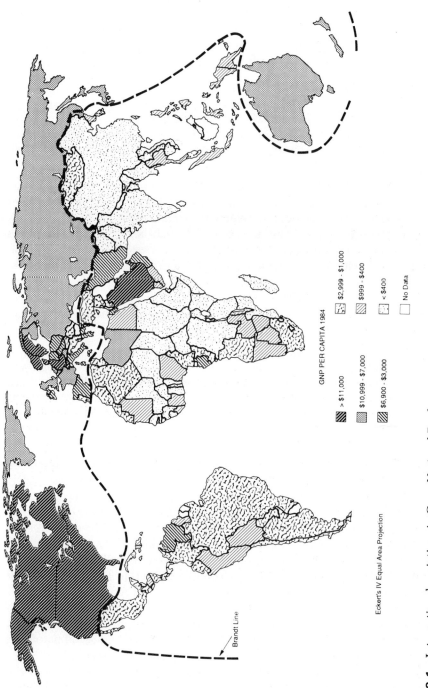

GNP PER CAPITA 1984

> $11,000

$10,999 - $7,000

$6,900 - $3,000

$2,999 - $1,000

$999 - $400

< $400

No Data

Eckert's IV Equal Area Projection

Brandt Line

Fig 2.1 International variations in Gross National Product per capita, 1984

acknowledged that there is also considerable variability within the North: GNP per capita is less than US$2,000, for example, in Hungary, Portugal and Yugoslavia; around US$10,000 in France and Japan; and over US$15,000 in the United States.

This variability, together with the very different forms of economic and political organization that exist in parts of the world, means that North–South or core–periphery contrasts are rather simplistic for many purposes. The World Bank, for example, divides the countries of the world into five main groups for statistical purposes:

Industrial market economies: all of the members of the Organization for Economic Co-operation and Development (OECD) [see Chapter 11], with the exception of Greece, Portugal and Turkey, which are included among the middle-income developing countries.

East European non-market economies: Albania, Bulgaria, Czechoslovakia, the German Democratic Republic, Hungary, Romania and the USSR.

High-income oil exporters: Bahrain, Brunei, Kuwait, Libya, Oman, Qatar, Saudi Arabia and the United Arab Emirates.

Low-income developing countries, with a 1984 GNP per capita of less than US$400.

Middle-income developing countries, with a 1984 GNP per capita of US$400 or more. These are subdivided into **oil exporters** (Algeria, Angola, Cameroon, the Congo, Ecuador, Egypt, Gabon, Indonesia, Iran, Iraq, Malaysia, Mexico, Nigeria, Peru, Syria, Trinidad and Tobago, Tunisia, and Venezuela) and **oil importers**. A subset of these middle-income oil importers, **major exporters of manufactures**, comprises Argentina, Brazil, Greece, Hong Kong, Israel, South Korea, the Philippines, Portugal, Singapore, South Africa, Thailand and Yugoslavia.

There are many other classifications of the world's economies, each based on different criteria and different sets of indicators. One other classification that should be mentioned here, however, is the division of the world into a *core*, a *semi-periphery* and a *periphery* (Fig. 2.2) in accordance with the perspective provided by the world-system theory of Immanuel Wallerstein (1984) and others. According to this perspective, the entire world economy is to be seen as an evolving capitalist market system in which the economic hierarchy of states is a product of the long-term economic cycles that dominate the dynamics of the system. It follows that the composition of this hierarchy is variable: countries can move from periphery to semi-periphery, core to periphery, and so on (Arrighi and Drangel, 1986). The labels 'core' and 'periphery' refer to the dominant *processes* operating in particular places. Core processes are characterized by economic relations that incorporate relatively high wages, advanced technology and a diversified production mix, whereas periphery processes involve low wages, more rudimentary technology and a simple production mix. The label 'semi-periphery' refers to places where there is, at present, a mix of both sets of processes. In essence, semi-peripheral countries

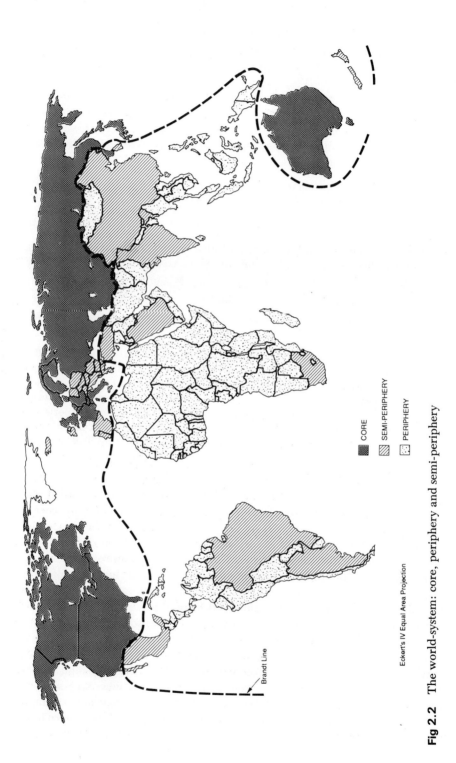

Brandt Line

Eckert's IV Equal Area Projection

CORE

SEMI-PERIPHERY

PERIPHERY

Fig 2.2 The world-system: core, periphery and semi-periphery

are seen as exploiting peripheral countries while being exploited by core countries. Figure 2.2 represents an attempt to capture the current composition of the three categories, based on the methodology of Timberlake and Lunday (1985), which uses an index that combines total GNP and GNP per capita. Countries with high scores on these two criteria, they suggest, are likely to have politically strong states, large internal markets, and predominantly high-wage, capital-intensive production – all theoretically defining characteristics of core status. Conversely, countries with a low national economic output and a low GNP per capita are likely to have weak states, and predominantly low-wage, labour-intensive production. These are rather sweeping assumptions; and the allocation of individual countries to particular categories can be somewhat arbitrary, being based on 'natural' breaks in the magnitude of the index scores. What is important in the present context is to recognize that the division of the world into a core, a semi-periphery and a periphery in this way represents more than an alternative classification of countries: it is a reflection of a particular conception of the dynamics of the world economy.

We shall be examining world-system theory in more detail in Chapter 3. It will by now have become clear, however, that major international economic cleavages, however categorized or labelled not only reflect differences in prosperity but also reflect different forms of economic organization, different kinds of resource bases, different demographic characteristics, different political systems, and different roles in the system of international specialization and trade. Defining and measuring development is therefore a difficult and contentious task. As we shall see, there are strong grounds for thinking in terms of *under*-development rather than development as far as the peripheral countries are concerned, since the term 'development' implies a trajectory of improvement, in both relative and absolute terms. This qualification notwithstanding, it is now widely accepted that development must be conceived in broad terms of social well-being. Narrowly economic definitions, while admirably precise, provide only part of the picture. They encompass changes in the amount, composition, rate of growth, distribution and consumption of resources but they do not extend to the effects these changes have on people's lives.

Development, then, should really be thought of not only in terms of income and consumption but also in terms of people's health, education, housing conditions, security, civil rights, and so on (Coates, Johnston and Knox, 1977; Hilhorst and Klatter, 1984). Seen in this light, development is clearly a normative concept, involving values, goals and standards that make it possible to compare a particular situation against a preferred one. It follows that development can properly be evaluated only in the context of the human needs and values as perceived by the very societies undergoing change. It also follows that although 'development' implies economic, social, political and cultural transformations, these should be seen not as ends in themselves but as means for enhancing social well-being and the quality of human life. In this book we shall be concerned with both the means and the ends, addressing our subject matter from a broad perspective that sees economic geography as the dynamic core of human geography. In the present context, this brings us first to an examination of some of the international patterns that reflect the 'means' of transformation: global patterns of resources, population, manufacturing, trade, investment, aid and debt. We shall then summarize the 'ends', or net outcomes, in terms of an overall typology of socio-economic development.

Resources and Population

The distribution of natural resources clearly has a very important influence on patterns of international economic activity and development. Not only are key resources – energy, minerals, cultivable land – unevenly distributed, but the *combination* of particular resources in particular nations and regions makes for a complex mosaic. Deficiencies in resources can, of course, be remedied through international trade (Japan is the prime example here: see p. 151); but for most countries the resource base is an important parameter of development.

In overall terms, a very high proportion of the world's non-renewable natural resources are concentrated in the Soviet Union, the USA, Canada, South Africa and Australia. The United States, for example, has 44 per cent of the world's known resources of hydrocarbons (oil, natural gas, oil shales, etc.), 38 per cent of the lignite, 38 per cent of the molybdenum, 21 per cent of the lead, 19 per cent of the copper, 18 per cent of the bituminous coal, and 15 per cent of the zinc. The Soviet Union has 75 per cent of the vanadium, 50 per cent of the lignite, 40 per cent of the bituminous coal, 38 per cent of the manganese, 30 per cent of the iron, 20 per cent of the cultivable land, and 18 per cent of the hydrocarbons. As Chisholm (1982) points out, this concentration is largely a function of geology and physical geography, but it is also partly a function of the uncertainties surrounding domestic politics in much of ex-colonial Africa, Asia and Latin America: uncertainties that have been a serious hindrance to exploration and exploitation. Current estimates of the distribution of resources will inevitably understate, therefore, the relative size of the resource base of many peripheral nations. It should also be noted that the significance of particular resources is sometimes very much dependent upon prevailing technologies. As technologies change, so resource requirements change: the switch from coal to oil, gas and electricity early in the twentieth century, for example; and the switch from natural to synthetic fibres for mass-produced textiles. This also means that regions and countries that are heavily dependent on one particular resource are very open to the consequences of technological change. This is particularly true of countries such as Bolivia, Chile, Guinea, Guyana, Liberia, Mauritania, Sierra Leone, Surinam and Zambia, whose economies are heavily dependent on non-fuel minerals.

Meanwhile, the rate of exploitation of some of the world's natural resources can also be a cause for concern. The indiscriminate logging of sub-tropical forests, for example, means that global deforestation is now of the order of between 10 and 40 hectares per *minute* (Blaikie, 1986). Apart from the overall loss of forest resources, this has also resulted in other economic and ecological problems: the loss of livelihood of local inhabitants, the silting of reservoirs, damage to hydro-electric plant, and an increase in flash floods with consequent damage to property, crops and livestock. Similarly, large-scale commercial agriculture has contributed to the 'desertification' of marginal environments such as the Sahel (Dinham and Hines, 1983; Goudie, 1981). Concern over issues such as these prompted the Club of Rome to commission a major research project on world resources, and their report, *The Limits to Growth* (Meadows *et al.*, 1972), was the catalyst for a great deal of concern. The major energy crisis that followed the Organization of Petroleum Exporting Countries (OPEC) price increases of 1973 served to emphasize the issue. Within a few years, however, the momentum of concern had largely fallen away, leaving only a residual concern over specific 'green' issues (saving whales and pandas, doing without nuclear energy, and conserving 'wilderness areas, for example). The 'Limits to Growth' thesis – that population growth and resource consumption will inevitably lead to a global economic/ecological/demographic crisis – lost a great deal of its force because the computer simulations on which the argument was based were quickly shown to be unsophisticated. They failed, for example, to take account of the probability of major technological advances, and of the multiple relations and feedback loops between resources, populations, production and pollution. Unfortunately, the technical critique of the argument was strongly linked to an ideological perspective that sought to defend a free-enterprise system with no constraints on the exploitation of scarce and non-renewable resources (O'Riordan, 1976; Sandbach, 1980).

Two Key Resources: Energy and Cultivable Land
Two particularly important resources in terms of the world's economic geography are energy and cultivable land. The major sources of commercial energy are oil, natural gas and coal, all of which are unevenly distributed across the globe (Manners, 1971; Odell, 1986). Most of the world's core economies are reasonably well-off in terms of energy *production*, the major exceptions being Japan and parts of Europe. Within the periphery and semi-periphery, most countries are energy-poor. The major exceptions are Algeria, Ecuador, Gabon, Indonesia, Libya, Nigeria, Venezuela and the Persian Gulf states – all major oil producers. Because of this unevenness, energy has come to be an important component of world trade. Oil is in fact the most important single commodity in world trade, making up around 13 per cent of the total by value. For many peripheral countries, the costs of energy imports represent a huge burden. Consider, for example, the predicament of countries like India, Pakistan, El Salvador and the Dominican Republic, where in the mid-1980s the cost of energy imports amounted to more than half of the value

Table 2.1: Energy consumption per capita (kilograms of oil equivalent), 1984

Low income economies	288
Middle income economies	
—oil exporters	615
—oil importers	856
High-income oil exporters	3593
Industrial market economies	4877
East European non-market economies	4360

Source: World Bank, *World Development Report,* 1986, Washington, DC, Table 8.

of exported merchandise. Nevertheless, few peripheral countries can afford to consume energy on the scale of the core economies, so that patterns of commercial energy *consumption* tend to mirror the fundamental core–periphery cleavage of the world economy (Table 2.1).

It should be noted that these figures do not reflect the use of firewood and other traditional fuels for cooking, lighting, heating, and, sometimes, industrial needs. In total, such forms of energy probably account for around 20 per cent of total world energy consumption. In parts of Africa and Asia they account for up to 90 per cent of energy consumption. This points us to yet another core–periphery contrast, for, whereas massive investments in exploration and exploitation are enabling more of the developed, energy-consuming countries to become self-sufficient through various combinations of coal, oil, natural gas, hydro-electric power and nuclear power (Odell, 1986), 1.5 billion of the people who depend on fuelwood as their principal source of energy are cutting wood faster than they can grow it (World Resources Institute, 1986). The problem is most serious in arid and semi-arid areas and in cooler mountainous areas, where the regeneration of shrubs, woodlands and forests is particularly slow. Nearly 100 million people in 22 countries (16 of them in Africa) cannot meet their minimum needs even by overcutting remaining forests. Given the consumption rates of the early 1980s, the fuelwood deficit will double by the year 2000 (Table 2.2).

The distribution of cultivable land represents another important environmental influence on international economic differentiation. Much more than half of the earth's land surface is unsuitable for any productive form of agriculture, as suggested by Figure 2.3. This map gives an approximation of the world's cultivable land by excluding regions that have too short a growing season (less than 90 days), are too dry (less than 25 cm annual rainfall), or too mountainous (elevations over 500 metres). This does not mean that agriculture is absent from the unshaded areas of the map – rather, that agriculture in these regions is likely to be marginal. By this measure, it will be noted, the distribution of the world's cultivable land is highly uneven, being concentrated in Europe, European and Central Soviet Union, eastern North America, the Australian littoral, Latin America, West Africa, India, and eastern China. In detail, of course, some of these regions may be marginal for agriculture because of marshy soils or other adverse conditions; while

Fig 2.3 The world's cultivable land
Source: after Berry, Conkling and Ray (1976) Fig 2.2, p. 16

Table 2.2: Fuelwood deficits by region, 1980 and 2000

Fuelwood situation	Region	Populations involved and Fuelwood deficit in 1980	Countries mainly concerned[d]
Acute scarcity[a]	Africa	13 million people 6 million m^3	Burkina Faso, Cape Verde, Chad, Djibouti, Mali, Mauritania, Niger, Sudan, Kenya, Ethiopia, Somalia, Botswana, Namibia
Arid and semi-arid areas	Asia	9.5 million people 3.6 million m^3	Afghanistan, Pakistan
	Latin America	6.8 million people 3.5 million m^3	Chile, Peru
	Africa	36 million people 40 million m^3	Burundi, Rwanda, Lesotho, Swaziland
Mountainous areas	Asia	29 million people 34 million m^3	Nepal
	Latin America	2 million people 2 million m^3	Bolivia, Peru
	Total	96.3 million people 89.1 million m^3	23 countries
Deficit[b]	Africa	131 million people 66 million m^3	Cameroon, Congo, Zaire, Malawi, Kenya, Madagascar, Uganda, Tanzania, Gambia, Guinea, Benin, Togo, Senegal, Sierra Leone, Nigeria, Mozambique
Areas with rapidly increasing population and agriculture	Asia	288 million people 75 million m^3	India, Nepal, Pakistan
	Latin America	143 million people 36 million m^3	Brazil, Colombia, Peru, Cuba, Dominican Republic, Guatemala, Mexico, Trinidad and Tobago

	Region	Figures	Countries
Densely populated lowlands	Asia	412 million people 120 million m³	Bangladesh, India, Sri Lanka, Thailand, Indonesia (Java), Philippines, Vietnam
	Latin America	9 million people 6 million m³	El Salvador, Haiti, Jamaica
	Total	983 million people 303 million m³	37 countries
Prospective deficit[c]	Africa	(in year 2000: 175 million people facing a 40 million m³ deficit)	Ghana, Ivory Coast, Central African Republic, Angola, Zimbabwe, Guinea-Bissau
	Asia	(in year 2000: 239 million people facing a 50 million m³ deficit)	Burma, India, Indonesia, Philippines, Vietnam
	Latin America	(in year 2000: 50 million people facing substantial degradation of fuelwood supplies)	Ecuador, Paraguay, Uruguay, Venezuela
	Total	464 million people	15 countries
Surplus potential for wood-based energy	Africa	Surplus potential 50 million m³	Cameroon, Congo, Equatorial Guinea, Angola, Zaire, Central African Republic
Low population tropical forest area	Asia	Surplus potential 200 million m³	Bhutan, Laos, Democratic Kampuchea, Indonesia (except Java)
	Latin America	Surplus potential 200 million m³	Amazon Basin

Notes:
a. Acute scarcity: available supplies of fuelwood are insufficient to meet minimum requirements, even with overcutting.
b. Deficit: fuelwood supplies are being consumed faster than they are replenished by natural regeneration and forest growth.
c. Prospective deficit: fuelwood supplies will be in a deficit situation by the year 2000, if present trends continue.
d. Data not available for China.

Source: World Resources Institute (1986) Table 5.8, p. 70

irrigation, for example, sometimes extends the local frontier of productive agriculture.

Similarly, it will be clear that not all cultivable land is of the same quality. This leads us to the concept of the *carrying capacity* of agricultural land: the maximum population that could be fed a minimum daily diet, given the particular soils and climate. The UN Food and Agriculture Organization (FAO) recently attempted to measure the carrying capacity of developing nations, drawing on UNESCO (UN Educational, Scientific and Cultural Organization) soil maps and climate data from their own Agroecological Zones project, and using a computerized routine to determine the particular food crops that would provide the greatest amounts of calories for each land/climate unit. The theoretical carrying capacity of each region was then calculated by dividing the total potential calorie production of each by the FAO's minimum daily requirement (United Nations, 1984). The results were expressed as ratios by dividing this figure by the actual (1975) population and by the projected population for the year 2000. Because agricultural output depends so heavily on technological inputs, the exercise was run for low, medium and high input levels, involving different assumptions about the use of fertilizers, biocides, improved crop varieties, and soil conservation. The results, summarized in Table 2.3, suggest that the developing world as a whole is in reasonable shape, potentially able to support twice its 1975 population even at low input levels. On a country-by-country basis, however, the results are less comforting. At the 1975 low input level, 55 countries were 'critical', i.e. they had a ratio of less than 1.1 and were not even able to support their existing population. By 2000, 64 countries are projected to be in critical condition, including the entire region of South West Asia. In fact, the FAO model is overly optimistic, since it assumes that all potentially cultivable land is used to grow nothing but staple food crops or to provide pasture for live-

Table 2.3: Potential population-supporting capacities divided by 1975 and 2000 populations

Input level	Africa	SW Asia	South America	Central America	SE Asia	Average
1975 ratios						
Low	3.0	0.8	5.9	1.6	1.1	2.0
Intermediate	11.6	1.3	23.9	4.2	3.0	6.9
High	33.9	2.0	57.2	11.5	5.1	16.6
2000 ratios						
Low	1.6	0.7	3.5	1.4	1.3	1.6
Intermediate	5.8	0.9	13.3	2.6	2.3	4.2
High	16.5	1.2	31.5	6.0	3.3	9.3

Source: UN Food and Agriculture Organization (FAO), *Land, Food, and People* (FAO, Rome, 1984).

stock. In reality, land has to be set aside for lumber and fuelwood production and for growing fibres and other non-food crops.

Agricultural Patterns and the Food Question

These considerations move us from the abstract to reality, and to a consideration of the world agricultural map and the world food situation. Both of these are rather different in configuration from the patterns of cultivable land and carrying capacity described above. The pattern of world agriculture, as we shall demonstrate in later chapters, is but one of a vast number of possible realizations of the world's agricultural resources. It is the product of a variety of interpretations, at different times, of environmental possibilities, desirable products, and marketable opportunities – all conditioned by prevailing land-tenure systems, levels of technology, and global power politics. It is a legacy of the world's economic history, with the agriculture of the core having come to be dominated by corporate 'agribusiness' and strongly conditioned by government policy; and that of the periphery having come to be a mixture of commercial non-food crop production and peasant-based food production (Berardi, 1985; Bradley, 1986). In detail, the mosaic of world agricultural regions shows a very high degree of specialization (Grigg, 1975). At the same time, the broader international division of labour means that some countries depend much more on agriculture for employment and income than others. In low-income developing countries, agriculture employs roughly 70 to 80 per cent of the labour force and accounts for 35 to 45 per cent of the Gross Domestic Product (GDP); in developed core economies, agriculture employs around 7 per cent of the labour force and accounts for about 3 per cent of GDP. One corollary of this specialization is of course a large volume of trade in agricultural produce. The biggest exporters of *food*, however, are not developing countries but a few of the more developed countries – Argentina, Australia, Canada, France and the USA – with highly productive agricultural sectors specializing in cereal production (Grigg, 1985b; Morgan, 1980). In recent years, world trade in food has grown rapidly and there have been some significant changes in the pattern of trade. Until the 1950s the dominant flows were those of food grains into western Europe. These have now declined significantly, with the major flows currently originating in Canada and the United States with destinations in the Soviet Union, Japan and, increasingly, middle-income developing countries (Tarrant, 1985).

The net results of these patterns and flows are gross inequalities and daunting inefficiencies in the distribution of one of the most basic of all human needs. Measured in terms of calorie consumption per capita as a percentage of the minimum daily requirement (Fig. 2.4), there is a steady gradient between low-income countries such as Chad, Mali and Mozambique, with levels of only 70 per cent, to the industrial core economies, both market and non-market, almost all of which had levels, in the mid 1980s, of more than 130 per cent. Estimates of the incidence of chronic malnourishment range from 340 to 730 million people, with most of them concentrated in South and East Asia

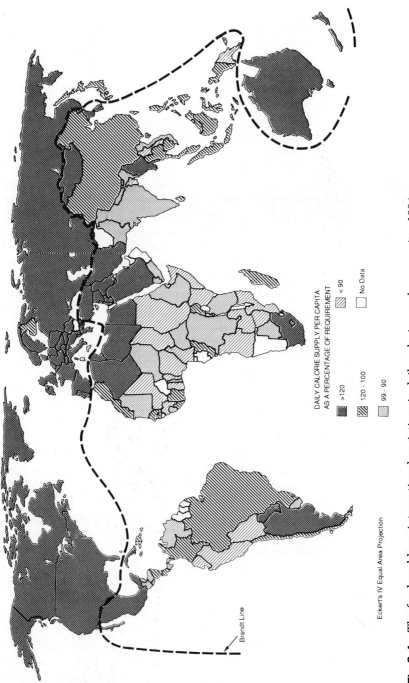

DAILY CALORIE SUPPLY PER CAPITA
AS A PERCENTAGE OF REQUIREMENT

>120	< 90
120 - 100	No Data
99 - 90	

Brandt Line

Eckert's IV Equal Area Projection

Fig 2.4 The food problem: international variations in daily calorie supply per capita, 1984

(Grigg, 1982, 1985a; World Bank, 1986a). The fact that almost half of them are located in countries that are net *exporters* (by value) of foods is a telling indictment of the world economic system. Because the food question is most dramatically high-lighted by localized famines, the most commonly cited causes of the food problem are climatic instability, inefficiencies in the allocation and transportation of food, and overpopulation. In fact, however, food production in developing countries has been growing faster than population; while the chief source of instability in food production is not climatic or the product of unfavourable population/resource ratios but, rather, the result of profit-motivated decisions and domestic and foreign policy considerations within the major grain-exporting countries (Currey and Hugo, 1984; D'Souza and Shoham, 1985).

> Thus in 1972, the crisis year of the sahelian drought in which starvation was wide-spread, the US government paid farmers $3 billion to take 50 million hectares out of production . . . The intent was quite clear. In order to remedy the 'glut' of previous years, which saw the grain reserve rise to 49 million tons with a commensurate fall in the world price, the US government determined to reduce production and create an effective shortage and thus raise again the world price. . . . The deliberately induced shortage was exacerbated by commercial sales to the Soviet Union; not, it seems, through deliberate government action, but via the combined efforts of a number of individual Russian buyers and the sales pitch of the controlling corporations in the USA. (Bradley, 1986, p. 97)

In this context, it is not surprising that surplus food has become an important component of international aid and, therefore, an important instrument in global power politics.

Demographic Patterns
The geography of population and the dynamics of population change are closely interrelated with patterns of economic development. Density, fertility, mortality and migration are often a direct reflection of economic, social and political conditions; and they are also important determinants of economic change and social well-being. Human resources are vital to economic development in terms of both production and consumption; but at the wrong time and in the wrong place they can be more of a liability than an asset. Although it is not always easy to unravel cause and effect, it is important to understand the broad context.

In global terms, this broad context is currently dominated by the sheer growth of population. Over one million people are added to the population of the world every five days. The current population of over 5 billion is likely to grow to over 6.5 billion by the year 2000, with nine-tenths of the increase taking place in the developing countries of the periphery, whose populations have been growing by between two and three per cent each year. In contrast, the population of the industrial core countries has been growing at an annual

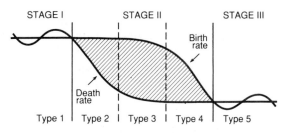

Fig 2.5   The demographic transition

rate of about 0.5 per cent, with some West European countries having virtually stagnant populations.

These core–periphery contrasts are the product of differences in fertility and mortality rates that are, in turn, related to differentials in the *demographic transition* that is associated with the broad sweep of economic development and social change. This transition is conventionally portrayed as involving three stages (Fig. 2.5). In the first, populations exhibit high birth rates and high, fluctuating death rates, with net growth rates of around 1 per cent. In the second stage, death rates fall sharply; birth rates also fall, but the decrease in fertility is lagged, resulting in an explosive increase in population. This stage was experienced by most western industrial countries during the nineteenth century. In the third stage, death rates even off at a low level; while birth rates are low but fluctuating, with net growth rates once again around 1 per cent.

It is clearly important to know whether a country is just entering the critical second stage of rapid population expansion and thus has the major part of its population growth ahead of it, whether it is in the middle of the population 'explosion', or whether it is on the verge of completing the growth stage. Accordingly, the UN has suggested a threefold division of the second stage, giving five categories of population growth types (Fig. 2.5). The map in Figure 2.6 shows how the countries of the world fit into this classification system. The core economies of the North are all in the final, slow-growth stage, while most of Latin America seems to be in the final phase of the growth stage. Most of Asia, the Middle East, and much of Africa are experiencing the most explosive phase of the growth stage, while the central and western regions of Africa seem poised to enter this explosive phase. A few African countries, meanwhile – including Burkina Faso, Chad, Ethiopia, Niger and Somalia – are at the very beginning of the demographic transition, with relatively high death rates that are suppressing the rate of natural increase.

Another important aspect of population change is *migration*. International labour migration has been an important part of the world economic system ever since the industrial revolution of the nineteenth century. Current estimates of the total number of international migrant workers stand at around 20 million, with a comparable number of dependents accompanying them. About 8 million of these, including three or four million illegal immigrants,

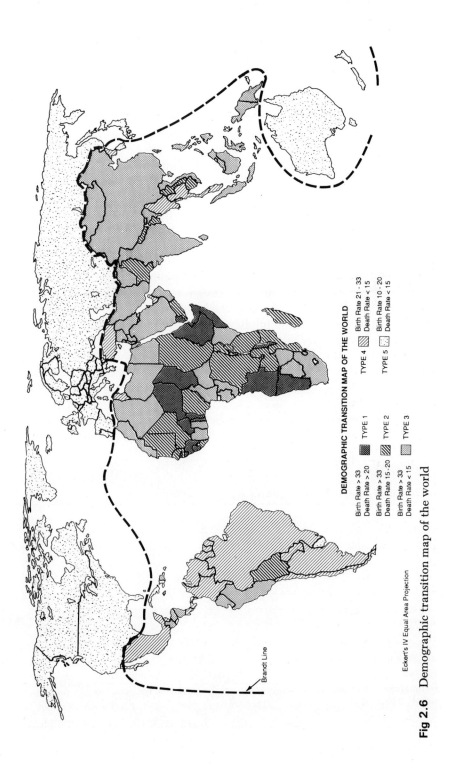

DEMOGRAPHIC TRANSITION MAP OF THE WORLD

TYPE 1
Birth Rate > 33
Death Rate > 20

TYPE 2
Birth Rate > 33
Death Rate 15 - 20

TYPE 3
Birth Rate > 33
Death Rate < 15

TYPE 4
Birth Rate 21 - 33
Death Rate < 15

TYPE 5
Birth Rate 10 - 20
Death Rate < 15

Eckert's IV Equal Area Projection

Brandt Line

Fig 2.6 Demographic transition map of the world

are working in the United States, which now draws most of its immigrants from Mexico. Northwestern Europe has about five million migrant workers, most of them from nearby semi-peripheral countries such as Spain, Turkey, Portugal and Yugoslavia or from ex-colonial countries such as Algeria and Jamaica. Since the early 1970s, large numbers of workers have also been attracted to the Middle East: about three million at present, two-thirds of them from the region itself and the rest from South and South East Asia. South Africa draws about 500,000 migrant workers from neighbouring countries; and there are also important flows of migrant labour among developing countries in parts of Latin America and in West Africa. Mention should also be made of the distinctive streams of highly skilled labour – physicians, engineers, scientists, etc. – the so-called 'brain drain'. The principal recipients of these streams have been the United States, Canada, Britain and Australia; while the principal countries of origin have been India, Pakistan, the Philippines and Sri Lanka (although typically the brain drain is a result of students and professionals choosing not to return home after the completion of educational courses or training programmes in developed countries). These streams are significant not because of the absolute numbers of people involved but because of the economic implications of the relative gains and losses of highly skilled manpower.

In terms of unskilled and semi-skilled workers, however, demand in the core economies has been decreasing since the mid 1970s, while the demographic transition continues to flood the labour markets of most developing countries. Without the option of migration or emigration to unsettled territories – an option that represents a crucial difference in the experience of

Table 2.4: Core-periphery contrasts in urbanization, 1980

	Low-income economies (excl. China)	Middle-income economies	High-income oil exporters	Industrial market economies	East European non-market economies
Average annual growth rate of urban population, 1973–1984	5.2	4.1	7.7	1.2	1.8
Percentage of urban population in largest city	29	29	28	18	7

peripheral countries compared to the historical experience of core countries – the increases in population resulting from the demographic transition have been channelled into internal, rural-to-urban migration streams. With young, reproductively active rural populations being pushed out by shortages of land and pulled to larger cities by a combination of real and perceived advantages in terms of employment opportunities, wages and modern amenities, the rate and scale of urbanization in developing countries represents yet another dimension of core–periphery contrasts (Table 2.4).

Industry, Trade and Finance: the New International Division of Labour

As with the agricultural map of the world, the international mosaic of industrial production and employment is highly complex, with a great deal of specialization in particular activities. Once again, what we want to stress here is the overall framework. Table 2.5 provides the necessary base information (though non-market economies are excluded because comparable data are not available). In terms of production, the United States is by far the most important source of manufactured goods, accounting for 24 per cent of the capitalist world's output in 1983. Just five countries – the United States, Japan, West Germany, France and China – produced over three-quarters of the world total. Of the 25 biggest manufacturing countries, a number were peripheral or semi-peripheral: Brazil, China, India, Iran, Indonesia, Mexico, South Korea, Spain, Turkey and Yugoslavia. Nevertheless, the vast majority of peripheral and semi-peripheral countries have a very small manufacturing output. Another important contrast implicit in Table 2.5 concerns *productivity*. In brief, the highly capitalized manufacturing industries of the core countries have been able to maintain high levels of productivity, with the result that (with the notable exception of the United Kingdom) their output has continued to grow appreciably even as the size of their manufacturing labour forces has tended to shrink.

Within the framework of this continuing dominance of the core industrial nations there are several important trends (Dicken, 1986). Although the United States has retained its leadership as the world's major producer of manufactured goods over the postwar period, its dominance has been significantly reduced. In 1963, for example, its share of world manufacturing production had been 40 per cent, compared to 24 per cent in 1983. The United Kingdom, meanwhile, has lost ground in both relative and absolute terms. In contrast, Japan has moved from fifth place with a share of 5.5 per cent in 1963 to second place and a share of nearly 16 per cent in 1983. We shall examine the reasons for these shifts in Chapters 5 and 6, where we discuss in detail the evolution and transition of the world's core economies. As we shall see, this has involved an increasing degree of international interdependence throughout the world economy. This interdependence is reflected, in turn, by some

Table 2.5: World manufacturing data, 1983[1]

Rank	Country	Manufacturing value added (millions of 1980 US$)	Per cent of world total	Average annual growth rate (%) 1965–73	Average annual growth rate (%) 1973–84	Share of GDP (%) 1965	Share of GDP (%) 1984	Share of labour force (%) 1960	Share of labour force (%) 1980
1	United States	592,504	24.0	2.9	1.4	29	21	36	32
2	Japan	387,272	15.7	14.4	7.2	32	30	30	39
3	West Germany	310,384	12.6	5.3	1.9	—	36	48	46
4	France	173,370	7.0	7.7	1.7	—	25	39	39
5	China	152,731	6.2	11.7	5.0	—	—	—	18
6	United Kingdom	120,228	4.9	2.6	-1.7	30	22	48	42
7	Italy	66,696[2]	2.7	8.0[3]	3.7	—	—	40	45
8	Brazil	56,898	2.3	11.2	4.9	26	27	15	24
9	Canada	46,210	1.9	5.4	1.1	23	—	34	29
10	Mexico	41,346	1.7	9.9	5.0	21	24	20	26
11	Netherlands	39,158	1.6	—	—	—	24	42	45
12	Spain	33,396[4]	1.4	9.8	—	25	—	31	40
13	Belgium	30,660	1.2	7.4	1.3	30	24	48	41
14	Australia	29,059	1.2	4.9	1.0	28	22	37	31
15	Sweden	27,151	1.1	4.1	-0.1	28	22	45	34
16	India	27,091	1.1	4.0	5.9	15	15	11	13
17	South Korea	21,788	0.9	21.1	11.5	18	28	9	29
18	Austria	21,534	0.9	6.9	2.5	33	27	46	37
19	Yugoslavia	19,512	0.8	—	—	—	—	18	35
20	Turkey	14,263	0.6	9.5	4.0	16	24	11	13
21	Finland	14,107	0.6	7.5	3.7	21	24	31	35
22	Argentina	12,682	0.5	4.6	-0.2	33	30	36	28
23	Denmark	11,935	0.5	4.7	2.4	20	17	35	31
24	Iran	11,596	0.5	13.7	—	12	—	23	34
25	Indonesia	9,611	0.4	9.0	14.9	8	—	8	15
.	.	.	.	.	.	.	.	.	.
.	.	.	.	.	.	.	.	.	.
119	Botswana	55	0.0	—	8.2	12	7	3	12
120	Mauritania	48	0.0	—	—	4	—	3	8
121	Guinea	39	0.0	—	-2.0	—	2	6	11

[1] Excluding non-market economies
[2] 1979
[3] 1960–1970
[4] 1980

important trends in manufacturing output within the periphery. Of particular importance is the emergence of ten or so semi-peripheral countries as major growth points for manufacturing (Table 2.6). The most important of these 'newly industrializing countries' (NICs) in absolute terms are Spain and Brazil, followed by Mexico, but in terms of the rate of manufacturing

Table 2.6: The growth of manufacturing production in the leading newly industrializing countries, 1960–1981

	Share of world manufacturing output (per cent)			Average annual growth in manufacturing (per cent)		Share of total labour force in manufacturing (per cent)	
	1963	1970	1980	1960–70	1970–81	1960	1980
Hong Kong	0.08	0.15	0.27	..	10.1	52	57
Singapore	0.05	0.06	0.16	13.0	9.7	23	39
South Korea	0.11	0.22	0.66	17.6	15.6	9	29
Taiwan	0.11	0.23	0.46[1]	15.5[2]	11.5[3]	16	32[1]
Brazil	1.57	1.73	3.01	..	8.7	15	24
Mexico	1.04	1.27	1.95	9.4	7.1	20	26
Spain	0.88	1.18	2.24	..	6.0[4]	31	40
Portugal	0.23	0.27	0.40	8.9	4.5	29	35
Greece	0.19	0.25	0.31	10.2	5.5	20	28
Yugoslavia	1.14	1.25	0.89	5.7	7.1	18	35
Total, 10 NICs	5.40	6.61	10.54				

[1]1977   [2]1961–1970   [3]1971–1978   [4]1970–1980

Source: Dicken (1986), Table 2.9, p.30

growth it has been the four Asian NICs – South Korea, Taiwan, Hong Kong and Singapore – that have experienced the most spectacular growth. As Dicken notes:

> By far the most dramatic increase in manufacturing production was experienced by South Korea which attained *annual average* growth rates of almost 18 per cent in the 1960s and 16 per cent in the 1970s. As a result, South Korea surged up the league table of developing market economies . . . The percentage of South Korea's labour force employed in manufacturing increased from 9 per cent to 29 per cent between 1960 and 1980. (1986, p. 30)

These shifts are part of a 'new international division of labour' that has emerged as the overarching component of the contemporary framework of the world's economic geography. As we shall see in Chapters 6 and 10, it has been corporate strategy, particularly the strategies of large multinational enterprises (MNEs – the acronym is used throughout this book as shorthand for multinational corporations and transnational corporations as well as multinational enterprises, though strictly speaking there are differences between the terms), that has created this new international division of labour. For the moment, however, it must be sufficient to take note of the magnitude of the phenomenon. One striking measure of the importance of MNEs in the world economy is given by the size of their annual turnover in comparison with the GNP of entire nation states. By this yardstick, all of the top 50 multi-national corporations – including the likes of Exxon, General Motors, Ford Motor Company, Matsushita Electronics, IBM, Unilever, Philips, ICI, Union Carbide, ITT, Siemens and Hitachi – carry more economic clout than many of the world's smaller, peripheral nation states; while the very biggest multi-nationals are comparable in size with the national economies of semi-peripheral states like Greece, Ireland, Portugal, New Zealand and Yugoslavia (see also Fig. 6.3). Collectively, the 500 largest US corporations now employ an overseas labour force as big as their domestic labour force. This overseas labour force is spread between parts of both the core and the periphery, but it is in peripheral countries and, in particular, the NICs where the most rapid growth has been taking place (Peet, 1983). Thus two-thirds of the radios made by Japanese manufacturing companies, are produced abroad, together with half the monochrome television sets and one third of the stereos and colour television sets – mostly in South Korea and other nearby East Asian locations (Grunwald and Flamm, 1985). This, clearly, has had much to do with the rise of the NICs. Over 90 per cent of South Korean exports of electronic equip-ment, for example, are produced by affiliates of Japanese companies.

These examples also serve to emphasize the point that the most important economic activities involved in the new international division of labour are electronics, together with textiles and clothing: industries where profits are difficult to maintain through increases in technological inputs but relatively easy to increase by substituting low-wage for high-wage labour. This means that the 'manufacturing' undertaken in peripheral settings by MNEs is more often than not merely *assembly*, with the manufacture of components that require high levels of skill and/or technology being undertaken in the core – albeit in settings that are often outside traditional manufacturing regions.

We should also note here that the new dimension of the world's economic geography that is manifest as the new international division of labour has, in turn, had an important impact on another dimension of economic geography: government policy. At one level, the governments of peripheral countries have sought to take advantage of multinational companies' need for assembly lines operated by cheap labour by setting up *export-processing zones* (see p. 315), adaptations of free trade zones in which favourable investment and trade conditions are created by waiving excise duties on components, provid-ing factory space and warehousing at subsidized rates, allowing tax 'holidays' of up to five years, and suspending foreign exchange controls. By the mid 1980s, over 50 developing countries either had established export processing zones or were planning to do so, while the total direct employment in these zones had exceeded one million. At a more general level, governments every-where – in both core and periphery – have responded to the 'global reach' of MNEs by intensifying their involvement with supra-national economic and political organizations such as the European Economic Community, the Asso-ciation of South East Asian Nations, and the Latin American Free Trade Association. We shall be reviewing the changing role of the state in the context of the internationalization of the world economy in Parts II and III of this book. In Part IV, we shall explore supra-national reactions to the internation-alization of the world economy.

Trade
The high degree of international specialization in agricultural and industrial production inevitably means that the geography of international trade is very complex. It is, moreover, changing rapidly in response to innovations in trans-port, communications and manufacturing technology, shifts in global poli-tics, and, most important of all, the increasing internationalization of production processes. As we have seen, the new international division of labour has created new flows of materials, components, information and fin-ished products. One recent estimate is that as much as 30 per cent of world trade now takes place within the 'internal markets' of multinational corpora-tions (UN Center on Transnational Corporations, 1983). The detailed geo-graphy of contemporary patterns of international trade is, surprisingly, an under-researched topic (McConnell, 1986). It is clear, however, that trade in general is of increasing importance as a component of the world economy. Between 1950 and 1980 the average annual growth rate of the value of world exports was 6.7 per cent in real terms: a figure that was well above the growth of world production and several times greater than that of world population growth.

Throughout the postwar period, the industrial core countries have domi-nated international trade (Fig. 2.7), though their share of world trade (by value) was trimmed back a little after the oil price increases of 1973, which increased the value of the exports of oil-exporting countries by a significant margin. Meanwhile, the share of world trade accounted for by the rest of the periphery has decreased. In general terms, then, there has been an intensi-fication of the long-standing domination of intra-core and inter-core trade at the expense of core–periphery trade (Freeman, 1973; Grimwade, 1988; Johnston, 1976) – with the major exception of trade in oil. In detail, however, there have been some very important shifts. Between 1950 and 1981, the United Kingdom's share of world exports shrank drastically, from 11.0 per cent to 5.7 per cent, with its share of world imports falling from 12.3 per cent to 5.3 per cent. The US share of exports fell from 17.8 per cent to 12.7 per cent, with imports falling rather less: from 16.0 to 14.3 per cent. As the United States was acquiring this trade deficit, Japan was moving in the opposite

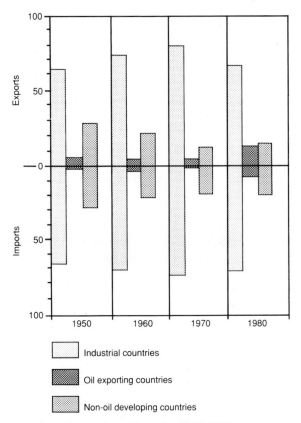

Fig 2.7 Shares of world trade, 1950–1980

direction and assuming a much more important role in world trade. In 1950, Japanese exports accounted for only 1.4 per cent of the world total; in 1981, they had risen to 8.2 per cent. Meanwhile, Japanese imports increased from 1.6 to 7.5 per cent of the world total. West Germany has also achieved a significant improvement in its trading position; while France and Italy have increased their share of world trade but at the same time have moved into a net trade deficit. Most of the other core countries have experienced a decrease in their share of world trade, as have the developing countries as a bloc.

Space does not permit a detailed examination of the dominant patterns of commodity flows or of the regionalization of international trade. Our purpose here is to illustrate the overall framework and note the major trends that provide the template and the context for the evolution of the world's economic landscapes. Suffice it to note, therefore, that the most striking aspect of commodity flows and the regionalization of trade is the persistence of the dependence of peripheral countries on trade with core countries that are geographically or geopolitically close. Thus, for example, the United States is the central focus for the exports and the origin of the bulk of the imports of most

Central American nations, while France is the focus for commodity flows to and from French ex-colonies such as Algeria, Cambodia, Dahomey and the Ivory Coast. These flows, however, represent only part of the action for the core economies, whose trading patterns are dominated by flows to and from other core countries. One of the implications of this situation is that the smaller, peripheral partners in these trading relationships are highly dependent on levels of demand and the overall economic climate in the core economies. Another aspect of dependency, in this context, is the degree to which a country's export base is diversified. Figure 2.8 shows one measure of this: the index of commodity concentration of exports. Countries with low values on this index have diversified export bases. They include Argentina, Brazil, China, India and North and South Korea as well as most of the core countries. At the other extreme are peripheral countries where the manufacturing sector is poorly developed and the balancing of national accounts and the generation of foreign exchange is dependent on the export of one or two agricultural or mineral resources: Bolivia, Chile, Iran, Iraq, Libya, Nigeria and Venezuela, for example.

Patterns of International Finance
The spatial organization of world production and trade is closely mirrored by patterns of international finance. Thus the long-standing dominance of flows of direct investment between the nations of the 'White North' (Buchanan, 1972) has been heavily modified by the emergence of the new international division of labour. Until the early 1970s, US-based multinational corporations accounted for about two-thirds of the total outflows of foreign direct investment, and about four-fifths of this was directed towards Canada and the more advanced industrial nations of Western Europe. By the mid 1980s, US multinational corporations' share of the total had dropped to less than half, while direct foreign investment by Japanese, Canadian and West German corporations had increased significantly. It should also be noted that another source of foreign direct investment has begun to show up: multinational corporations based in the NICs. Nearly 10 per cent of the top 500 non-US-based corporations in the world are now based in semi-peripheral countries. Hyundai, the South Korean shipbuilding firm, is now bigger than Michelin or Rio Tinto Zinc; and Taiwan's Walsin Likwa (an electronics group) is bigger than Distillers or De Boers (Thrift, 1986).

Along with these changes in the sources of investment have been changes in destination. The advanced industrial nations still absorb most of the inflows but, as we have seen, the new international division of labour has brought significant flows of capital into the NICs. The sharpness with which these investments have been focused is reflected by the fact that almost three-quarters of the total inflows to all peripheral and semi-peripheral countries are accounted for by just seven: Argentina, Brazil, Hong Kong, Malaysia, Mexico, Singapore and South Korea. Within the core countries, meanwhile, other significant shifts have occurred. Australia, Canada, West Germany,

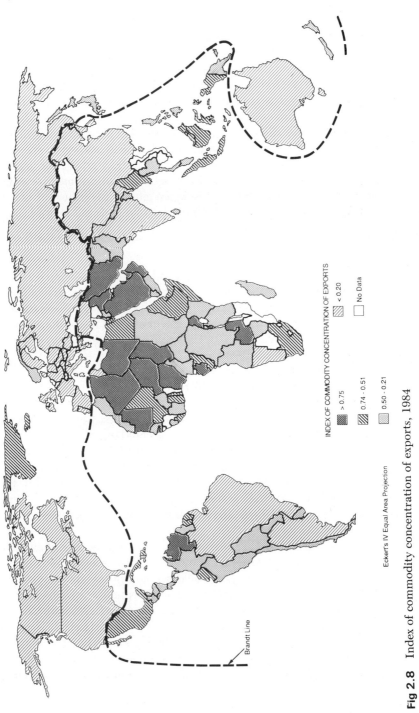

INDEX OF COMMODITY CONCENTRATION OF EXPORTS

> 0.75

0.74 - 0.51

0.50 - 0.21

< 0.20

No Data

Eckert's IV Equal Area Projection

Brandt Line

Fig 2.8 Index of commodity concentration of exports, 1984

Italy and the Netherlands have all lost ground in terms of their share of the inflow of foreign capital, while France, Spain, the United Kingdom and the United States have gained. The United States now *receives* almost one third of the total inflow of foreign direct investment, compared to less than 10 per cent at the beginning of the 1970s.

These shifts in international investment – and in particular the opening up of the United States to investment from Canadian, European and Japanese corporations – have been contingent upon other changes in the pattern of international finance. The pattern of international finance for the first part of the postwar period was set by the Bretton Woods agreement of 1944, which created what was virtually a US-run system, with fixed exchange rates and the US dollar serving as the convertible medium of currency with a fixed relationship to the price of gold. But, as the position of the United States deteriorated in terms of world manufacturing and trade, the system came under pressure.

> The result was that the Bretton Woods system crumbled. In particular, by the late 1960s fixed exchange rates effectively disappeared and every domestic currency became convertible into every other. Exchange rates 'floated' and, as a result, all domestic currencies became a medium that could be bought and sold and out of which a profit could be made. (Thrift, 1986, p. 28)

Meanwhile, there had developed a pool of 'Eurodollars' – US dollars held in banks located outside the United States – that was boosted after 1971 as the US government began to finance its budget deficit by paying in its own currency, flooding the world with dollars and fuelling worldwide inflation. Two years later, in 1973, the Eurodollar market was swollen still further as oil-producing countries rapidly acquired huge reserves of US dollars as a result of the quadrupling of petroleum prices in the wake of the OPEC embargo. The net result of the floating of currencies and the creation of a large market in Eurodollars was that a new, more sophisticated system of international finance emerged (Hamilton, 1986). Consequently, new patterns of investment were accompanied by an expansion and internationalization of key producer services such as stock exchanges, futures markets, banks, advertising agencies and business hotels. Indeed, as core economies have lost competitiveness in terms of industrial production, they have come to rely increasingly on these services in order to earn foreign currency and to balance national accounts.

Banking services provide a good example. Fostered by advances in telecommunications and data processing, the expansion and internationalization of the world's banking system has been explosive (Hamilton, 1986; Thrift, 1987), and has contributed to an 'electronic colonialism' (McPhail, 1986). In the race to become global, as Thrift observes, US banks were the most successful:

> The number of foreign branches of US banks increased from 124 to 723 between 1960 and 1976 . . . But the United States banks were soon followed by the British and French banks (with their experience of dealing with former colonial countries) and later by German, Italian, Arab and Japanese banks. Like

> Japanese multinational corporations, the Japanese-based banks have become a
> major force in global banking . . . They are now second only to the US-based
> banks. (Thrift, 1986, p. 32)

Although the major impetus for this internationalization of banking has been
the internationalization of production by multinational corporations, it has of
course been the objective of every bank to expand the business of overseas
branches by lending to local companies and foreign governments. In the
1970s, world monetary reserves increased twelvefold with the availability of
OPEC 'petrodollars' and as a by-product of the inflation that accompanied
the break-up of the Bretton Woods system. The international banking system,
awash with funds, found willing borrowers in developing countries, desperate as they were for capital in order to be able to maintain productivity by
investing in infrastructure and new technology (Fryer, 1987). The scale of
borrowing undertaken by some countries, however, has added another significant dimension to international economic patterns: debt. Servicing long-
term debts (i.e. meeting the costs of both interest charges and repayments) has
reached crisis proportions for some countries. The intensity of these crises is
highlighted by Figure 2.9, which shows countries' long-term debt service as a
proportion of their capacity to earn foreign exchange, as reflected by the value
of exports of goods and services. Because of lack of comparability in book-
keeping, the figures for non-market countries are based on estimates published by *The Economist.* A large number of peripheral countries are clearly in
serious trouble (including geopolitically important countries like Egypt,
Indonesia, Nigeria, and Pakistan); but it is within the semi-periphery that the
greatest debts and the heaviest burdens, in relation to earning capacities, have
accrued: in East European non-market economies such as Poland, Hungary
and East Germany; and in the NICs of Brazil and Mexico, where for every $10
earned through exports, $5 is owed in long-term debt servicing (Dornbusch
and Fischer, 1985; Massad, 1985; OECD, 1984; Pfister and Suter, 1987).

   The debt issue leads us logically to the question of aid. As with most of the
other issues raised in this chapter, we shall be pursuing various aspects of this
question in subsequent chapters. For the moment, therefore, we shall merely
outline the dominant patterns and the most striking trends.

   Large-scale movements of aid began shortly after World War II with the
Marshall Plan, financed by the United States to bolster war-torn European
allies whose economic weakness, it was believed, made them susceptible to
communism. During the 1950s and 1960s, as more developing countries
gained independence, aid became a useful weapon in Western and Sino-
Soviet cold war offensives to establish and preserve political influence
throughout the world. By the late 1960s, the list of donor countries had
expanded beyond the super-powers to include smaller countries such as
Austria, Denmark and Sweden, whose motivation in aid-giving must be seen
as more philanthropic or conscience-salving than political. In addition there
was a greater geographic dispersal of aid, thanks largely to the activities of
multilateral financial agencies such as the International Monetary Fund

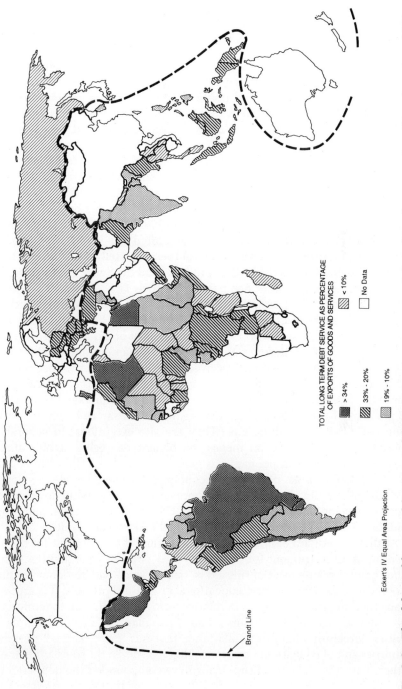

TOTAL LONG TERM DEBT SERVICE AS PERCENTAGE
OF EXPORTS OF GOODS AND SERVICES

	> 34%		< 10%
	33% - 20%		No Data
	19% - 10%		

Eckert's IV Equal Area Projection

Brandt Line

Fig 2.9 The debt problem: total long-term debt service as a percentage of the value of exports of goods and services, 1984

(IMF) and the World Bank (Krueger, 1986). Nevertheless, the geography of aid still has a strong political flavour: Asia, for instance, receives less aid per capita than the average for all recipient countries, yet within this region Western strategic involvement has led in the past to South Korea and South Vietnam receiving above-average amounts of aid. Similarly, Turkey and Yugoslavia have received above-average aid because of the special interest of the West in limiting the influence of the Soviet bloc. Bilateral aid from several countries also reflects localized political aspirations and colonial ties. Thus much British and French aid is directed towards former African colonies, while Japanese aid is disbursed largely within Asia, and aid from the OPEC countries has been directed mainly towards the 'front-line' Arab countries.

Moreover, it should be noted that international détente, together with the balance of payments difficulties of several of the core countries, has ensured that levels of aid have diminished. Thus, whereas official development assistance from OECD countries amounted to nearly 0.5 per cent of their total GNP in 1965, it had fallen to 0.36 per cent in 1985. The most striking decreases were those of the United States and the United Kingdom, whose overseas development assistance as a percentage of their GNP fell from 0.58 to 0.24 and from 0.47 to 0.33 respectively. The Japanese and the Swiss, meanwhile, have never exceeded one third of one per cent of their GNP in aid. It is true that some countries – Denmark, the Netherlands and Norway, in particular – have steadily increased their aid-giving; while France has maintained a relatively high level of donations. Equally, the impact of aid on some countries is clearly significant. Mali, for example, received aid amounting to 32.0 per cent of its GNP in 1984; Mauritania received aid equivalent to 24.6 per cent of its GNP; and six other countries – Burkina Faso, Burundi, the Central African Republic, Jordan, Lesotho and Togo – received aid equivalent to more than 15 per cent of their GNP. These figures, however, say as much about these countries' GNP as anything else. They are also exceptions. In general, the poorest countries are by no means the biggest recipients of aid; and the amount of aid received per capita is generally very low (Mabogunje, 1986). In 1984, low-income developing economies received an average of just US$4.60 per capita in overseas development assistance, while lower-middle income developing economies received US$15.00 per capita and upper-middle income developing countries received US$4.80 per capita.

At these levels, aid cannot seriously be regarded as a catalyst for development or as an instrument for redressing core–periphery inequalities. On the other hand, because most of this aid is 'tied' in some way to donor countries' exports or to specific military, educational or cultural projects, it is argued by many that, insignificant as it is in relative terms, it *is* sufficient to reinforce the initial advantages of the 'donors'. Thus Buchanan (1972), for example, has written forcefully of military assistance that has 'mercenarized' peripheral countries and of educational assistance that has 'stolen the souls' of their élite. Others have shown how 'cheap' loans have compounded the debt trap (see, for example, Payer, 1974). Paul Streeten has put the whole argument very graphically:

The Kings of Siam are said to have ruined obnoxious countries by presenting them with white elephants that had to be maintained at vast expense. In the modern setting this can be achieved best by tying a high-interest loan, called 'aid', to projects and to donors' exports and to confine it to the import content (or better still, some part of it) of the project. But even untied aid on soft terms can be used to promote exports of a white elephantine nature, because capital grants do not cover the subsequent recurrent expenditure which the elephant inflicts on its owners. Receiving aid is not just like receiving an elephant but like making love to an elephant. There is no pleasure in it, you run the risk of being crushed, and it takes years before you see the results. (Streeten, 1968, p. 154)

Summary

Brief reviews of the major aspects of international economic differentiation have been sufficient to have illuminated both the dominance of core–periphery patterns and the extent of the gradient between core and periphery. Other important points to have emerged include:

- The existence of a distinctive group of semi-peripheral countries with intermediate levels of living. This group includes two very different types: resource-exporting countries and newly industrializing countries

- The speed and intensity of changes in patterns of economic activity and development associated with the new international division of labour that is, in turn, largely the product of the strategies of multinational corporations.

- The degree of dependency of peripheral countries created by inequalties in resources, trading relationships, access to financial resources, and control of economic activity.

An Overall Typology

There have been several attempts to capture the net outcomes of this inequality through overall measures that respect the notion of development set out at the beginning of this chapter; i.e. that it extends beyond fundamental economic dimensions to encompass variations in social well-being (see, for example, Drewnowski's work on levels of living and 'levels of civilization' (1974; 1986), McGranahan et al. (1970) on a 'development index', and Morris (1980) on a 'Physical Quality of Life Index'). While there are obvious dangers in attempting to construct normative yardsticks from aggregate statistics on a variety of topics, it is often useful and sometimes necessary to take the more general view. A recent attempt to provide such a view is shown in Figure 2.10. This is based on the results of research on 'World Standard Distance Scales' undertaken by Ginsburg et al. (1986). Their composite index, shown in Figure 2.10, is based on 42 variables that measure a broad spectrum of economic, demographic and socio-economic characteristics (Table 2.7). A 'World

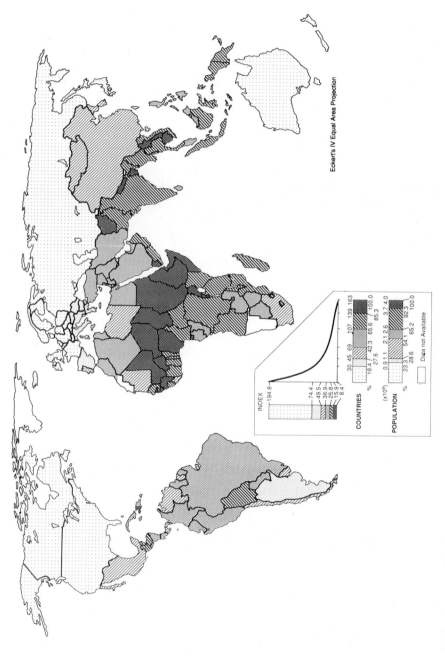

Fig 2.10 An overall index of international development
Source: Ginsburg *et al.* (1986) Fig. 7, p. 58

Table 2.7: Variables for index of development

1 Agriculture as per cent of gross domestic product, 1973, current factor cost
2 Agricultural population, per cent of economically active population
3 Agricultural population, 1975, per cent of total population
4 Calories per capita per day
5 Energy consumption: commercial consumption as per cent of gross consumption, 1975
6 Energy consumption per capita: commercial consumption, 1975, tons of coal equivalents per 100 population
7 Energy consumption per capita: electricity generation, 1975 kilowatt-hours per person
8 Energy consumption per capita: gross consumption, 1975, tons of coal equivalents per 10 persons
9 Energy consumption per capita: hydroelectric generation, 1975, kilowatt-hours per person
10 Export concentration, 1972, Hirschman Normalized index
11 Exports of raw materials, 1973, per cent of total exports
12 Fertilizer consumption, 1975, kilograms per square kilometer of arable land
13 Fertilizer consumption per capita, 1975, kilograms per 10 agricultural population
14 Infant mortality, 1970, deaths per 1,000 live births
15 Investment: gross domestic investment as per cent of gross domestic product, 1973
16 Literacy rate, adult, 1970, per cent
17 Newspaper circulation per capita, 1970, daily copies per thousand people
18 Life expectancy at birth, 1970, years
19 Manufacturing as per cent of gross domestic product, 1973, current factor cost
20 Paddy yield, 1975, tens of metric tons per square kilometer
21 Physicians and dentists per 100,000 people, 1970s
22 Radio ownership per capita, 1973–74, radios per thousand people
23 Rail route density, 1975, kilometers per thousands of square kilometers
24 Rail route length per capita, 1975, ton-kilometers per 100,000 people
25 Rail freight per route length, 1975, thousands of ton-kilometers per kilometer of rail route length
26 Rail freight per capita, 1975, ton-kilometers per million persons
27 Road network density, 1975, kilometers per thousand square kilometers
28 Road network length per capita, 1975, kilometers per 100,000 people
29 School enrolment, primary, gross enrolment ratio, 1970, per cent
30 School enrolment, secondary, gross enrolment ratio, 1970, per cent
31 School enrolment, third level, gross enrolment ratio, 1970, per cent
32 Steel consumption per capita, 1975, tons per thousand people
33 Tractors per capita, 1975, tractors per million persons agricultural population
34 Tractors per square kilometer of arable land, 1975
35 Trade turnover per capita, 1975, US Dollars per person
36 Urban population, 1975, per cent in cities over 100,000 people
37 Urban population, 1970s, per cent of total population, Census definition
38 Vehicles per capita, 1974, commercial motor vehicles per 100,000 persons
39 Vehicles per capita, 1974, motor vehicles per thousand people
40 Vehicles per road length, 1974, motor vehicles per hundred kilometers
41 Wheat yield, 1975, metric tons per square kilometer
42 Youthfulness, 1970s, per cent of population age 14 or less

Standard' was derived for each variable by averaging the scores of 17 benchmark countries with populations of three million or more and high levels of economic and socio-economic performance that are not dependent on oil exports. The value for each country on a particular variable was then converted to a percentage of this standard value; the index is a simple unweighted average of these percentages.

Ginsburg *et al.* claim that this index provides a real measure of attainment among countries, since it gives a measure of the relative 'distance' that separates countries from the benchmark level of the world's core economies. The results show that 30 countries, accounting for 23 per cent of the world's population, are at levels of 74.4 per cent or more of the world standard, including northwestern Europe, Eastern Europe, Japan, Australia, Canada, the United States, and several island micro-states. Countries at approximately 50 to 75 per cent of the standard account for only 5.3 per cent of the world's population and are clustered largely in southern Europe. The next group of countries, with index values in the 36.9 to 49.5 range, includes China, several of the NICs, and several of the more prosperous resource-exporting countries and accounts for over 25 per cent of the world's population. Where the index is most useful, however, is in differentiating between the 94 countries in the three lowest categories at less than 36.9 per cent of the world standard:

> Of the major realms, Latin America, Sub-Saharan Africa and East Asia are the more heterogeneous. The Near East, South Asia and Southeast Asia are the more homogeneous. The 'worlds' of *low*, *lower* and *least* development into which these developing countries fall (corresponding to categories of 25.8–36.9 per cent, 15.9–25.8 per cent, and less than 15.9 per cent of the world standard) display a regional quality that is important both for analytical and for policy-making purposes. The 'world of low development' clusters in central South America, the Near East, the Caribbean, and southern Africa, with two major outposts in Southeast Asia – Malaysia and the Philippines. The 'world of lower development' covers much of the rest of Sub-Saharan Africa and South Asia, but that of 'least development' consists of a striking band of poverty running across Sahelian Africa, with a few outliers such as Afghanistan, Nepal, Laos and Haiti. (Ginsburg *et al.*, 1986, p. 62)

Regional Patterns

Within nations, the patterns fundamental to economic geography can be observed at many different spatial scales: we cannot possibly do justice here to all of them, or to every nation. This section will concentrate on fairly broad patterns, as displayed by data for major administrative or statistical subdivisions, drawing briefly on examples from the world's core, semi-periphery and periphery to illustrate the gradient and the configuration of inter-regional contrasts. It should be emphasized that it is both difficult and dangerous to draw detailed generalizations from these individual cases. Regional economic landscapes are deeply rooted in the history of economic development and closely conditioned, as at the national scale, by physical geography, natural resources, demographic composition, political organization, and so on. Our examination of regional patterns, therefore, must be restricted to high-level generalizations about regional economic patterns. In essence, these are fairly straightforward. Regional patterns within core economies tend to be characterized by core–periphery cleavages. Core regions have typically been centred on urban-industrial heartlands, but have recently been modified by the geography of service activities, particularly producer services. Regional patterns within peripheral and semi-peripheral economies also tend to reflect core–periphery cleavages but are also characterized by sharp urban–rural contrasts. Core regions in these settings are typically centred on major metropolitan areas that have, because of the geography of colonialism and neo-colonialism, developed around port cities.

The Core: Britain

Britain provides a good example of the kind of regional differentiation that is characteristic of capitalist core economies. Figure 2.11 shows the geography of 'economic performance' of local labour market areas, as measured by an index consisting of five variables: unemployment in 1985 (given double weighting), employment change 1971–78, employment change 1978–81, population change 1971–81, and households with two or more cars, 1981 (Champion *et al.*, 1987). The economic 'core' of Britain stretches eastward from Somerset, extending around the southern and northern sides of London, and reaching into the southern parts of the Midlands and East Anglia. At the heart of this core is a virtually continuous arc around the western half of the London region, stretching from Crawley and Haywards Heath in the south to Milton Keynes and Aylesbury in the north. This zone focuses on the M4 motorway corridor and embraces the M3 belt of western Surrey and northern Hampshire. Champion *et al.* point out that, in general, high economic performance in Britain is associated with a southeastern location, with relatively small labour markets (60,000–100,000), with planned expansion and proximity to the motorway system, and with relatively high levels of employment in finance, banking, insurance, and related producer services. Britain's traditional industrial heartland (labour markets in the Northwest, Yorkshire and Humberside, and the northern Midlands), it will be noted, now fares only marginally better than the long-recognized periphery of Northern England, Wales and Scotland. Within this broad periphery, the worst-performing labour market areas are widely scattered around the coalmining and heavy industrial districts of Central Scotland, South Wales, Tyneside, Teesside, and Merseyside, with an outlier at the steel-closure town of Corby on the very edge of the core region. The fundamental cleavage reflected in this core–periphery pattern is echoed by a broad spectrum of social and economic data, to the

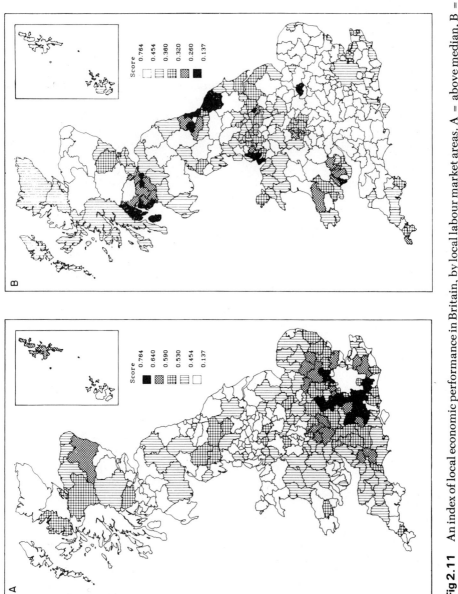

Fig 2.11 An index of local economic performance in Britain, by local labour market areas. A = above median, B = below median

Source: Champion *et al*. (1987) Fig. 8.2

point where it has become common to refer to Britain's political economy in terms of the 'Two Nations' of North and South (Knox, 1982).

The Periphery: Costa Rica

Costa Rica provides a useful example of regional differentiation at the other extreme of world development. It is representative of many peripheral countries in its heavy dependence on a narrow range of agricultural exports, its widespread poverty, its rapidly growing population, and its high rate of urbanization. As a case study, it also has the advantage of publishing official statistics that are both wide-ranging and reliable; and of having developed under a stable democracy in which economic development has never been retarded by political emergencies. The socio-economic geography of Costa Rica has been analysed in detail by Hall (1984), using data for over 400 districts that provide an exceptionally fine level of resolution. Her analysis of 31 variables (measuring aspects of resources, income, employment, housing, education, demography, health and social security) pointed to two geographically distinct components of socio-economic well-being: one contrasting districts in terms of 'affluence' (as reflected by income, the incidence of telephones, televisions, refrigerators, etc., and levels of formal education) and the other in terms of 'social well-being' (reflected by housing amenities, levels of literacy, and levels of social security insurance). Figure 2.12 shows a fourfold classification of districts based on the results of this analysis. Hall's description of these four categories provides a neat encapsulation of patterns that are exemplars of regional economic differentiation in peripheral countries:

> The districts in group I cover less than 1 per cent of the country but contain almost 30 per cent of the population. These relatively affluent, developed portions are predominantly urban and suburban, including most of the metropolitan area of San José, the cities of Cartago, Heredia, Alajuela, Grecia, Palmares, and San Ramón, all in the Central Valley, as well as Puntarenas, the principal port of the country on the Pacific coast. Founded during the colonial or early republican periods, these urban centres are among the oldest in Costa Rica. Their growth during the nineteenth and early twentieth centuries was associated with the development of the coffee industry in their hinterlands. In recent years they have received substantial immigration from rural areas and small urban centres throughout the country. Employment, including many activities that yield only irregular work and low incomes, is concentrated in the tertiary sector. . . .

> The districts in group II account for approximately one-sixth of the country and contain almost half of its population. The level of affluence was much lower than in the districts of group I, because there was a smaller proportion of the very rich and the urban middle class. The level of social well-being, however, was as high, if not higher, possibly because fewer people lived in shantytowns. Located mainly in the central and western parts of the country on the Pacific slope, the districts in group II comprised rural areas and market towns. They included the

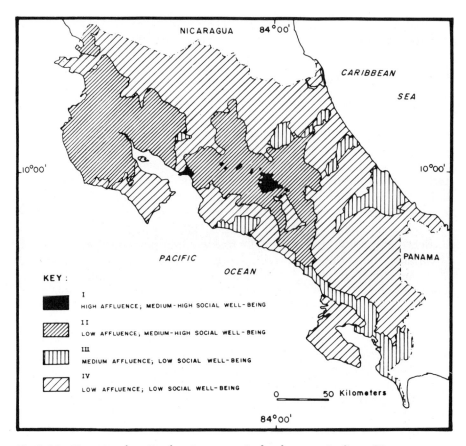

Fig 2.12   Patterns of regional socio-economic development in Costa Rica
Source: Hall (1984)

two principal regions of colonial Spanish settlement. . . . During the past two or three decades, the districts in group II received substantial investment of government funds in basic economic infrastructure and social services.

Group III . . . comprises rural areas and ports in the humid tropical lowlands on the Caribbean coast and the southern Pacific slope, which with one exception were initially colonized as plantation enclaves for the cultivation of bananas. The districts in this group cover approximately 10 per cent of the area of the country and account for 7 per cent of its population. . . . All districts in this group are areas of intensive commercial farming. Wages on the banana and oil-palm plantations are among the highest in the agricultural sector and contribute to relatively high scores for ['affluence']. The provision of services and amenities in these enclaves was done by foreign companies that controlled banana production, and investment by the government in social well-being lagged behind the districts in groups I and II.

The districts in group IV occupy more than 70 per cent of the area of Costa Rica but have only 16 per cent of its population. They are located in the humid tropical lowlands in the north of the country, the rugged Cordillera de Talamanca in the south-east, and three small areas on the Pacific slope. . . . Colonization by migrants from the centre of the country has accelerated in recent decades, but land use is dominated by extensive cattle ranching and subsistence cultivation. These districts have few roads and no urban centres, so the majority of population lives in poverty and isolation with no regular access to social services. (Hall, 1984, pp. 57–9)

The Semi-Periphery: South Korea and China

In many ways, South Korea is the archetypal NIC. With a relatively inexpensive but well-disciplined labour force and a relatively stable political climate, South Korea has been a major focus of investment by US and Japanese corporations. At the same time, South Korea has been able to exploit a reasonably large and varied resource base and a large domestic market. The net result is a broadly-based economy with an emphasis on manufactured goods – principally textiles and electronics – and a relatively high level of living: the average household income in 1985 was US$5,150. This figure masks acute spatial variations, however, since South Korea's development has been very uneven. Because the locus of economic growth has been in the manufacturing sector, the larger industrial cities and the highly urbanized provinces have experienced high levels of economic performance. Rural incomes have been supported vigorously through price-support subsidies, but rural incomes and per capita consumption remain at less than half those of towns and cities (Hasan and Rao, 1979). It is the largest cities and their metropolitan regions, however, where levels of living are, on average, highest: these are the settings where both public investment and private investment have been greatest. The net result is that Seoul, Incheon, Anyang and the surrounding province of Gyeonggi, in the north western corner of the country, constitute a clear 'core' of prosperity. Figure 2.13, which is based on a composite index of social well-being derived from 29 socio-economic indicators (Kim, 1984), shows this very clearly, together with a fragmented 'periphery' that corresponds to the highland regions of the south and the northeast.

China is another important semi-peripheral country, with a very different form of economic organization. There are, nevertheless, some similarities in the broad pattern of spatial differentiation. Although China's past emphasis on local self-sufficiency has resulted in a diversity of economic activity in most localities, there are large differences in per capita output between regions and provinces (Fig. 2.14). Both per capita agricultural and industrial output tend to be much higher on the coast than in the interior. The difference, for example, between Jiangsu, a prosperous coastal province at the centre of the coastal 'core', and Gansu, a province in the interior 'periphery', is substantial: per capita gross agricultural output in 1982 was 390 Yuan in Jiangsu and Y 160 in Gansu; per capita gross industrial output was Y 820 in Jiangsu and Y 410 in Gansu. Despite fiscal and other redistributive measures, the pattern, if not the

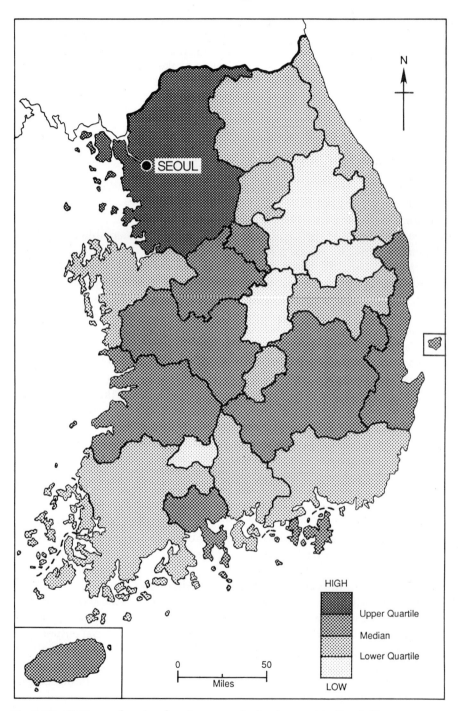

Fig 2.13   Patterns of regional socio-economic development in South Korea
Source: Kim (1984) p. 59

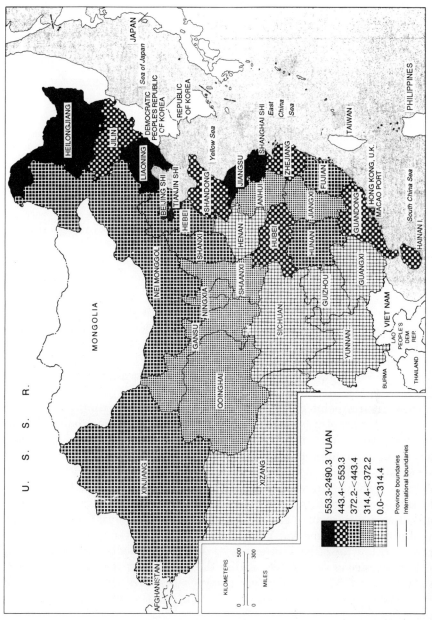

Fig 2.14 China: per capita material product, by Province
Source: World Bank (1985) Map 5.1, p. 75

The following labels appear on the map:

U. S. S. R.

MONGOLIA

AFGHANISTAN

XINJIANG

XIZANG

QINGHAI

GANSU

NINGXIA

NEI MONGGOL

SHANXI

SHAANXI

SICHUAN

YUNNAN

GUIZHOU

GUANGXI

HUNAN

HUBEI

HENAN

HEBEI

BEIJING SHI

TIANJIN SHI

SHANDONG

JIANGSU

SHANGHAI SHI

ANHUI

JIANGXI

ZHEJIANG

FUJIAN

GUANGDONG

HAINAN I.

HEILONGJIANG

JILIN

LIAONING

HONG KONG, U.K.

MACAO PORT

VIET NAM

LAO PEOPLE'S DEM. REP.

THAILAND

BURMA

DEMOCRATIC PEOPLE'S REPUBLIC OF KOREA

REPUBLIC OF KOREA

JAPAN

TAIWAN

PHILIPPINES

Sea of Japan

Yellow Sea

East China Sea

South China Sea

553.3–2490.3 YUAN
443.4–<553.3
372.2–<443.4
314.4–<372.2
0.0–<314.4

Province boundaries
International boundaries

KILOMETERS 0 — 500
MILES 0 — 300

Table 2.8: China: per capita income in urban and rural areas, 1983

Area	Urban		Rural		Total	
	Per capita income (yuan)	Percentage of population	Per capita income (yuan)	Percentage of population	Per capita income (yuan)	Percentage of population
National average	574	21	269	79	333	100
Shanghai						
municipal average	668	63	437	37	582	100
Jiangsu						
provincial average	593	16	309	84	354	100
Wuxi County	572	7	412	93	423	100
Qianzhou Township	..	..	560	100	560	100
Hubei						
provincial average	550	18	286	82	334	100
Gansu						
provincial average	648	15	228	85	245	100
Dingxi County	562	9	108	91	149	100
Dongye Township	..	..	55	100	55	100

Source: World Bank (1985) Table 5.6, p. 87

intensity, of these inequalities is replicated in inter-regional variations in personal incomes (World Bank, 1985). The gap in personal incomes between Jiangsu and Gansu in 1983, for example, was 1.4 to 1; between Wuxi county, Jiangsu and Dingxi county, Gansu, it was 2.8 to 1; and between Qianzhou Township, Wuxi, and Dongye Township, Dingxi, it was over 10 to 1 (Table 2.8).

These figures point to another broad parallel with patterns elsewhere: core–periphery contrasts are overlain by a large gap between urban and rural incomes, and by substantial variations in income within rural areas, largely because of wide differences in the quality and quantity of agricultural land per person, coupled, in China's case, with tight restrictions on geographical mobility. Table 2.8 shows that per capita income in urban areas is more than double the rural level. In terms of variations between rural areas, the example of Gansu province reveals an even sharper gradient: whereas Gansu's average rural per capita income was Y 228 in 1983, 41 per cent of its population had incomes below the official poverty level of Y 140. Its poorest county, Dingxi, had an average of only Y 108, and in the sub-district of Dongye, the average was only Y 55 – and this was Dongye's best-ever year for agricultural production.

National Development and Regional Inequality

As we shall see in Chapter 3, the relationship between overall levels of development and the intensity of regional disparities is central to theory in economic geography. We conclude this section on regional patterns, therefore, by reviewing the available empirical evidence on the issue. Much of the conventional wisdom on the subject is derived from a major study by Williamson (1965), who examined inter-regional income disparities in a sample of 24 countries. The results of this analysis suggested that the greatest regional disparities were associated with countries at an intermediate level of development, with much smaller disparities in both the most- and the least-developed countries. Williamson interpreted these cross-national results dynamically, suggesting that the onset of development precipitates sharp increases in regional inequality that are subsequently attenuated as the economy matures. This interpretation was supported by evidence of time-series data of the sort represented in Figure 2.15, which shows the clear convergence of regional per capita incomes in the United States.

Both the results and the interpretation of Williamson's work have been questioned on several grounds, however. As Krebs (1982) points out, the reliability of data and the appropriateness of measurement techniques is crucial: depending on the researcher's selections, anything can be proved. The case of Italy illustrates this impressively:

> The differences between northern and southern Italy *increased* during the period 1951–64, if measured in net regional product at market prices per capita in real terms . . . ; but it *decreased*, however, if measured in net regional product at market prices per capita . . . in current prices. (Krebs, 1982, p. 73, emphases added)

Reviewing the large number of empirical studies that have followed Williamson's work, Krebs shows that, even allowing for different measurement techniques, the idea of divergence followed by convergence in regional disparities does not meet with strong support. In the core economies, it seems, the evidence of statistics on regional per capita income is broadly consistent with Williamson's hypothesis of convergence. But in terms of the spatial

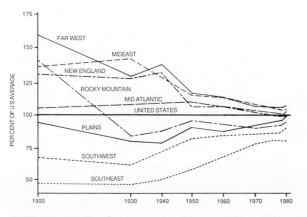

Fig 2.15 Regional convergence in per capita incomes in the United States

concentration of economic activity, the evidence points to spatial polarization or, at best, no change. This apparent paradox is explained by migration flows: in short, regional convergence of per capita incomes can be accounted for by the migration of poor people from poor regions. Taking this into account, Krebs suggests, there is little evidence for regional convergence in any of the core economies except Belgium and West Germany. Within peripheral economies, Krebs found strong evidence of marked and intensifying disparities (both in terms of regional per capita incomes and in terms of measures of economic activity), both in low-income developing countries (which, according to the conventional wisdom, should exhibit relatively low levels of interregional disparity) and in the NICs.

Inter-Urban Patterns

Even more than regions and nations, cities are specialized in terms of their economic functions and activities. Indeed, towns and cities are in many ways the basic 'motors' of economic development and differentiation (Jacobs, 1984). In this section, however, we are concerned not so much with patterns of individual functional specialization as with the patterns and regularities that can be observed among towns and cities as members of urban systems. Throughout the world, urban centres and the regions they serve are organized into spatial hierarchies – systems of settlements of different sizes that represent settings for particular groupings of economic activities and that are functionally linked to one another by flows of goods, people, money and information. These spatial hierarchies provide a fundamental framework for the world's economic landscapes, and they exhibit some important attributes in terms of the distribution of city sizes and the location of cities of different sizes.

Urban Hierarchies

Regularities in the size distribution of towns and cities have been observed for many decades, despite large increases in both the number of towns and cities and their populations. These regularities are based on a consistent relationship between the rank order of a city and its population. In many instances, this relationship has been found to conform to the so-called rank–size rule, which states that the population of any town or city in an urban hierarchy is approximately given by dividing its rank position into the population of the largest city. Thus, if the largest city in a particular system has a population of 10 million, the fifth-largest city should have a population of 2 million, the hundredth-ranked city should have a population of 100,000 and so on. Urban hierarchies approximating to this rank–size rule have been characteristic of some countries for more than a century. Figure 2.16 shows the classic example of the persistence of the rank–size distribution in the United States, from 1790

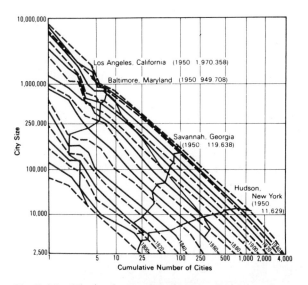

Fig 2.16   The rank–size distribution of cities in the United States
Source: based on Madden (1956) Fig. 1, p. 239

to 1950. Despite considerable changes in the rank-order of particular cities, the rank–size relationship has been remarkably consistent.

Central Places and Economic Landscapes

There is also evidence of a certain degree of regularity in the spatial form of urban hierarchies, particularly in settings where both the topography and the the distribution of natural resources are relatively even. In such settings, towns and cities can be considered as 'central places' whose rank-position in the urban hierarchy is reflected both in the range of functions, activities and amenities present and in the size of cities' immediate service area or hinterland. In short, major cities tend to dominate large regions that are, in turn, sub-regionalized by successively smaller centres at progressively lower levels of the hierarchy. The classic example here is provided by the central-place system of southern Germany in the 1930s (Fig. 2.17).

This kind of regularity inspired a great deal of deductive theorizing about the economic landscapes that might develop under various circumstances (Christaller, 1933, 1966; Lösch, 1943; Berry, 1967), and this theorizing in turn contributed in large part to the emergence of positivist approaches to economic geography under the banner of regional science (see, for example, Isard, 1975). Empirical support for the economic landscapes predicted by these deductive approaches is at best rather patchy, however; and, as we argue in Chapter 3, there are severe limits to the usefulness of regional science in explaining the reality of economic landscapes. Nevertheless, the spatial form of urban hierarchies must remain central to our thinking about

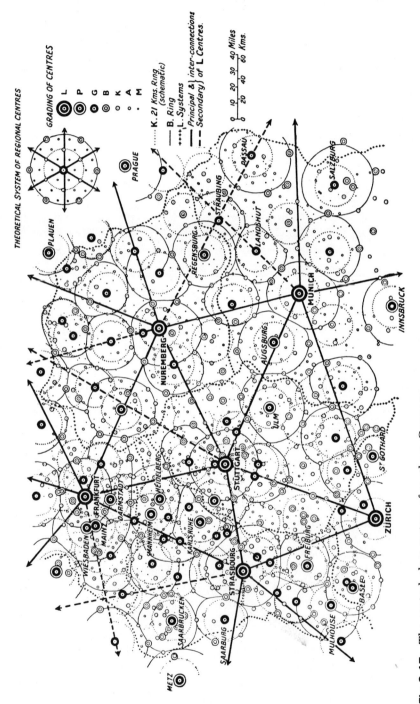

Fig 2.17 The central place system of southern Germany
Source: Berry *et al.* (1976) Fig. 12.8, p. 232. After Christaller (1966) p. 224–5

economic organization and spatial change. Patterns of diffusion from dominant metropolises to smaller centres at lower levels in the hierarchy, and from
urban centres in general to their respective hinterlands, serve to structure how
and when change takes place, as we shall see very clearly in relation to the
evolution of the world's core economies (Part II).

Primacy

Another long-standing observation about urban systems is the so-called 'law
of the primate city' based on the observation that in many countries the
rank–size distribution is distorted by the largest city being markedly more
than twice the size of the next-largest city. Primacy is most often associated
with the urban systems of peripheral countries, particularly those with a
history of foreign dependence and low levels of internal economic integration.
But strong primacy is also found in the urban systems of some core countries –
Austria, France and the United Kingdom, for example. In overall terms, there
is no clear-cut relationship between primacy and patterns of economic
development (Berry, 1961), though there is some evidence to suggest that
primacy is positively related to the degree of 'closure' of national economies in
terms of dependence on exports (Vapnarsky, 1969). What is perhaps most
significant about urban primacy is the *rate of increase* of primacy within the
urban systems of many peripheral and semi-peripheral countries: a product of
the hyper-urbanization consequent upon uneven development coupled with
acute rural poverty. In this context, urban primacy translates into a very striking form of economic primacy. Bangkok, for example, with 10 per cent of
Thailand's population, accounts for over 30 per cent of the country's GDP;
Lagos, with about 10 per cent of the Nigerian population, accounts for over 55
per cent of the country's value added in manufacturing; Lima, with just over
25 per cent of the Peruvian population, accounts for 43 per cent of Peruvian
GDP; and Managua, with about 25 per cent of the Nicaraguan population,
accounts for nearly 40 per cent of Nicaraguan GDP (Hardoy and Satterthwaite, 1986).

World Cities
These primate cities themselves are of course linked to one another as part of
an *international* urban system. Indeed, the increasing internationalization
of the world-economy makes it less and less realistic to think only in terms of
national urban systems. As we have seen, however, the new international
division of labour has been very localized in its impacts, so that just a few cities
within the international urban system have emerged as 'world cities', dominant centres and sub-centres of multinational business, international finance,
and international business services – what Friedmann (1986) calls the 'basing
points' for global capital. These 'world cities', it should be stressed, are not
necessarily the biggest within the international system of cities in terms of
population, employment or output. Rather, they are the 'control centres' of

the world-economy: places that are critical to the articulation of production and marketing under the contemporary phase of world economic development. Because these properties are difficult to quantify, it is not possible to establish a definitive list or hierarchy of world cities. Following Cohen (1981) and Friedmann (1986), however, it is possible to identify dominant, major and secondary world cities on the basis of the location of major financial centres, major corporate headquaters, international institutions, communications nodes, and concentrations of business services (Fig. 2.18). On this basis, all but two of the dominant and major world cities – São Paulo and Singapore – are located in core countries. The relative importance of secondary world cities is very much a function of the strength and vitality of the national economies that they articulate. In overall terms, notes Friedmann,

> The complete spatial distribution suggests a distinctively linear character of the world city system which connects, along an East–West axis, three distinct sub-systems: an Asian sub-system centred on the Tokyo–Singapore axis, with Singapore playing a subsidiary role as regional metropolis in Southeast Asia; an American sub-system based on the three primary core cities of New York, Chicago and Los Angeles, linked to Toronto in the North and Caracas in the South, thus bringing Canada, Central America and the small Caribbean nations into the American orbit; and a West European sub-system focused on London, Paris and the Rhine Valley axis from Randstad and [sic] Holland to Zurich. The southern hemisphere is linked into this system via Johannesburg and São Paulo. (Friedmann, 1986, pp. 72–3)

Summary

This chapter has outlined the broad framework of economic geography that is constituted by patterns of resources, population and economic activities at international, regional and inter-urban scales. Several important patterns have emerged from this review:

- The dominance of core–periphery cleavages at the international level

- The selective changes in patterns of development associated with the new international division of labour

- The existence of core–periphery cleavages *within* core countries and peripheral countries

- The intensity of urban–rural disparities within peripheral countries

- The increasing divergence of economic well-being between regions in peripheral countries

- The persistence of rank–size regularities in certain urban systems

- The increasing primacy of urban systems in peripheral settings

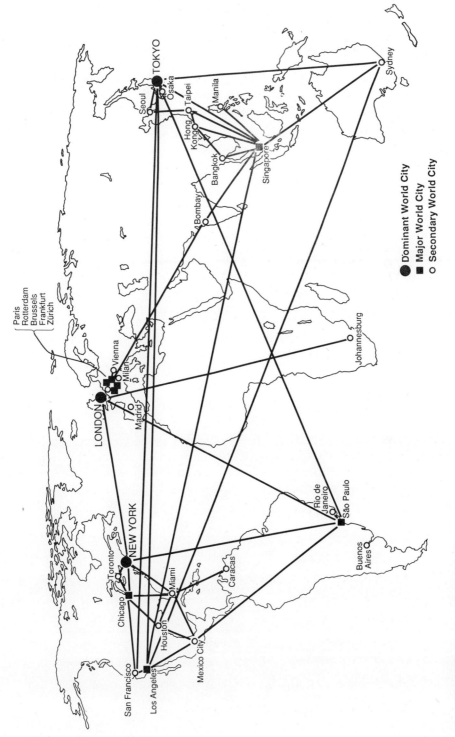

Fig 2.18 The system of World Cities

Paris
Rotterdam
Brussels
Frankfurt
Zürich

TOKYO
Seoul
Osaka
Taipei
Manila
Hong
Kong
Bangkok
Bombay
Singapore
Sydney

Vienna
Milan
LONDON
Madrid
Johannesburg

Toronto
NEW YORK
Chicago
Miami
Houston
Mexico City
Caracas
San Francisco
Los Angeles

Rio de
Janeiro
São Paulo
Buenos
Aires

● Dominant World City
■ Major World City
○ Secondary World City

- • The emergence of a global urban system in which a few 'world cities' operate as control centres for international business.

These patterns raise a number of critical questions about process and theory in economic geography. What are the locational principles that govern patterns of economic activity? What are the processes that initiate core–periphery cleavages? What is the role of trade? And how should the development process be conceptualized? It is to such questions that we now turn our attention.

3

Understanding Economic Landscapes: From Statics to Dynamics

Understanding the dominant and recurring patterns in the economic land-scape has been a major challenge to economic geography. The challenge has been met, though in a limited number of ways. The purpose of this chapter is to survey the major contributions and to give some sense of the recent shift towards more comprehensive historical approaches to understanding the pro-cesses that contribute to the dominant patterns. The overall trend in academic economic geography has been away from a cross-sectional or 'time-slice' mod-elling of sectoral (agricultural, industrial, etc.) and regional economic land-scapes towards an historical geography of economic development based upon the historical phases of the world-economy and the macroeconomic activities of states. This does not signify the 'eclipse' of sectoral or regional approaches as much as it indicates a progressive elaboration in understanding as economic geography has moved from static, partial perspectives to a more dynamic, all-encompassing historical perspective. Indeed, the basic principles of dis-tance and movement central to traditional location theory have been real elements in the growth of the dominant patterns described in Chapter 2 and the global historical geography of economic development described later in this chapter. The point we want to stress here is that they have been used by location theorists and regional scientists in limited and over-specified ways to build static models rather than viewed as geographical principles guiding the practices of an historically changing, global, and dynamic macroeconomic system.

We begin with a survey of sectoral approaches to understanding economic landscapes, paying special attention to the 'principles' of distance and move-ment that underpin them. Attention then turns to the major approaches to regional economic change. Finally, the historical approach to understanding economic landscapes is detailed.

The Economic Landscapes of Different Sectors: Location Theory

The term location theory is often used to refer to those approaches to understanding the economic landscape that focus on different 'sectoral' landscapes and which share a common set of 'principles' of distance and movement. Location theory involves building and applying models in an avowedly deductive way to agricultural, mercantile and industrial landscapes. Models can be seen as either simplified representations of reality that purport to explain it, albeit selectively and incompletely, or simplified representations of reality whose main function is heuristic (hypothesis generating). In either case, however, the focus is upon simplification or reduction of a more complex reality to a simpler set of 'locational principles'.

One limitation of this conception of explanation is that it isolates and then generalizes simplifications that are specific to certain historical periods and certain places (Gregory, 1978). Another limitation is that the models are often viewed as equivalent to theories. But, as Chorley (1972; 188) has observed:

> . . . it is important to differentiate between models and theories . . . . A model becomes a theory about the real world only when a segment of the real world has been successfully mapped onto it, both by avoiding the disregarding of too much information in the stage of abstraction and by carrying out a rigorous *interpretation* of the model results in real world terms.

Location theory, however, has become an important part of economic geography. As the intellectual kernel of the field of 'regional science' it has been the major way in which the positivist conception of explanation has been brought to bear in economic geography (Szymanski and Agnew, 1981).

Basic Principles of Distance and Movement

There are a number of ways in which the 'basic principles' can be expressed (e.g. compare Haggett, 1966 with Abler, Adams and Gould, 1971). Basic to all, however, is the idea that economic geography is about the impact of *distance* or space, *sui generis*, upon economic activities. Most locational models consequently begin with the assumption of an isotropic plain upon which a certain economic activity is located and then deduce the independent effect of distance – measured in terms of physical relationship, cost, or perception by a decision-maker – in determining where the economic activity is located, *ceteris paribus*. In most locational models, cost and perceived distances are much more important 'explanatory variables' than absolute distances measuring physical space. As geographers shifted from 'normative' to 'behavioural' models with less restrictive assumptions about economic behaviour (for example, allowing for information constraints and mixed motives in decision-making), perceived distance became even more important. An important continuity, however, lies in the premise that distance or space is an independent variable producing predictable and recurring spatial patterns of economic activities (Abler, Adams and Gould, 1971).

A second basic principle of location theory concerns *accessibility*. All locations are not equal, even on an isotropic plain. Some are more accessible than others. Usually this means that they are easier to travel to or more central. This reflects the importance of the assumption of 'least-effort' in human behaviour and the associated assumption of 'distance-decay' in the importance and intensity of economic activity as one moves away from the most accessible location. People in general are viewed as effort-and-distance-minimizers (Haggett, 1966).

A third principle concerns *interaction and movement*. Movement occurs on the isotropic plain under three conditions: (1) complementarity: in order for two locations to interact there must be a demand in one and a supply in the other; (2) intervening opportunity: complementarity generates interaction only if no intervening source of supply is available; and (3) transferability: if the distance between the locations of demand and supply is too great or too costly, interaction will not take place even if there is perfect complementarity and lack of intervening opportunity (Ullman, 1956). This principle applies to interaction based on physical movement, both of goods and of people. One model that exemplifies this principle is the so-called 'gravity model.' This postulates that an attracting force of interaction between two locations is created by the population masses of the two locations, and a friction against interaction is caused by the intervening space and intervening opportunities (Carrothers, 1956).

The fourth principle involves *diffusion*. Ideas and innovations spread across the isotropic plain both contagiously (friction of distance) and hierarchically (directly between more accessible locations). Barriers, such as mountains and rivers, cultural and political boundaries, and limitations of information availability, restrict spatial diffusion. Adoption of innovations is viewed as largely dependent on nearness to previous adopters, *ceteris paribus* (Abler, Adams and Gould, 1971).

The fifth principle concerns *transportation and networks*. The accessibility of locations is fundamentally affected by the transport networks that integrate the isotropic plain. Interaction is channelled by these networks (Ullman, 1956).

Sixth, and finally, the more accessible locations acquire advantages over others in the form of *agglomeration economies* or returns to centralization. As they are more accessible they attract activities which in turn attract other activities that are attracted by the ones already there. The principle of agglomeration as a function of accessibility, therefore, is the ultimate determinant of why some economic activities tend to cluster and others are distributed relative to the demands of the cluster. Attempts at developing general location theories have tended to regard agglomeration/centralization as a 'higher-order' principle from which the operation in practice of the other principles derives (e.g. Isard, 1956; Ullman, 1960).

These principles – distance, accessibility, interaction, diffusion, transportation, and agglomeration – have been the guiding geographical principles within the world-economy that originated in the sixteenth century and spread out to encompass the world in the years since. *The core–periphery, urban-rural, urban system and spatial division of labour* contrasts identified in Chapter 2 are the cumulative product of the increasing global operation of these principles of geographical differentiation and integration. The final section of this chapter describes how these principles have worked together in different ways and changed in relative significance during different phases in the evolution of the world-economy.

However, these basic principles typically have been given expression in sectoral accounts of economic landscapes. Consequently, most textbook accounts of location theory proceed by sector (e.g. Conkling and Yeates, 1976; Berry, Conkling and Ray, 1987). This is also the approach taken in this section. The agricultural landscape is examined first. This is followed by the mercantile landscape of market towns and service centres, and, finally, by the industrial landscape. It is important to note, however, that the discussion here is intended to be illustrative rather than comprehensive.

The Agricultural Landscape

Models concerned with the spatial distribution of agricultural activities attempt to account for variations in land use patterns. They focus on why some uses are located where they are rather than elsewhere. The choice of one location over another is seen as a function of the farmer's or land-owner's calculus of advantages. For the most part, advantages are defined in monetary terms but they really represent such things as soil fertility, location near transport nodes, location in a prosperous market area, good water supply, etc.: the expression of these characteristics at any one particular location will be translated into a money output obtained from exploiting them as advantages.

Above all, however, the use of a particular location is determined by a *competition* between potential land uses. Most land areas are suitable for a variety of uses and many uses have the ability to generate a net return on any given land unit. In normative agricultural location models the assumption is that through the maximization of profit the farmer engages in the 'highest and best use' in order to maximize productivity and return on investment. For every land use, therefore, there is an optimum set of locations. The optimal locations possess optimal sets of factors for the conduct of a particular agricultural activity.

The concept of *rent* is used to represent the comparative productivity and profit yield of particular locations. Rent is thus a return or surplus generated by the differential use of a particular land area. The highest rent is produced by the 'best' use. To Ricardo and other classical economists this was seen as a return to differential fertility, even if it did accrue to the land-owner. However, a more influential conception of rent is that provided by J.H. Von Thünen, who can be regarded as the foremost of the early agricultural location theorists.

To Von Thünen rent accrued to land on the basis of its locational attributes rather than its fertility. Since the (market) price the farmer received was determined by the costs of production plus the cost of transporting the product, a surplus occurred but at a diminishing rate of return up to as distant a point as was necessary to satisfy market demand. The surplus is realized, therefore, from savings in transportation costs and is a direct function of accessibility. In addition to the locational sources of surplus, Von Thünen identified two other sources from which rent *might* arise: (1) return on intensification when all usable land is under cultivation, and (2) return on capital invested in fixed improvements.

To demonstrate his conception of location and differential rents, Von Thünen set up a model that has served as a major inspiration for location theory in general. His first step was to assume the following:

1   A state isolated from all others
2   A city located at the centre of the state
3   One agricultural hinterland surrounding the city
4   The city is the market for agricultural products
5   All farmers desire to maximize profit
6   Farmers can adjust operations to maximize profits
7   A uniform plain with respect to soils, topography, climate, etc.
8   Only one means of transportation – horsedrawn wagons
9   Transportation is available equally in all directions
10 Transportation costs vary directly with distance but vary by product
11 Transportation costs are borne by the farmer
12 The farmer delivers his products to market
13 Market prices and production costs are the same for all farmers
14 Market prices differ by product

Von Thünen's second step was to ask: what land use pattern will result and how will distance to market affect the possible use of land? The answers followed from his assumptions (Fig. 3.1). In particular, using empirical information from the region in eastern Germany in which he lived (Rostock), Von Thünen demonstrated that:

1   The spatial distribution of land uses depends on the comparative rent-paying ability of different land uses
2   Each use occupies that area for which its marginal revenue is greater than its marginal (transportation) costs
3   As distance increases from market intensive agriculture plays a progressively smaller part in land use
4   Concentric zones of land use develop around market centres

Von Thünen's model was later elaborated in greater detail by Lösch (1954) and formalized mathematically by Dunn (1954). It has also served as the focus for an important book on rural land use (Chisholm, 1962) and extended to the contexts of urban land use (Alonso, 1964) and continental and global patterns

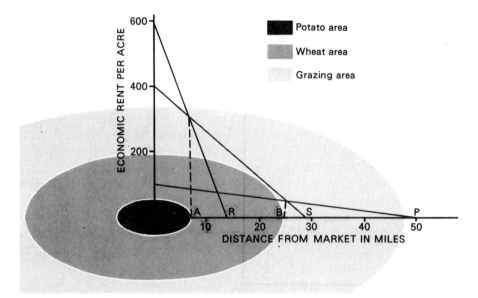

Fig 3.1 Von Thünen's rings
Source: Conkling and Yeates (1976) p. 17

of agricultural production (Schlebecker, 1960; Peet,1969). It seems clear, however, that the processes involved in these other contexts are quite different from those Von Thünen was concerned to demonstrate in a nineteenth-century regional setting. In particular, the shift to continental and global scales involves movement into a realm where what is easily swept into a *ceteris paribus* clause by Von Thünen (assumptions 1 to 14) is probably of vital *causal* importance.

More generally, however, Von Thünen's model itself has become viewed increasingly as representing the workings of an idealized *laissez-faire* space economy that has little contemporary relevance. The behavioural critique of normative locational models has been particularly popular among students of agricultural land use. The multiple motives of farmers and the constraints on their activities are more likely to attract attention today than is the Von Thünen model. For example, Ilbery (1985), in his major text on agricultural geography, pays very little attention to the Von Thünen model except to criticize it. The tendency is to focus on the farm as a decision-making unit and to see distance and transportation costs as relatively minor elements in the list of locational and decision-making factors facing farmers. (See also Watts, 1983 on why Nigerian farmers do not conform to Von Thünen's model.) Behavioural models such as those of Wolpert (1964) and Pred (1967) emphasize the importance of both farmers' choices and external constraints in reaching decisions about what to grow where. However, they maintain an emphasis on deductive modelling and fitting 'expected' to actual behaviour but without the aesthetic simplicity and logical clarity of a normative model such as Von Thünen's.

The Mercantile Landscape

One of the major purposes of location theory is to put location into economic theory. Location theorists criticize classical and neo-classical economists for holding location in a *ceteris paribus* clause – i.e., for assuming away the effects of distance, accessibility, and transportation costs (Isard, 1956; Amedeo and Golledge, 1975). Two writers in particular, Walter Christaller (1933, 1966) and August Lösch (1954), attempted to build models of spatial marketing by incorporating spatial considerations into neo-classical economic theory. These attempts characterize space as a 'theatre' or context for the competitive market forces of neo-classical theory.

Although there are important differences between the models of Christaller and Lösch there are a number of commonalities in terms of reasoning and assumptions. In particular, each was concerned with modelling a mercantile landscape: an economic landscape of market centres and retail distribution in which different-sized centres offer different combinations of goods and services to different-sized trade areas (Fig. 2.17). Settlements are thus viewed as primarily *local* trade centres serving rural hinterlands. Being Germans, both Christaller and Lösch could look back on a settlement history that conformed to a considerable degree to their characterizations. Towns and local trade had indeed developed together.

Christaller published his *Central Places in Southern Germany* (in German) in 1933. In it he presented a theory about the number, distribution, and size of towns. His first step was to make a number of critical assumptions:

1   There is an isotropic plain (i.e., there are no environmental differences such as rivers or variable relief)
2   Rural population is evenly distributed
3   Everyone has the same income
4   Each person can travel in every direction
5   Travel costs are the same per kilometre in every direction
6   Towns act as *central places* for the surrounding countryside
7   Each person demanding a good or service goes to the nearest town in which it is available, thus minimizing their travel expenses.

From these assumptions Christaller (1966) deduced that each central place should be surrounded by a hexagonal service area, that for each service all service areas are the same size, that for each service the central places are the same size and located at equal distances from one another. However, some goods and services are in greater demand on a more regular basis than others. These lower-order central-place functions are provided by the smaller central places that are located closer together. Larger central places are located further apart and provide higher-order functions as well as lower-order ones. But they too are evenly distributed and have equal (if larger) hexagonal service areas (see Fig. 2.17).

Christaller's model, therefore, produces a hierarchical spatial structure of central places and service areas based on a hierarchy of functions. At the top of the urban hierarchy is the highest-order centre with many specialized as well as all other functions, at the bottom there are a great many small central places with a few lower-order functions serving small rural hinterlands.

In addition to the focus on marketing, however, Christaller also proposed that criteria such as transportation and administration can be more important in the location of central places than marketing. He thus elaborated two other central place hierarchies: one in which location on transportation routes is the primary determinant of location and one in which location within a bounded administrative area was primary. Christaller found that a 'mix' of the three 'principles' worked well for southern Germany. He was clear that his model was a beginning rather than a substitute for the analysis of real economic landscapes. He also stressed the significance of historical conditions in determining the relative importance of marketing considerations. Unfortunately, these *caveats* were lost when Christaller's model became popular in the 1960s.

To Lösch (1954), the spatial outcomes of Christaller's three principles of location were special cases of a more general hierarchical/hexagonal relationship. In addition, Lösch argued that the process involved was *entirely* due to economic conditions of monopolistic competition created by space itself. Hierarchies of hexagons exist because the hexagon is the ideal economic form of market area and goods differ in the size of market area they require. Within each market area a producer acquires a monopolistic advantage but the space commanded is restricted and bounded by competition from neighbouring producers.

However, the scope for monopolistic advantage and thus the size of market area differs by good. Essentially, different goods will have different sized hexagonal market areas. As a consequence, central places arise at the intersection of multiple hexagonal areas rather than being uniquely associated with a particular type of good or order of function and its hexagonal unit. The Löschian ideal economic landscape, therefore, results in a much less distinct hierarchical structure than that proposed by Christaller because (1) settlements of the same size need not have the same range of functions, and (2) higher-order centres need not have all of the functions of lower-order centres.

Lösch's formulation has not been without its critics, even if sympathetic ones. Isard (1956), for example, notes the paradox that at the same time that production is concentrated at central places, the consuming population is supposed to be distributed uniformly. Isard has attempted to deal with this problem by modifying Lösch's economic landscape in such a way that hexagons decrease in size as the larger centres are approached. While maintaining the hexagonal form, the Löschian landscape is transformed in order to account for agglomeration. Isard has also attempted to include spatial variation in the availability of raw materials in his elaboration on Lösch's model.

There is a large volume of literature reporting on empirical research into the uses of central place models. Some of this is reviewed in Berry (1967). Much of the research has been on various parts of the United States but there are also works on China (Skinner, 1964–65), South America (Snyder, 1962), India (Mayfield, 1967), and West Africa (Abiodun, 1967). These are alleged to 'lend cumulative support to the basic concepts of the central place model' (Conkling and Yeates, 1976 p. 171) but usually it is the *forms* of the model (hierarchies and hexagons) that are 'discovered' rather than evidence for the economic processes that underpin the different central place models.

The work of Skinner (1964–65) is an important and interesting example of both an application of the central place approach to the context of a peasant society in which local trading and periodic markets predominate and the form–process confusion. Skinner's work in general and the hexagons he uses to characterize the market areas of Szechuan in pre-Communist China in particular, constitute the most well known example of periodic market research (Szymanski and Agnew, 1981). Skinner attempted to show that in the Chinese case 'the service area of each market should approach a regular hexagon' (Skinner, 1964–65, p. 17). Although he provided no numerical data with regard to either the location of consumers or the markets they used, he claimed that

> . . . in six areas of China where I have been able to test the proposition, a majority of market towns have precisely six immediately neighbouring market towns and hence a marketing area of hexagonal shape, albeit distorted by topographical features. (Skinner, 1964–65, p. 17)

Of course, the claim concerning hexagonal market areas does not follow from the existence of six neighbouring markets, neither is any information provided about the size-ranking of market centres even though Skinner identifies six higher-level central places in one region and five in another.

When one examines the bulk of the literature on periodic and daily markets, however, it becomes clear that Skinner's findings were an aberration. Most peasant marketing systems just do not fit the classical central place patterns (Bromley, 1974; Smith, 1978). Replication of Skinner's 'research' has not been possible given its context and the paucity of data available. Yet Skinner's findings have acquired a certain celebrity. One text includes Skinner's hexagons as an important part of a chapter entitled 'Empirical Evidence of Spatial Order' (Lloyd and Dicken, 1972).

Another area of empirical research into the efficacy of central place models concerns the settlement hierarchies that the models predict. In fact, some empirical research suggests that city-size distributions in general are positively skewed; that is, there are many small but relatively few large cities, with a *tendency* for the number of cities in each of a set of size classes to decline as city size increases (Richardson, 1973). This has been known for many years. What is at issue is how to explain it. The predilection of location theorists has been to explain it in terms of the so-called 'rank–size rule' (Fig. 2.16) which conforms closely to predictions from central place models.

The rank–size rule states that the *normal* (i.e., rank–size) distribution of city sizes is the result of 'stochastic' growth processes. The problem with this is threefold. First, many countries do not have rank–size city-size distributions: as we saw in Chapter 2, primacy is widespread. Second, the instability and, often, irrelevance, of national boundaries to city growth processes makes the use of national city-size distributions questionable. Third, the term *stochastic* masks an incredible variety of causal processes (Szymanski and Agnew, 1981). While there *are* clearly demarcated international and national urban hierarchies, the *form* that they take and the processes that produce them cannot be predicted by deduction from central place models.

The Industrial Landscape

The final sectoral landscape is that created by the 'forces' of industrial location. The same factors of production that influence agricultural land use – land, labour, capital and 'entrepreneurship' – also enter into models of industrial location. In manufacturing, however, there are a number of other considerations, particularly raw materials, energy, and economies of scale (internal (firm) and external (agglomeration)), that have come to play an important part in models of industrial location.

Identifying the range of influences affecting manufacturing location does not resolve the problem of how to relate them to one another. Numerous location theorists have attempted to do this but in different ways. The least-cost model of industrial location is the oldest approach. This model combines the various locational influences so as to determine the site where production can take place at minimum cost. A very different model is that involving market-area analysis. In this case the location of a factory is viewed as the result of a search for that site from which a firm can command the largest share of the market and thereby maximize total revenue. A third model focuses on managerial decision-making and actual firm locational decisions rather than the question of the 'best' location.

An early and important *least-cost model* of industrial location was provided by Alfred Weber (1929). He first considered the problem of where to locate an industrial plant when the locations of its markets and raw materials were fixed and known. His major assumptions were:

1 Fuels and raw materials used in production are fixed in location and not ubiquitous
2 Markets are separate locations and the amount of product consumed in each is known
3 The cost of transportation is the major cost in plant location
4 The plant operates within a competitive market so monopolistic advantage derived from location is of no consequence.

On the basis of these assumptions he built his simplest model, 'the location triangle', which he used to find the location of minimum transportation costs for a plant. In this model transportation costs were considered a function of weight to be carried and distance to be travelled (Fig. 3.2).

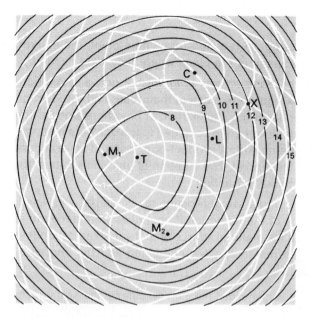

Fig 3.2 Weber's location theory
Source: Conkling and Yeates (1976), p. 92

Weber moved on from this simple model to consider various complicating factors:

1 If a raw material 'loses weight' in manufacture then a plant will be drawn towards the location of that raw material; the plant is *raw-material oriented*.

2 If distribution costs are higher than assembly costs then the plant will be *market oriented*. This will be particularly the case if there is a weight gain in manufacturing either through the combination of raw materials that expand or through the addition of ubiquities (e.g. water).

3 If labour costs are higher than transportation costs this will shift plant location, especially in labour-intensive industries.

4 If there are cost savings from agglomeration (sharing services, greater division of labour) then a plant will be deflected towards industrial clusters but if there are increased costs (higher rents) it will be deflected away.

He 'solved' successively more complex scenarios for different industries, from one raw material and one market to multiple sources of raw materials and one market plus the complicating factors. Multiple markets were outside the scope of the model.

Although Weber's approach remained 'buried' for many years, in the 1950s and 1960s there were numerous attempts to formalize and operationalize his model using a variety of linear and non-linear programming algorithms (e.g.

Kuhn and Kuenne, 1962). There was also one attempt, by Hoover (1948), to examine transportation costs in more detail by considering such factors as the tapering effect of freight charges, break-of-bulk points, the type of transport mode used and the influence of political boundaries and tariffs. Isard (1956) introduced the idea of 'substitution principles' whereby firms could limit output and choose between alternative proportions of input and thus reduce dependence on particular sources of raw materials. Finally, Moses (1958) stressed the role of plant economies of scale in industrial location. It is important to stress that Weber was explicitly concerned to develop a model of industrial location that could apply equally to any political-economic context. This was why he stressed minimizing costs rather than maximizing profits. But in so doing he avoided the issue of the motivations that are characteristic of different political-economic settings and thus the reasoning process that lies behind industrial location decisions.

The single market assumed by Weber is a case in point. This unrealistic treatment of demand is especially important in those contexts, such as the US, where firms have tended to be oriented towards enhancing market share and increasing profits through increasing demand. *Market-area analysis* has developed as a way of thinking about industrial location that is oriented towards a firm's attempt to maximize sales through monopolizing and increasing the size of a sales territory (Fetter, 1924; Greenhut, 1956).

The analysis begins with the following assumptions:

1   Buyers are distributed evenly in space and all have the same level of demand for a given product.
2   Competing products are identical in all respects.
3   Products are sold f.o.b., i.e., the buyer pays all freight charges from the plant.
4   Prices are based on the manufacturer's costs plus mark-up that is the same for all producers.
5   Freight charges are the same for all producers of the same products.
6   Each firm is located separately from its competitors, and each producer monopolizes the trade of those buyers who are closest because of savings in freight charges.

The locational pattern that appears as a result of these assumptions is first determined. Then the assumptions are relaxed one by one to discover the separate effects of the added variables upon the shapes and sizes of market areas and thus on the location of production. This approach is useful when the products are standardized and transportation costs are a substantial part of the final price. But for many products transportation costs are usually a small parts of total costs, and standard *delivered* prices predominate. So, even though it compensates for the least-cost model's neglect of markets, it is itself of limited utility.

As a result there has been less and less interest in normative models of industrial location and much more interest in examining *firms as decision-*

making units and discovering the motivations, information sources, and managerial techniques that lead to the selection of particular sites for production facilities. Even for their advocates, normative models, especially the least-cost model, remain of value largely as a 'norm' against which to measure actual locational patterns (Conkling and Yeates, 1976). But behavioural studies also have important limitations. Without some normative, simplified framework they often amount to no more than descriptive accounts. At the level of firms and consumers, however, the normative models are clearly deficient, as we have seen. In particular, they split behaviour into two parts: (1) an essential core described by the model and (2) deviations specified at the level of the individual case, and described as deviations from the model (Massey, 1974).

The alternative is to move away from the *ideal type* models that have characterized location theory in general (both normative and behavioural) towards a concern for the historical-structural contexts in which firm locational decisions are made (Markusen, 1985; Storper, 1985). This does not mean abandoning a focus on firms and markets but does involve placing them in historical and institutional contexts.

For example, the electrical machinery and electronics industries in Britain in the late 1960s were faced by a new macroeconomic context that affected decisions about where to locate operations (Massey, 1974). Two were dominant: the influx of US capital and the balance-of-payments deficit. The first produced a retrenchment in certain high-technology and military-oriented sectors. The second stimulated British industry, especially export-oriented industry, to be more internationally competitive. So firms faced an environment specific to their *industrial sector*, *time period*, and *national situation*: a worried but friendly government, retrenchment through merger/acquisition/ rationalization aimed at increasing competitiveness, defensiveness in relation to established markets and aggressiveness in relation to potential ones.

This was what the firms had in common at a particular period of time. Of course, they had their own particular characteristics which varied between them: different sizes, different product groups, different capital structures. These influenced the specific ways in which the macroeconomic processes produced locational responses. But these characteristics were not themselves the causes of locational response. Firms, both old and new, were responding to changing external circumstances and adjusting as best they could.

It is not difficult, therefore, to agree with Massey (1974, p. 86) when she writes: 'If we are to understand locational behaviour, we must be prepared to relinquish the formalism of non-historical models, and turn to the structural context which determines that behaviour.'

Approaches to Regional Economic Change

An alternative to the sectoral approach in understanding the economic land-scape has been a focus on the differential economic condition of different regions or other spatial units. Sometimes the term region refers to a relatively large area within a country. But sometimes larger world regions are also implied. Arguments are often transferred from one scale to another without much care as to whether there is *processual* continuity. The major concern has been to provide frameworks for thinking about the general mobilization of resources and the spread of economic activity in spatial terms. Economic geography, therefore, becomes from this point of view the geography of regional development.

There are two major types of approaches: (1) neo-classical economic/liberal models and (2) structuralist models that originated as critiques of the other models. The first type assumes that differences in economic develop-ment between regions are due to short-run disequilibrum between supply and demand within each region. Ultimately, however, growth will shift, spread or trickle down from the more developed regions to the less developed ones, as long as 'market forces' are unimpeded (neo-classical) or government acts (liberal). The second type is the *mirror-image* of the first. Regional disequilibrium is viewed as a *structural* feature of the capitalist market: the development of one region presupposes the non-development or underdevelopment of others. Rather than a balancing up between regions or long-run equilibrium, as expected in the neo-classical/liberal models, structuralists expect a permanent imbalance between regions in levels of economic growth. Regional economic change, therefore, always involves a perpetuation or a deepening rather than a mitigation of regional imbalance.

Neo-Classical/Liberal Models

Compared to the sectoral models, the regional models are relatively new, dating mainly from the 1950s. There are four major ones: (1) export base models; (2) income inequality models; (3) growth pole models; (4) centre–periphery models.

The claim that 'regional growth typically has been promoted by the ability of a region to produce goods or services demanded by the national economy and to export them at a competitive advantage with respect to other regions' (Perloff and Wingo, 1961, p. 200) led to the development of models stressing the role played by the export base. North (1955), for example, proposed a five-stage regional export base model which he suggested was appropriate for all capitalist countries where population pressure has been limited. After a brief subsistence stage, he envisaged a stage of specialization in staple exports. This in turn was followed by the expansion and diversification of the export base. A fourth stage involved the growth of locally-oriented industries.

Finally, the local industries became export-oriented and thus further diversified the region's export base.

North's model is an explicit generalization from the experience of the Pacific Northwest region in the United States. it has been criticized, however, for ignoring regional differences in wage rates and labour supply. Borts and Stein (1964) use a careful statistical comparison with US experience to suggest that wage levels are at least as important as exports in stimulating or restricting regional economic growth.

More widely accepted than export base models have been models that focus on regional income inequality. Rather than isolating one region and assuming an essential identity in regional experience, these models assume a short-run inequality between several regions that is only overcome in the long run. Perhaps the most important of these models is that of Myrdal (1957). This model is based on the contention that in a market economy changes in the location of economic activities produce cumulative advantages for one region rather than a straightforward equalization of advantages across all regions. In the short run, growth in one region is at the expense of others. But in the long run 'spread effects' can counteract the 'backwash effects' of regional concentration as demands in backward regions are met locally (Fig. 3.3).

Myrdal's model was followed by others, such as those of Hirschman (1958) and Hicks (1959). Hirschman's model assumes 'polarization' and 'trickling-down' effects but argues that early polarization eventually produces a countervailing trickling-down (and thus interregional equilibrium) rather than cumulative returns to initial advantage. Hicks's model is similar to Myrdal's in its emphasis on cumulative causation but gives greater attention to

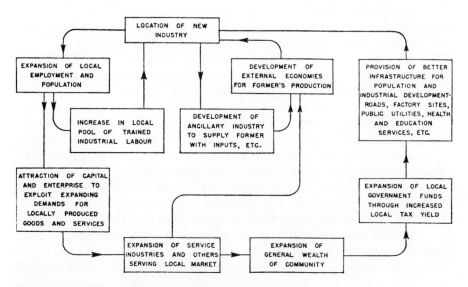

Fig 3.3   Myrdal's model of cumulative causation

flows of labour and capital from growing to lagging regions rather than vice versa.

Some empirical work, especially that of Williamson (1965), suggests that if the world is divided into 'developed' 'developing' and 'underdeveloped' countries, the developing display the regional inequality predicted by the models for the early stage of 'development' whereas the developed exhibit the convergence predicted for later. In fact, however, as described in Chapter 2, regional inequalities are characteristic of *all* countries whatever their 'stage' of development. Moreover, the regional scale of analysis often obscures more localized patterns of growth and underdevelopment that can deepen even as the region or the nation is experiencing aggregate growth (Massey, 1984; Bensel, 1984).

In response to the perceived lack of regional uniformity in economic growth, a number of writers have proposed 'growth pole' or 'growth centre' models. These are predicated upon the concentration of growth in regions at urban-industrial poles. To Perroux (1955, 1961) the growth pole owes its existence to the location within it of one main 'growth industry'. As this industry grows it attracts other linked industries by virtue of local external economies. Other agglomeration economies encourage further growth. Perroux drew the model from his study of the Ruhr in Germany and Lyons in France. The insistence on the key role of a single propulsive growth industry probably arose from the selection of these cases for study. There are clearly many situations where growth has not been based on a single industry; where there have been a number of unrelated but propulsive growth industries (think of almost any major urban centre). In addition, the very presence of a single dominant industry may inhibit rather than stimulate long-run economic growth by reducing diversification and increasing dependence on a single industry or industrial sector. There are, therefore, serious empirical and logical problems with growth pole models of economic growth.

Finally, some centre–periphery models, particularly that of Friedmann (1956, 1961), have been proposed to account for the failure of regional convergence, even in the very long run. Friedmann (1956) argued that as economic development proceeds, an economy's spatial structure changes from one characterized by 'small, isolated, and functionally undifferentiated communities' to one of interdependent regions with a centre–periphery structure. Only government comprehensive planning with a focus on projects and their regional coordination is seen as a plausible solution. Interregional equilibrium cannot occur 'naturally' as most models expect: 'even the advanced economies of Western Europe and the USA continue to be plagued with problems of depressed areas' (Friedmann, 1963, p. 45). Unlike the other models, therefore, this one does not expect equalization, even in the long run, without intervention.

But like the others, Friedmann's centre–periphery model does accept spatial equilibrium as a norm towards which planners and governments should strive. Yet, as Gore (1984, pp. 47–9) has pointed out, conditions of general equilibrium are logically inconsistent with the implications of a space economy:

1   Perfect competition assumes the independence of individual decisions, but *as soon as a spatial dimension is added to an economy*, it is apparent that decisions are interdependent in the same way as they are under conditions of oligopoly . . . [when] locational interdependence in terms of market share means that there is in fact no stable solution. (Gore, 1984, pp. 47–8)

2   Agglomeration economies are an important influence on locational decisions, and they can in no sense be regarded as 'imperfections'. But once they are allowed into a space economy, the whole notion of equilibrium becomes untenable. For the achievement of equilibrium is posited on the assumption that economic changes are created by changes in *exogenous* variables. The presence of agglomeration economies and, indeed, any increasing returns to scale, means that the forces for change are *endogenous*. . . . The economy is not equilibriating, but characterized by progressive and cumulative change. (Gore,1984, p. 49)

The neo-classical/liberal models, therefore, are based on a criterion of welfare, spatial equilibrium, that is logically impossible to attain – either through the market or by means of government intervention.

Structuralist Models

The problems with the neo-classical/liberal models are not solely logical, however. In the late 1960s it became clear the the 'trickling-down' process was not working in many countries. Indeed, the so-called 'backwash effects' were apparently much stronger than the anticipated 'spread effects' or diffusion of economic growth. Spatial inequalities at a range of scales – international, regional and urban – had become more rather than less pronounced.

In this context, a virtual avalanche of critical writings appeared with many new terms and concepts such as metropolis and satellites, core and periphery, dominance–dependence relations, neo-colonialism, growth-without-development, dependent development, unequal exchange, and enclave economy. These writings were highly critical of the 'stages' approach to development and the idea that the previous historical experience of particular 'developed' countries (such as the US) could be used to build models that had universal validity. Rather, development and prosperity in the developed core of the world (the US and/or Europe) were seen as being based on under-development and squalor in the periphery. By means of unequal trade, foreign investment, and profit extraction, the underdeveloped countries were becoming *increasingly* impoverished. The development of the core thus *depends* on the systematic underdevelopment of the periphery: it is a structural necessity.

Three writers exemplify the alternative models of regional economic change that arose from this critique: André Gunder Frank, David Slater, and Milton Santos. They invert the propositions of the neo-classical/liberal models

– impoverishment rather than growth is now diffused – but, they do so in rather different ways.

In his best-known work, Frank (1967) rejected the idea that under-development is an original condition, equivalent to 'traditionalism' or 'back-wardness'. Rather, it is a condition *created* by integration into the world-wide system of exchange originating in the sixteenth century: the 'world capitalist system'. Poverty is not, therefore, a consequence of isolation or the failure of western technology, capital and values to spread. It stems directly from the nature of relationships within the world capitalist system.

This system is described by Frank as follows:

> As a photograph of the world taken at a point of time, this model consists of a world metropolis (today the United States) and its governing class, and its national and international satellites and their leaders – national satellites like the southern states of the United States, and international satellites like São Paulo. Since São Paulo is a national metropolis in its own right, the model con-sists further of the satellites; the provincial metropolises, like Recife or Belo Horizonte, and their regional and local satellites in turn. That is, taking a photo-graph of a slice of the world we get a whole chain of metropolises and satellites, which runs from the world metropolis down to the hacienda or rural merchant who are satellites of the local commercial metropolitan centre but who in their turn have peasants as their satellites. If we take a photograph of the world as a whole, we get a whole series of such constellations of metropolises and satellites. (Frank, 1967, pp. 146–7)

This structure of metropolises and satellites has been in place since Europeans ventured out into the world in the sixteenth century. Although the form of the monopoly power of metropolis over satellites has changed (for example, fol-lowing political independence or with the switch from merchant to industrial investment in the nineteenth century), the system of 'surplus expropriation' and transfer from satellites to metropolis has continued to fuel growth in some places essentially at the expense of others.

One writer who has taken up the logic of Frank's model and applied it to the case of regions within 'underdeveloped' countries is David Slater (1975). His view of the world economy is very similar to that of Frank described above. But his main concern is to examine the spatial structure of underdevelopment and how it has changed over time. He identifies four stages of spatial organi-zation in African development:

1   Pre-colonial spatial structure (pre-1880s)
     Colonial penetration, initial concentration and the beginning of inter-nal expansion (1880–1914)
3   Colonial organization and continued extension (1919–60).
4   Neo-colonial concentration and limited attempts at restructuring (1960-present)

The first stage was not characterized by the isolated, local economies of Friedmann's model but by inter-regional trading networks. In stage 2 these networks disintegrated as capitalist penetration from the coast reoriented regional economies to external ties. The older inter-regional networks were atomized both by the imposition of new political boundaries that bore little relationship to them and by the construction of railways to service new plantations, mining concerns and settler estates. In the third stage, export crop production was extended into new areas and transportation networks became clearly focused upon ports and colonial capitals. In the final stage, even with political independence, the external dependence and internal atomization continue.

The models of Frank and Slater are examples of what can be called 'dependency theory'. They are in fact fairly extreme examples. Some other work, including other writing by Frank and Slater, puts more emphasis on the nature of the social and political structures created by external dependence and how these structures, in conjunction with the external relationships, limit 'real' development.

Milton Santos (1979), for example, is a writer who argues that the economies of urban areas in underdeveloped countries are characterized today by two circuits: an *upper circuit*, comprising such activities as banking, industry, export trade, 'modern' services, wholesaling and trucking; and a *lower circuit*, consisting of 'non-capital intensive forms of manufacturing, non-modern services generally provided at the 'retail' level and non-modern and small-scale trade' (Santos, 1979, p. 16). The upper circuit tends to be controlled by multinational corporations and other monopolies. There are few linkages. But not all this activity is externally-oriented. Some industry is oriented to supply the domestic economy. Because this is dependent on local markets it tends to locate disproportionately in the main metropolises. At the same time externally-oriented industries are more locationally flexible but often without any multiplier effects. Thus the upper circuit leads to both increased concentration and the spread of industries that are both more capital-intensive and less dynamic.

The lower circuit exists to serve the needs of urban populations. Within the cities the bulk of the population is forced to eke out a living in petty production and 'informal' distributional activities in which employment 'is seldom permanent and its remuneration is often at or below the subsistence level' (Santos, 1979, p. 21). In this circuit capital circulates but is not accumulated. Within urban areas and within regions, therefore, there are major disparities in income and wealth between those involved in the two circuits. The lower circuit is also subordinated to the upper one (Santos, 1979).

The 'shared space' of the two urban circuits is the latest form that 'modernization' has taken in peripheral countries. To Santos this represents the spatial outcome of a *technological* phase to the world economy that began after World War II and is associated with the application of new technologies to industrial processes in peripheral as well as core countries and the spread of a 'consumption ethic' all over the world. Older phases are a *commercial* phase that lasted from the sixteenth century to the Industrial Revolution in Western

Europe, dependent on the transport revolution in world shipping; and an *industrial* phase from the mid eighteenth to mid twentieth century, dependent on industrialization in Western Europe and the United States. What is important in each phase, however, as far as development is concerned, is a function of both contemporary external ties and the internal structures inherited from past external dependence.

If the neo-classical/liberal models are based on an ideal of spatial equilibrium, it is plain that the structuralist models are based (without stating it) on an ideal of spatial disequilibrium in which there is a permanent imbalance between metropolis and satellites. Yet, as Santos's 'phases' suggest, even if proposed within a structuralist framework, the logic and demands of the world economy are in a continual state of reconstitution. The rise of the USA from satellite to metropolis, the challenge of the Soviet Union, the appearance of the NICs, and the increasing role of multinational capital, in the core as well as the periphery, are all contradictory to the 'fact' of permanent spatial disequilibrium. Most important of all, just as the neo-classical/liberal models of regional economic change completely isolate regions from any wider context, the structuralist models completely subordinate them to a world economy in which the identity of regions of growth and exploitation, development and underdevelopment has been determined from the beginning. The structuralist models are therefore as ahistorical and static, whatever their references to phases and stages, as the sectoral models and the neo-classical/liberal models of regional economic change described previously.

Geographical Dynamics: The Historical Geography of the World-Economy

For the years after World War II, the period when most of the models described above became accepted in economic geography, economic growth was viewed as a constant. Even the structuralists assumed that even if there was not growth everywhere there was always growth somewhere. Since the late 1960s, however, confidence in the permanence and inevitability of economic growth has been shaken. Perhaps the clearest indication of the onset of a profound crisis in expectations of growth occurred in the aftermath of the dramatic increases of world oil prices in 1973. This led many commentators and scholars towards a *historical-global* perspective on questions of economic growth and change. In particular, questions of location and spatial structure could no longer be separated from questions concerning the dynamics of an evolving world-economy.

But is this 'world' context just something new? In one sense it is new. Beginning in the 1960s a new, more interdependent and 'internationalized' world-economy did start to emerge. Faced with dramatic drops in their rates of profit many firms operating in Western Europe and United States, and elsewhere, were forced to reorganize and improve their returns by internationalizing their operations (Chapter 6). But in another sense there was already a world-economy in existence that could be 'globalized'. Beginning in Western Europe in the sixteenth century a world-economy began to evolve out of more localized economic systems and empires. But as it has become progressively more integrated, covering ever wider geographical areas and more and more activities (resource extraction, capital investment, trade in manufactures, services, etc.), it has also undergone shifts in its mode of operation. The change beginning in the late 1960s is the most recent manifestation of this mutational process.

The purpose of this section is to sketch the historical development of the modern world-economy, identify the locational principles and 'spatial divisions of labour' operative over time, and indicate the significant geographical effects of state regulatory and macroeconomic policies. This section should provide both a framework for understanding economic landscapes, such as those described most generally in Chapter 2 and more specifically in Parts II and III, and an overview of an important theoretical trend in contemporary economic geography.

The World-Economy

At one time all societies were 'minisystems': 'A minisystem is an entity that has within it a complete division of labour, and a single cultural framework' (Wallerstein, 1979, p. 17). Such minisystems would include very simple agricultural or hunting and gathering societies. But they no longer exist. As soon as they became tied to empires by the payment of tribute they ceased to be separate systems.

Then there came 'world-systems': 'units with a single division of labour and multiple cultural systems. It follows logically that there can be two varieties of such world-systems, one with a common political system and one without' (Wallerstein, 1979a, p. 17). The former are called 'world-empires', and the latter 'world-economies'.

Until the advent of capitalism in Europe, world-economies were unstable and tended towards disintegration or conquest by one group and hence transformation into world-empires. Examples of such world-empires emerging from world-economies are all the so-called great civilizations of pre-modern times, such as China, Egypt, Rome. World-empires, however, undermined the economic growth of their territories by using too much of their surpluses to maintain their bureaucracies and military establishments.

Around AD 1500 a new type of world-economy, the modern capitalist one, began to take form:

> In a capitalist world-economy, political energy is used to secure monopoly rights (or as near to them as can be achieved). The state becomes less the central economic enterprise than the means of assuring certain terms of trade and other economic transactions. In this way, the operation of the market (not the *free* operation but nonetheless its operation) creates incentives to increased

> productivity and all the consequent accompaniment of modern economic development. The world-economy is the arena within which these processes occur. (Wallerstein, 1974, p. 16)

How and why Europe alone embarked on the path of capitalist development is beyond the scope of the present study. Suffice it to say that a set of practices and beliefs evolved in Europe that emphasized the centrality to life of the commercial-economic in the form of capital accumulation and production for the market. As Meyer (1982, p. 266) points out: 'not every politically anarchic economy generates capitalism'. The *cultural* system of exchange and accumulation that emerged in late medieval Europe was what made the peculiarily *modern* world-economy possible (Jones, 1981; Hall, 1985; Schama, 1987).

The causes of capitalism's success as a means of organizing a world-economy are also complex, but two seem fundamental. First, new transportation technology *allowed* far-flung resource areas to be connected with markets, and European military technology provided the means to enforce favourable terms of trade. Second, released from the burden of maintaining relations of tribute within their economic zones by the growth of territorial states, merchant capitalists could attend to the expansion of their interests. Of special importance were Dutch and English capitalists, who were able in the sixteenth century to beat back the Spanish-Habsburg attempt to turn the emerging modern world-economy into a world-empire dominated by one or other hegemonic state (Wallerstein, 1974).

Six basic features of the modern world-economy can be identified. First, the modern world-economy consists of a single world market. Within this, production is for exchange rather than use: producers exchange what they produce for the best price they can get. As the price of a product is not fixed but set by the market there is competition between producers, at least for periods of time. More efficient producers can undercut other producers to increase their share of total production and achieve monopoly control. Until this century, control was largely achieved through territorial division among national enterprises that aimed for localized rather than more global monopoly.

There is a controversy over whether the world-economy can properly be labelled 'capitalist' before the late eighteenth century. Only since that time has the world-economy provided a price-fixing market. Previously, the argument runs, the world-wide movement of commodities took place without labour becoming a commodity. Thus, there may have been a world-economy but it was not as yet a capitalist one. This need not detain us here since most commentators seem agreed that between 1500 and the late eighteenth century there was a vast expansion of trading relations between Europe and other parts of the world. The major point is that there was a qualitative change in the nature of the world-economy in the late eighteenth century associated with European industrialization. It is from this more recent time that the self-regulating world market dates (see Brenner, 1977).

Second, in the modern world-economy there has always been a territorial division between political states. This division both pre-dates and grew along with the spread of the world-economy. It ensures that the world-economy cannot be transformed into a world-empire. At the same time it provides for the protection of developing industries and a means for groups of capitalists to protect their interests and distort the market if it is to their advantage. The major result of this process is a competitive state system in which each state attempts to the best of its ability to insulate itself from the rigours of the world market while attempting to turn the world market to its advantage.

Third, the modern world-economy has established a basic 'three-tiered' geography as it has expanded to cover the globe. This geography is defined by the international division of labour at a particular time. The initial world-economy consisted of Europe and those parts of South and Central America under Spanish-Portuguese control. The rest of the world was an 'external arena'. Spanish activity in America was fundamental in forming the world-economy. Later, by means of plunder, European settlement in place of aboriginal groups and the reorientation of local economies to the world-economy, the rest of the world was transformed from an external arena into a periphery. The world-economy thus came to consist of a core (Western Europe at first, later joined by the United States and Japan) and a periphery. The core is defined in terms of processes in the world-economy that have led to relatively high incomes, advanced technology and diversified production, whereas a periphery is defined in terms of processes leading to low incomes, primitive technology and undiversified production. The core needs the periphery to provide the surplus to fuel its growth. Uneven development, therefore, is not a recent phenomenon or a by-product of the world-economy; it is one of the modern world-economy's basic components.

There is movement between the two categories of core and periphery as attested to by the 'rise' of the United States and Japan. A third geographical tier, the semi-periphery, applies to the processes operating in certain parts of the world to provide movement between periphery and core (and vice versa). These are zones in which a mix of core and peripheral processes are at work. Essentially, political conditions determine whether core processes come to dominate and allow 'upward mobility' within the world-economy. In particular, the timely application of protectionism and other autarkic measures can allow for development but only in conjunction with favourable global economic conditions. Wallerstein emphasizes the importance of the third tier, the semi-periphery. Not only do economies in this group stand between the core and the periphery, some may eventually fall into the periphery, as Spain did in the seventeenth century, and others may eventually rise into the core as the United States did in the nineteenth century. The semi-periphery thus provides a geographical dynamism to the world-economy (Agnew, 1982).

Fourth, the modern world-economy has followed a temporally cyclical pattern of growth and recession. The causes of this pattern are the subject of controversy (Kindleberger, 1978; Mandel, 1975; Marshall, 1987; Rostow, 1978). But there is now considerable evidence that, at least since the

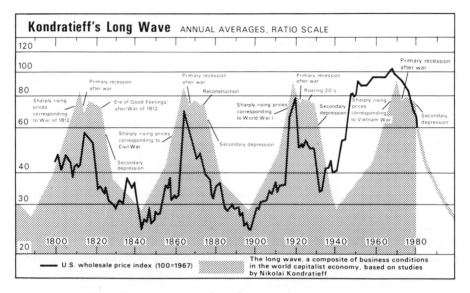

Fig 3.4   Kondratieff's long-wave cycle and American experience
Source: Agnew (1987), p. 22

eighteenth century, the world-economy has gone through four major cycles of growth (A) and stagnation (B) (Kondratieff, 1984) (Fig. 3.4). These have been identified in time-series data for a wide range of economic phenomena (approximate dates):

> I: 1780–90 → A → 1810–17 → B → 1844–51
> II: 1844–51 → A → 1870–5 → B → 1890–96
> III: 1890–96 → A → 1914–20 → B → 1940–45
> IV: 1940–45 → A → 1967–73 → B → ?

A widely accepted, if not definitive, explanation of these regular 50-year cycles (often called Kondratieff cycles after the Russian economist who first identified them) focuses on the contradiction between the short-run interests of individual firms, on the one hand, and the long-run collective needs of business as a whole, on the other. In times of growth, profits are higher and firms tend to overinvest in production and new technology. With no central control over production this leads to overinvestment and overproduction. Stagnation follows.

The correlation with technological change is high. Growth or A-phases are associated with major periods of technological innovation. For example, the first A-phase is the period of the original 'industrial revolution': Abraham Day's discovery of smelting iron ore with coal and the mechanization of the English textile industry. Subsequent periods fit the pattern as well, with steam engines, railways and Bessemer steel in II A, chemicals, electricity and automobiles in III A, and aerospace and electronics in IV A. But there are also important political–cultural correlates. Wallerstein *et al.* (1979) postulate the competition between states involves the geographical redistribution of cyclical effects to the benefit of some strong states and to the cost of other, weaker ones. Thus, states can differentially exploit or suffer from cyclical shifts depending on their productive efficiency, commercial supremacy and ability to restrict competition from rivals (Bousquet, 1980). According to Wallerstein *et al.* (1979) the four Kondratieff cycles, when put in a political context, can be described as two 'paired Kondratieffs' (see Table 3.1). The first pair covering the nineteenth century involves the rise and demise of British dominance and the second pair describes a similar trend for the United States in this century.

No inevitability should be read into this pattern of paired Kondratieffs. In particular, this should not be seen as a case of 'history repeating itself'. Rather, there is a similar pattern to the ways in which first Britain and then the United States gained and then lost pre-eminence. The extent and nature of the

Table 3.1: A dynamic model of hegemony and rivalry

	Great Britain		USA	
A₁ Ascending hegemony	1790–8 Rivalry with France (Napoleonic Wars) Productive efficiency: industrial revolution		1890–6 Rivalry with Germany Productive efficiency: mass production techniques	
B₁ Hegemonic victory	1815–25 Commercial victory in Latin America and control of India: workshop of the world		1913–20 Commercial victory in the final collapse of British free trade system and decisive military defeat of Germany	
A₂ Hegemonic maturity	1844–51 Era of Free Trade: London becomes financial centre of the world-economy		1940–5 Liberal economic system of Bretton Woods based upon the dollar: New York new financial centre of the world	
B₂ Declining hegemony	1870–75 Classical age of imperialism as European powers and USA rival Britain. 'New' industrial revolution emerging outside Britain		1967–73 Reversal to protectionist practices to counteract Japan and European rivals	

Source: Agnew (1987) Table 1 p. 6

dominance exerted by each has been different. For example, Britain followed a 'mixed' strategy of formal and informal imperialism whereas the United States has largely eschewed the territorial control outside its own borders required by formal imperialism. Moreover, US dominance has generally involved direct investment overseas and manipulation of the global monetary system rather than the raw-materials and markets bias of the British.

More importantly, the US hegemony has been constantly challenged by the existence of, and military competition from, the Soviet Union, a state representing a different image of world order. British dominance in the nineteenth century never faced such a challenge. Finally, American hegemony has been achieved through an internationalization of the world-economy to an extent unknown in the eighteenth and nineteenth centuries. Large American-based multinational corporations have been major instruments of American hegemony. But they, as much as other states such as the Soviet Union or Japan, have now become the major threat to American hegemony.

Central to American hegemony has been, in Daniel Boorstin's memorable phrase, the 'democracy of things'. Or, as Emily Rosenberg puts it in more detail:

> American traders would bring better products to greater numbers of people; American investors would assist in the development of native potentialities; American reformers – missionaries and philanthropists – would eradicate barbarous cultures and generate international understanding; American mass culture, bringing entertainment and information to the masses, would homogenize tasks and break down class and geographical barriers. A world open to the benevolence of American influences seemed a world on the path of world progress. The three pillars – unrestricted trade and investment, free enterprise, and free flow of cultural exchange – became the intellectual rationale for American expansion. (Rosenberg, 1982, p. 37)

That the flow was all in one direction struck few as contradictory to the gospel of 'free exchange'.

The recent emergence of Japan as a challenger to American hegemony also involves the deployment of a distinctly different 'cultural logic', one based around a peculiar isomorphism of state-oriented values and policy efforts (Vogel, 1980). This challenges the legitimacy of the entire American approach to capital accumulation as it proves more effective at accumulating capital. The capitalist world-economy, therefore, not only persists, it changes as rising powers deploying new cultural logics impose new hegemonies.

Fifth, the world *resists* or *adapts* to domination rather than simply accepting or succumbing to it (Corbridge, 1986). The danger of elevating the concept 'world-economy' to a key position is that local histories can be deprived of their integrity and specificity. All too often the world outside of Europe and North America is painted in drab, uniform colours and as reacting to 'core' influences in a uniform manner. Facile use of concepts such as the 'less developed world' and 'the Third World' can lead to an easy over-homogenization of a much more variegated pattern. Different parts of the world have reacted quite distinctively to the expansion of the world-economy. A key variable has been the ability of local systems of political-cultural organization to resist and/or adapt to outside influences (T. Smith, 1979). For example, in the nineteenth century some regions

> . . . such as the Kingdoms of West Africa which had been built up partly through a preceding period of trade with the North [Europe], were taken by assault; others, like the Ottoman Empire and Manchu Dynasty, collapsed – for reasons fundamentally caused more by internal factors than by the overwhelming power of the North; Japan managed to mount a rival establishment; and the Latin American states drew strength from the international connection – albeit of a sort that made them satellites of the economic dynamism of the North. (Smith, 1979, 277)

In this century cultural monitoring, resistance and adaptation have continued. At one extreme, as with Japan, lies the conjunction of adoption and adaptation, at the other, as in Iran since 1979, lies rejection. In the writings of Ayatollah Khomeini, 'the West', through its association with corruption and decadence, is viewed as the enemy of the legitimate system of Islamic rule:

> The colonialists have spread in school curricula the need to separate church from the state and have deluded people into believing that the ulama [ministers] of Islam are not qualified to interfere in the political and social affairs . . . When their wish of separation is realized, the colonialists and their lackey can take away our resources and rule us. (Quoted in Beeman,1983, 216–17)

The Iranian example illustrates a more general point; that Western-style states and their associated political ideas are often incompatible with local subordinate cultural logics (Birnbaum and Badie, 1983). In the face of 'totalizing' cultures, such as that exemplified by Khomeini's *Shi'ite* Islam, the principles of structural differentiation and autonomy upon which distinctions such as 'the political', 'the economic', and 'the religious' rest, and from which Western views of development derive – essentially the 'freeing' and nurturing of the economy – fail to take root and gain popular legitimacy.

Sixth, and finally, every part of the world has had its own particular and peculiar relationship to the evolution of the world-economy. In the case of the United States, for example, the existence from an early period of two contrasting and incompatible modes of socio-economic organization: a plantation agriculture based on slavery in the South and 'classic' capitalist or free enterprise economy in the North, was peculiarly American. Likewise today, *apartheid* as a system of socio-economic organization is a peculiarly South African response to the history of settlement and economic exploitation in southern Africa. The whole process of development therefore is mediated culturally – and regionally (Agnew, 1987; Cell, 1982).

Spatial Divisions of Labour and Shifting Locational Principles

There remains the general problem of how the development of the world-economy relates to the spatial distribution of specific economic activities. This has recently begun to preoccupy economic geographers, and both those concerned with early periods and those concerned with the operations of the world-economy today have found themselves confronted with the changing and dialectical relationship between its national and international aspects. They have come to see the evolution of the world-economy as dynamically related to the spatial distribution of economic activities through shifting spatial divisions of labour and changing 'principles' of locational organization.

Imposing a relatively crude division of the modern world-economy into three periods helps to understand the more complex evolution that has gone on over the past 300 years. In the first period (see Chapter 4), development was largely independent of territorial states, except to the extent that certain trading, financial and manufacturing centres tended to develop as politically independent entities (e.g. 'city-states') from which long-distance activities emanated. Interaction between producers and consumers was largely unaffected by state organization, apart from the problems of acquiring government loans and paying taxes to difficult rulers. To this extent, the early modern 'world-economy', or that thin layer of production that was exchanged beyond the confines of the locality, was essentially *transnational*.

In the second period, between the seventeenth and the mid twentieth centuries, development came to be based upon a number of 'developed' national economies whose boundaries were politically defined. Until the ascent of Japan these were exclusively European in origin (see Chapter 5). The rest of the world, as it was integrated into the world-economy, was without the state-economy structure. Not that it was always and invariably integrated through formal colonialism. Formal colonialism was more often than not a function of competition between developed national economies rather than a necessity for economic subordination (Mommsen, 1980). During this phase the world-economy tended increasingly to consist of a set of rival developed 'national economies', a 'dependent' world being increasingly penetrated by them, and a set of economic flows (1) within each national economy, (2) between the national economies of the core, and (3) between the core and the dependent world. However distinctive the flows were, they served primarily to aid capital accumulation and the spatial division of labour at the *national* scale. Even the largely transnational component of the world-economy, international trade, shipping and finance, was itself clearly tied to national bases.

What is important to note is that not only were the various *sectors* of the world-economy politically separate and affected by the particularities of national policies, but that this separation largely determined the spatial division of labour within the core. In a minor sense it determined whether the unevenly distributed factors of production (labour, capital, resources) entered into domestic as opposed to international exchanges. More importantly, the basic division of labour within the productive process was organized *within* national economies or regional parts of them. In terms of production, plant, firm and industry were national phenomena; organized around national markets, generating national industries and creating national social divisions. International trade was largely an exchange of raw materials and foodstuffs and products manufactured within single national economies. Although capital, labour and technology were often imported and exported, they were subject to intensive national regulation.

The division between the developed and underdeveloped economies, which had been moderate before the Industrial Revolution in the core, grew dramatically during this period (Bairoch, 1979). This is the insight basic to the structuralist models of regional economic change. The conditions for the development of 'national economies' did not exist nor were permitted to develop in the dependent world (Baker, 1981). Meanwhile, the internal geography of a national economy such as that of Britain reflected its international position. In the 1930s, for example, a small group of industries – coal-mining and exporting, iron and steel manufacture, shipbuilding – owed their significance within the British economy to the role of Britain in the international division of labour operative since the late nineteenth century. Massey elaborates both generally and in terms of locational principles as follows:

> It was the United Kingdom's position as an imperial power, its early lead in the growth of modern industry, and its consequent commitment to free trade and its own specialization in manufacturing *within* this international division of labour, which enabled the rapid growth, up to the First World War, of these major exporting industries. The spatial structures that were established by those industries were those where all the stages of production of the commodity are concentrated within single geographical areas. The comparatively low level of separation of functions within the process of production, and the relatively small variation in locational requirements between such potentially separable functions, were not sufficient to make geographical differentiation a major attraction. (Massey, 1984, pp. 128–9)

The spatial division of labour of key industries within 'national economies' during the second period, therefore, was based primarily on different sectoral specializations by locality and region. These economies were as a consequence regionally differentiated. Physical accessibility and agglomeration were major features of economic organization. This was why the models of Von Thünen, Christaller, Weber, etc., ever made any sense at all. Thus, the United States in this period was clearly associated with the development of an industrial core in the northeast, areas of specific specialization within it, and regions of agricultural and raw material specialization elsewhere (Bensel, 1984).

Since the Second World War, however, the world-economy has entered a third phase of development in which there has been a re-emergence of the transnational element in its operation. The pace of this shift has quickened, especially in the United States, since the late 1960s. The extent of the change is such that the export of some industrialization to underdeveloped countries is now taken for granted and multinational corporations are no longer seen as external extensions of some specific national economy (see Chapter 6).

The most important innovation is a new international division of labour in the actual process of production, as in the automobile and electronics industries, and the involvement of parts of the dependent world in this (Thrift, 1986). Paralleling this has been the emergence of international devices for coordinating and steering capital beyond national control (e.g., the Eurodollar market), and of 'mini-states ', somewhat like the old city-states, whose economic specialty is servicing the new international division of labour (e.g., Singapore, Hong Kong). Indeed, some small states, including many European ones (e.g. Switzerland), have successfully cashed in on the new world-economy such that they now have higher median living standards than the old imperial 'national economies' such as Britain and the United States.

The national economy, therefore, is no longer the sole building block of the world-economy. It has a rival in the form of the 'immediately global' market which can be supplied directly by firms capable of organizing their production and distribution (in agriculture, manufacturing and services) without reference to national boundaries (e.g., on agriculture, see Dorel, 1985 and Morgan, 1979; on the automobile industry, see Fieleke, 1981). For many multinational firms, national markets for capital, labour, or commodities (and plant and office location) exist only as parts of a global market. Some German data suggest that even small firms have acquired the propensity and capability to operate globally (Fröbel et al., 1977). So the new conditions cannot be identified solely with 'giant' multinationals.

The degree of 'globalization' has accelerated tremendously since the 1960s. Between 1961 and 1976, for example, the number of persons employed abroad by German firms increased tenfold. The number of firms with production operations outside of West Germany doubled during the same period (Fröbel et al., 1977).

The 'internationalized' world-economy has been both accompanied and *enabled* by the development of new transport and communication technologies that have provided a 'permissive' environment in which firms could decentralize manufacturing and agricultural operations yet maintain central control, e.g., computers, telecommunications, air travel (Bluestone and Harrison,1982). There is now the possibility of intensive interaction and diffusion without physical proximity. Firms can thus remain head-quartered in, for example, Hamburg or New York, but locate manufacturing facilities in places with isolated, disorganized labour forces (Clark, 1981), with particular combinations of labour force skills, costs, militance and captivity (Storper and Walker, 1984), or close to highly concentrated regional markets. These trends all suggest, as Gertler puts it:

> . . . that the greater economies of 'scale' and 'agglomeration' are now realizable in a situation in which production is spatially dispersed. (Gertler, 1986, p. 77)

Table 3.2: 'Hymer's stereotype', in which the space-process relationship takes the form A→B→C.

Level of corporate hierarchy	Type of area		
	Major metropolis (for example, New York)	Regional capitals (for example, Brussels)	Periphery (for example, South Korea, Ireland)
1 Long-term strategic planning	A		
2 Management of divisions	D	B	
3 Production, routine work	F	E	C

Source: Sayer (1985) Table 1 p. 13

This tendency for interaction-at-a-distance has led some commentators to argue for a 'space–process' relationship in which firm control and operations activities are completely separated geographically (e.g., Hymer. 1975; Lipietz, 1980). Thus, in the terms of Table 3.2 the space–process relationship takes the form A → B → C. Even though D, E, and F are present they are assumed to be less potent. In fact, a major metropolis may dominate *all* levels in *absolute* terms, as Sayer (1985) has pointed out with respect to the electronics industry in the London–South East region of England. This example shows that it is important not to overstress the role of unskilled labour-intensive production across all industries and overstate the significance of standardized, mass production (or customized production for that matter). The danger lies in presenting 'as universal, relationships which are contingent and historically specific' (Sayer,1985, p. 17) to particular industries and places.

In fact, spatial divisions of labour can be structured in a number of different ways depending upon the needs and characteristics of particular industries. If in the past *regional specialization* was most characteristic of many manufacturing industries and commercial agriculture, a number of other possibilities have emerged as competitors to both it and the *regional dispersal* that has always characterized consumer services and certain manufacturing industries (e.g., shoe production, food processing) (Urry, 1985). These are (1) *functional separation* between management/research in a 'core' region, skilled labour in old manufacturing areas, and unskilled labour in a regional 'periphery'; (2) *functional separation* between management/research in a 'core' region and semi-skilled and unskilled labour in a regional 'periphery' (e.g., UK electrical engineering); (3) *functional separation* between management/ research and skilled labour in a 'core' economy and unskilled labour in a 'peripheral' economy (this is the Fröbel *et al.*, 1977 case); and (4) *division* between one or several areas, on the one hand, with investment, technical change and job expansion, and other areas, on the other hand, with stagnant and progressively less competitive production and job loss. These are largely distinctions of scale but they do reflect the fact that the 'new' internationalized division of labour has a number of different processes associated with it rather than being 'a simple unitary trend' (Sayer, 1982, p. 80).

Nevertheless, for an increasing proportion of industrial and agricultural commodities and services, production and markets have become world-wide (Scott and Storper, 1986). This shift has had important consequences for the spatial distribution of economic activity both globally and within the economies of the developed world. Globally it has given rise to the growth of the NICs such as South Korea, Taiwan, Hong Kong, Singapore, Brazil and Mexico. Multinational corporations now employ 9 per cent of the labour force in 'underdeveloped' countries in general and the number of such workers has been growing much faster than in most of the developed nations (Thrift, 1986). However, it is important to stress that the 'successes' of the NICs in attracting *industrial* investment are outnumbered by the failures among other countries in the periphery of the world-economy.

Within the national economies of the core the new international division of labour has led to both shifts in employment from manufacturing to services and massive regional and urban restructuring. In Britain, for example, three sorts of locality have fallen victim to the loss of 'traditional' manufacturing industries and the failure of new ones to replace them. First of all are the centres of nineteenth-century industrialization in the north of England, South Wales and Central Scotland. Second are the 'inner cities' of London and other large metropolitan areas. Third are the centres of the growth industries of the 1950s and 1960s (vehicles and engineering) in the West Midlands and North-west (Martin and Rowthorn, 1986). There have been compensations, for example the expansion of administrative and producer services, but these have been largely elsewhere (Daniels, 1985a). One effect has been to encourage the growth of London (and some other cities) as primarily centres for corporate headquarters and services. The international services economy is thus a major stimulus to the primacy of London in the British urban hierarchy (Thrift, 1986).

In the United States the traditional manufacturing industries have also gone into decline. The national economy has undergone a massive restructuring as a result of increased foreign competition and the emergence of more profitable activities for firms than manufacturing (e.g., real estate and financial services). One major feature has been the growth of the southern and western states (the 'Sunbelt') relative to the manufacturing belt (the 'Snowbelt') (Agnew, 1987; Knox *et al.*, 1988). In 'Sunbelt' states the new economic growth is so diversified that it cannot be satisfactorily described sectorally (Keinath, 1985). But it is also very localized and 'patchy' without many interregional linkages, except branch plant to headquarters location (Agnew, 1988). Another feature has been, as in Britain, the emergence and concentration of the international services economy in such centres as New York, Los Angeles, San Francisco and Miami (Bensel, 1984; Ginzberg *et al.*, 1986). But many metropolitan areas have also maintained important manufacturing industries because, for some emerging industries and new forms of production, external economies (and especially subcontracting) *are* still of great significance (Storper and Christopherson, 1987).

These changes in the economic geography of 'core' countries have drawn attention to the increased variety of geographical linkages between firms and plants. Markusen (1985), for example, has explained the shifts in economic activity between American regions largely in terms of the 'maturation' of products as they move through a cycle of production requirements (especially technological ones) as the products change from being 'innovative' to being 'mass-produced'. As production requirements change so do locational requirements. In particular, standardized production is regarded as labour intensive and hence requires access to different labour forces than those required at earlier stages in the product-cycle. This model was originally applied at an international scale (Fig. 3.5; see p. 193). However, this model neglects, among other things, location-specific advantages other than cheap labour that might *attract* investment and production to other locations, the substitution of automation for labour in many product-cycles, and the increased importance of customized production (as opposed to mass production) in many new product categories (Sabel, 1982; Storper, 1985; Taylor, 1986).

An alternative approach has been to focus on firm types and industrial sectors in an attempt to link together firm strategies with the changing geography of production (Taylor and Thrift, 1983; Sayer, 1985; Cooke and da Rosa Pires, 1985). The major premise is that each type of firm has a particular 'establishment structure' laid out over space, ranging from 'the highly localized clustering of craftsmen/smaller firms to the world-wide networks that have been established by business organizations in the global corporation

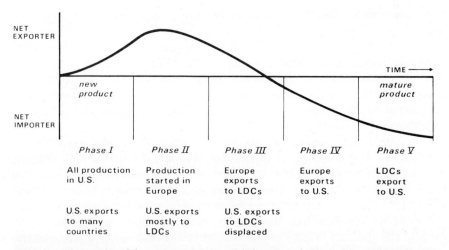

Fig 3.5   The product life-cycle and its possible locational effects upon US production and trade
Source: Dicken (1986) p. 130

segment' (Taylor and Thrift, 1983, p. 458). There is then no *general* model of firm locational behaviour, although some palpably general models (such as those of Lösch, Weber, etc.) and general principles of location (such as agglomeration economies) *do* have utility in connection with certain types of firms' locational characteristics. For example, 'agglomeration' is important still for craftsmen and subcontractor firms while it is of reduced importance for global manufacturing enterprises.

When examined historically in terms of shifts in the world-economy it becomes clear that the geography of economic activity cannot be explained for all time by a set of *immutable* principles of location. Rather, concepts such as distance, accessibility, interaction, diffusion and agglomeration take on meaning in determinate historical contexts. They are dependent on specific firm-organizational, technological, cultural and political conjunctures. Recently, for example, with the emergence of a more internationalized division of labour, distance means something rather different from what it meant under the previous regime of 'national' economies. In particular, physical proximity between control and operations functions within large firms is now less critical in some important industries (e.g. electronics) (Scott, 1982). Agglomeration economies also appear less significant for many industries than they were at one time for others (e.g. steel, automobiles) (Wardwell, 1980; Vining, 1982; Beeson, 1987). Interaction costs, especially transportation ones, are also much less of a barrier than they once were. Finally, diffusion is probably less contagious and more urban-hierarchical than formerly. The world-economy is dynamic; it is time that our concepts reflected this.

Bringing in the State

The emergence of the modern world-economy in Western Europe coincided with and was dependent on the territorial consolidation of Europe's nation-states (Tilly, 1986). From 500 political entities in Europe in 1500, there were not more than 25 nation-states in 1900 (Tilly, 1975). The modern state has been the political form of the modern world-economy. Thus, the continued expansion of the world-economy has been accompanied by the expansion of the inter-state system as the sole form of political, military and territorial organization (Giddens, 1981).

The 'state' is not a standard thing in all countries. It includes very different institutions, products of peculiar histories, that adapt in phase with shifts in national development and the world-economy. The relative power of states has three dimensions: (1) relative to one another, (2) relative to their inhabitants, and (3) relative to the 'globalized' world-economy (Harris, 1986, pp. 145–69). The first has shown important variation – in the decline of Britain, the rise and decline of the United States, the rise of Japan and the NICs. The second seems to grow incessantly – in terms of regulation, taxation and surveillance. However, the third appears to be declining in general, and to decline more as countries develop. Ironically, in this respect, the relative power of governments in underdeveloped countries is greater than in the more developed ones: 'the more industrialized the country, in contemporary conditions, the more the condition of continued growth of the wealth and power of the state depends upon permitting the integration of the local with the world economies' (Harris, 1986, p. 148).

Of particular importance, the international financial system is much more integrated in the late 1980s than even 10 years ago. This has increased the vulnerability to external financial shocks (shifts in investment, stock market crashes, currency revaluations, etc.) of even the most economically powerful countries such as Japan and the United States (Strange, 1986; Parboni, 1981). However, individual governments 'can still *affect* the international financial system in all kinds of ways, from industrial strategy to running up budget deficits, but they can often only *control* the system in concert with other governments and even then, as the recent decline of the US dollar has shown, concerted action by central banks is not always effective' (Thrift and Leyshon, 1988, p. 56).

It is clearly *not* the case, therefore, that the world-economy now runs rampant *over* national economies without check or restraint in either under-developed or developed countries. The crux of the present situation is rather the coexistence of the national and global structures within the world-economy and attempts by states to *manage* the tensions between them. Transnational activities operate within states and under conditions imposed by them (trade and tariff policies, monetary policies). For political reasons national economies cannot be confined solely to creating optimal conditions for the operations of businesses within them, because political life involves considerable inter-group and inter-regional bargaining for public sector resources (Bensel, 1984; MacLaughlin and Agnew, 1986). At the same time, the global economy is developing explicitly to optimize conditions for private business activity, at whatever cost to this or that national economy, including the firm's 'own'.

This is a major theme of authors such as Aglietta (1979) and Lipietz (1987). They argue, as in Lipietz's words (1987, pp. 18–19), that 'The formation of the international division of labour cannot be regarded as the deliberate or functional organization of a system. . . . The development of capitalism in any given country is first and foremost the outcome of internal class struggles which result in embryonic regimes of accumulation being consolidated by forms of regulation that are backed up by the local state.' In particular, it would be 'quite wrong to conclude that the new international division of labour is simply the outcome of organizational activity on the part of multi-national companies' (p. 26). Rather, 'the actual existing division of labour is simply the outcome of various nations' attempts to control one another or to escape one another's control, of one or another class alliance's unremitting efforts to achieve or surrender national autonomy' (pp. 25–6).

The continuing importance of states within the world-economy is manifested in a number of ways: first, in the organizing and mobilizing roles of the states in the NICs; second, in the continuing geopolitical rivalry of the developed countries; third, in the macroeconomic policies pursued by national governments to stabilize and reorganize their economies; and, fourth, in the latitude and initiative of local governments in attracting economic activity to their localities.

It is remarkable that if the *larger* underdeveloped countries (i.e., excluding Hong Kong and Singapore) are examined in detail, the fast growing and otherwise best-performing countries have all had national governments that have directly and actively intervened in economic and social *planning*. In South Korea, for example, the government has played a major part in fostering economic growth. Adding government savings to deposits in nationalized banks, the South Korean government controlled two-thirds of the investment resources in the country during the period of most rapid growth in the late 1970s (Sen, 1981a). This power was used to guide investment in chosen directions through differential interest rates and easy credit terms. Korean export expansion was itself built on an industrial base that was severely protected from foreign imports. Economic growth was directly orchestrated by an activist national government.

There is not a little difficulty, therefore, in reading the recent experience of Korea, or some other NICs such as Taiwan, Brazil, Mexico (and Japan), as an entirely 'market' phenomenon. Economists on both right (e.g., Beenstock, 1983) and left (e.g., Harris, 1986) err when they ignore or systematically understate the importance of the state in organizing and mobilizing resources for economic growth.

States in the developed world have not disappeared either. Indeed, under the conditions of crisis and restructuring that have affected most developed economies over the past 20 years, there has been a strengthening of rivalry between countries over trade, monetary policy and foreign policy (Corbridge, 1986). The key 'geographical fact' has been the relative decline of the USA within the world-economy but its refusal to give up military and monetary hegemony (Kaldor, 1978; Parboni, 1981; Agnew, 1987). David Harvey captures the geopolitical context dramatically when he writes:

> At times of savage devaluation inter-regional rivalries typically degenerate into struggles over who is to bear the burden of devaluation. The export of unemployment, of inflation, of idle productive capacity become the stakes in the game. Trade wars, dumping, international interest-rate wars, restrictions on capital flows and foreign exchange, immigration policies, colonial conquest, the subjugation and domination of tributary economies, the forced reorganization of the division of labour within economic empires, and finally, the physical destruction and forced devaluation of a rival's capital through war are some of the methods at hand. (Harvey, 1982, p. 438).

In terms of the geography of economic activity, the responses of states to their external rivalries lead them to adopt various macroeconomic policies to stabilize and reorganize their economies. It is not a 'spatial division of labour' in itself but in a macroeconomic context that brings about geographical-economic restructuring. For example, from the late 1940s onwards, American governments have stimulated and stabilized the US economy through various indirect fiscal and monetary policies. One industry has been given a high priority: housing and real estate. This happened for political reasons. In the legislative battles of the late 1940s over what would remain of the government intervention from the 1930s (the 'New Deal'), debate focused on housing. What is important in the present context is that the Housing Act of 1949 locked the federal government into a massive stimulus of the US economy through a transformation of the American landscape. Suburbanization by means of housing subsidies and highway construction funds served both as a fiscal regulator and a massive stimulus to the relocation of industry and other economic activities (including agriculture) (Walker, 1978; Agnew, 1987; Knox *et al.*, 1988).

For a second example, the contemporary situation of the US economy, and of particular sectors, industries and regions within it, cannot be understood without giving attention to the federal deficit (Rees, 1987). This deficit is the direct result of the tax cuts of 1981–82 and large increases in military spending for ideological and economic-stimulative reasons. To finance the deficit, the US government must attract large amounts of foreign investment. Within the country the deficit has stimulated an economic revival in those regions of the country with large financial service sectors (servicing the deficit) (e.g., the New York metropolitan area) and with large amounts of defence-related industry (e.g. southern California) (Malecki, 1984a; Ó hUallacháin, 1987). Government policies, therefore, can play an important, if often indirect, role in local and regional economic change.

Finally, in some countries, such as the United States and Canada, local tiers of government are often able to pursue policies of their own with respect to attracting and keeping economic activities. As many industries have become more 'footloose' with technological and organizational change, a variety of factors once marginal to a firm's locational calculus have assumed greater prominence. Some of these can be subsumed under the heading 'business climate'. In the United States, for example, the northern states of the old manufacturing belt tend to have higher personal tax rates and much greater provision of public goods and services. They therefore provide a rather *less* favourable climate for businesses and. capital accumulation than do the 'growing' regions of the South and the West.

In a number of respects, therefore, nation-states and the political regulation of the economy they provide are of continuing relevance in understanding the economic landscape. But states, far from being primordial and pre-existing essences, are intertwined in complex and contradictory ways with the world-economy. The world-economy and the states within it are always changing. Thus, today states must coexist with a world-economy that is much more 'globalized' than in the past. This does not mean, however, that states give up or are ineffective in pursuing their objectives. A major challenge to contemporary economic geography lies in assessing how in specific circumstances specific economic activities are affected by states' attempts at meeting these objectives.

Summary

The economic events of the past 20 years present a serious challenge to those approaches to understanding economic landscapes that have been dominant in economic geography. This chapter has reviewed these dominant approaches in a critical manner and proposed an alternative historical-geographical framework that places understanding of the location of economic activities at international, regional, and inter-urban scales in the context of an evolving world-economy. In particular, this alternative view-point sees the 'principles' of location (distance, accessibility, interaction, diffusion, agglomeration) as historically changing rather than fixed in meaning and significance. Thus, the contemporary 'spatial division of labour' involves rather less emphasis on accessibility and agglomeration and more on inter-action and diffusion. Or, to put it another way, under contemporary conditions the central concern of 'classical' models with transportation costs and agglomeration economies as the definitive geographical variables seems, at best, quaint.

But the major point of this chapter is not to demean previous approaches. It is to provide a sense of their inadequacy as static perspectives and then move on to provide an alternative. The alternative, though more-or-less within the world-system tradition, has a number of important differences from it. Most importantly, we choose to stress the importance of states in regulating and directing economic activities, qualitative change in the nature of spatial divisions of labour, and the shifting importance of different locational principles.

The argument of this chapter has been largely abstract with a few empirical illustrations. Unlike the 'classic' models which assume a simple necessary relationship between their predictions and geographical patterns, the histori-cal-geographical framework proposed here does not assume the necessity of particular patterns. From this point of view, for example, the terms 'core' and 'periphery' around which this book is organized are heuristic and suggestive rather than definitive. There are *always* anomalous instances because of contingency effects (Sayer, 1982). In other words, it is no longer the spatial out-comes – hexagonal grids, regional clusters – that are the focus for under-standing but the historical-geographical processes out of which geographical patterns emerge and change. The rest of the book is concerned with these processes *and* the patterns they have produced, rather than vice versa.

Part Two

The Rise of the Core Economies

In the next three chapters we trace the emergence of the world's core economies, following their different paths towards increasing scale and complexity with case histories that illuminate many of the patterns, models and theories outlined in Chapters 2 and 3. Taking our cue from Johnston (1984), we seek to show that the world's economic landscapes, however unique or exceptional they seem, are now part of a single, overarching world-economy. In Chapter 4 we describe the way in which this world-economy came to be centred on Europe, how it came to be consolidated by the emergence of merchant capitalism, and how the nature and organization of merchant capitalism came to be reflected in particular kinds of urban and regional change. In Chapter 5 we describe the very different trajectories that have marked the ascent of Western Europe, North America, Japan and the Soviet Bloc within the world-system, emphasizing the spatial changes consequent upon the emergence and evolution of industrial capitalism and, in the case of the Soviet Bloc, industrial socialism. In Chapter 6 we describe the spatial implications of the latest, advanced, form of economic organization on the capitalist countries of the world's core. But, although the emphasis throughout this part of the book is on the interaction of dominant forms of economic organization and major dimensions of spatial change, there is an important sub-theme. This is the role of human agency in shaping and differentiating the mosaic of regional landscapes. What is done, where and how – under any form of economic organization – reflects human interpretations of how resources should be used. As Johnston notes, these interpretations 'are shaped through cultural lenses (which may be locally created, or may be imported); they reflect reactions to both the local physical environment and the international economic situation; they are mediated by local institutional structures; they are influenced by historical context; and they change that context, and hence the environment for future operations' (Johnston, 1984, p. 446).

4

Pre-Industrial Foundations

In this chapter, we trace the gradual emergence of an embryonic world economy centred on Europe and describe the way in which Europeans became, as Robert Reynolds put it, the 'leaders, drivers, persuaders, shapers, crushers and builders' (1961, p. viii) of the rest of the world's economies and societies. It was as a result of these changes that the core areas of Western Europe acquired the foundations for the development of the industrial revolution which was to forge the template for the economic geography of the modern world. It must be recognized from the outset, however, that pre-industrial economic development was by no means exclusively – or even always dominantly – a European phenomenon: the early socio-economic trajectories of other parts of the world often eclipsed that of Europe (and, in particular, of Western Europe), and were sometimes important in conditioning events in Europe itself. Moreover, their legacy can be seen as an important dimension of the world's economic, social and cultural geography. We begin, therefore, with a brief review which spans the origins and diffusion of the first, crucial 'revolution' in the development of agricultural systems, the rise of ancient empires, the establishment of urban systems, and the spread of feudalism as the dominant mode of production. Our purpose here is not so much to attempt to provide a thumbnail sketch of early economic history as to point to the emergence and spatial implications of certain fundamental socio-economic forces.

Beginnings

Relatively little is in fact known about the first transitions from primitive hunting/gathering minisystems to larger-scale, agriculturally based world-empires and world-economies: despite rapid advances in the accuracy of archaeological research, we still have to rely on speculation as much as established facts. It is generally agreed, however, that the transition began in the Proto-Neolithic period (between 9000 and 7000 BC), when the *pre-conditions* for agriculture were established through a series of innovations among certain hunter-gatherer peoples. These innovations included the use of fire to process food, the use of grindstones, and the improvement of basic tools for catching, killing and preparing animals, fish, birds and reptiles. Given these pre-conditions, it was a relatively straightforward transition to the most simple system of long-fallow agriculture, sowing or planting familiar species of wild cereals or tubers on scorched land. No special tools are required for such a system, nor are weeding or fertilization necessary, provided that cultivation is shifted to another burned plot after a few crops have been taken from the old one.

Meanwhile, the domestication of herbivorous animals had begun, and by Neolithic times (7000 to 5500 BC), farming had developed to the point where stock breeding and seed agriculture were established techniques of food production. The switch from hunting and gathering to food production seems to have occurred very slowly, however: it was not a revolutionary change which suddenly transformed local practices. Archaeological evidence from a Neolithic village in western Asia, for example, shows that the wild legumes which were the major food item in 7500 BC were gradually replaced by cultivated grains over a span of almost 2,000 years (Flannery, 1969). Ester Boserup (1981) suggests that, because hunting and gathering often provided adequate levels of subsistence with relatively low workloads, there was little incentive to switch to food production until population densities began to increase and/or wild food sources became scarce. From this perspective, then, demographic conditions as well as technological innovations were a critical precondition for economic change.

The weight of available archaeological evidence suggests that the transition to food production took place *independently* in several different agricultural 'hearths'. The earliest hard evidence comes from the Middle East, in the foothills of the Zagros Mountains of what are now Iran and Iraq, where radiocarbon analysis has dated the remains of domesticated sheep at around 8500 BC (Clark, 1977). In addition, evidence of early Neolithic activity has been found in other parts of the Middle East, particularly around the Dead Sea Valley in Palestine and on the Anatolian Plateau in Turkey. A second early Neolithic hearth area was in South Asia, along the floodplains of the Ganges, Brahmaputra and Irawaddy rivers. Later, from around 5000 BC, a third hearth area seems to have emerged in China, around the Yuan River valley in Western Hunan. Finally, there is evidence of independent agricultural rganization in four regions of the Americas: the southern Tamaulipas area and the Tehaucán Valley in Central America, coastal Peru, and the North American Southwest. In these regions, however, agricultural development not only came later but it was painfully slow, with widespread food production coming to dominate the exploitation of wild plants and game only after AD 1000. Meanwhile, the agricultural 'revolution' had been diffused from the Middle East. By 5000 BC it had begun to spread eastwards, to southern Turkmenia, and westwards, via the Mediterranean and the Danube, into Europe; by 3000 BC it had reached the Sudan and Kenya (via the Nile), much of India (via Afghanistan and Baluchistan) and had penetrated Europe as far as the British Isles and southern Scandinavia. By 1500 BC the last European stronghold of pure hunter-gatherer economies was the zone of tundra and coniferous forest stretching eastwards from the Norwegian coast.

Archaeological evidence is inevitably rather patchy, however, so that the patterns of diffusion from agricultural hearth areas remain a topic of considerable academic debate. Thus, for example, Carl Sauer's influential treatise on *Agricultural Origins and Dispersals* (1952) argued that hearth areas logically had to fulfil six criteria:

1   plentiful natural food supplies: 'People living in the shadow of famine do not have the means or time to undertake the slow and leisurely experimental steps . . . [to develop] a better and different food supply' (p. 21).
2   a diversity of species in order to provide a large reservoir of genes for hybridization. This implies well-diversified terrain and varied climatic conditions.
3   freedom from the necessity to drain or irrigate land. This implies, however, that river valley sites were unlikely hearth areas.
4   natural vegetation dominated by woodland, which is much easier to open up than grassland.
5   a population whose economy and technology was oriented towards gathering rather than hunting.
6   a sedentary rather than nomadic population, in order to facilitate the protection of growing crops from 'all manner of wild creatures that fly, walk and crawl to raid fruits, leaves and roots' (p. 23).

On this basis, it was deduced that the first hearth area must have been in South Asia, and that Middle Eastern agriculture was a later, more sophisticated outgrowth. Whether or not such deductions are vindicated by future archaeological findings is of less importance to us here, however, than the eventual outcomes of the transition to food production:

1   The increased volume and reliability of food supplies allowed much higher population densities and encouraged the proliferation of settled agricultural villages. This, in turn, facilitated:
2   The development of non-agricultural crafts, such as pottery, weaving, jewellery and weaponry. Such specializations in their turn encouraged:
3   The beginnings of barter and trade between communities, sometimes over substantial distances.

The Framework of Early Urbanization

These outcomes of the transition to food production were effectively the preconditions for another 'revolutionary' change in the economic and spatial organization of the world: the emergence of cities and city systems. As with the evidence on the agricultural transition, our knowledge of the earliest cities is partly a function of where archaeologists have chosen to dig and partly a function of fortuitous factors like the durability of building materials and artifacts. It now seems firmly established, however, that urbanization developed independently in different regions, more or less in the wake of the local completion of the agricultural transition. Thus the first region of independent or 'nuclear' urbanism was in the Middle East, in the Mesopotamian valleys of the Tigris and Euphrates and the Nile Valley (together making the so-called Fertile Crescent) from around 3000 BC. By 2500 BC cities had appeared in the Indus Valley, and by 1000 BC they were established in northern China. Other areas of nuclear urbanism include Central America (from around AD 500), Peru (from around AD 1500) and the Niger Valley in West Africa (from around AD 1500). Meanwhile, of course, the original Middle Eastern urban hearth had spawned successive generations of urban world-empires, including those of Greece, Rome and Byzantium.

Explanations of these first transitions to city-based economies have given emphasis to each and all of the preconditions which emerged as a result of the agricultural revolution. Boserup (1981), for instance, stressed the role of local concentrations of population; while Jane Jacobs (1969) interprets the emergence of cities mainly as a function of trade; and the classical archaeological interpretation rests on the availability of an agricultural surplus large enough to facilitate the emergence of specialized, non-agricultural workers (Childe, 1950; Woolley, 1963). But, in addition to the impetus and interaction of these preconditions, we must also recognize the catalytic role of socio-political changes. Specifically, it was the emergence of groups who were able to exploit these preconditions that marked the transition from primitive, egalitarian, subsistence-oriented minisystems to more complex, urbanized, 'rank-redistributive' societies. This exploitation took place initially through what is called 'primitive accumulation': the collection of fixed assets and/or the control of labour power, usually through some form of religious persuasion or despotic coercion. Once established, the parasitic élite provided the stimulus for urban development by investing its appropriated wealth in displays of power and status. This not only created the kernel of the monumental city but also required an increased degree of specialization in non-agricultural activities – construction, crafts, administration, the priesthood, soldiery, and so on – which could only be organized effectively in an urban setting (Wheatley, 1971).

This kind of expansion, however, could only be sustained in the most fertile agricultural regions, where the peasant population could produce enough to support not only the parasitic élite but also the growing numbers of non-productive workers. In this context, the development of irrigation seems to have been a critical factor. It not only intensified cultivation and increased productivity; it also required the kind of large-scale cooperation that could only be organized effectively in a hierarchical, despotic society (Wittfogel, 1957). Hence the shift within the Middle East from the agricultural hearth areas in the foothills and plateaus surrounding the Mesopotamian plains to the neighbouring plains themselves, where flow irrigation and waterwheels enabled a sophisticated and productive system of multicropping. Yet, even in the most fertile and intensively farmed regions, rank-redistributive economies could only expand beyond a certain point if overall levels of productivity could be increased: through harder work, improvements in technology, or improvements in agricultural practices. As Ron Johnston points out, all three of these solutions will have required more non-agricultural specialists and so will have reinforced the incipient process of urbanization:

> administrators and, perhaps, an army to oversee the harder work (their actions may have been accompanied by the élite taking to itself the ownership of land) in the first, craftsmen to create the tools in the second, and also, probably, miners and others to provide the raw materials; and 'researchers' to develop the new strains and the new technology (notably irrigation) in the third. Thus the demands for more production are reflected in the urban node as well as in the countryside, and continued growth of the society, to meet the never-satisfied demands of an expanding élite and its associates, leads to self-propelling urban growth. (1980a, p. 52)

Such developments are ultimately constrained by the size of the society's resource base, however, so that successful expansion eventually reached the point of diminishing returns to the productivity of both labour and land. The obvious response – the enlargement of the resource base through territorial expansion – also tended to reinforce and extend the process of urbanization. Thus,

> To enable successful colonial activity, the structure of the society would need to be reorganized and several new functions created. Among the latter, the most important in the new areas would be administration – both civil and military – probably accompanied by religious colonization of the new subject population; to ensure contact between the colonies and the 'heartland', and the movement of surplus production back to the élite centre, a transport infrastructure would have to be established and maintained, and the ability to move substantial quantities of goods created. (Johnston, 1980a, p. 53)

All these changes would involve the creation of city-based jobs. Moreover, whereas small-scale colonial expansion could be organized from one centre and controlled by a single élite group, expansion beyond easy reach of the main settlement (beyond, perhaps, a day or two's journey) would require 'the establishment of secondary settlements, to act as the nodes for parts of the controlled territory, as intermediate centres in the flow of demands from élite to producers and of goods in return' (Johnston, 1980a, p. 54). As long as growth was maintained, therefore, the empire would have to be continually enlarged, with an increasing number of urban control centres. Hence the expansion of the Greek and Roman empires which laid the foundations of an urban system in Western Europe (Fig. 4.1). Meanwhile, another important change was occurring in terms of the political organization of space. Whereas the limits of subsistence economic systems were their social limits, bounded by

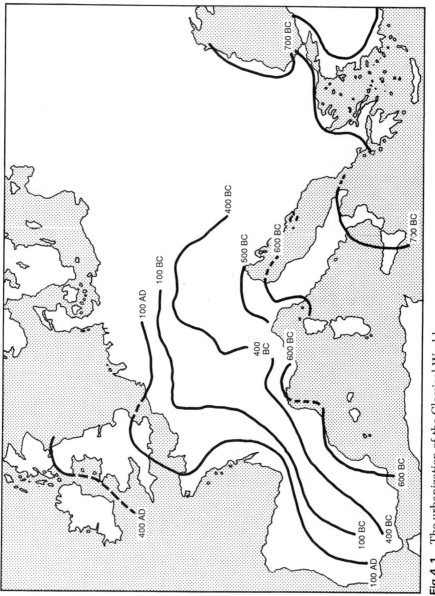

Fig 4.1 The urbanization of the Classical World
Source: Carter (1983) Fig. 2.2 p. 21

the limits of kinship and kinship alliances, rank-redistributive systems were defined, first and foremost, in spatial terms: as the area ruled over by a particular dynasty. The question of what the state comprised in social terms was reduced to a secondary consideration, a matter of whoever lived within the territorial bounds of the state (Fig. 4.2; see also Chapter 7, p. 228). 'In this simple but profound change', Dodgshon observes (1987, p. 137), 'we are confronted with one of the decisive revolutions in human spatial order.'

It would be wrong, however, to draw a picture of the steady growth, expansion and succession of ancient and classical empires. Urbanized economies were a precarious phenomenon, and many relapsed into ruralism before being revived or recolonized. In a number of cases, this was a result of demographic setbacks (associated with wars and epidemics) which left too few people to maintain the social and economic infrastructure necessary for urbanization. An early example of this kind of relapse occurred in the Indus Valley, where the urban economy was displaced by Aryan pastoralists in the middle of the second millenium BC. Elsewhere, it was changes in resource/population ratios which precipitated the breakdown and decay of urban economies. Irrigation systems were enlarged and made more complex in step with population increase,for example, while the extension of cultivation and the pasturing of ever-larger herds of livestock required careful management of the soil in order to prevent erosion. As a result, the demands of repair and upkeep, on top of the need for increasing productivity, sometimes put over-whelming strains on the available peasant labour. After a while, investments were neglected, armies grew small, and the strength and cohesion of the empire was fatally undermined (Boserup, 1981). This kind of sequence seems to have been the root cause of the eventual collapse of the Mesopotamian empire and may also have contributed to the abandonment of much of the Mayan empires more than 500 years before the arrival of the Spanish.

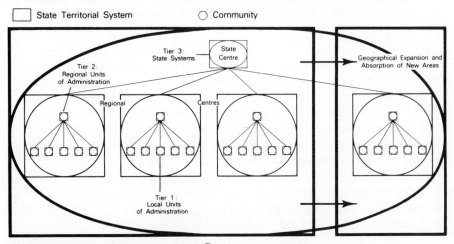

Fig 4.2 Early states and the political integration of space
Source: Dodgshon (1987) Fig. 5.1 p. 136

Similarly, the population of the Roman empire began to decline in the second century AD, giving rise to contemporary references to labour shortages, abandoned fields and depopulated towns (Pounds, 1974), and allowing the infiltration of 'barbarian' settlers and trades from the German lands of east-central Europe.

Rural consolidation

Although the emergence of urbanism provided an important framework for the future development of the world's space-economies, the reorganization and consolidation of rural areas was to provide the immediate platform for the critical transition to merchant capitalism and the emergence of a European world-economy. At the heart of this rural consolidation was the penetration of decentralized and hierarchical rank-distributive systems which eventually evolved into the elaborate feudal systems of Medieval Europe, China, India and Japan (Anderson, 1974).

In economic terms, feudal systems were characterized by being almost wholly agricultural, with 80 or 90 per cent of the workforce being engaged in mixed arable and pastoral farming, and most of the rest occupied in basic craft work. Moreover, most production was for immediate needs: very little of a community's output ever found its way to wider markets. The basis of the feudal system was the feudal estate, owned by lay or ecclesiastical lords, who delegated parcels of land to others in return for allegiance and economic obligations, the latter being fulfilled mainly in the form of money dues. The lords in their turn would normally owe allegiance and homage to higher lords from whom they held delegated grants of land.

> In other words, a feudal system would at least initially be associated with the existence of a chain of dependent tenures and of a corresponding hierarchy of territorial lords composed, at the bottom, of local notables and, at the top, of great magnates owning immense stretches of land. (Dunford and Perrons, 1983, pp. 91–2)

The labour power which ran each estate and which provided the wealth to be appropriated along the feudal hierarchy consisted of a peasant population, most of whom were serfs – descended from slaves and therefore not free in public law, or tenants whose freedom of movement, freedom of marriage, freedom to leave property to their heirs and freedom to buy goods and sell their labour was closely circumscribed by public law (Duby, 1974). It was this socio-political institution – serfdom – that was the key to feudal economic systems in that it formed the basis on which feudal lords were able to accumulate wealth, through a combination of labour services, rents in kind, taxes, seigneurial dues and payments for the use of essential services – milling, baking, olive pressing, and so on – monopolized by the lords.

In western Europe, feudalism evolved from a synthesis of the legacy of the slave-based economic system of the disintegrating Roman empire and the communal chiefdoms of the invading Germanic tribes. It reached its most developed form in northern France and southwestern Germany, where the overlap of its two progenitors was most evenly balanced. In Mediterranean Europe, the feudal system was heavily conditioned by the legacy of Roman law, while in northern Europe the development of feudalism was equally modified by the strong tribal influence of the barbarian heritage – except where, as in England, a centralized feudal system was directly imposed from the continental core region (in this case, as a result of the Norman Conquest). Only the most marginal peripheral and mountainous regions, however, were left relatively untouched by the economic and social organization involved in feudalism (East, 1966; Pounds, 1974).

By 1000 AD the countryside of most of Western Europe had been consolidated into a series of agricultural sub-systems which were largely autonomous. Every estate was more or less self-sufficient in terms of basic foodstuffs and most regions were self-sufficient in the raw materials for simple industrial products. Some of the members of every rural household would be capable of specialized, non-agricultural, part-time activities such as cloth-making or basketry; and nearly every community supported a range of specialist artisans and craft workers. In addition, most regions were able to sustain at least some small towns, whose existence hinged mainly on their role as ecclesiastical centres, defensive strongholds, and administrative centres for the upper echelons of the feudal hierarchy. It was this economic landscape – inflexible, slow-motion and introverted – which, as we shall see, nurtured the essential preconditions for the by-passing of feudalism and the rise of merchant capitalism in Western Europe: the resurgence of trade and the revival of cities.

Emerging imperatives of economic organization

Before moving on to examine the transition to merchant capitalism and the emergence of the European world-system, it is useful to pause briefly in order to review some of the organizing principles which seem to have been important in delineating the formative stages of pre-industrial economic geography at the macro-scale:

- Major changes in patterns of economic activity were gradual and incremental, even in 'hearth' or 'core' regions.

- Such changes were generally preceded by the development of critical innovations, particularly in technology and economic organization.

- Such innovations were a necessary but not sufficient condition to bring about radical change: institutional and socio-political changes were also necessary in order to exploit them.

- Demographic factors were also critical. Insufficient absolute numbers of potential workers sometimes hindered economic development, while changes in the balance between a population and its local resource base could be important in precipitating *either* progressive *or* regressive economic change.

- The law of diminishing returns provided an early impetus for territorial expansion. In addition to the obvious spatial consequences in terms of establishing dominant/subordinate territorial relationships, colonization was pivotal in the development of hierarchical urban systems and improved transportation. Colonization also stimulated the development of militarism, which itself induced important changes in spatial organization: through the influence of defensive sites for key settlements, for example. Not least, the environmental and social circumscription which translated into the law of diminishing returns was responsible for the emergence of a new geo-political phenomenon – the state (Carneiro, 1970).

These organizing principles will be recurring themes as we go on to examine successive epochs of economic development; they must also be reconciled, together with the principles which emerge from our examination of subsequent epochs, within any comprehensive theoretical approach to regional economic development.

The Emergence of the European World-System

This section deals with the period from the first stirrings of the transition from feudalism to merchant capitalism in the thirteenth century, through the creation of the European world-system in the sixteenth and seventeenth centuries, to the proto-industrialization of the early eighteenth century which laid the foundations for the Industrial Revolution. A comprehensive and detailed review of the period can be found in the works of Cipolla (1981), De Vries (1976), and Wallerstein (1980); our purpose here is merely to point to the emergence, interaction and spatial implications of the salient aspects of economic change. We must begin our examination of the emergence of the European world-system, however, with an obvious but somewhat neglected question: why Europe?

Why Europe?

In the twelfth century, before Europe embarked on the path of capitalist development which was to shape – directly or indirectly – virtually the entire global economy, there were several well-developed 'economic worlds' in the Eastern Hemisphere. One was the Mediterranean region, whose principal elements included Byzantium, the Italian city-states and Muslim North Africa. A second was the Chinese Empire. The central Asian land mass from Russia to Mongolia was a third; the Indian Ocean/Red Sea complex was a fourth; and the Baltic area was on the verge of becoming a fifth (Wallerstein, 1974). Why, therefore, did Europe become the locus of innovatory economic change? In particular, *why not China?*, which had approximately the same total population as Europe and for a long time – well into the fifteenth century – was at least as far advanced in science and technology. Moreover, because China had retained an imperial system, it held a potentially telling advantage in that its centralized decision-making, extensive state bureaucracy, well developed internal communications and unified financial system were well suited to economic development and territorial expansion.

China's failure to take off in the way that Europe did must be attributed in part to its failure to pursue economic opportunities overseas. The Chinese had in fact matched early European exploratory successes by spanning the Indian Ocean from Java to Africa in a series of lucrative and informative voyages; but they simply lost interest in further exploration. One explanation for this lack of a colonizing mission is that they saw their own 'world' as the only one that mattered (Willetts, 1964; see also p. 234). Another is that they were distracted by the growing menace of Mongol nomad barbarians and/or Japanese pirates. A third explanation is that the centralized power structure of imperial China did not contain enough different interest groups for whom overseas exploration was an attractive proposition.

This last point is seen by some to be part of a broader set of structural constraints imposed by the imperial form. In particular, the administration and defence of a huge population and land mass is held to have been a drain on attention, energy and wealth which might otherwise have been invested in capital development (Wallerstein, 1974), while the centralization of decision-making is seen as having been insensitive to the economic potential of China's estimated 1700 city states and principalities (Jacobs, 1984). There is a link too between China's imperial framework and its failure to develop military technology (after having gained a flying start) in the way that enabled Europeans to turn exploration into domination: quite simply, the Imperial court suppressed the spread of knowledge of gunnery because it feared internal bandits and domestic uprisings (Cipolla, 1965).

> So China, if anything seemingly better placed *prima facie* to move forward to capitalism in terms of already having an extensive state bureaucracy, being further advanced in terms of the monetization of the economy and possibly of technology as well, was nonetheless less well placed after all. It was burdened by an imperial political structure. (Wallerstein, 1974, p. 63)

Another important difference in the trajectories followed by China and Europe was that European agriculture had become focused on the production of cattle and wheat, whereas Chinese agriculture was dominated by rice production. The implications of this difference, it has been suggested, were as follows. Because rice production requires relatively little land, China did not feel such a great need for territorial expansion. At the same time, the high labour input required for rice cultivation meant that the Chinese economy was potentially short of manpower. Conversely, Europe's reliance on wheat and cattle provided a strong impetus for territorial expansion and exploration, while the more extensive use of animal power meant that 'European man possessed in the fifteenth century a motor, more or less five times as powerful as that possessed by Chinese men' (Chaunu, 1969, p. 336). Finally, some writers have emphasized the lack of autonomy of Oriental towns compared to their European counterparts. As we shall see, the legal and political autonomy of European towns was a crucial 'pull' factor in attracting rural migrants whose labour and initiative were central to the emergence of merchant capitalism. So much, then, for China; it remains for us to explain just how Europe became the hub of the embryonic world-economy.

The Crisis of Feudalism in Europe

It has to be accepted that the transition from feudalism to merchant capitalism remains an issue of considerable debate, largely because we simply do not know enough about the details or timing of the critical economic and social changes which took place between 1300 and 1450. As a result, a variety of theoretical interpretations have emerged, each emphasizing different elements in the transition (for a review, see Peet, 1980). It is generally agreed, however, that the overall context for the transition was a phase of economic, demographic and political 'crisis' which was precipitated by the conjuncture of steady population growth, modest technological improvements, and limited amounts of usable land. As Perry Anderson put it: 'the basic motor of rural reclamation, which had driven the whole feudal economy forwards for three centuries, eventually over-reached the objective limits of both terrain and social structure' (1974, p. 197).

As a result of improvements in ploughing techniques, harnesses and basic equipment in the early feudal period, wheat yields rose significantly (from a seed-to-output ratio of 1:4 to 1:25, leading to a steady rise in population over the twelfth and thirteenth centuries (England's population, for example, increased from between 1 and 2 million in 1100 to between 4 and 5 million in 1300). In response, the feudal economy kept up by reclaiming rough pastureland and woodland; and when this began to prove difficult (from around 1250) the response was to improve crop rotations and shorten the period of fallow. There were limits, however, to such adjustments. The number of cattle which could be kept, for example, was fixed by climatic constraints which limited the quantity of available winter forage; and this in turn imposed a limit on the supply of fertilizer for arable farming. In the absence of further advances in agrarian technology, food shortages were an inevitable outcome; and in their wake, just as inevitably, came epidemics such as those of the Black Death (bubonic plague) in the 1340s, 1360s and 1370s. These problems were compounded by climatic fluctuations: the cold winters and late springs of the fourteenth century aggravated the food shortages, while some exceptionally hot summers helped to swell the population of the black rat, the host to the rat flea, one of the two vectors of bubonic plague (Duby, 1968).

Another aggravating factor was the beginning of the Hundred Years War in

1335–45, which put many economies on a war footing, with the particular result that there was a marked increase in taxation. This, in turn, initiated a downward economic spiral as levels of consumption fell, causing liquidity problems for noble treasuries and eventually leading to a rise in prices and further rounds of tax increases which provoked a political climate of endemic discontent. The combined result of these pressures was 'not only to exhaust the goose that laid the golden eggs for the castle, but to provoke, from sheer desperation, a movement of illegal emigration from the manor' (Dobb, 1963, p. 21).

The destination of all these fugitives from feudalism was the town, where different laws and tax systems prevailed. The late medieval European town, writes Cipolla (1981, p. 146):

> was the 'frontier', a new and dynamic world where people felt they could break their ties with an unpleasant past, where people hoped they would find opportunities for economic and social success, where sclerotic traditional institutions and discriminations no longer counted, and where there would be ample reward for initiative, daring and industriousness.

That the towns should appear so attractive was not simply the result of the legal status of their inhabitants, however. They had, ironically, begun to prosper at the height of feudal economic development. In order to meet the nobility's more sophisticated and ostentatious requirements, seigneurial incomes had been increasingly realized in the form of cash. This obliged peasants to sell part of their produce on the market in order to pay rents and taxes, and generally facilitated the trading of commodities. There developed an embryonic pattern of regional trade in basic industrial and agricultural produce, and even some long-distance, international trade in luxury goods such as spices, furs, silks, fruit and wine. One consequence of this trade was an increase in the size and vitality of towns, as more and more merchants and craft workers emerged to cope with the demands of the system (Dunford and Perrons, 1983). It has been suggested that this urban vitality was a major agent in the eventual crisis of feudalism, because it helped to highlight the relative inefficiency of the self-sufficient feudal estate and transformed attitudes towards the pursuit of wealth (Sweezy, 1957).

Meanwhile, the endemic discontent of the remaining peasantry in Western Europe had led to the abolition of serfdom and the introduction of village institutions for economic regulation and political emancipation. Conflict between the nobility and the peasantry had rather different outcomes in different regions, however, depending on the local balance of power. In England, for example, the nobility managed to retain their position as landlords while the peasantry managed to achieve the status of tenants and wage labourers. This formed the basis of what was to become a capitalist system of agriculture, with relatively stable food prices, the incentive for investment and innovation, and, as a consequence, the release of rural labour into industrial pursuits. In France, the peasantry was even more successful, forcing the break-up of feudal estates into small parcels of land under peasant proprietorship. But, far from initiating progressive change, the French reforms led to rural stagnation: the freed peasantry, unlike the English tenant farmers, were under no compulsion to farm efficiently or profitably. Subsequently, population growth, the subdivision of holdings, and the steady growth of taxation hampered the ability of the peasantry to increase productivity, leading to a self-perpetuating cycle of rural backwardness (Brenner, 1976; Dunford and Perrons, 1983).

The Resurgence of Trade and Expansion of Towns under Merchant Capitalism

It follows from the preceding paragraphs that increased trade and urban growth were both a cause and an effect of the transition from feudalism. But they were also the hallmarks of the new economic order. As the feudal system faltered and disintegrated, it was displaced by an economy which was dominated by market exchange, in which communities increasingly came to specialize in the production of the goods and commodities which they could produce most efficiently in comparison with other communities. The key actors in this system were the merchants who supplied the capital required to initiate the flow of trade – hence the label merchant capitalism. In marked contrast to feudalism and earlier rank-redistributive and primitive subsistence-oriented systems, merchant capitalism was a self-propelling growth system, in which the continued *expansion* of trade was vital: without it, neither merchants nor those dependent on their success – producers, consumers, financiers, etc. – could maintain their position, let alone advance it. Johnston summarizes the dynamics of the system as follows:

> Mercantile success required the merchants to buy as cheaply as possible, and to sell as expensively as possible; it also demanded that they trade in as large a volume of goods as possible . . . This created a contradiction, however, for the producers were also consumers (though not of the goods they produced), so that if the prices they received were low, they could not afford to buy large quantities of other goods and thus satisfy the demands of the merchant class as a whole. A consequence of this was a great pressure on producers to increase the volume of goods offered for sale, which meant increasing their productivity, while merchants put pressure on consumers to buy more, even if this meant them borrowing money in order to afford their purchases. Both processes . . . involved producers raising loans which they had to repay with interest; to achieve the latter, they had to produce more (or, if they were employees rather than independent workers, to work harder). (1980a; pp. 33–4)

The regional specializations and trading patterns which provided the foundations for early merchant capitalism were predetermined to a considerable degree by the long-standing patterns which had been developed by the traders of Venice, Pisa, Genoa, Florence, Bruges, Antwerp and the Hanseatic League (which included Bremen, Hamburg, Lübeck, Rostock and Danzig) from the twelfth century. As the self-propelling growth of merchant capitalism took hold, centres of trade multiplied in northern France and the lower Rhineland, new routes across Switzerland and southern Germany linked the commerce of Flanders more closely to that of the Mediterranean, and sea lanes – across the English Channel, North Sea and Baltic – began to integrate the economies of the British Isles, Scandinavia and the hansa territories with those of the continental core. Very quickly, a trading system of immense complexity came to span Europe from Portugal to Poland and from Sweden to Sicily, based not on the luxury goods of earlier trade routes but on bulky staples such as grains, wine, salt, wool, cloth and metals (Glamann, 1974; Pounds, 1974).

The increased volume of trade fostered a great deal of urban development as the merchants involved in long-distance trade began to settle at locations that were of particular significance in relation to the major lines of movement, and as local economies everywhere came to focus on market exchange (Pirenne, 1937). But, once the dynamics of trade had been initiated, the key to urban growth was a reciprocal process of *import substitution*. Although some regional specialisms were hard to copy because of the constraints of climate or basic resource endowment, many imported manufactures could be copied by local producers, thus increasing local employment opportunities, intensifying the use of local resources and increasing the amount of local investment capital available. Moreover, as Jane Jacobs (1984) argues, cities which replaced imports in this way could then afford *new* types of goods being produced in other cities. The newly imported innovations, in their turn, might then be replaced with local production, opening up the market for still more innovations from elsewhere. So the cities of Europe, as Jacobs observes:

> were forever generating new exports for one another – bells, dyes, buckles, parchment, lace, carding combs, needles, painted cabinet work, ceramics, brushes, cutlery, paper, sieves, riddles, sweetmeats, elixirs, files, pitchforks, sextants – and then replacing them with local production, to become customers for still more innovations. They were developing on one another's shoulder. (1984, p. 50)

As a result, patterns of trade and urban growth were very volatile; and long-term local success within the new economic order became increasingly dependent on

- sustained improvisation and innovation,

- repeated episodes of import substitution, and

- the discovery and control of additional resources and new kinds of resources.

Consolidation and Expansion

The consolidation of merchant capitalism that took place throughout western Europe in the fifteenth and sixteenth centuries must be attributed in large measure to the diffusion of a broad spectrum of innovations in business and technology. Central among these were innovations in the organization of business and finance: banking, loan systems, credit transfers, company partnerships, shares in stock, speculation in commodity futures, commercial insurance, courier/news services, and so on (for a detailed review of the emergence of 'modern' finance in Europe, see Parker, 1974). The importance of these innovations lay not only in the way that they oiled the wheels of industry, agriculture and commerce but also in the way that they helped to encourage savings and to facilitate their use for investment. Furthermore, the routinization of complex commercial and financial activity brought with it the codification of civil and criminal legislation relating to property rights (patent laws, for example): a development which is seen by some as being of critical importance in providing an incentive for a sufficient number of innovators and entrepreneurs to channel their efforts into the embryonic capitalist economy (North and Thomas, 1973).

Meanwhile, technological innovations succeeded each other at an accelerated rate in response to the imperatives of the new economic order. Some of these were adaptations and improvements of Oriental discoveries – the windmill, spinning wheels, paper manufacture, gunpowder, and the compass, for example. But in Europe there was a real passion for the mechanization of the productive process as a means of increasing productivity, and in addition to improvements based on others' ideas there emerged a welter of independent engineering breakthroughs, including the more efficient use of energy in water mills and blast furnaces, the design of reliable clocks and firearms, and the introduction of new methods of processing metals and manufacturing glass.

The advantages conferred by these breakthroughs were jealously guarded by the centres of innovation – northern Italy up to the fifteenth century; England and Holland in the sixteenth and seventeenth centuries – while competitors in other regions went to considerable lengths to acquire new technology at the first opportunity. Thus, for example, the Venetian government strictly prohibited the emigration of caulkers; and the Grand Duke of Florence gave a reward for the return, dead or alive, of emigrants from key positions in the brocade industry. On the other hand, the French actually kidnapped skilled iron workers from Sweden; while many governments were happy to provide shelter and handsome rewards for migrant craftsmen who had knowledge of new techniques (Cipolla, 1980). These early examples of a 'brain drain' were complemented by the practice of temporary migration in the opposite direction in order to acquire new expertise, sometimes legitimately, sometimes covertly. But the most important vector for the diffusion of technological innovations came with the invention of the printing press using movable type. Within 20 years of its introduction in Mainz, printing shops had spread throughout Europe, opening up vast new possibilities in the fields of knowledge and education.

It was the combination of innovations in shipbuilding, navigation and naval ordnance, however, that literally had the most far-reaching consequences for the evolution of the European space-economy. By the fourteenth century, European shipwrights were building ships skeleton first, at a vast saving of labour in comparison with previous methods. In the course of the fifteenth century, the full-rigged ship was developed, enabling faster voyages in larger and more manoeuvrable vessels that were less dependent on favourable winds. Meanwhile, the quadrant (1450) and the astrolabe (1480) were developed and a systematic knowledge of Atlantic winds had been acquired. By the mid sixteenth century, England, Holland and Sweden had perfected the technique of casting iron guns, making it possible to replace bronze cannon with larger numbers of more effective guns at lower expense. Together, these advances made it possible for the merchants of Europe to establish the basis of a world-wide economy in the space of less than a hundred years.

Mercantilism and Territorial Expansion
As we have already seen in relation to China, however, economic strength and technological ability do not necessarily lead to overseas expansion. What, then, were the factors which translated Europe's economic power and technological superiority to a broader arena? Among those that were undoubtedly important was the large number of impoverished aristocrats produced by western European inheritance laws and by expensive Crusades and local wars. Discouraged from commercial careers by sheer snobbery and encouraged by a culture which romanticized the fighting man, these poverty-stricken gentlemen provided a plentiful supply of adventurers who were willing to die for glory and even more willing to exercise greed and cruelty in the name of God and Country (Reynolds, 1961). This points to two other important factors: the evangelical zeal of the Church and the political competitiveness of the monarchies.

Above all, however, overseas expansion was impelled by the logic of merchant capitalism and the law of diminishing returns. Self-propelling growth could only be sustained as long as productivity could be improved, and after a point this required food and energy resources which could only be obtained by the conquest – peaceful or otherwise – of new territories. Similarly, merchant capitalism required new kinds of commodities in order to stimulate demand and so sustain the continuing growth of commerce. And, last but not least, merchant capitalism required new supplies of gold and silver to make up for the leakage through trade with Byzantium, China and Arabia.

Collectively, these motivations found expression in the dogma of Mercantilism – the economic counterpart of political Absolutism – to which most European countries adhered from the sixteenth century to the early eighteenth century. The basis of Mercantilism was that national wealth was to be measured in terms of gold or silver and that the fundamental source of economic growth was a persistently favourable balance of trade. This was the economic 'logic' that justified not only overseas colonization but also the coercion of cash-crop labour and the prohibition of manufacturing in the colonies. It was also the logic which, on the domestic front, promoted thrift and saving as a means of accumulating capital for overseas investment and which required a high degree of economic regulation, sponsorship and protection by the government.

There is no need for us to reiterate here the pattern and sequence of European expansion and conquest; though it is worth noting that the overall thrust, overseas from Atlantic Europe rather than inland to the east, was essentially because the technological superiority of the Europeans was not as marked on land as it was on the seas: Asians could counterbalance technological inferiority with weight of numbers until after the mid seventeenth century, when European technology succeeded in developing more mobile and rapid-firing guns. Nevertheless, Europeans soon destroyed most of the Muslim shipping trade in the Indian Ocean and captured a large share of the intra-Asian trade. By bringing Japanese copper to China and India, Spice Island cloves to India and China, Indian cotton textiles to southeast Asia and Persian carpets to India, European merchants made good profits and with them paid for some of their imports from Asia.

It was the gold and silver from the Americas, however, which provided the first major economic transformation, allowing Europe 'to live above its means, to invest beyond its savings' (Braudel, 1972, p. 268). In effect, the bullion was converted into effective demand for consumer and capital goods of all kinds – textiles, wine, food, furniture, weapons, ships – thus stimulating production throughout the economic system and creating the basis for a 'Golden Age' of prosperity for most of the sixteenth century. Meanwhile, overseas expansion made available a variety of new and unusual products – cocoa, beans, maize, potatoes, tomatoes, sugar cane, tobacco and vanilla from the Americas, tea from the Orient – which opened up large new markets to enterprising merchants.

Just as the fruits of conquest stimulated the European economy, so did the superiority of its merchant fleets. As European traders came to monopolize intra-oriental trade routes, they were literally able to govern the flow and pattern of trade between potential rivals. Moreover, because of this monopoly, European traders could identify foreign articles with a tested profitable market and ship them home to Europe where skilled workmen could learn to imitate them. Once Europeans had begun manufacturing these products, it was their goods which were shipped to the rest of the world:

> For example, Europeans long prized the shawls which were made in the north of India in the Kashmir region; much later Scotchmen [sic] were making imitations of those shawls by the dozens per day; called 'Paisley' shawls, they swept the Kashmir shawls off the general market. Europeans admired the very hard vitrified china of the Chinese, and for a long while bought it to sell to other peoples, taking it from China and distributing it. But then the Europeans began to make it in France and elsewhere, and shortly true Chinese china had become a rare article on the world market while Europe was making and selling enormous amounts of its own 'china'. For a good while Europeans bought cottons of a very fine quality from India for markets in Africa, Europe, and America, but before

too long they had imitated them in England and were shipping cheaper machine-made cottons back to India where they ruined the Indian cotton-weaving industry in its own home. (Reynolds, 1961, pp. 45–6)

For Europe, the benefits of overseas expansion thus extended well beyond the basic acquisition of new lands and resources. In this context we should note that it also stimulated further improvements in technology and business techniques, thus adding a further dimension to the self-propelling growth of merchant capitalism. New developments were achieved in nautical mapmaking, naval artillery, shipbuilding and the use of sail; maritime insurance emerged as one of a growing number of tertiary industries; and the whole experience of overseas expansion provided a great practical school of entrepreneurship and investment. Most important of all, perhaps, was the way that the profits from overseas colonies and trading overflowed into domestic agriculture, mining and manufacturing, representing an accumulation of capital that was undoubtedly one of the main preconditions for the emergence of industrial capitalism in the eighteenth century.

Outside Europe, the most important features of the economic landscape to emerge as a result of merchant capitalism were the gateway towns and entrepôts that were established along the coastal rims of the Americas, Africa and South Asia. These transoceanic rim settlements were of three main kinds (Haggett, 1983):

1   *Trading stations*, such as Canton (China), Madras (India) and Goa, which grew up as the points of contact between Europe and the – as yet – relatively autonomous economic worlds of the Orient. Few Europeans lived in these towns and cities, and only in India was it possible to exercise any secure measure of political control over the large hinterland areas that served the ports.

2   *Entrepôts and colonial headquarters for tropical plantations*, such as Rio de Janeiro (Brazil), Georgetown (British Guiana), Port of Spain (Trinidad), Penang (Malaysia), Lagos (Nigeria), Lourenço Marques (Mozambique) and Zanzibar. Substantial numbers of European settlers were required for administrative and military purposes, whereas the indigenous population provided field labour and manual labour in the towns. The colonial plantation system made intensive demands on labour, however, and when the indigenous supply was insufficient it was made up by enforced movements of slave labour from other regions, thus creating distinctive ethnic cleavages among the populations of many colonies.

3   *Gateway ports* for the 13 farm-family colonies on the northeastern seaboard of America (similar settlements were later established in South Africa, Australia and New Zealand). Although there were several distinctive groups – the Tidewater Colonies of Virginia (e.g. Jamestown, Baltimore), the New Towns of New England (e.g. Boston, Newport), the Middle Colony towns (e.g. New York, Philadelphia) and the

Colonial Towns of the Carolinas (e.g. Charleston, Savannah) (Reps, 1965) – they were essentially a direct extension of the West European urban system, peopled by West Europeans and oriented much more to their homelands than their hinterlands.

The Shifting Locus of Economic Power

Up to now, our discussion has been couched in terms of Europe as a whole, mainly for the sake of convenience in dealing with a very broad sweep of economic history. We can no longer sustain this convenience, however, since one of the distinctive features of the era of merchant capitalism was the changing economic geography of Europe itself and, in particular, the shifting centre of gravity of economic leadership and power. Once again we must be content with a brief review of the salient points insofar as they are relevant to later patterns of economic development; detailed accounts can be found in the works of Earle (1974), and Cipolla (1981).

The dominant feature of the changing economic geography of Europe in the sixteenth and seventeenth centuries was a dramatic shift in the focus of economic activity from the Mediterranean to the North Sea. At the end of the fifteenth century, the Mediterranean was the most highly developed region in the world, with central and Northern Italy as the hub of economic activity. During the sixteenth century, the relative prosperity of the Mediterranean was further enhanced as Spain and Portugal benefited immensely from the influx of treasure from the Americas. By the end of the seventeenth century, however, the Mediterranean had become a backward region in relation to the levels of prosperity generated by the Dutch economy; while England, hitherto a very marginal economy in European terms, stood poised to threaten the position of the Dutch as world leaders. Between these two extremes of stagnation/regression and dynamic expansion was the experience of France, Scandinavia, Germany and much of the rest of continental Europe, where there was a general penetration of economic development and maturing of local economies: a consolidation of merchant capitalism which helped to maintain the coherence of the European economy during a period of volatile change in its spatial organization. In detail, therefore, the changing centre of gravity of the European economy involved a complex of overlapping, inter-locking and interacting regional struggles and transformations. The basic processes involved, however, were more general, and they can be illustrated with reference to the decline of Spain and Italy and the rise of Holland and England.

Spain provides a good example of the importance of import substitution. Quite simply, Spain declined because it had never been fully 'developed' to begin with; it·had only been rich. The increased demand generated by its acquisition of bullion from the Americas did not stimulate domestic production as much as it might have done because of bottlenecks in the productive system – the restrictive practices of guilds and the lack of skilled labour, for example – and the complacent attitude of the Spanish élite. In 1675 Alfonso Nuñez de Castro wrote:

> Let London manufacture those fabrics of hers to her heart's content; Holland her chambrays; Florence her cloth; the Indies their beaver and vicuña; Milan her brocades; Italy and Flanders their linens, so long as our capital can enjoy them; the only thing it proves is that all nations train journeymen for Madrid and that Madrid is the queen of Parliaments, for all the world serves her and she serves nobody. (quoted in Cipolla, 1976, p. 25)

The treasure of the Americas provided Spain with purchasing power but ultimately it stimulated the development of England, France, Holland and the rest of Europe. Meanwhile, Spain's artificial prosperity had led the government to pursue a persistently warmongering policy, which represented a serious drain on the treasury. In the course of the seventeenth century then, as the influx of bullion from Spain's colonies declined (partly through depleted mines), the momentum of the economy evaporated, leaving insufficient entrepreneurs and artisans to counterbalance the mounting national debt and an overabundance of bureaucrats, lawyers and priests.

Italy's decline was more complex, but its beginning can be dated more accurately: the end of the fifteenth century, when for almost 50 years Northern Italy became the battlefield for an international conflict involving Spain, France and Germany. As a result there were not only famines and epidemics but also severe disruptions to trade at a time when trade was beginning to expand elsewhere. Buoyed up by the international boom in demand during the late sixteenth century, the economy made something of a recovery (Fig. 4.3); but it was a recovery based on traditional methods of organization

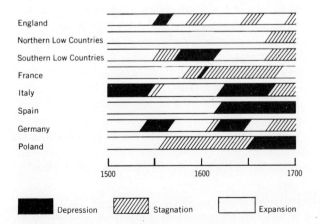

Fig 4.3   Economic trends in selected European countries, 1500–1700
Source: Cipolla (1976) Fig 10.1, p. 249

which meant, among other things, that competition and innovation were suppressed by the renewed strength of craft guilds. Between 1610 and 1630 a series of external events led to the collapse of some of the Italians' major markets – the decline of the Spanish economy, disruptive wars in the German states, and political instability within the Turkish empire. At the same time, many of Italy's competitors had been able to substitute domestic products for Italian imports. At this point, the self-propelling growth of merchant capitalism broke down. Unable or unwilling to respond through innovation and increased productivity, Italian entrepreneurs began to disinvest in manufacturing and shipping. By the end of the seventeenth century Italy was importing large quantities of manufactures from England, France and Holland while exporting agricultural goods for which the terms of trade were poor: oil, wheat, wine and wool. Foreign trade had thus been transformed from an 'engine of growth' to an 'engine of decline'.

Holland's 'economic miracle' of the seventeenth century was launched from a fairly solid platform of trading and manufacturing. Although over-shadowed in the early phases of merchant capitalism by the prosperity of nearby Bruges and Antwerp, Holland (and Amsterdam in particular), had steadily developed an entrepôt function for Northern Europe (importing flax, hemp, grain and timber, and exporting salt, fish and wine), around which it had begun to establish a manufacturing base. From the stability of this base, the Dutch successfully rebelled against Spanish imperialism and emerged, in 1609, with political independence and religious freedom. Thereafter, a combination of factors helped the Dutch to become leaders of the world economy for more than 150 years. One was the 'modernity' of Dutch institutions: relatively few restrictive guilds, a small nobility of landowners, and a relatively weak church after the departure of the Spanish. Another was the vigorous pursuit of Mercantilist policies, including not only a strong colonial drive and a massive commitment to merchant shipping but also an uncompromising stance towards competitors: for example, the Dutch blockaded Antwerp's access to the sea from 1585 to 1795, taking over its entrepôt trade and its textile industry. In relation to their drive to dominate trade, the Dutch were able to turn their geographical situation to great advantage, both developing ocean ports and exploiting the inland waterways that penetrated the heart of continental Europe. They were also able to benefit from a highly developed and very innovative shipbuilding industry whose output completely overshadowed that of the rest of Europe. Finally, the Dutch were the major beneficiaries of the flight of skilled craftsmen, merchants, sailors, financiers and professionals from the fanaticism and intolerance of the Spanish in Flanders and Wallonia.

England, at the end of the fifteenth century, was distinctly backward, with a small population (around 5 million, compared to more than 15 million in France, 11 million in Italy and 7 million in Spain) and a weakly developed economy. The only significant comparative advantage the English held was in the manufacture of woollen cloth; though Mediterranean supplies and German merchants had long dominated the European trade in woollen textiles. The first real break for the English economy came in the first half of the sixteenth century, when Italian production and trade collapsed because of war and its ensuing disasters, leaving the English literally to capitalize on a sustained increase in woollen exports – a trend which was further enhanced by the progressive deterioration of English currency resulting from Henry VIII's extravagant military expenditures. The boom was halted in the mid-sixteenth century however, by the recovery of the Italian textile industry and by the war between the Dutch and the Spanish, which disrupted English exports (Fig. 4.3). By this time, though, English entrepreneurial and expansionist ambitions had become established and were articulated through a strong Mercantilist philosophy. Like the Dutch, the English were able to take advantage from their geographical situation, at least in relation to trans-oceanic trade. They had also developed a strong navy and gave high priority to establishing a large merchant fleet and to acquiring colonial footholds. Like the Dutch, they also benefited from the skills of immigrants driven from France and the Low Countries by religious persecution. Innovation, improvisation and import substitution also played their part in ensuring a rapid escape from the mid-century economic crisis and, indeed, in building an economy to challenge that of the Dutch. The development of iron artillery in the 1540s, for example, enabled the English to arm their merchant ships, privateers and warships more extensively *and* at lower cost. Meanwhile, the exploitation of coal as a substitute for her relatively sparse and rapidly diminished timber reserves not only helped England to avoid an energy crisis but also helped to develop new processing techniques. 'Concentrating on iron and coal', writes Cipolla (1976, p. 290), 'England set herself on the road that led directly to the Industrial Revolution'.

Summary: Dominant Features of the Emergent Space-Economy

At this stage it is useful to review the major organizing principles which had been important in delineating the evolving space-economy from the transition to merchant capitalism to the eve of the Industrial Revolution. The first observation that should be made in this context is that the observations we made in relation to early economic systems (p. 111) appear as recurring elements in subsequent economic epochs. Thus we can confirm the gradual and incremental nature of major economic change (though we should note that increasing economic sophistication and territorial integration make for a more rapid diffusion of short-run changes).

We can also confirm the continuing importance of innovations in technology and business organization (though we should note the innovative process to this point was carried out in small steps, by way of the gradual cumulation of improvements rather than by distinct bursts of invention which, as we shall see, have characterized economic change since the industrial era).

The importance of institutional and socio-political factors was also a recurring theme (as, for example, in the constraints of a centralized imperial system on the evolution of the Chinese economy, in the stimulus provided by European laws on property rights, and the role of European governments in implementing Mercantilist policies). Similarly, we must acknowledge the continuing interaction between demographic change and economic development and, finally, the continuing impetus for territorial expansion provided by the law of diminishing returns. In addition, though, we can identify several new dimensions of spatial-economic organization:

- The emergence of a true 'world-economy', involving long-distance economic interaction based on a sophisticated division of labour but distinctive from earlier economic worlds of Rome, Byzantium and China in that, rather than being dominated by a single imperial structure, there was a discontinuity between economic and political institutions. This discontinuity was both a cause and an effect of the creation of capitalist forms of production in agriculture, industry and commerce (Wallerstein, 1974; 1979).

- The progressive elaboration of the world-economy, with competitive ('price-fixing') markets penetrating into more and more space and more and more commodities, was *uneven*. Some sectors, nations, and regions expanded more quickly than others, and some spheres of opportunity and lines of communication were penetrated more quickly than others, so that its early spread was in a selective, spatially discontinuous fashion (Fig. 4.4).

- The pattern of specialization and the nature of economic interaction within the world economy resulted in the emergence of *core* areas, characterized by such mass-market industries as had emerged (e.g. textiles, shipbuilding), international and local commerce in the hands of an indigenous bourgeoisie, and relatively advanced forms of agriculture; *peripheral* areas, characterized by the monoculture of cash crops by coerced labour on large estates or plantations; and *semi-peripheral* areas, characterized by a process of de-industrialization but retaining a significant share of specialized industrial production and financial control.

- The spatial organization of these components was based around a cluster of core areas in northwestern Europe – southeastern England and Holland, together with the Baltic states, the Rhine and Elbe regions of Germany, Flanders and northeastern France. Peripheral regions included northern Scandinavia, Britain's Celtic fringe, east-central Europe and all of the trans-oceanic rim settlements and colonies. The semi-periphery consisted of the Christian Mediterranean region which

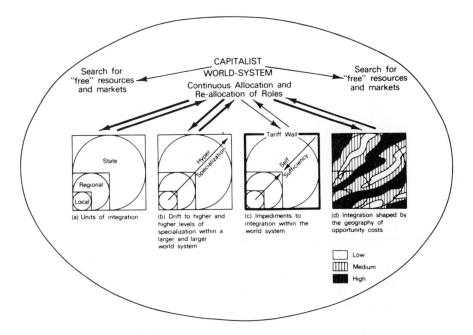

Fig 4.4   Competitive 'price-fixing' markets and the economic integration of space. With the emergence of a world-system of competitive markets, the organization of space becomes an economic process that envelops and even transcends political space. This drift to a global system of economic integration via economic specialization develops at each level of scale order, the local, regional and national, the whole process being advanced or retarded by the georgraphy of opportunity costs, costs that could be varied by natural factors (such as navigable rivers) or residual political barriers (for instance, tariff walls).
Source: Dodgshon (1987) p. 290, Fig. 9.1

had been the advanced core area at the beginning of the merchant capitalist era.

- This last feature points to a further important characteristic of the emergent European world-economy: a system of internal dynamics involving conflicting forces – both economic and political – which held the entire structure together by tension while reorganizing it as each group sought persistently to remould it to its advantage (Wallerstein, 1974). Among the key mechanisms of change in this context we can identify:

  1 The switching of investment from one area to another by merchants in response to the shifting comparative advantages enjoyed by local producers. These shifts in comparative advantage, in turn, are associated with technological innovations and improvements, institutional changes, currency fluctuations, and so on. A good illustration of such change is provided by the rapid and almost continuous

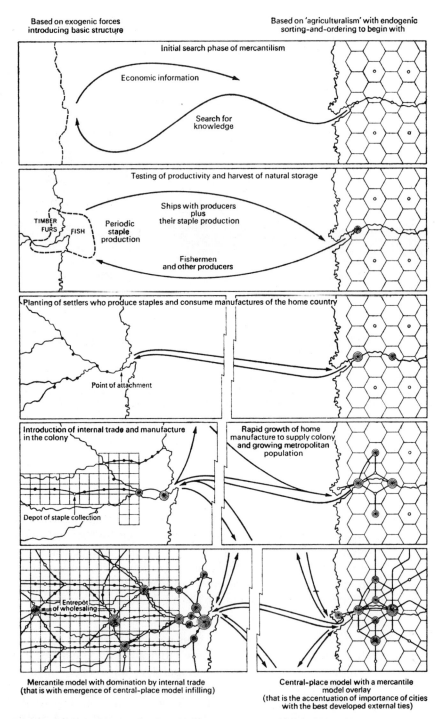

Based on exogenic forces introducing basic structure

Based on 'agriculturalism' with endogenic sorting-and-ordering to begin with

Initial search phase of mercantilism

Economic information

Search for knowledge

Testing of productivity and harvest of natural storage

Ships with producers plus their staple production

TIMBER FURS   FISH   Periodic staple production

Fishermen and other producers

Planting of settlers who produce staples and consume manufactures of the home country

Point of attachment

Introduction of internal trade and manufacture in the colony

Depot of staple collection

Rapid growth of home manufacture to supply colony and growing metropolitan population

Entrepôt of wholesaling

Mercantile model with domination by internal trade (that is with emergence of central-place model infilling)

Central-place model with a mercantile model overlay (that is the accentuation of importance of cities with the best developed external ties)

Fig 4.5   Colonialism and urban settlement patterns (after Vance)
Source: Johnston (1980) Fig. 5.8, p. 75

redrawing of the map of textile production in early modern Europe (Dunford and Perrons, 1983).

2   Import substitution. Communities able to achieve repeated episodes of import substitution, as Jacobs (1984) points out, benefit from five aspects of economic development:
   (a)   enlarged markets for new imports and innovations
   (b)   an expanded and more varied employment base
   (c)   new applications of technology to increase rural productivity
   (d)   a spillover of employment to rural areas as older, expanding enterprises are crowded out of cities
   (e)   growth of city capital

   The corollary, of course, is that communities that are unable or, like Spain, unwilling to substitute their own manufactures for imports remain – or become – peripheral.

3   Militarism and geopolitical change

• The articulation of the European world-economy produced a distinctive pattern of settlement and urbanization. Merchant capitalism was reflected in the urban landscape by a strengthening of the hierarchical system of settlements and the development of the kind of *central place system* described above (p. 69). The overseas territorial expansion associated with Mercantilism was also reflected in a distinctive urban landscape as illustrated in Figure 4.5. Johnston once again provides a succinct description:

In the initial stages of mercantile exploration no permanent settlement is established in order to obtain the required products (fish, timber and furs). Then the colony is settled by agriculturalists; the export of their products moves through local articulation points to the colonial port, and thence to the port in the homeland, which grows in size and status relative to its inland competitors. As settlement of the colony expands further inland, so both of the ports increase in size, railways replace rivers as the main traffic arteries within the colony, and internal gateways develop to articulate the trade of areas some distance from the port, while in the homeland places near to the original port benefit from the imports and a new outport is built to handle the larger volume of trade and the bigger vessels. (1980a, p. 74)

5

Evolution of the Industrial Core Regions

From the second half of the eighteenth century, industrialization brought a new pattern and tempo to the economic organization of the world-economy, and new dimensions to the world's economic landscapes. Today, the economic geography of the 'advanced' nations of the West is dominated by the legacy of industrial capitalism, while the economic geographies of the Soviet Union and Eastern Europe, having had their foundations cast by industrial capitalism, are at least as much the product of industrialization as they are of socialism. Moreover, the economic geography of the world's peripheral regions has been strongly conditioned by their role in sustaining the industrial expansion of the core economies. In short, there are few of the world's economic landscapes that are not largely a product, directly or indirectly, of the industrial era. In this chapter, we outline the evolving economic geography of the industrial core regions, analysing the major processes which govern the relative ascent and decline of nations and regions within the industrial core.

The Industrial Revolution, Industrial Capitalism and Spatial Change

The transition during the late eighteenth and early nineteenth century from merchant capitalism to industrial capitalism as the dominant mode of production is conventionally ascribed to the industrial revolution. The industrial revolution, in turn, is conventionally depicted as a revolution in the techniques and organization of manufacturing, based on a series of innovations in the technology of production (e.g. Kay's flying shuttle (1733), Hargreaves's spinning jenny (1765), and Cartwright's machine loom (1787)), in the technology of energy (James Watt's steam engine (1782)), and in transport technology and engineering (particularly the development of canal and railway systems). But technological advance was part of a wider economic, social and political transition, and the industrial revolution must be seen as a conjunction of changes whose origins and preconditions are to be found in the era of merchant capitalism.

In particular, it was the existence within merchant capitalism of *industry* organized on capitalist lines by entrepreneurs employing wage-labour and producing commodities for sale in regional and national markets that provided the immediate setting and stimulus for technological advance; and it was the capital that had been accumulated in trading that provided the means for entrepreneurs to finance investment in the capital-intensive but highly productive technology of the industrial revolution. From these roots, machine production and the organizational setting of the factory – 'machinofacture' – emerged as the central characteristics of industrialization. While machinery provided the basis for higher levels of productivity, it was the factory setting that enabled this productivity to be exploited to the fullest possible extent: through specialization – the 'division of labour' – and internal economies of scale. At the same time, the concentration of workers in big industrial units generated urban environments which themselves represented a new dynamic force for economic, social and political change.

Once initiated, industrial capitalism, like all forms of capitalism, was impelled by a fundamental need for growth:

> More must be produced, and then sold, to ensure the needed returns on investment. Again, this leads to the contradictory situation whereby forcing down wages so as to increase returns on investment (profits), while at the same time attempting to maintain if not increase prices, produces a reduction in consumption and thus capitalist failure. Wages must rise, to keep pace with prices, in the system as a whole, and this could only be ensured by growth – more production, more productivity, more consumers, more people. The resulting greater profits lead to a greater pool of investment capital, seeking the best returns; to attract this investment, the productivity potential of workers is increased by improving the tools with which they work. Better and more complex machinery means more production, more and bigger factories, and more goods seeking purchasers. Growth demands more growth. (Johnston, 1980a, p. 37)

But, like merchant capitalism before it, industrial capitalism has also had to confront the twin obstacles of market saturation and the law of diminishing returns. In response, industrialists have pursued a variety of strategies. In addition to the constant search for technological advances, these have included:

- the pursuit of new ways of exploiting internal and external economies of scale

- the exploitation of new, cheaper sources of labour and/or raw materials and energy

- the penetration of new (i.e. overseas) markets for existing products

- the development of new products, either through new inventions (e.g. video recorders, microcomputers) or by the 'commodification' of activities previously performed within the household (e.g. food processing and preparation)

As a result, the changes engraved on economic landscapes by the first waves of the industrial revolution have been overwritten by a succession of episodes of industrial development, restructuring, and reorganization. Moreover, while there are some generic similarities in terms of spatial outcomes, it is important to recognize the differences which have been created between the major industrial regions as a result not only of variations in resource endowment and previous patterns of economic development but also because of variations in the relative timing and interaction of these episodes of industrial change.

The Spread of Industrialization in Western Europe

The European experience demonstrates that there was in fact not one industrial revolution but several distinctive transitional phases, each having a different degree of impact, in different ways, on different regions and nations. As new technologies shifted the margins of profitability in different kinds of enterprise, so the character of industrial capitalism was modified, with parallel changes in patterns of spatial organization. In some cases, and for certain periods, such changes were superimposed one on the other in the same region. In other cases, the imperatives of profitability excluded whole regions from particular phases while exposing others to industrial development for the first time. Meanwhile, these regional differentials, in turn, helped to condition the changing character of capitalism itself. The following account is drawn largely from Knox (1984).

First-Wave Industrialization: Britain

It is in fact possible to identify three major waves of industrialization in Europe, each consisting of several phases and each highly localized in their impact (Pollard, 1981). 'Above all,' Pollard emphasizes, 'the industrial revolution was a regional phenomenon' (p. 14). The springboard for the first wave of industrialization, which began in Britain around 1760, consisted of several local hearths of 'proto-industrialization': areas with long-standing concentrations of industry based on a wage-labour force using the most advanced of the industrial processes that were available (for a discussion of proto-industrialization, see Butlin, 1986). In part, this early industrial activity had become localized because of the pull of mineral resources and water power and the importance of local canal systems (Langton, 1984). In part, its localization had been dictated by the principle of comparative advantage, with industry being displaced into areas which were least profitable for agriculture.

This pattern of proto-industrialization, with its external economies, infrastructural advantages and well-developed markets, helped to determine the loci of industrial development precipitated by the first phase of the first wave of industrialization between 1760 and 1790. These included north Cornwall, eastern Shropshire, south Staffordshire, North Wales, upland Derbyshire, south Lancashire, the West Riding of Yorkshire, Tyneside, Wearside and parts of the central lowland of Scotland. Although these sub-regions shared the common impetus of certain key resources and innovations, each retained its own distinctive business traditions and industrial style. Much of the required capital was raised locally, labour requirements were drawn (in the first instance) from the immediate hinterland, and industrialists formed themselves into regional organizations and operated regional cartels.

From the start, then, industrialization was articulated at the *regional* level; and this has been a feature of subsequent phases and waves. The second phase of the first, 'British', wave, between 1790 and 1820, reinforced the position of those embryo industrial regions with a coalfield base and saw the emergence of Ulster and South Wales as industrialized regions. Meanwhile, the prosperity of four of the early starters – Cornwall, North Wales, eastern Shropshire and upland Derbyshire – declined markedly as their relative advantages were eclipsed by a combination of three different factors. One was the exhaustion of minerals, or the discovery of cheaper alternative supplies of them. The second was inaccessibility to markets because of poor communications and/or relatively remote locations. The third was a question of size. As Pollard puts it, 'A small compass may be an ideal milieu for the first halting steps in an innovation, but beyond a certain point an industrial region has to be of a certain size to remain viable' (1981, p. 20). The third phase of the 'British' wave, between 1820 and 1850, was dominated by the expansion of the railway system. This did not foster any new industrial regions, but it did widen the market area of the existing industrial regions, at once drawing more of Britain into the sphere of industrial capitalism and further exaggerating the differences between the industrialized regions and the rest.

The Second Wave: Inner Europe

It was at this point that industrialization began to spread to continental Europe. It should be emphasized, however, that this did not take the form of a straightforward spatial diffusion of industrialization or 'modernization'. The British process of industrialization had come about as an autonomous and organic process, drawing not only on preconditions which were the legacy of its past economic history (i.e. an established tradition of industrial employment and commercial enterprise, a high level of accumulated wealth, a virtual absence of feudal structures, and a relatively enlightened political and legal climate) but also on a series of 'natural' geographical advantages: a compact territory with a large population, favourable conditions for intensive agricultural production, and a rich variety of minerals, including coal.

But it was the *initial advantage* enjoyed by British industries over their would-be competitors on the Continent that provided the most distinctive element to British industrialization, for it meant that later-industrializing regions in Europe (and North America) had to confront a situation in which

British industries, having secured comfortable advantages in technology, had been able to dominate world markets. This competitive disadvantage was compounded, in Europe, by the consequences of the revolutionary and Napoleonic Wars of the early nineteenth century (as it was in the United States by the Civil War of 1861–65). Conscription, conflict and military occupation disrupted production and suppressed industrial expansion, allowing British industries to forge still further ahead. On the other hand, Continental entrepreneurs and governments did not have to industrialize by trial-and-error in the way that the British had: they could benefit from British experience and they could import British managers, workers, capital and technology.

Just as the British wave of industrialization was based on localized concentrations of proto-industrialization, so the second wave was launched from the proto-industrial regions of Continental Europe. Here, the first phase of industrialization, from around 1850, was concentrated in the Sambre–Meuse region of Belgium and in the valley of the Scheldt in Belgium and France. Subsequent phases saw the spread of industrialization to the Aachen area, the right bank of the River Rhine around Solingen and Remscheid, the Ruhr, Alsace, Normandy, the upper Loire valley and the Swiss industrial district between Basel and Glarus. As Pollard notes, these regions of 'inner' Europe were differentiated one from another not only by their different mix of industries, but also by what he calls the *differential of contemporaneousness*, whereby new technologies, ideas and market conditions reached different regions simultaneously but affected them in very different ways because they were differently equipped to respond to them. Thus, for example:

> Legislation permitting the easy formation of joint-stock companies spread quickly across Europe in the 1850s, and their contribution to overspeculation and wide-spread bankruptcies in the less sophisticated European economies has often been commented on. In banking, the backward economies, using the experience of the pioneers, could bypass some of the difficulties of the latter by enjoying the benefits of more efficient banks, ahead, as it were, of their own stage of economic growth . . . At the same time, however, banks and particularly central banks were internationally meshed into the same system, and those in the less advanced areas, and their economies, had to absorb shocks transmitted by the advanced world of a nature to which they were not yet properly fitted. On balance, the transmission of these trade and crisis cycles emanating from more advanced economies could not but be damaging to the less developed ones. (Pollard, 1981, pp. 188–9)

In general, however, the cumulative impact of innovations in first- and second-wave industrializers made for convergence: the French Nord began to look and function increasingly like the central belt of the Scottish lowlands, and the Ruhr began to look and function increasingly like the Sambre–Meuse region. On the other hand, there was increasing divergence between those areas which had adopted an industrial base and those which had yet to follow suit. By 1875, the latter still covered a great deal of the map (Fig. 5.1), but

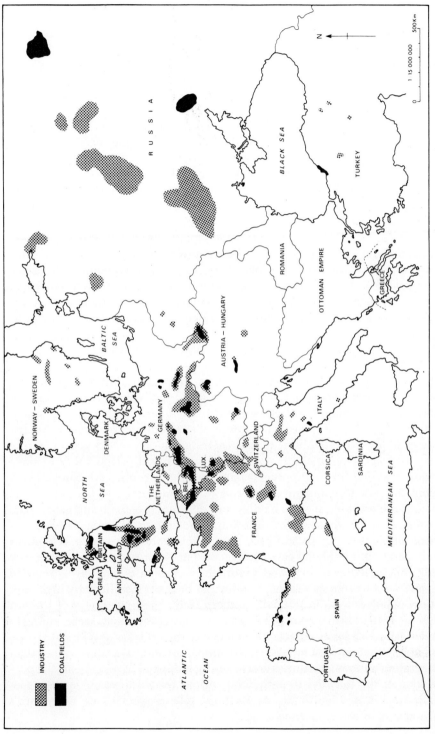

Fig 5.1 Europe in 1875
Source: Pollard (1981) Map 2, p. xv

many of them were incorporated in the third wave of industrialization between 1870 and 1914.

The Third Wave: Intermediate Europe

The third wave of industrialization included parts of Britain, France, Belgium and Germany that had not been directly affected by the first two waves, together with most of the Netherlands, southern Scandinavia, northern Italy, eastern Austria, and Catalonia. In these regions of 'intermediate' Europe, the path of industrialization was different in several important respects, since there was little by way of antecedent development on which to base industrialization (apart from small enclaves in Barcelona, Milan–Turin and Vienna) and the relative amount of capital they were required to find in order to support industrialization was ten times greater than during the first wave. This, together with the increasing sophistication of industrial technology and its related services, compelled central governments to take on ever-increasing responsibilities (Gerschenkron, 1966). The economic role of the state among the later industrializers therefore tends to be more pronounced than in the countries of 'inner' Europe, though they too experienced a marked increase in state economic activity from the early twentieth century onwards.

Peripheral Europe

The residual territories of Western Europe – most of the Iberian peninsula, northern Scandinavia, Ireland, southern Italy, the Balkans and east-central Europe, which Pollard collectively terms the 'outer periphery' – remained, like the interstices of 'inner' and 'intermediate' Europe, mainly outside the fold of industrial capitalism, to be penetrated to different degrees over the next 50 years. One of the reasons for the continued peripherality of these regions was that their entrepreneurs and governments often felt compelled to adopt the new technologies and forms of organization that had served the pioneer regions well, despite having very different economic and geographic settings. Railway systems provide a simple illustration. Whereas railway networks in pioneer regions had been able to integrate industrial development and operate profitably by carrying regular passenger traffic as well as heavy bulk freight like coal, ore and grain, the extension of railway systems to regions with neither an emerging industrial base nor a sufficiently high density of population (as in Ireland, southern Italy, Spain, and most of Eastern Europe) invited heavy losses. The fact that most governments were willing to underwrite such losses reflects the potency of the railways as political virility symbols. What was not foreseen at the time, however, was that, rather than integrating national territories and fostering industrial development, the penetration of the railways to peripheral regions tended to result in their specialization in a subordinate, agricultural role: a special case of Pollard's 'differential of contemporaneousness'.

Another reason for continued peripherality is to be found in the very different nature of *urban* development within the later-industrializing regions. In Britain, 'inner' Europe and 'intermediate' Europe there had been a symbiotic relationship between urban and industrial development (with cities providing capital, labour, markets, access to transport systems, and a variety of agglomeration economies). In much of peripheral Europe, the 'demonstration effect' of these events led to a very different relationship, largely because of the attitudes of the elite:

> Railways were laid to royal palaces, gas or water mains supplied a narrow layer of privileged classes . . . innovations intended for mass markets were misused for a narrow luxury market and either diverted resources, or led to burdensome capital imports. . . . Above all, the city became the gate of entry to new technology manufactures from abroad, spreading outward from Naples, Madrid, Budapest or St Petersburg, to kill off native industry as unfashionable. (Pollard, 1981, p. 212)

In short, conspicuous consumption precluded import substitution, creating cities that inhibited rather than fostered industrial growth.

Dislocation and Depression

In the first half of the twentieth century, the economic development of the whole of Europe was punctuated twice by major wars. The disruptions of the First World War were immense. The overall loss of life, including the victims of influenza epidemics and border conflicts which followed the war, amounted to between 50 and 60 million (Aldcroft, 1978). About half as many again were permanently disabled. For some countries, this meant a loss of between 10 and 15 per cent of the male workforce. In addition, material losses caused a severe dislocation to economic growth: it has been calculated that the level of European output achieved in 1929 would have been reached by 1921 if it had not been for the war (Lewis, 1952). Economic dislocation was further intensified by several indirect consequences of the war. In terms of tracing the evolving economic geography of the core regions, two of these were particularly important:

- The *relative* decline of Europe as a producer compared with the rest of the world. Europe accounted for 43 per cent of the world's production and 59 per cent of its trade in 1913, compared with only 34 per cent of production and 50 per cent of trade in 1923 (Hardach, 1973). The main beneficiaries were the USA and Japan for manufactures, and Latin America and the British dominions for primary production.
- The redrawing of the political map of Europe. This created 38 independent economic units instead of 26, 27 currencies instead of 14, and 20,000 extra kilometres of national boundaries. The corollary of these changes was a severe dislocation of economic life, particularly in east-central Europe: frontiers separated workers from their factories,

factories from their markets, towns from their traditional food supplies, and textile looms from their spinning sheds and finishing mills;
while the transport system found itself only loosely matched to the new
political geography.

Just as European economies had adjusted to these dislocations, the cyclical
financial crisis of 1929–35 – the Great Depression – created a further phase
of economic damage and reorganization throughout Europe. It should be
emphasized, however, that the effects of the Depression varied a good deal
from one sector of the economy to another and from one region to another.
The image of the 1930s depends very much on whether attention is focused on
Jarrow or Slough, on Bochum or Nice, on Glasgow or Geneva. These contrasts
are reflected in the unequal distribution of the unemployed – the 'casualties
of peace' – in the United Kingdom. Even at the depth of the Depression, in
the winter of 1932–33, the steep regional gradient persisted. Local variations,
meanwhile, were sharper still: in parts of South Wales, for example, up to 80
per cent of the civilian labour force was out of work. In northeast England the
figure approached 70 per cent in towns like Jarrow; and in Scotland it
approached 40 per cent in the Glasgow area. Meanwhile, unemployment
never rose above 5 per cent in places such as Guildford, St Albans and
Romford in southeast England.

Furthermore, recovery, when it came, affected the depressed regions only
slowly. Economic revival was concentrated in the southeast and the Midlands, where industries based on new consumer products – domestic appliances, mass-produced clothes and furniture, etc. – were assured of a large
and relatively buoyant market. Nevertheless, the availability of cheap manufactured products also affected patterns of consumption in the depressed
regions, producing the contradictory situation noted by George Orwell in *The
Road to Wigan Pier*:

> Twenty million people are underfed but literally everyone . . . has access to a
> radio. What we have lost in food we have gained in electricity. Whole sections of
> the working class are being compensated, in part, by cheap luxuries which
> mitigate the surface of life. . . . It is quite likely that fish-and-chips, art-silk
> stockings, tinned salmon, cut-price chocolate, the movies, the radio, strong tea
> and the football pools have between them averted revolution. (Orwell, 1962,
> pp. 80-1; first published in 1937)

Meanwhile, the coherence of the European economic world had begun to
disintegrate as individual countries attempted to protect their industries with
import quotas and restrictions, currency manipulation, and exclusionary
trade agreements. The net result was a substantial fall in trade, both in
absolute terms and as a proportion of output, with the USA and Japan, once
again, as the major beneficiaries.

The Second World War and Recovery

The Second World War resulted in a further round of destruction and dislocation. The total loss of life in Europe was 42 million, two-thirds of which were
civilian casualties. The German occupation of Continental Europe involved
ruthless exploitation. By the end of the war, France was depressed to below 50
per cent of her pre-war level of living and had lost 8 per cent of her industrial
assets. The United Kingdom lost 18 per cent of her industrial assets (including
overseas holdings) and the USSR lost 25 per cent. Germany herself, however,
lost 13 per cent of her assets and ended the war with a level of income *per
capita* that was less than 25 per cent of the pre-war figure (Pollard, 1981).

After the war, the political cleavage between Eastern and Western Europe
that resulted from the imposition of what Churchill called the 'Iron Curtain'
along the western frontier of Soviet-dominated territory resulted in a further
erosion of the coherence of the European economy and, indeed, of its economic geography. Ironically, it was this cleavage which led to a surprisingly
rapid economic recovery in Western Europe: the USA, believing that poverty
and economic chaos would foster communism, embarked on a massive programme of aid under the Marshall Plan (Aldcroft, 1978). This pump-priming
action, together with the pent-up backlog of demand in almost every sphere of
production, provided the basis for a remarkable recovery. By the early 1950s
most of Europe had exceeded pre-war levels of prosperity; by the early 1960s,
European central banks were in a position to step in, when necessary, to
support the US dollar. As Table 5.1 illustrates, growth rates throughout Western Europe surged forward to impressive levels.

Centre and Periphery in Western Europe

Once again, however, we must acknowledge the persistence of regional differentials. The cumulative effect of the differential impact of successive waves
of industrialization and reorganization has often been interpreted in terms of
centres of capital accumulation and economic power and peripheries of
limited – or suppressed – potential for economic development. Yet different
criteria yield different definitions of 'centre' and 'periphery' (Knox, 1984).
The West European centre, for example, has variously been interpreted as the
triangular region defined by Lille–Bremen–Strasbourg (the 'Heavy Industrial
Triangle'), as an axial belt stretching between Boulogne and Amsterdam in
the north and Besançon and Munich in the south, as a T-shaped region whose
horizontal axis runs from Rotterdam to Hanover and whose stem extends
down the Rhine to Stuttgart; and so on.

Such definitions are confusing in their variability, but their major weakness
is that they overlook the *interdependence* which exists between centre and
periphery. It is therefore more satisfactory, as King (1982) points out, to think
in terms of a centre consisting of a number of structural socio-economic components which are linked to the structural components of peripheral regions

Table 5.1: Growth rates in Europe

	Annual average compound growth rate of real output per capita	
	1913–50	1950–70
Austria	0.2	4.9
Belgium	0.7	3.3
Denmark	1.1	3.3
Finland	1.3	4.3
France	1.0	4.2
Germany (W.)	0.8	5.3
Greece	0.2	5.9
Ireland	0.7	2.8
Italy	0.8	5.0
Netherlands	0.9	3.6
Norway	1.8	3.2
Portugal	0.9	4.8
Spain	– 0.3	5.4
Sweden	2.5	3.3
Switzerland	1.6	3.0
UK	0.8	2.2
Av. Western Europe	1.0	4.0

Adapted from Pollard (1981), Table 9.2, p. 315

by a series of *flows* (capital, migrants, taxes, tourists, consumer fashions) which bind centre and periphery together, reinforcing their unequal but symbiotic relationship. Using similar criteria, Seers (1979) has defined the West European centre as an incomplete egg-shape centred on Kassel in West Germany, with its long axis stretching 2,700 kilometres from Barcelona in the southwest to Helsinki in the northeast (Figure 5.2).

As Gottmann (1980) has noted, the existence of a centre/periphery structure implies not only the functional organization of space but a degree of conflict between the dominant centre and the subordinate periphery. Economic dominance, in other words, tends to go hand in hand with political control and cultural standardization. This, in turn, points to the existence of different *kinds* of peripheral regions as a result of the interplay of economic, political and cultural factors. Rokkan (1980), for example, demonstrated how the changing patchwork of European nation states created a number of peripheral regions as *interfaces* between major politico-economic core territories. These include parts of Seers's centre such as Flanders/Wallonia, Alsace-Lorraine, the Bernese Jura and the Austro-Hungarian interface (Fig. 5.2). Rokkan also recognized *external* peripheries, characterized by their relative distance from national centres. These include Brittany, Galicia, Scotland and Wales. At the same time, differentiation along the major lines of cleavage between centre and periphery – economic, political and cultural – are also

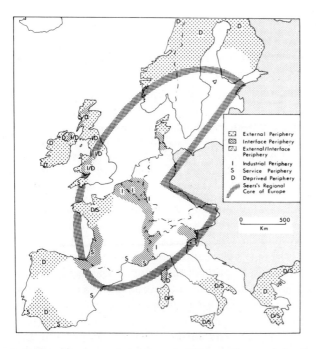

Fig 5.2   Centre and periphery in Western Europe (after Seers (1979) and Aarebrot (1982)
Source: Knox (1984) Fig. 5.8, p. 147

recognized as important. In terms of economic profiles, for example, peripheral regions can be grouped into *industrial peripheries* (e.g. northern England, northern Italy), *service peripheries* dependent on tourism (e.g. southwestern England, the Italian Riviera, and the French southern Atlantic and Mediterranean coasts) and *deprived peripheries* (southern Italy, the Republic of Ireland, Scotland, Wales, Sardinia and Corsica). Finally, it must be acknowledged that a second 'centre' of the West European space-economy has emerged: that of the United States, which is now a major supplier of capital, technology and consumer trends to the whole of Western Europe – centre and periphery.

The Geography of North American Industrialization

The emergence of North America as the dominant component of the core of the world-economy was essentially due to the fact that it had vast natural resources of land and minerals, a large and – thanks to immigration – rapidly-growing market and labour force, and was big enough to breed giant corporations with large research budgets, which helped to institutionalize the innovation process in a way which European industry had never done. Within

North America, the evolving pattern of spatial organization can be interpreted in terms of the interaction of (i) the geography of resources, (ii) the introduction of major technological innovations (particularly in transport), and (iii) movements of population (Knox *et al.*, 1988). Thus:

> Major changes in technology have resulted in critically important changes in the evaluation or definition of particular resources on which the growth of certain urban regions had previously been based. Great migrations have sought to exploit resources – ranging from climate or coal to water or zinc – that were either newly appreciated or newly accessible within the national market. Usually, of course, the new appreciation or accessibility had come about, in turn, through some major technological innovation. (Borchert, 1967, p. 324)

As Borchert and others have noted, the history of the development and evolution of the American economy found its clearest spatial expression in changing patterns of urbanization. At the time when Europe was experiencing the first waves of industrialization, the spatial organization of the North American economy was focused on the gateway ports of the Atlantic seaboard, each of which controlled a limited hinterland in which the economy was dominated by the production of agricultural staples for Europe and the consumption of manufactured goods from Europe. From the end of the eighteenth century, however, the North American economy began to break loose from this dependent relationship, and within 100 years it had become the dominant component of the world-economy, articulated around a closely integrated but highly differentiated urban system. The following account is drawn largely from Knox *et al.* (1988).

Getting Started: 1780–1840

A major factor in this metamorphosis was the political independence of the United States, which was formally achieved in 1783. This stimulated economic development in several ways. First, independence from Britain and national political integration under a federal system provided an important stimulus for economic links to be forged between the component parts of the old colonial system. Second, it meant that a much greater proportion of investment was financed by American capital, with the result that less of the profits were 'leaked' back to Europe. Third, it stimulated a proliferation of government employment at all levels. Finally, the territorial expansion of the new nation provided a large, rich resource base.

Both urban and economic development in this period, however, were constrained by the relatively primitive transportation system of the 'sail and wagon' epoch (Borchert, 1967). Consequently, foreign commerce began a long decline in its contribution to economic growth; so that the most vigorous development occurred in areas of westward expansion and, in particular, the gateway cities located at strategic points along the inland waterways that linked the new western lands with the major centres of the Atlantic seaboard (Johnston, 1982). Thus New Orleans grew particularly rapidly in the first two decades of the nineteenth century because of its situation at the mouth of the Mississippi system and the comparative advantage of water-borne transport over the primitive turnpike network. The extent of this advantage is illustrated by the fact that European goods destined for Cincinnati were shipped inland via New Orleans and the Mississippi rather than overland through one of the east coast ports. East coast merchants, however, were not content to let the lucrative trade from western and southern hinterlands slip from their grasp. Their response was to invest in the intensive development of their immediate hinterlands, tapping the waterways of the Great Lakes and the Hudson, Ohio and Mississippi river systems with networks of canals. As a result, New York gained an early dominance which has never been seriously challenged, while, further west, St Louis emerged as a major gateway, with its location at the confluence of the Missouri and Mississippi allowing it to tap its own hinterland to the west while capitalizing on the trading routes both to the east and to the south.

1840–1920: Expansion, Realignment and Differentiation

The process of industrialization accelerated strikingly during the late 1830s and early 1840s. In part, this was the result of the diffusion of industrial technology – particularly the wider industrial application of steam and the accompanying changes in the iron industry – and methods of industrial and commercial organization from the hearth of the industrial revolution in Europe. In addition, the demand for foodstuffs and other agricultural staples, both in North America and abroad, stimulated the growth of industrial capitalism as farmers sought to increase productivity through mechanization and the use of improved agricultural implements. Increasing agricultural productivity, in turn, helped to sustain the growing numbers of immigrants from Europe, thus allowing them to be channelled into industrial employment in North America's mushrooming cities.

The development of the railway system was central to the evolution of this new economic order. Initially, the railways were complementary to the waterways as competitive long-haul carriers of general freight; but by the end of the 'iron horse' epoch (Borchert, 1967) the railway network had not only realigned the economic system but also extended it to a continental scale. In 1869, the railway network reached the Pacific when, at Promontory, Utah, the Union Pacific railway, building west from Omaha, met the Central Pacific railway, building east from Sacramento; and by 1875 intense competition between railway companies had began to open up the western prairies as far as Minneapolis-St Paul and Kansas City. The significance of this has been stressed by Hamilton (1978, p. 26, emphasis added):

> Not only did this permit American enterprise to exploit fully the commercial advantages and scale economies of large, diversified natural resources and of the revolutionary technologies evolved in those decades, but it generated rapid, large-scale functional and spatial concentration of finance and management

unimpeded by world events, creating a '*transcontinental*' business mentality. Wide spatial separation of major resources, cities and markets, and adjacency to the easily penetrated Canadian economy all induced mental thresholds for thinking '*intercontinental*' once imported resources and markets overseas became a necessary ingredient to sustain business activity at home, especially during and after the Second World War.

In short, the railways can be seen as the catalyst which allowed regional economies to develop into a continental economy which stood poised to become the leading component of the world economic system. Meanwhile, the westward extension of the railways affected the relative fortunes of the inland gateway cities. Buffalo and Louisville, for instance, slowed their rate of growth and came to rely increasingly on more diversified regional functions, while, further west, St Paul and Kansas City grew rapidly to become major wholesaling depots. It is also important to note that the development of improved transportation networks led to adjustments in spatial organization within the northeast, where fierce competition between the railways and water-borne transport, coupled with equally fierce rivalry between neighbouring cities, led to a marked increased in *intra*-regional trade (Pred, 1980). This, in turn, helped to lay the foundations of what was to become the Manufacturing Belt.

At the same time, the entire system became increasingly differentiated as the industrialization of the economy created new kinds of specialist towns. Thus emerged a variety of specialist mining towns (mainly in Appalachia), a whole series of specialist manufacturing towns based on the water-power resources of the Fall Line (in New England and along the eastern margins of the Appalachians), and the production of agricultural machinery in some Midwestern towns. The economic base of most of the longer-established cities, on the other hand, became more diversified as manufacturing establishments and service industries were opened to serve local markets; while the very largest (including the mushrooming Chicago, San Francisco and Toronto), with more local capital, bigger markets, larger pools of skilled labour, and a high degree of nodality in relation to newspaper, postal and telegraphic services, were able not only to expand and diversify their economic base but also to become the major control centres of industrial activity for the entire continent.

It would be misleading, however, to convey the impression of unmitigated growth. The changing logic of industrial location eventually worked to the disadvantage of manufacturing towns at historic waterpower sites along the Fall Line, while the continued expansion of east–west wholesaling chains based on the railways ensured the relatively sluggish growth of St Louis, Louisville and many of the smaller towns on the great waterways. Furthermore, inertia and conservatism among the leading entrepreneurs of *some* of the older cities resulted in a failure to invest in more profitable industries such as iron and steel, machinery and machine tools, leaving the local economy to depend on slower-growing industries such as printing and publishing, confectionery, clothing and furniture, which relied heavily on *local* rather than regional or national markets.

The Manufacturing Belt and Regional Economic Specialization

In essence, the consolidation of the Manufacturing Belt as the continental economic heartland was the result of initial advantage. With its large markets, well-developed transport networks and access to nearby coal reserves, it was ideally placed to take advantage of the general upsurge in demand for consumer goods, the increased efficiency of the telegraph system and postal services, the advances in industrial technology and the increasing logic of scale economies and external economies which characterized the late nineteenth century. The net effect was twofold:

1 Individual cities began to specialize, as producers were able to gear themselves to *national* rather than regional markets:

> Between 1870 and 1890, advances in milling technology and concentration of ownership supported the emergence of Minneapolis as a milling centre. Furniture for the mass market centralized in fewer, larger plants using wood-working machinery. . . . The rise of national brewers between 1880 and 1910 is an example of national market firms encroaching on local-regional firms. The brewers in Milwaukee and St Louis achieved economies of scale in manufacture, used production innovations such as mechanical refrigeration, and capitalized on distribution innovations made possible by the refrigerated rail car and an integrated rail network. (Meyer, 1983, p. 160)

Similarly, musical instrument manufacture and men's clothing emerged as specialties in Boston; meat packing, furniture manufacture and printing and publishing in Chicago; coachbuilding and furniture manufacture in Cincinnati; textile manufacture in Philadelphia; and so on. In smaller cities, specialization was often much more pronounced, as in the production of iron and steel and coachbuilding in Columbus, furniture in Grand Rapids, agricultural implements in Springfield, and boots and shoes in Worcester. Overall, there emerged a three-part segmentation of the Manufacturing Belt (Fig. 5.3), with a heavy bias towards consumer-goods production in the ports of Baltimore, Boston and New York, a producer-goods axis between Philadelphia and Cleveland, and a western cluster of rather less specialized consumer-oriented manufacturing cities.

2 This specialization provided the basis for increasing commodity flows between individual cities, thus binding the Manufacturing Belt together. These linkages, in turn, generated important multiplier effects through the intermediary functions of wholesaling, finance, warehousing and transportation, thus adding to the cumulative process of regional industrial growth (Pred, 1977) and increasing the region's comparative advantage in terms of further industrial growth. These advantages meant that the Manufacturing Belt was able to attract a large proportion of any new industrial activities with

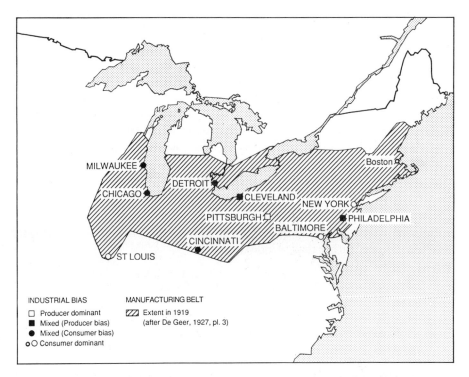

INDUSTRIAL BIAS

☐ Producer dominant
■ Mixed (Producer bias)
● Mixed (Consumer bias)
o○ Consumer dominant

MANUFACTURING BELT

▨ Extent in 1919
(after De Geer, 1927, pl. 3)

Fig 5.3   The American manufacturing belt in 1920 (after Conzen)
Source: Knox *et al.* (1988) Fig 5.1 p. 117

large or national markets, *and this in turn stifled the chances* of comparable
levels of industrialization in late-developing regions.

This does not mean, of course, that other regions did not become industrialized. Rather, it was the scale and the intensity of industrialization which
differed: later-developed regions were able to support an array of locally-
oriented manufacturers, together with some nationally-oriented activities
based on particular local advantages or raw materials; but they were rarely
able to attract manufacturers of producer-goods for the national market.

The Inter-War Years: Growth and Depression

If the template of North American economic geography had been established
by 1920, the full details of industrial capitalism were etched in between 1920
and 1940, when the arrival of truck and automobile transportation and the
acceleration of the functional integration of the economy triggered a further
series of shifts and adjustments. As Borchert has pointed out, the mass production of the internal combustion engine 'put the farmer in an automobile and
thus encouraged the centralization of urban growth at the larger, diversified
centres in all the commercial farming regions' (1967, p. 305). In addition, air

passenger transport helped to encourage centralization of the national business management function in a few cities, and the auto stimulated the decentralization of most metropolitan functions. Another consequence of the transition from steam to internal combustion was the relative decline of coal and railway centres and, conversely, the rapid growth of metropolitan areas in the oilfields.

Road and air travel, along with improvements in electronic communications, also increased the *capacity* and *efficiency* of the economy and facilitated the functional integration of both businesses and regions at an unprecedented pace. The 1920s were the 'New Economic Era', and the liberal reactions to industrialism which had characterized the Progressive Era before the First World War were quickly edged aside by consumerism and boosterism. The larger companies based in the major metropolitan centres were best placed to exploit the increased capacity and efficiency of the economic system. A flurry of company mergers just before the war had transformed the business structure of the economy, resulting in a relatively small number of very powerful corporations which now stood poised to dominate the economy. By 1920, over 30 per cent of all jobs and nearly 50 per cent of the country's production was accounted for by just 1 per cent of all firms.

> The Captains of Industry were clearly in charge. Across the country, territorial communities watched effective control over local production slip out of their grasp. Political power came to focus on the national level of territorial integration which, for the time being, effectively bounded the operation of most businesses. (Friedmann and Weaver, 1979, p. 22)

But the New Economic Era fostered some serious problems. Mechanized agriculture became so 'over-productive' that commodity prices plummeted; while the industrial market became unstable as a result of the labyrinth of holding companies which had been created. In October 1929 the stock market collapsed, initiating the Great Depression in which millions of workers lost their jobs. Because of the regional division of labour which had emerged over the previous 50 years, some areas suffered particularly acute social and economic problems. In Canada, exports were cut by over half in value as the Depression pushed the price of wheat down from Can$1.05 to Can$0.49 a bushel, so that it was the prairie regions that bore the brunt of the Depression, while southern Quebec and Ontario were cushioned by their more diversified economic base (Kemp, 1978; Blackbourn and Putnam, 1984).

With the outbreak of war in Europe in 1939, however, the entire North American economy entered a phase of accelerated growth; and in the aftermath of the war the United States and Canada emerged not only with stronger and more efficient industries but also with new technologies and with control over new international markets. Furthermore, the United States, in its new, outward-looking role as leader of the capitalist world, was able to dictate, through the terms of Marshall Aid, its control of the Organization for European Economic Co-operation, and the Bretton Woods agreement (which established a new framework for international economic relations). By 1960,

GNP *per capita* stood at $2,513 in the US, compared with $1,909 in Canada, $1,678 in Sweden, $1,259 in the UK, $1,200 in West Germany, $1,193 in France, and $421 in Japan. By this time, however, the economic geography of North America had begun to respond to the imperatives of advanced capitalism: a theme which we explore in detail in Chapter 6.

Japanese Industrialization

The rise of the Japanese economy to join Western Europe and North America at the core of the modern world-economy represents a major achievement, and it poses some important questions in relation both to the theory and the reality of economic organization and spatial change. In particular, how was it that a relatively resource-poor country like Japan was successful in industrialization while resource-rich regions elsewhere in Asia and in Latin America were not? In other words, in what way was Japan an exception to the rest of the periphery?

Broadly speaking, the answer lies in the fact that the Japanese economy, although organized along feudal lines until well into the nineteenth century, was autonomous; it had never been penetrated by the capitalism of the core regions. Moreover, the transition from feudalism to capitalism took place as a deliberate attempt to preserve national political and economic autonomy. But, even though Japan was 'lucky' in not having been politically and economically subordinated, the path to progress via industrialization was still obstructed by the core regions' pre-emption of the technology, the infrastructure and the capital for industrial development. This raises a second important question: how were these obstacles overcome? The answer, again in general terms, lies in the combination of military aggression, flooding overseas markets with cheap products, and copying and adapting Western technology: a strategy that was achieved at the expense of authoritarian government, widespread exploitation and acute regional disparities.

From Feudalism to Industrial Capitalism

Japan's transition from feudalism to industrial capitalism can be pin-pointed to a specific year – 1868 – when the feudal political economy of the Tokugawa regime was toppled by the restoration of imperial power. For 250 years, the Tokugawa regime had consistently pursued the objective of sustaining traditional Japanese society. To this end, the patrimonial government of the Tokugawa family excluded missionaries, banned Christianity, closed Japanese ports to foreign vessels (Nagasaki was the single exception), and deliberately suppressed commercial enterprise. At the top of the feudal hierarchy were the nobility (the *shogunate*), their barons (*daimyos*), and warriors (*samurai*). Farmers and artisans represented the productive base exploited by these ruling classes; and only outcasts and prostitutes ranked lower than merchants.

In terms of spatial organization, the economy was built around a closed hierarchy of castle towns, each representing the administrative base of a local shogun. The position of a town within this hierarchy was dependent on the status of the shogun which, in turn, was related to the productivity of their agricultural hinterland. As a result, the largest cities – which were to become the foundations for subsequent economic growth – emerged among the alluvial plains and the reclaimed lakes and bay-heads of southern Honshu. At the top of the hierarchy was Edo (now Tokyo), which the Tokugawa regime had selected as its capital in preference to the traditional imperial capital of Kyoto, and which, bloated by soldiery, administrators and the entourages of the nobility in attendance at the Tokugawa court, reached a population of around a million by the early nineteenth century (Kornhauser, 1982). Kyoto and Osaka were next largest, with populations of between 300,000 and 500,000; and they were followed by Nagoya and Kanazawa, both of which stood at around 100,000.

With cities of this size, it was very difficult to suppress commerce and prevent the breakdown of the traditional political economy. As in feudal Europe, the peasantry fled the countryside in increasing numbers in response to a combination of taxation, technological improvements in agriculture, and the lure of the relative freedom and prosperity of the cities. Meanwhile, prolonged peace had reduced both the influence and the affluence of the samurai, drawing increasing numbers of them towards commercial and manufacturing activities. Thus 'former peasants mingled with former warriors in secular occupations coordinated as much by market forces as by feudalistic regulations. A class-based commercial society thus developed despite the efforts of the Tokugawa leaders to maintain the pre-industrial, status-oriented society of old Japan' (Light, 1983, p. 158). By the early nineteenth century, Japan had moved into a period of crisis: famines and peasant uprisings, presided over by an introverted and self-serving leadership. In 1853 US Admiral Perry arrived in Edo Bay to 'persuade' the shogunate to open Japanese ports to trade with the US and other foreign powers. This neo-colonialist threat galvanized feelings of nationalism and xenophobia and precipitated a period of civil war among the shogunate. The outcome was the restoration of the Meiji imperial dynasty in 1868 by a clique of samurai and daimyo who were convinced that Japan needed to industrialize in order to maintain national independence. Under the slogan 'National Wealth and Military Strength', the new élite of ex-warriors set out to modernize Japan as quickly as possible. A distinctive feature of the entire process was the very high degree of state involvement. Successive governments intervened to promote industrial development by fostering capitalist monopolies (zaibatsu). In many instances, whole industries were created from public funds and, once established, were sold off to private enterprise at less than cost. Because early manufacturing was motivated strongly by considerations of national security, it was iron and steel, shipbuilding and armaments that were prominent in the early phase of Japanese modernization. The latest industrial technology and equipment were bought in from overseas, and advisers (chiefly British) were bought in to supervise the initial stages of development. Meanwhile, the state indulged in high levels of expenditure on highways, port facilities, the banking system and public education in its attempt to 'buy' modernization. Similarly, the railway system was financed by the state under British direction before being sold to private enterprise.

Hampered by the legacy of Tokugawa treaties that restricted their ability to manipulate international trade as a source of capital, the Japanese financed this modernization by harsh taxes on the agricultural sector. As a result, there began a sharp polarization between the urban and the rural economies, characterized by the impoverishment of large numbers of peasant farmers. Yet the more productive components of the agrarian sector were able to contribute significantly to Japanese economic growth. Improved technology, better seedstock and the use of fertilizers provided an increase of 2 per cent per annum in rice production during the last quarter of the nineteenth century and the first part of the twentieth century, thereby helping to feed the growing non-farm sector without great dependence on food imports. In this context, it is important to note that these increases in agricultural productivity were not absorbed by population growth, as has been the case for most late-comers. The Japanese demographic transition arrived later – after increases in agricultural productivity had helped to finance an emergent industrial sector but in time to provide an expanding labour force and market for industrial products.

Several other factors helped to foster rapid industrialization in Japan in the late nineteenth and early twentieth centuries. One was the cultural order that allowed the Japanese to follow government leadership and accept new ways of life: a recurring theme in modern Japanese economic history (Kornhauser, 1982; see also p. 236). Another was the success of educational reforms: by 1905, 95 per cent of all children of school age were receiving an elementary education (Fairbank et al., 1973). Third, Japanese sericulture (silk production) provided the basis for a lucrative export trade with which to help finance expenditure on overseas technology, materials and expertise. It has been estimated that between 1870 and 1930 the raw silk trade alone was able to finance as much as 40 per cent of Japan's entire imports of raw materials and machinery (Lockwood, 1954). Finally, and most important, were the benefits deriving from military aggression. Naval victories over China (1894–95) and Russia (1904–05) and the annexation of Korea (1910) not only provided expanded markets for Japanese goods in Asia but also provided indemnities from the losers (which paid for the costs of conquest) and stimulated the armaments industry, shipbuilding, and industrial technology and financial organization in general.

By the early 1900s, a broad spectrum of industries had been successfully established. Most were geared towards the domestic market in a kind of pre-emptive import-substitution strategy. The textile industry, however, had already begun to establish an export base. Unable to compete with Western nations in the production of high-quality textiles, the Japanese concentrated on the production of inexpensive goods, competing initially with Western producers for markets in Asia. Their success derived largely from labour-intensive processes in which high productivity and low wages were maintained through a combination of (a) exhortations to personal sacrifice in the cause of national independence, and (b) strict government suppression of labour unrest.

Japan Advances

With the First World War there came a major stimulus to industrial advance. With the rest of the Allied powers preoccupied with the situation in Europe, Japan was able to become a major supplier of textiles, armaments and industrial equipment on world markets, to almost double its merchant marine tonnage, and to establish a balance of payments surplus. Between 1919 and 1929 this position was consolidated, again under government sponsorship. Steel manufacturing, engineering and textiles were further developed, and aircraft and automobile industries were established. Meanwhile, Japanese innovations began to emerge, at once weakening the dependence on Western technology and providing an important competitive advantage (Kornhauser, 1982). This pattern of progress was halted, however, by the stagnation of international trade which followed the stock market collapse of 1929 and the subsequent Depression. Once again, state intervention provided a critical boost. A massive devaluation of the yen in 1931 allowed Japanese producers to undersell on the world market, while a Bureau of Industrial Rationalization was set up to increase efficiency, lower costs, and weed out smaller, less profitable concerns.

Although these interventions helped to sustain Japanese industrialization and improve her overall economic independence, they led directly towards crisis. Western governments – particularly the United States – began seriously to resist the purchase of Japanese goods while, at home, the austerity resulting from devaluation and rationalization precipitated social and political unrest. The government response was to indulge in further military expenditure and to adopt a more aggressive territorial policy. In 1931 the Japanese army advanced into Manchuria to create a puppet state. In 1936 a military faction gained full political power and, declaring a Greater East Asian Co-Prosperity Sphere, set about full-scale war with China the following year. In 1939 Japan attacked British colonies in the Far East and by 1940 the Japanese 'had become heavily committed to an industrial empire based on war. In that year, 17 per cent of the entire national output was for war purposes' (Kornhauser, 1982, p. 119). By this time, as the rest of the world quickly realized, Japan had attained the status of an advanced industrial nation. The military leaders overplayed their hand, however, by attacking the United States. With defeat in 1945, Japanese industry lay in ruins. In 1946, output was only 30 per cent of the pre-war level; and the United States, having begun to weaken the power of the zaibatsu and to impose widespread social and political reforms, was set to impose punitive reparations.

Postwar Reconstruction and Growth

Within five years, the Japanese economy had recovered to its pre-war levels of output. Throughout the 1950s and 1960s the annual rate of growth of the economy held at around 10 per cent, compared with growth rates of around 2 per cent per annum in North America and Western Europe (Harris, 1982). After beginning the postwar period at the foot of the international manufacturing league table, Japan had risen to the top by 1963 (Fig. 5.4). By 1980, Japan had outstripped, even in *absolute* terms, all of the major industrial core countries in the production of ships, automobiles and television sets, and only the Soviet Union was producing more steel (Fig. 5.5). The Japanese, in short, have not only achieved a unique transition direct from feudalism to industrial capitalism, they have presided over a postwar 'economic miracle' of impressive dimensions.

Explanations of this 'miracle' have identified a variety of contributory factors (Morishima, 1982; Murata, 1980). One of the most important, in the first instance, was the reversal of United States policy. Cold War strategy, in response to China's pursuit of a communist path to development, dictated

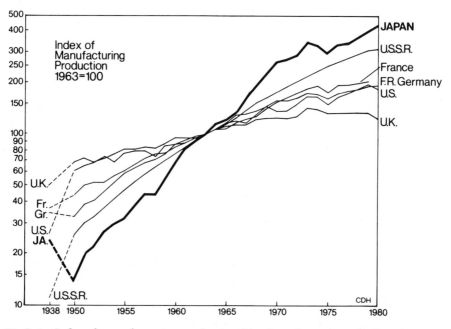

Fig 5.4 Index of manufacturing production for selected countries, 1950–1980
Source: Harris (1982) Fig. 10, p. 63

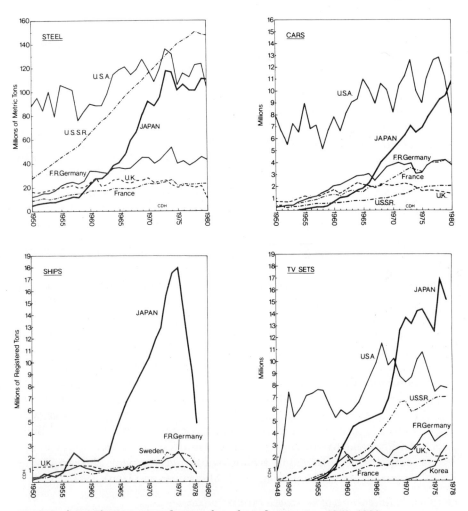

Fig 5.5 Manufacturing production for selected countries, 1950–1980
Source: Harris (1982) Figs. 11–14, p. 64

that the punitive stance should be replaced by massive economic aid in order to create a bastion against the spread of communism in East Asia. The Korean conflict (1950–53) helped to reinforce this logic and at the same time stimulated the Japanese economy through United States expenditure on Japanese supplies and military bases. Once under way, the reconstruction of the Japanese economy was able to draw on some of its previously established advantages: a well-educated, flexible, loyal and relatively cheap labour force, a large national market with good internal communications, a good geographical situation for trade within Asia, a high degree of cooperation between industry and government, and a mode of industrial organization – derived from the zaibatsu – big enough to compete with the multinational corporations of Western Europe and North America. In addition, several *new* factors helped to metamorphose reconstruction into spectacular growth. These include:

1   Exceptionally high levels of personal savings (19.5 per cent of personal disposable income in 1980, compared with 4.7 per cent in the United States), which have helped to fund high levels of capital investment.

2   The acquisition of new technology: between 1950 and 1969 Japan was able to acquire, for around $1.5 billion in royalties and licenses, a body of thoroughly tested US technology that had cost the United States $20 billion *per year* in research and development (R & D). More recently, Japanese investment in domestic R & D has overtaken (in relative terms) that of both Western Europe and North America, providing important advantages in production technology and product design. Overall, Japanese investment in technology in 1980 amounted to 6 per cent of her industrial turnover, compared with 1 per cent in the United States.

3   New means of government support. On the one hand, the construction of a rigid and sophisticated system of import barriers – both tariff and non-tariff – has protected domestic markets from overseas competition. On the other hand, the growth of domestic industry was fostered by a multitude of tax concessions and by the provision of investment finance through the Japan Development Bank. Most important of all, however, was the orchestration of industrial growth by the Ministry of International Trade and Industry (MITI). In particular, MITI identified key recovery sectors (e.g. steel, shipbuilding) and potential growth sectors (e.g. automobiles, electronics, computers) and facilitated their development by providing finance, ensuring protection from foreign competition, subsidizing technological development and arranging corporate mergers (Johnson, 1982; Magaziner and Hout, 1980)

Regional Dimensions of Japanese Industrialization
The pace and weight of postwar industrialization has dramatically rearranged the economic landscape that existed at the close of the Tokugawa period. In many ways, the changes wrought on the Japanese landscape parallel those which occurred in response to the industrialization of Western Europe and North America. Existing urban centres (the castle towns) grew differentially according to their adaptability as regional industrial, commercial or administrative centres; while new kinds of specialist settlements – ports, mining towns, heavy manufacturing towns and transport centres – emerged and grew rapidly to become major nodes of urbanization. Similarly, the expansion and diversification of the industrial economy imposed a progressive spatial division of labour as the logic of agglomeration and economies of scale made for regional specialization: the concentration of the silk industry in central Honshu, the gravitation of the cotton industry towards the port cities which serve the Asian market, and the location of heavy industry around

deposits of raw materials in Hokkaido and northern Honshu, for example (for a full account of the economic geography of Japan, see Kornhauser, 1982; Murata, 1980).

Within this overall transformation one distinctive feature to emerge was the large company town. This, of course, is a reflection of the unique role of the zaibatsu in Japanese industrialization. Thus the early leaders among the zaibatsu – Mitsui, Mitsubishi and Sumitomo – inevitably came to dominate their host cities (which included Omuta, Niihoma, Nobeoka and Nagasaki); while later-established zaibatsu, as well as some of the corporate giants spawned by postwar growth, sponsored new company towns in newly-industrializing regions: the city of Hitachi, northeast of Mito, for example.

What was most distinctive about the geography of industrialization in Japan, however, was the sheer intensity of development that was crammed into the relatively limited amount of suitable land. The 'megalopolitan' corridor between Tokyo and Kobe represents the apotheosis of this development, and it has inevitably brought serious problems: notably crowding, congestion, environmental pollution and ground subsidence. Moreover, the corollary of the concentration of economic activity in the Tokyo–Kobe corridor is a relative lack of development elsewhere. Japan is thus characterized, like Western Europe and North America, by a *centre–periphery* pattern. In the Japanese case, the periphery consists of northern Honshu, Hokkaido, Kyushu and Shikoku. Like peripheral regions within older core nations, they have experienced the backwash effects of metropolitan development: selective out-migration, restricted investment (both public and private), and limited employment opportunities. In addition, much of the periphery has a climate that most Japanese find severe, thus compounding feelings of deprivation and remoteness.

Industrialization under Socialism: the Soviet Union and Eastern Europe

The economies of the Soviet Union and Eastern Europe provide a very different case study of industrial development, though in terms of spatial organization the differences between them and capitalist industrial countries are fewer than might be expected. It should be emphasized at the outset that the economies of the Soviet Union and Eastern Europe have *not* been based on a true socialist or communist mode of production in which the working class has democratic control over the processes of production, distribution and development. Rather, they seem to have evolved as something of a hybrid in terms of economic organization (despite the persistence of 'pure' socialist ideology in government and Communist Party rhetoric). Chase-Dunn (1982) has identified four different characterizations of this hybridization:

1   *Beaureaucratically deformed workers' state*: transitional between

capitalism and socialism, with the state dominated by a privileged beaureaucracy but also influenced by world market forces (see, for example, Mandel, 1981).

2　*Post-revolutionary society*: neither capitalist nor socialist, with the state used by a beaureaucratic/technocratic class to exploit workers (see, for example, Sweezy, 1980).

3　*State socialism*: economic organization is dominated by central planning for social use, under the direct control of the working class (Szymanski, 1979).

4　*State capitalism*: state power is used by a bureaucratic class to exploit workers and to compete for power and economic advantage in the larger world-economy (Binns and Haynes, 1980).

Alternatively, some observers have interpreted the development of the Soviet Union and Eastern Europe not so much in terms of the (distorted) expression of an alternative and separate political economy as the pragmatic response of late-comers who could only industrialize under highly centralized and rigidly enforced government control (Gerschenkron, 1970; von Laue, 1960; Wallerstein, 1979a). What is not in doubt, however, is that the Soviet Union and Eastern Europe have been able to achieve a relatively advanced stage of industrial development by disengaging from their semi-peripheral role under the industrial capitalism of the European world-economy.

Revolutionary Economic Reorganization

Since the time of Peter the Great (around 1700), Tsarist Russia had been attempting to modernize. By 1861, when Alexander II decreed the abolition of serfdom, Russia had built up an internal core with a large beaureaucracy, a substantial intelligentsia and a sizeable group of skilled workers. The abolition of feudal serfdom was designed to accelerate the industrialization of the economy by compelling the peasantry to raise crops on a commercial basis, the idea being that the profits from exporting grain would be used to import foreign technology and machinery. In many ways, the strategy seems to have been successful: grain exports increased fivefold between 1860 and 1900, while manufacturing activity expanded rapidly (Black, 1977). Further reforms, in 1906, helped to establish large, consolidated farms in place of some of the many small-scale peasant holdings. But the consequent flood of dispossessed peasants to the cities created acute problems as housing conditions deteriorated and labour markets became flooded. These problems, to which the Tsar remained indifferent despite the petitions of desperate municipal governments, nourished deep discontent which eventually, aggravated by military defeats and the sufferings of the First World War, spawned the revolutionary changes of 1917. It was not the peasantry or the oppressed provincial industrial proletariat, however, that emerged from the chaos to take control. It was the Bolsheviks, a dissatisfied element drawn from the internal core of the nation, whose orientation from the beginning favoured a strategy of economic development in which the intelligentsia and skilled industrial workers would play the key roles (Tylecote and Lonsdale-Brown, 1982).

In the first instance, however, the ravages of war and the upheavals of revolution precluded the possibility of planned economic reorganization of any kind. Thus the centralization of control over production and the nationalization of industry resulted as much from the need for national and political survival as from ideological beliefs. Similarly, it was rampant inflation that led to the virtual abolition of money, not revolutionary purism. By 1920, industrial production was still only 20 per cent of the pre-war level, crop yields were only 44 per cent of the pre-war level, and national income *per capita* stood at less than 40 per cent of the pre-war level. In 1921, a New Economic Policy was introduced in an attempt to catch up. Central control of key industries, foreign trade and banking was codified under *Gosplan*, the central economic planning commission; but in other spheres – and in agriculture in particular – a substantial degree of freedom was restored, with heavy reliance on market mechanisms operated by 'bourgeois specialists' from the old intelligentsia. Improvement in national economic performance was immediate and sustained, with the result that recovery to pre-war levels of production was reached in 1926 for agriculture and the following year in the case of industry (Grossman, 1974).

Soon afterwards, however, there occurred a major shift in power within the Soviet Union which swept aside both the New Economic Policy and its 'bourgeois specialists'. They were replaced by a much more centralized allocation of resources: a 'command' economy operated by a new breed of engineers/managers/apparatchiks drawn from the new intelligentsia that had developed among the membership of the Communist Party. With this shift there came a more explicit strategy for industrial development. Like Japan, the Soviet Union gave national economic and political independence the highest priority; but, in contrast to the Japanese strategy of aggressive international trade, the Soviet Union chose to withdraw from the capitalist world-system as far as possible, relying instead on the capacity of its vast territories to produce the raw materials needed for rapid industrialization. As in Meiji Japan, the capital for creating manufacturing capacity and the required infra-structure and educational improvements was extracted from the agricultural sector: the foundation of Stalin's industrialization drive was the collectivization of agriculture. This involved the compulsory relocation of peasants into state or collective farms where they were expected to produce bigger yields. The state would then purchase the harvest at relatively low prices so that, in effect, the collectivized peasant was to pay for industrialization by 'gifts' of labour.

In the event, the Soviet peasantry was somewhat reluctant to make these gifts, not least because the wages they could earn on collective farms could not be spent on consumer goods or services: Soviet industrialization was overwhelmingly geared towards manufacturing *producer* goods. It proved very difficult to regiment the peasants. Requisitioning parties and tax inspectors were met with violence, passive resistance and the slaughter of animals. At this juncture Stalin employed police terror to compel the peasantry to comply with the requirements of the Five-Year Plans that provided the framework for his industrialization drive. Severe exploitation required severe repression. Dissidents, along with enemies of the state uncovered by purges of the army, the beaureaucracy and the Communist Party, provided convict (zek) labour for infrastructural projects. Altogether, some 10 million people were sentenced to serve in the zek workforce, to be imprisoned, or to be shot. The barbarization of Soviet society was the price paid for the modernization of the Soviet economy.

Economic and Territorial Expansion
The Soviet economy *did* modernize, however. Between 1928 and 1940 the rate of industrial growth increased steadily, reaching levels of over 10 per cent per annum in the late 1930s: rates which had never before been achieved, and equalled since only by Japan. The annual production of steel had increased from 4.3 million tons to 18.3 million tons, coal production had increased nearly five times, and the annual production of metal-cutting machine tools had increased from 2,000 to 58,400. In short, 'An industrial revolution in the Western sense had been passed through in one decade' (Pollard, 1981, p. 299). When the Germans attacked the Soviet Union in 1941 they took on an economy which in absolute terms (though not *per capita*) had output figures comparable with their own.

The Second World War cost the Soviet Union 25 million dead, the devastation of 1,700 towns and cities and 84,000 villages, and the loss of more than 60 per cent of all industrial installations. In the aftermath, the Soviet Union gave first priority to national security. The *cordon sanitaire* of independent East European nation states that had been set up by the Western nations after the First World War was appropriated as a buffer zone by the Soviet Union. That this buffer zone happened to be relatively well-developed and populous meant that it also provided the basis of a Soviet world-empire as an alternative to the capitalist world-economy, thus providing economic as well as military security. It should be acknowledged at this point that both socialism and authoritarianism had been latent forces throughout much of Eastern Europe before and during the Second World War. Moreover, the radical reforms of socialist governments in Eastern Europe between 1945 and 1947 can be regarded as largely autonomous national achievements (Turnock, 1988).

But the Soviet Union felt vulnerable to the growing influence and participation of the United States in world economic and political affairs, and Stalin felt compelled, in 1947, to intervene in Eastern Europe. In addition to the installation of the 'iron curtain' which severed most economic linkages with the West, this intervention resulted in the complete nationalization of the means of production, the collectivization of agriculture, and the imposition of rigid social and economic controls. The Communist Council for Mutual Economic Assistance (CMEA, better known as COMECON) was also established to reorganize the Eastern European economies in the Stalinist mould, even to

the point of striving for autarky for individual members, each pursuing independent, centralized plans. This proved unsuccessful, however, and in 1958
COMECON was reorganized by Stalin's successor, Kruschev (see Chapter
11). The goal of autarky was abandoned, mutual trade among the Soviet bloc
was fostered, and some trade with Western Europe was permitted.

Meanwhile, the whole Soviet bloc gave high priority to industrialization.
Between 1950 and 1955, output in the Soviet Union grew at nearly 10 per cent
per annum, though it has subsequently fallen away to more modest levels
(Table 5.2). The experience of the East European countries has varied considerably, but, in general, rates of industrial growth have been high. Equally
important has been the structural transformation of industry, for although
producer-goods remain dominant, the economic base of all Soviet bloc
countries has expanded to the point where *per capita* consumption of food,
clothing and consumer goods is much closer to that of the capitalist core
countries than to that of the peripheral and intermediate countries of the
capitalist world-economy.

A New Socialist Economic Geography?

As in Western Europe, North America and Japan, industrialization brought
about radical changes in the economic landscapes of the Soviet Union and
Eastern Europe (for detailed economic geographies, see Dewdney, 1976;
Cole, 1984; Mellor, 1982; and Turnock, 1988). But did the different economic
and political organization that guided Soviet bloc industrialization result in
qualitatively different economic landscapes? At face value, there are sound
reasons for anticipating substantial differences. On the one hand, there are

Table 5.2: Industrial growth in the Soviet bloc, 1950–1978.

	1950/2–1958/60		1958/60–1967/9		1971–1975		1976–1978	
	A	B	A	B	A	B	A	B
Bulgaria	15.5	7.5	11.5	6.4	9.1	6.6	6.9	6.1
Czecho-slovakia	8.0	4.6	5.5	5.1	6.6	5.4	5.4	4.6
GDR	10.1	3.6	5.2	5.7	6.5	5.4	5.6	4.8
Hungary	7.1	8.5	8.7	7.8	6.4	6.2	5.5	5.8
Poland	9.4	3.1	8.3	7.0	10.4	7.7	7.3	6.7
Romania	11.9	8.4	13.2	10.7	12.9	6.2	11.0	7.5
Soviet Union	10.7	6.6	8.7	4.9	7.4	5.9	5.1	3.4

A = Average annual % change in industrial output
B = Average annual % change in labour productivity

Source: UN Economic Commission for Europe, *Economic Survey of Europe in 1971*,
      New York, 1972; and *The European Economy in 1978*, New York, 1979.

ideological reasons: the socialist bloc has been committed from the start to egalitarian principles that extend to the explicit objective of minimizing inter-regional differences in affluence and opportunity. On the other hand, there are practical reasons: central planning and control of economic development means that ideological objectives can be translated into administrative fiat, while the absence of a competitive market eliminates risk and uncertainty, precludes the influence of powerful monopolies, and facilitates the rapid dissemination of technological innovations.

In practice, however, spatial organization within the Soviet bloc does not exhibit any really distinctive dimensions. As in the industrial core regions of the West and Japan, the industrial landscape is dominated by the localization of manufacturing activity (Fig. 5.6), by regional specialization, centre–periphery contrasts in levels of economic development, and by agglomeration and functional differentiation within the urban system. The reasons for this are several. At the most fundamental level is the unevenness of natural resources and the consequent unevenness of population and economic development inherited from the pre-socialist era. Second, the principles of rationality and the primacy of *national* economic growth have taken prece-dence over ideological principles of spatial equality. As a result, Soviet plan-ners have probably applied Weberian location principles (see pp. 72–4) more comprehensively than the corporate planners of the West, particularly in relation to heavy industry. Similarly, the logic of agglomeration economies has resulted in the policy of developing *territorial production complexes:* planned groupings of industries designed to exploit local energy resources and environmental conditions (Probst, 1977; Rutt, 1986). As developed by the Tenth Five-Year Plan (1976–80), these territorial production complexes are broadly defined (Fig. 5.6), designed to foster broad-scale agglomeration economies among specialized sub-regional territorial production complexes. Third, the extensive beaureaucracy required by 'command' economies has meant that a pronounced 'control hierarchy' has developed. As David Smith points out:

> Central places in the spatial control hierarchy will have disproportionate num-bers of high-level business and party posts. This, along with the tendency for the world of culture, the arts and education to concentrate spatially, will create local élites, as in Moscow, enjoying living standards substantially better than those of the mass of people. (1979, pp. 341–2)

Conversely, places at the lower end of the control hierarchy will offer limited occupational opportunities and limited access to upper-level jobs. Smith also points out that internal politics can also play an important part in regional differentiation, citing the failure of Stalin's chairman of State Planning, Voznesensky, to prevent the patronage by Beria (the NKVD Chief) that stood in the way of a more even distribution of Soviet resources. The fourth and final reason is that centralized economic planning has been unable to redress *unwanted* spatial disparities because large parts of the system have come to be

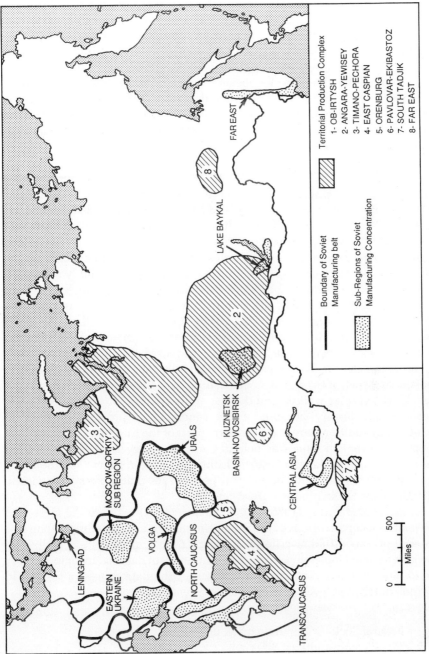

Key:

Boundary of Soviet Manufacturing belt

Sub-Regions of Soviet Manufacturing Concentration

Territorial Production Complex
1- OB-IRTYSH
2- ANGARA-YEWISEY
3- TIMANO-PECHORA
4- EAST CASPIAN
5- ORENBURG
6- PAVLOVAR-EKIBASTOZ
7- SOUTH TADJIK
8- FAR EAST

Fig 5.6 Manufacturing regions and territorial production complexes in the Soviet Union, 1980

characterized by inertia, insensitivity, conservatism and compartmentalization. As a result, resource allocation has been strongly conditioned by *incrementalism*, whereby those places already well-endowed by past allocations get proportionally large shares of each successive round of budgeting. In addition, places and regions which were able to establish an initial advantage (by proximity to market or raw materials, for instance) have generally been able to maintain a significant comparative advantage over other regions. David Turnock, reviewing the outcomes of 'socialist' location principles, observed that 'Despite oft-repeated assertions forecasting the impending elimination of backward regions, through appropriate allocations of investment under the system of central planning, growth rates continue to show wide spatial disparities' (1984, p. 316). In other words, spatial outcomes are similar to those in the West, but for rather different reasons.

Centre and Periphery in Socialist Countries
Two brief examples serve to illustrate both the extent of the resultant unevenness in economic development and the degree to which the economic landscapes of industrial socialism, like those of industrial capitalism, are dominated by centre–periphery contrasts.

In the *Soviet Union*, the major contrast has always been between, on the one hand, the richly endowed, relatively densely peopled, highly urbanized core of the manufacturing belt that stretches across European Russia from Leningrad in the north and the eastern Ukraine in the south, through the Moscow and Volga regions to the Urals (Fig. 5.6) and, on the other, the rest of the country. Within the latter there are vast reaches where physical isolation and harsh environmental conditions have prevented all but a veneer of modern economic development and where tribal folk still pursue local subsistence economies. Much of the rest of Soviet Central Asia and the southern portion of Kazakhstan also lag well behind the rest of the country in terms of economic development, largely because of the fundamental problem of physical isolation. In addition, however, there are parts of the European portion of the country that remain some way behind the levels of development achieved in the centre. These include Belorussia, Lithuania, eastern Latvia and the Western Ukraine: regions with large rural populations that were systematically excluded from Stalin's industrialization drive.

Granberg and Suslov (1976) found the differential between the most- and the least-developed regions of the Soviet Union to be a factor of more than two on each of four different criteria: per capita GNP, per capita contribution towards national income, *per capita* consumption of national income, and *per capita* non-productive consumption. Overall, the data suggest a seven fold division in terms of levels of economic development:

1   The Baltic area and the northwestern region of the Russian Soviet Federal Socialist Republic (most developed)
2   The Ukraine and East Siberia
3   The Volga region, North Caucasus and Kazakhstan

4   Belorussia, the Volga-Vyatka and the Central Black Soil regions
5   Western Siberia
6   Moldavia and the Trans-Caucasian republics
7   The republics of Central Asia (least developed)

A similar pattern, with equally steep gradients between centre and periphery, was documented by Schroeder (1973) in relation to levels of living and by Koropetckyj (1975) in relation to differences in per capita GNP. It is not entirely clear, however, whether the gradient between centre and periphery is increasing or decreasing. Schroeder's evidence suggests that the gradient increased, in per capita terms, during the 1960s as the more rapid population growth of the Asian republics more than offset their aggregate economic gains. Cole and Harrison (1978), on the other hand, taking 1940 as their point of reference, suggest that the gradient has been narrowed significantly. What is not disputed is that centre–periphery contrasts are still sharply defined. Moreover, within every region, from the poorest to the best-off, *urban–rural* cleavages persist as an important secondary dimension of social and economic well-being (Fuchs and Demko, 1979; Yanowitch, 1977).

Studies of spatial variations in socio-economic development in *Poland* also point to clear core–periphery and urban–rural contrasts (Karaska, 1975; Gruchman and Kasinski, 1978, D.M. Smith, 1979). Most indicators reveal a sharp gradient between the best- and worst-off regions: levels of retail turnover, electricity consumption and television ownership per capita, for example, are all twice as high in the better-off regions as they are in the worst-off. Some indicators reveal even greater differentials: levels of savings and capital investment in 1975 varied by a factor of four. Moreover, the spatial expression of these gradients is very consistent. On almost every criterion, the highest levels of socio-economic development are registered by Warszawa, followed by the country's other major urban/industrial areas: Lodz, Poznan, Wroclaw and Krakow. At the foot of the scale are the predominantly agricultural regions of southeastern Poland: Kieleckie, Krakowskie, Lubelskie and Rzeszowskie. Overall, there is a striking relationship between levels of industrialization and levels of living. Once again, it is difficult to establish whether this gradient is increasing or decreasing. The available evidence, based on different criteria and different units of analysis, is contradictory. Fallenbuchl (1975), for example, noted increasing absolute differences in per capita private expenditures on the consumption of material goods; while Karaska (1975) and Koropeckyj (1977), using different data, suggest that the centre–periphery gradient is decreasing.

An Overview and Some Points of Departure

It will be clear from the case studies in this chapter that the increasing complexity of economic organization and spatial change under industrial capitalism and industrial socialism make it difficult to generalize about organizing principles or characteristic features. What we can do, however, is to emphasize once more the recurring importance of certain elements and the emergence of others in interacting to produce the economic landscapes of the industrial core regions. Among those which carried over from previous eras are:

- the distribution of natural resources – with iron ore and coal now exercising a central role.

- demographic change – particularly (i) the timing of the demographic transition in relation to industrialization and (ii) the role of large-scale migrations in relation to changing labour markets.

- technological change – including improvements and innovations in transport and communications.

- colonialism and territorial expansion as responses to the law of diminishing returns.

- changes in institutional and socio-political settings.

- changes in the spatial distribution of investment in response to the shifting comparative advantages enjoyed by producers in different areas.

- import substitution as a mechanism of ascent within the world-system.

- militarism and geopolitical change as a mechanism of ascent within the world-system.

In addition, the industrial era saw the emergence of several new dimensions of spatial-economic organization and the increased prominence of others:

- the extension of the world-economy to a global scale with a corresponding extension of the spatial division of labour (Fig. 5.7) and the consequent intensification of the interdependencies between core, semi-periphery and periphery.

- the replacement of 'liberal' merchant capitalism with a competitive and, later, an increasingly organized form of industrial capitalism characterized by distinct, specialized regional economies organized around growing urban centres.

- the eclipse of the European core of the world-economy by the ascent of the United States and Japan.

- the partitioning of the world-economy with the emergence of a Soviet world-empire.

- the emergence of distinctive centre–periphery contrasts within the industrial core territories of the world-economy.

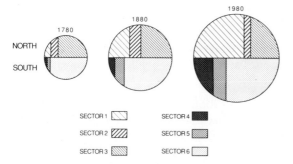

Fig 5.7 A model of the international division of labour
Source: Stuckey (1987) Diagram 1, p. 21
Sector 1 = commodity production using waged labour; sector 2 = commodity
production without waged labour (e.g. family farms producing for the market, self-
employed); sector 3 = non-commodity production without waged labour (e.g.
homemakers, family vegetable gardens, do-it-yourself work); sector 4 = commodity
production using waged labour, originally in the form of colonial enterprises; sector 5
= commodity production without waged labour (e.g. forced labour, peasant farming,
handicrafts); sector 6 = non-commodity production without waged labour – the work
of the extended family in subsistence farming, herding, hunting and fishing

- the agglomeration of industrial activity as a result of the logic of
  economies of scale and the multiplier process.

- the modification of urban systems by the addition of new kinds of
  towns and cities – mining towns, heavy manufacturing centres, power
  centres and transport nodes – and the rapid growth of larger pre-
  industrial cities as they benefited disproportionately (because of their
  established markets, entrepreneurship, trading links and commercial
  infrastructure) from the various growth impulses that characterize
  industrialization (Johnston, 1980a).

- the increasing intervention of governments in economic development.

- cyclical fluctuations in the pace and nature of economic activity.

- the 'differential of contemporaneousness' in regional economic development: a phenomenon linked to the process of technological diffusion
  and changing industrial processes.

Four of these – the emergence of 'organized' capitalism, governmental intervention, global interdependence, and cyclical economic fluctuations – represent important points of departure for the arguments presented later in this
book in relation to patterns of regional development in both the core and the
peripheral territories of the world-economy. Some of the salient characteristics of each are therefore reviewed below.

The Emergence of 'Organized' Capitalism

The maturation of industrial economies brought with it a number of important changes in the nature of economic, social, political and cultural relations, each of which became woven into the urban and regional landscapes of the industrial core regions. Collectively, these changes characterize what has been called 'organized' capitalism. Its principal features include (Lash and Urry, 1987, pp. 3–4):

1   The concentration and centralization of industrial, banking and commercial capital as markets became increasingly regulated; the increased interconnectedness of finance and industry; the proliferation of cartels.

2   The emergence of extractive and manufacturing industry as the dominant economic sector.

3   The concentration of industrial capitalist relations within relatively few industrial sectors and within a small number of nation states.

4   The expansion of empires and the control by the core economies of markets and production in overseas settings.

5   The increasing separation of ownership from control and the elaboration of complex managerial hierarchies.

6   The growth of a new managerial/scientific/technological intelligentsia and of a bureaucratically employed middle class.

7   The emergence of 'Modernism' – a cultural-ideological configuration involving the glorification of science and technical rationality, a machine- and future-oriented aesthetic, and a nationalistic frame of reference.

8   The growth of collective organizations in the labour market: trade unions, employers' associations, nationally organized professions, etc.

9   Regional economic specialization.

10   The dominance of particular regions by large metropolitan areas.

11   An increasing inter-articulation between nation states and large monopolies and between collective organizations and nation states as states increasingly intervene in social conflicts and become involved in welfare state legislation.

Clearly, not all of these changes occurred simultaneously or in the same way everywhere. Lash and Urry (1987) point out that there are three main factors that determine the timing of these changes and the extent to which a particular national economy develops the characteristics of 'organized' capitalism. First is the *point in history* at which it begins to industrialize: the earlier this is, the less 'organized' capitalism will be, because later industrializers need to begin at higher levels of concentration and centralization of capital in order to compete with established industrial economies. Second is the extent to which *pre-industrial institutions survive* into the capitalist period: 'Britain and Germany became more highly organized capitalist societies than France and the United States: this is because the former two nations did not experience a 'bourgeois revolution' and as a result, guilds, corporate local government, and merchant, professional, aristocratic, university and church bodies remained relatively intact' (Lash and Urry, 1987, p. 5). Third is the *size* of the country:

for the industry of small countries to compete internationally, resources had to be channelled into relatively few sectors and firms. This, in turn, meant that coordination between state and industry was facilitated. Lash and Urry argue that German capitalism became 'organized' during the last quarter of the nineteenth century, but that American capitalism was organized fairly early on at the top (e.g. through the concentration of industry, increasing inter-articulation of banks, industry and the state, and the formation of cartels) but very late and only partially at the bottom (e.g. the development of national trade union organizations, working-class political parties, and the welfare state). British capitalism, in contrast, was organized rather early at the bottom but late at the top; while French capitalism only came to be organized, at both top and bottom, after the Second World War.

The characteristics of organized capitalism thus came to be woven into the urban and regional landscapes of the core regions rather unevenly. Meanwhile, they came to represent not just a distinctive set of economic, social, political and cultural relations but also to represent the context – the preconditions – for further transformations of capitalism and the new economic landscapes to emerge with the onset of 'advanced' capitalism (Chapter 6).

The Changing Role of the State

It is no accident that the rise of competitive capitalism and the evolution of industrial economies took place side by side with the emergence of the modern nation state. Within Europe, it was the system of nation states, once established in place of the earlier dynastic kingdoms and empires, that fostered the economic, social and political organization required by the Industrial Revolution. At the same time, strong competitiveness between nation states provided a strong incentive to technological innovation. It is important to bear in mind, however, that few nation states were 'natural' entities developed from distinctive cultural or philosophical bases. Rather, they were *constructed* in order to clothe, and enclose, the developing political economy of industrial capitalism (Poulantzas, 1978; Tivey, 1981). It follows that the process of building nation states involved the resolution of successive crises arising from the interaction of territory, economy, culture and government. One series of crises arose from the long struggle to make state boundaries fit populations with feelings of (or at least the potential for) common identity. This struggle involved (i) states attempting to build 'nations' from a diversity of peoples, and (ii) peoples with a common identity, 'nations', attempting to create an autonomous state (Grillo, 1980; Knight, 1982). The former has often involved the penetration by powerful regions or groups of neighbouring territories with different cultures, languages and economic institutions. As a result, many nation states came into being with inbuilt centre–periphery contrasts, with socio-political tensions compounding economic differentials. We examine the reaction to these developments in Chapter 12.

Another series of crises arose from the changing degree of organization required by capitalism. The evolution of the industrial core regions posed a succession of problems which resulted in *more* state intervention in a *greater variety* of fields. The initial advantage gained by British manufacturers with the advent of the Industrial Revolution soon prompted businessmen elsewhere to realize that the old doctrine of *laissez-faire* and free trade only served the interests of the dominant economy. As a result, the state was looked to everywhere as a protector – through tariffs and quotas – against low-priced British imports. Meanwhile, the coming of the railway involved the state in another sphere – investment in infrastructure – because of the railways' economic and strategic importance. Problems of public health, working conditions, housing and civil disorder induced further kinds of state involvement, as did the need to provide a stable price system for the successful operation of private industry, the need to manage the cyclical fluctuations of the industrial economy, and the need to improve the quality of the workforce and its managers through formal education. Of course, the *capacity* of governments to intervene in all these matters was dependent on economic growth. Nevertheless, it was by no means the wealthiest economies which led the way in terms of state activity, since public expenditure is mediated through the complex arena of politics.

In detail, then, the development of state functions has been complex. It is possible, however, to identify two major trends in the nature of the changes which have taken place. One has been the *centralization* of the functions of states, whereby local and regional activities have been rationalized into centralized national bureaucracies as the organization of government has attempted to keep up with the changing scale of economic organization. With increasingly powerful central bureaucracies, the power of politicians at both local and national levels has been constrained and this, in turn, has led to crises in the legitimacy of political institutions. One response has been the intensification of demands for the devolution of power by the representatives of communities in peripheral areas. Another has been the growth of forms of direct action in the shape of grass-roots pressure groups. These are both examined in more detail in Chapter 12. The second major change has been the dramatic expansion of the *public economy* as governments have become increasingly drawn into the creation of welfare states. Italy, Sweden and the United Kingdom had by the 1970s reached the stage where more than 50 per cent of their GNP was committed to public expenditure, and most of the other industrial core nations are approaching this figure, having almost doubled their share of their respective national economies since the 1950s (Nutter, 1978). The public sector of advanced economies has therefore come to exert a major influence on regional development, and this is a theme which we take up in Chapter 6.

Global Interdependence

Although the industrial core regions have been the focus of this chapter, the historical process of industrialization must be seen in a global perspective.

Quite simply, the ascent of the industrial core regions could not have taken place without the foodstuffs, raw materials and markets provided by the rest of the world. In order to ensure the availability of the produce, materials and markets on which they were increasingly dependent, the industrial core nations vigorously pursued a second phase of colonialism and imperialism, creating a series of 'trading empires'. As soon as the industrial revolution had gathered momentum, European nation states embarked on the inland penetration of midcontinental grassland zones in order to exploit them for grain or stock production – although the detailed pattern and timing of this exploitation was heavily conditioned by innovations such as the railways, barbed wire and refrigeration. Hence the settlement of the prairies and the pampas in the Americas, the veld in Africa, and the Murray-Darling and Canterbury Plains in Australasia. It should be noted that the emigration which fuelled this colonization was itself a major factor in the economic development of the core regions, siphoning off the 'surplus' population that was generated by the demographic transition and swollen by the rationalization of rural economies. Meanwhile, as the demand for tropical plantation products increased, most of the tropical world came under the political control – direct or indirect – of one or another of the industrial core nations.

The outcome of this expansionism was that the colonies and client states of the industrial core began to specialize in the production of those foodstuffs and raw materials (a) for which there was an established demand in the industrial core, and (b) for which they held a comparative advantage. This specialization, in turn, established a complex pattern of interdependent development that was articulated, above all, in patterns of international trade. From the start, however, this expanded and more closely integrated international system was unevenly balanced. On the one hand, the influence of the core countries on the cultural and institutional organization of the peripheral countries has moulded their economic organization to fit core-oriented needs and core-inspired philosophies of 'development' (Chapter 8). On the other, a variety of barriers and imperfections have blunted the effectiveness of international trade as an 'engine of growth'. While the economies of *some* of the semi-peripheral and peripheral nations were able to achieve considerable momentum as a result of the stimulus provided by rapidly increasing levels of demand transmitted from the industrial core regions, many were not (Lewis, 1978a). In very general terms, the type and profitability of activity in semi-peripheral and peripheral nations was determined, as in the von Thünen model (see p. 66), by effective distance from the industrial core regions which represented their major market (Chisholm, 1962; Peet, 1969, 1972). Within the resultant zones of specialization, the beneficial effects of trade were conditioned by a variety of factors, including variations in climate, topography, pre-existing systems of agriculture, and population densities. In practice:

> The trade impetus to growth was . . . immensely important for Argentina and Uruguay in Latin America, South Africa and Zimbabwe (formerly Southern Rhodesia) in Africa, Australia and New Zealand, and, to a lesser extent, in Sri

Lanka (formerly Ceylon). Elsewhere, there was a significant impact, *but this was inadequate to get sustained development going*, for example on the west coast of Africa. For countries such as India, Pakistan, Bangladesh, Iraq and Iran, the *export trades were too small relative to the total population* to provide much impetus for development, except in very restricted areas. (Chisholm, 1982, p. 88, emphasis added)

In short, the once-for-all benefits of specialization and international trade enabled some regions and some nations to ascend within the world-system while enhancing the position of those at the top. For the rest, the subsequent prospects of economic growth through trade have been further diminished by the in-built differential between themselves and the better-off in terms of access to capital, since this translates into a differential in the use of technology; and this, in turn, keeps productivity at relatively low levels. As a result, the amount of labour power required to produce a given quantity of exports from the industrial core will generally be much less than that needed to produce an equivalent value of exports from peripheral countries. From this point of view, the international trade system is characterized by *unequal exchange* (see, for example, Amin, 1973). Attempts to short-circuit this built-in handicap by borrowing capital with which to purchase new (but not always appropriate) technology have almost always resulted in a *debt trap* as interest rates have outpaced increases in the rate of productivity (Colman, 1986; Payer, 1974). In addition, many peripheral countries have been affected by another built-in handicap: the differential elasticities of demand for their products *vis à vis* those of their trading partners in the industrial core. In general, elasticities of demand for the primary products that have become the staples of the periphery are low, so that even fairly large price reductions in overseas markets elicit only a modest rise in demand. Similarly, demand for these products will only increase very slightly in response to increases in the purchasing power of consumers in the core nations. Conversely, elasticities of demand for manufactured goods are generally very high. The net result is that the *terms of trade* have tended to work to the cumulative advantage of the industrial core (Coates *et al.*, 1977).

In other words, although the world-economy has come to be characterized by interdependent relationships as a result of the spatial division of labour, it is the periphery that has carried the burden of *dependency*, and this is one of the themes that we explore in detail in Part III.

Cyclical Fluctuations

We have seen, from the case studies of Europe, North America and Japan, how fluctuations in the international business climate sometimes have important effects on regional economic development: periods of depression can seriously affect the economic trajectory of major nations, and they are also highly selective *within* nations in terms of the degree of socio-economic dislocation. Comparative studies have established that the economies of the industrial core regions have in fact been characterized by a variety of different cyclical fluctuations. The inter-war depression referred to in each of our case studies was a particularly severe product of *short-term business cycles*. In the United States, there were 28 such cycles between 1857 and 1978, each lasting from two-and-a-half to nine-and-a-half years (Maddison, 1982). It is the longer-term cyclical fluctuations that are generally more important in terms of large-scale regional and international transformations, however. Unfortunately, problems of measurement and the statistical analysis of time-series data make the whole field rather speculative, but it is possible to identify at least three different kinds of cyclical fluctuation, each with different amplitudes.

Logistic Cycles
The longest of these are the 'logistics' identified by Cameron (1973), with an amplitude of 150–300 years. They are called 'logistics' because, rather than conforming to wavelike curves of expansion and recession, they conform to the shape of a statistical logistic curve, with an expansion phase followed by a phase of stagnation. Two such cycles have been completed: 1100–1450 and 1450–1750. The industrial era, representing the third, is still in progress. In the first cycle, the expansion phase (between 1100 and 1300) was the period of expanding population and territorial colonization of the late Middle Ages; the second phase, between 1300 and 1450, saw the crisis of feudalism and the stagnation, throughout Europe, of economic development. In the second cycle the expansion phase, from 1450 to 1600, saw a further increase in population and economic growth with the transition to merchant capitalism. The second phase, as Wallerstein (1979b) points out, was a period of relative stagnation only in an *overall* sense. It was 'a vector of several curves: some zones expanding, others staying level and still others declining' (p. 75), the reason being, of course, that the economic landscape had become sharply differentiated, with the core, semi-periphery and periphery experiencing asymmetrical trajectories as a reflection of the overall consolidation of the European world-economy. The mechanisms of change associated with these two cyclical periods have been outlined in Chapter 4. The asymmetries underlying the expansion phase of the third cycle have been the focus of this chapter; and the emergent asymmetries of the second phase of the third cycle – which seems to have begun between 1960 and 1970 – are the subject of Chapter 6.

Climacteric Cycles of Centre–Periphery Development
The interdependence of centre–periphery relationships within the third logistic has been associated with a further kind of long-term cycle: the 'climacteric' eclipse of core economies by emergent rivals from the periphery (Lewis, 1978b). The first large-scale climacteric involved the relative decline of Britain and the ascent of the United States, Germany, France and Russia between 1870 and 1900. Beenstock (1983, pp. 162–3) summarizes the British climacteric as follows (see also Figure 5.8):

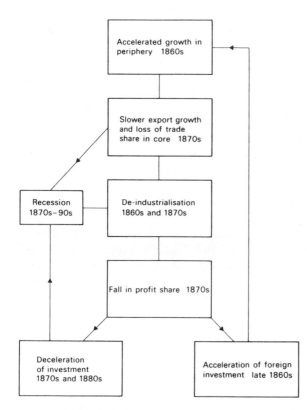

Fig 5.8 Stages of transition in Britain in the late nineteenth century
Source: Beenstock (1983) Fig 6.12, p. 176

1 Industrial growth in the periphery adversely affects the relative price of manufactures and/or threatens the trading power of the core (Britain).
2 The new set of relative prices and/or the trade threat to the core on the part of the periphery causes *deindustrialization* in the core as the share of industrial production in GDP declines from what it otherwise would have been.
3 This in turn raises the wage share, reduces the profit share and adversely affects the return on capital in the core.
4 The lower returns to capital cause a reduction of investment in the core and increased foreign investment by the core in the periphery.
5 While deindustrialization takes place there is a temporary if protracted period of 'mismatch' unemployment and slower economic growth in the core.

Lewis (1978b) has argued that while the climacteric was induced by foreign competition this was only a necessary and not a sufficient condition for decline, since Britain could have moved up-market by taking advantage of the new science-based industries that emerged during the latter part of the nineteenth century. According to Lewis, Britain's failure to adapt reflected (i) rigidities imposed on the labour market by growing trade unionization and (ii) snobbery on the part of the bourgeoisie, who did not understand the need for technological and vocational education upon which the new industries would be based. As well shall see in Chapter 6, these events have been echoed during the era of advanced capitalism. Beenstock (1983), indeed, suggests that a second major climacteric cycle began around 1970, with an expanded core (represented by the OECD countries) experiencing deindustrialization, while parts of what were formerly peripheral regions – South Korea, Taiwan, Mexico, Brazil, Hong Kong and Singapore – begin to ascend rapidly within the world-economy, creating a new category of Newly Industrializing Countries.

'Kondratieff' Cycles

Interwoven with the spatial articulation of the third logistic and the two climacteric cycles described above have been the series of 50-year Kondratieff cycles described in Chapter 3. Although the mechanics of these cycles remain, to some extent, in dispute, it is clear that each of the 50-year cycles consists of a long climb up from recession followed by a sharp slide into another one. During the recession period of each cycle, it seems, there have occurred exceptional clusters of new inventions, the application of which, as clusters of innovations, have triggered succeeding upswings. As this new technology is exploited, profits rise and economies expand; but when the possibilities of the new technologies are exhausted, profits fall and recession begins. According to Mensch (1983), key clusters of innovations occurred around the years 1764, 1825, 1866, and 1935, to be followed between 11 and 17 years later by a climb away from recession. Mensch predicted that the fifth Kondratieff cycle should begin around 1989, and will probably be based on the likes of microchip technology, biotechnology, superconductors and new energy-related technologies such as heat pumps and solar energy systems. The point about these cycles is that *the ups and downs of each have been imprinted differentially* on the economic landscapes of industrial core regions in response to the changing locational logic of each cluster of technologies – as we have seen in the case studies in this chapter. In Chapter 6 we shall preview the geography of the fifth Kondratieff cycle by examining the emerging locational dynamics of the high-tech activities of advanced capitalism.

Cyclical Fluctuations and Changes in Economic Organization

These cyclical fluctuations provide a useful framework around which to set some of the other key features of the development of industrial capitalism. In this context, we can divide the development of industrial capitalism into three main periods (Fig. 5.9): a 'competitive' period, consisting of two Kondratieff cycles from the late eighteenth to the late nineteenth century; the period of 'organized' capitalism that consists of the next two Kondratieff cycles, and an emerging period of 'disorganized' capitalism. The upward-turning points of

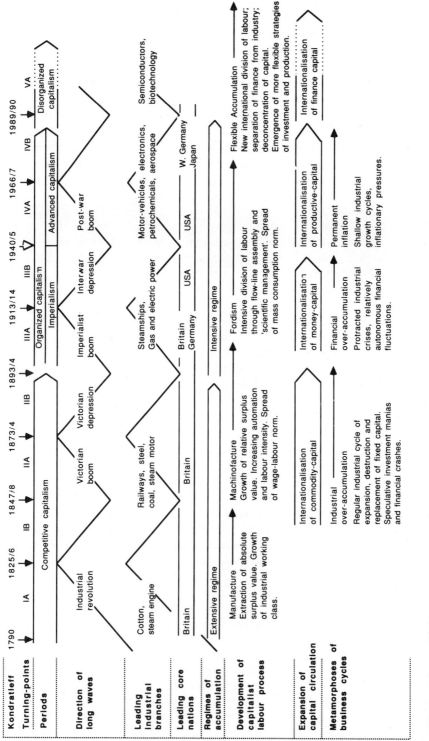

Fig 5.9 Schematic representation of the major features associated with long-wave economic cycles
Source: Adapted from Marshall (1987)

the Kondratieff cycles presume prior crises which had the function of trans-forming economic organization, precipitating significant social and spatial changes, and preparing the path for a new phase of economic expansion. As we have seen, the two Kondratieff cycles of competitive capitalism were marked by the appearance of the factory system of production and by the rise of 'machinofacture' – which entailed 'the increasing subordination of the workforce to machine-regulated production through an intensive division of labour' (Marshall, 1987, p. 98). Subsequently, as we shall see in the next chapter, these forms of economic and social organization were consolidated under the advanced capitalism of the fourth Kondratieff, only to be followed by a decade of crisis which seems now in the process of being resolved as the beginning of the fifth Kondratieff is accompanied by the emergence of a 'disorganized' capitalism.

6

Advanced Capitalism: Towards a Global Economic Order

After the Second World War, the economies of the industrial core regions began to enter a substantially different phase in terms of *what* they produced, *how* they produced it, and *where* they produced it. This phase is sometimes referred to as 'postindustrial capitalism', 'late capitalism' or 'corporate capitalism' as well as 'advanced capitalism'. Its principal characteristics are:

- a shift away from agriculture and manufacturing activities towards service activities in the use of labour and the investment of capital,

- a trend away from labour-intensive methods of production as firms in every sector of economic activity introduce techniques of mass-production and automation,

- a trend towards oligopoly as larger and more efficient corporations drive out their competitors and diversify their range of activities, and

- a redeployment of capital by large corporations in response to the search for new markets and the changing costs of factors of production in different regions and nations.

Crisis and Transition

The structural shifts which characterize advanced capitalism stem from the cumulative interaction of a variety of processes. As in all of the previous major economic transitions we have described, these processes have drawn on a number of *preconditions* developed during the preceding era ('organized', industrial capitalism); and their importance has been revealed only after a period of 'crisis' for the old order. In this case, we may number among the most important preconditions (i) the high levels of productivity and (ii)

increasing saturation of consumer markets resulting from the process of industrialization, (iii) the unionization of labour, (iv) the growth of the public
economy, (v) the intensification of global interdependence, and (vi) the development of new and improved transport and telecommunications
technologies.

The *crisis* for industrial capitalism emerged rather abruptly in the early
1970s, throwing into reverse the postwar industrial boom that had been
'almost without precedent' (OECD, 1983). This reversal is clearly illustrated
by the performance of the US economy. In overall terms, the US economy
performed exceptionally well from the late 1940s right through to the early
1970s. Real disposable income per capita rose from just over $2,200 (in con-
stant 1972 dollars) in 1947 to over $3,800 in 1972. The 1960s were particularly
prosperous, with economic growth averaging over 4 per cent per year, thus
expanding the GNP by 50 per cent over the decade. Meanwhile, the average
family obtained a real increase of over 30 per cent in its disposable income:
these were the years of Galbraith's 'affluent society' (Galbraith, 1977). Since
the early 1970s, however, US economic growth has averaged only 2.2 per
cent, while productivity in the private business sector, having increased at
around 3.3 per cent per year up to 1970s, fell away to 1.3 per cent per year in
the 1970s. 'By 1979, the typical family with a $20,000 income had only 7 per
cent more real purchasing power than it had a full decade earlier. The years
had brought a mere $25 more per week in purchasing power for the average
family' (Bluestone and Harrison, 1982, p. 4). Unemployment, having
remained steady at around 4.5 per cent until the early 1970s, almost doubled
over the next five years, leveling off at around 10 per cent by the mid 1980s.
The rate of inflation doubled from around 2.5 per cent per year in the 1960s to
over 5 per cent per year in the mid 1980s. Meanwhile, in 1971, the US economy had moved, for the first time this century, into a negative trade balance
with the rest of the world: a performance repeated in 15 of the next 17 years.

The 'system shock' precipitated by the rise in oil prices in 1973 as a result of
the OPEC cartel has been widely cited as a major cause of this downturn (in
1973–74, petroleum prices quadrupled as a result of the cartel's actions), but
the evidence is inconclusive (Denison, 1979; Freeman, 1980). Similarly, it has
been difficult to establish the 'guilt' of other popular scapegoats, such as the
role of labour unions in obtaining wage increases in excess of productivity
(Freeman, 1982; Reischauer, 1981). Rather, the crisis of the 1970s must be
seen as the product of a conjunction of trends whose origins can be traced to
the 1960s or before (Armstrong *et al.*, 1984). Hamilton (1984) has identified
seven such trends:

1 A slowing down of economic growth and steadily falling profits
   (Fig. 10.1), particularly in the industrial core countries of the OECD
   (which accounted for 80 per cent of the non-communist world's industrial output in 1982) that was associated with falling levels of demand
   for capital goods, particularly transport, building, mining and factory

equipment (e.g. ships, vehicles, machinery, machine tools) and, hence, steel. Overall, rates of growth in the OECD countries fell from an annual average of 5 to 6 per cent between 1963 and 1973 to around 2.5 per cent between 1973 and 1978 and less than 1 per cent between 1979 and 1982.

2   Rising levels of inflation. This generally reduced profits and hampered capital accumulation, resulting in greater dependency on financing investment via the banking sector. This, in turn, meant high interest rates that retarded technological investment and so hindered competitiveness. Meanwhile, inflation also raised labour costs, thus increasing the urgency of technological investment (particularly automation) at a time when capital was expensive. The net result was the widespread depression of both capital-intensive industries (e.g. steel, shipbuilding, vehicles, appliances) *and* labour-intensive industries (e.g. textiles, clothing, footwear).

3   Increased international monetary instability, which took two major forms:

(a)   under- or over-valuation of exchange rates as a result of the transition (in the early 1970s) from fixed exchange rates to floating exchange rates. Where currencies were under-valued (e.g. the Deutschmark, the Swiss franc and the Japanese yen), industrial production was stimulated by increased demands for exports; but where currencies were over-valued (e.g. the currencies of oil and/or gas producers such as the Netherlands, Norway and the United Kingdom, and, more recently, the US dollar), the loss of international competitiveness resulted in *import penetration* and a consequent decline in industrial capacity (Fig. 6.1). In the United States, import penetration in clothing and textiles increased from 34 per cent in 1980 to 55 per cent in 1986; import penetration in shoes increased from 50 per cent to 81 per cent, in computers from 7 to 25 per cent; and in automobiles from 35 to 40 per cent

(b)   problems of indebtedness among NICs and some underdeveloped countries following massive borrowing from the 'petrodollar' surpluses created in the OPEC countries (see p. 39). In addition to the international financial instability associated with the uncertainty attached to debt rescheduling and fears over national bankruptcies, this created a strong incentive for NICs and underdeveloped countries to increase their exports – of cheap manufactured goods as well as traditional staples – to the core regions in order to obtain the necessary foreign exchange. This, in turn, increased the competitive pressure on the labour-intensive sectors of the core economies.

4   The rise of new social values associated with social welfare and environmental protection. Although this created new markets for some products and services, it also raised some industrial costs and contributed to a higher tax burden on both consumers and producers.

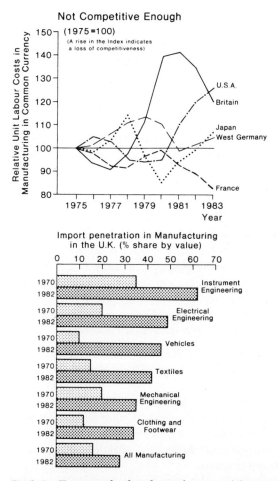

Fig 6.1   Forces in the deindustrialization of the United Kingdom: dramatic loss of competitiveness (1978–1983) and resultant import penetration, converting the country from a net exporter to a net importer of manufactures
Source: Hamilton (1984) Fig 2, p. 352

5   The introduction of innovations and technological changes in response to escalating energy and labour costs created feedback effects that depressed demand in 'traditional' industrial activities. Energy-saving designs in transport and heating, for example, reduced the demand for steel; while innovations in microelectronics reduced the demand for electro-mechanical products.

6   A resurgence of political volatility that reduced the extent of stable business settings and so inhibited several dimensions of world trade, including East–West trade and trade involving much of Central America, the Middle East and South-East Asia.

7   An increasing intensity of international competition arising from the postwar liberalization of trade, the spread of industrialization to the

periphery, the aggressive role of governments in NICs, and the post-1970 stagnation of world markets.

Meanwhile, advances in computing and telecommunications technology contributed to a *destabilization* of the economic environment, with more frequent alterations in interest rates, currency exchange rates and commodity prices requiring industrial organizations to make decisions at shortening intervals with respect to changes in investment, labour requirements, stock levels and wage rates (Fig. 8.13). The net effect has been to accelerate the processes of industrial reorganization and structural change that signal the transition to advanced capitalism.

Towards a 'Disorganized' Capitalism

As new models of economic, social, political and cultural organization are being established, the capitalist world-economy is now emerging from the period of crisis (1973–82) that was rooted in these secular economic and social trends. *New technologies* have also been of critical importance here, as both companies and governments have exploited them to restructure the relationships that underpin the operation of the world-economy. According to Castells (1988), this restructuring has relied on three main processes:

1   A transformation of the relationship between capital and labour, with capital recapturing the initiative over wage rates and conditions that had been established under 'organized' industrial capitalism. New technologies are playing a major role in this transformation through robotics in factories and information-processing technologies in offices. These make for dramatic increases in productivity but also create a long-term threat of substituting machines for workers, thus placing labour in a weak bargaining position.

2   The development of new roles for the state and the public sector, not only in reducing government intervention in the economy but also shifting its emphasis away from collective consumption (schools, hospitals, community services, etc.) towards militarization. It has been this militarization that has fostered a core of very profitable and dynamic high-tech manufacturing industries – particularly microelectronics – that have already begun to recast the economic landscapes of the core economies (Boddy, 1987; Markusen, 1986b).

3   The creation of a new international and inter-regional division of labour, as large corporations pursue flexible strategies (Guile and Brooks, 1987; Piore and Sabel, 1984) to deal with, and exploit, the 'time–space compression' introduced by new transport and telecommunications technologies such as long-distance fibre-optic systems, regional telecommunications systems, satellite teleports, 'smart' buildings, telefax, and microwave communications (Bakis, 1987; Goddard and Gillespie, 1987; Hepworth, 1986; Moss, 1986). As Harvey (1987)

points out, this 'annihilation of space' and 'electronic colonialism' (McPhail, 1986) has, paradoxically, heightened the importance of geography: the reduction of spatial barriers has had the effect of magnifying greatly the significance of what local spaces contain since the new flexibility of the business world means that relatively small differences between places can be quickly, if temporarily, exploited to good effect. As a result, there has been an acceleration of shifts in the patterning of uneven development on the basis of particular local mixes of skills and resources: a continuously variable geometry of labour, capital, production, markets and management.

Together with the structural shifts (p. 176) which characterize advanced capitalism, the restructuring of social, economic, cultural and political relationships taking place as a result of these processes represents a clear departure from the 'organized' capitalism of the past. For Lash and Urry (1987) this transition amounts to the emergence of a *'disorganized'* capitalism, characterized by:

1   A deconcentration of capital within national markets, a growing separation of finance from industry, and the decline of cartels (as a result of the growth of a world market, the increasing scale of industrial commercial, and banking enterprises, and the general decline of tariffs)
2   A decline in the absolute and relative size of the core working class and the expansion of a service class of professional, white-collar workers in core economies as they are deindustrialized
3   A decline in the importance and effectiveness of national-level collective bargaining and a growth in company and plant-level bargaining (as companies exert their new leverage in order to impose more flexible forms of organization)
4   An increasing independence of large monopolies from direct control and regulation by individual nation states
5   A decline in average plant size because of shifts in industrial structure, substantial labour-saving capital investment, the hiving off of various sub-contracted activities, and the export of labour-intensive activities to underdeveloped countries and to peripheral regions within core nations
6   The decline of metropolitan dominance within core nations: the loss of jobs and population from inner-city areas and an increase of jobs and population in smaller towns and some rural areas
7   A weakening of the degree to which industries are concentrated in specific nations and regions as a result of the new, variable geometry of the division of labour: 'each nation or locality develops its own kind of industrialization process even as it may depend on, and partake of, global investment flows and multinational industrial production systems' (Storper, 1987a, p. 591)
8   A decline in the salience and class character of political parties, an

increase in cultural fragmentation and pluralism, the emergence of a 'global' culture and an international consciousness and the ascendance of a 'postmodern' cultural-ideological configuration (in response to shifting class and occupational composition, the commodification of leisure, the internationalization of the economy and the time–space compression of new communications technologies, among other things) (Lash and Urry, 1987, pp. 5–7)

In this chapter we examine the outcomes of this transition. First, we discuss the extent of some of the structural shifts that have emerged under advanced, 'disorganized' capitalism: the decline of the manufacturing base, the rise of the service sector, changes in the occupational composition of labour markets, and the effects of changes in the public economy on the economic geography of the core economies. We then examine in some detail the effects of the reorganization and redeployment of capital on economic landscapes at the international, regional and inter-urban scales, including an examination of the 'new' geography of the high-tech industries that represent, in several ways, the leading edge of advanced capitalism.

The Decline of the Manufacturing Base

One of the most striking results of these changes has been the decline in the manufacturing base of the industrial core regions. Initially, this took the form of a relative decline: growth in the postwar boom period was much greater in the service sector of most economies. With the transition to advanced capitalism, however, there has been an *absolute* decline in manufacturing. Whereas in 1960 manufacturing in the 15 most industrialized OECD countries generated between 25 and 42 per cent of their GDP and accounted for similar proportions of their employment, the comparable figures for 1982 were 15 to 32 per cent and 18 to 33 per cent respectively (OECD, 1983).

The decline has been most pronounced in the early-industrializers of north-western Europe. In the United Kingdom, for example, more than one million manufacturing jobs disappeared, in *net* terms, between 1966 and 1976: a fall of 13 per cent. This decline affected almost every sector of manufacturing: not just the traditional pillars of the manufacturing sector – shipbuilding (–9.7%), metal manufacture (–21.3%), mechanical engineering (–14.5%) and textiles (–27.6%) – but also its former growth sectors and the bases of the fourth Kondratieff cycle – motor vehicles (–10.1%) and electrical engineering (–10.5%). In the West Midlands – widely regarded as a 'leading' region within Britain, a net loss of 151,117 manufacturing jobs between 1978 and 1981 helped to redefine the region as part of Britain's 'rust belt' (Flynn and Taylor, 1986). It is within the peripheral regions of the United Kingdom that the problem has been most acute, however. In Lancashire, for example, the textile industry alone has shed over half a million jobs (Martin and Rowthorn, 1986; Townsend, 1983). It would be unfair, however, to portray a picture of unmitigated decline throughout the developed nations. Some aspects of manufacturing have prospered, both relatively and absolutely. These can be grouped into three types:

1 *R & D intensive industries* such as aircraft, computers, industrial robots, nuclear power, integrated circuits, fine chemicals, new synthetics, new metals and special ceramics.
2 *Sophisticated assembly industries* such as communications equipment, pollution control devices, industrially-produced housing, automated warehousing, and high-grade plant.
3 *Fashion-oriented industries* such as high-quality clothing, furniture, household fittings, and electronic musical instruments.

The Rise of the Service Sector

The rise of the service sector has been the product of several inter-related processes (Gershuny and Miles, 1983). First, the increasing geographical specialization that characterized the industrial era had the effect not only of stimulating trade but also of generating new opportunities for employment and investment in trade-related services: transport, communications, utilities and wholesaling (*distribution services*) and services that have enabled firms and regions to maintain their specialized roles: marketing, advertising, administration, finance and insurance (*producer services*). Meanwhile, the market for some basic manufactured goods has become saturated, leaving consumers free to spend a larger proportion of their incomes on leisure and various personal services (*consumer services*) thus making, in turn, for increased investment opportunities in the service sector. Market saturation in the manufacturing sector has also encouraged firms to seek ways of making existing products less expensively or, better still, of developing new products altogether, thus fostering the growth of another kind of producer service: scientific research and development (R & D). Finally, a large number of service jobs has been created in the public sector as central and local governments have expanded their range of activities in response to changing social values and to the increasing complexity of economic and social organization.

These shifts have been most pronounced in the United States where, between 1947 and 1980, the service sector increased its share of total employment by about 12 per cent and its contribution to GNP by almost 4 per cent. Between 1975 and 1985, four service industry groups (wholesale and retail trade, transportation and utilities, finance, insurance and real estate, and other services) collectively accounted for 80 per cent of all the new jobs created in the United States: a substantial increase from their share of roughly 55 per cent during 1955–65 and 67 per cent during 1965–75 (Table 6.1). However, there were in fact substantial variations in the performance of the different types of services. Retailing and consumer services, although they have come to be closely associated with the idea of advanced capitalism, have not in

Table 6.1: Sectoral composition (per cent) of new jobs in the US economy

Sector	1955–1965	1965–1975	1975–1985
Manufacturing	11.9	1.9	4.8
Mining and construction	2.0	2.5	6.3
Transportation and utilities	– 1.0	3.1	3.4
Wholesale and retail trade	21.8	26.5	29.0
Finance, insurance, and real estate	6.9	7.4	8.7
Other services	27.7	30.2	39.1
Government	31.7	28.4	8.2

fact grown very rapidly. Rather, it has been producer services, public-sector services and non-profit services (mainly higher education and certain aspects of health care) that have contributed most to the expansion in service-sector employment. Of these, producer services and non-profit services also increased their relative contribution to GNP; public services, although employing more people, contributed proportionally less.

Changes in Occupational Composition

These sectoral shifts have also been accompanied by some important changes in the size and composition of the workforce in the core nations. To begin with, it must be acknowledged that the growth of service-sector employment has not been sufficient to cancel out the shrinkage of employment opportunities in the manufacturing sector. The result, of course, has been rising *unemployment*. The effects of recession, structural change and economic reorganization have, however, been highly differential in their impact on regional unemployment rates. Within Western Europe, for example, the worst change, in *relative* terms, has occurred in the industrial heartlands of northeast France and western Belgium, where unemployment rates surged from between 1 and 2 per cent in 1973 to between 8 and 12 per cent in the mid 1980s. Other regions which have experienced a relative deterioration include several which had for a long time been regarded as leader regions (the West Midlands and East Anglia in England, Hamburg and Nordrhein-Westfalen in West Germany, and the Paris Basin in France) as well as some of the 'traditional' industrial regions (Saarland in West Germany, Northern England, Northern Ireland and Wales) and peripheral regions (Campania and Sardinia in Italy and Languedoc-Roussillon and Auvergne in France). Figure 6.2 shows the extent of net job losses within Britain during the slump of the early 1980s, when total unemployment more than doubled to more than 2.5 million people. Such patterns now represent a significant dimension of the economic geography of the core nations.

Meanwhile, the structural economic transition of the core nations has resulted in a substantial decrease in blue-collar employment and a commensurate increase in *white-collar* employment. Currently, less than 20 per cent

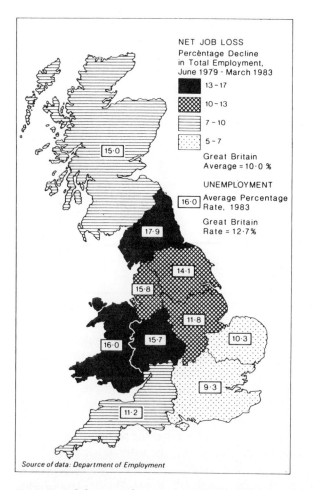

NET JOB LOSS
Percèntage Decline
in Total Employment,
June 1979 - March 1983

■ 13 – 17

▨ 10 – 13

▤ 7 – 10

▫ 5 – 7

Great Britain
Average = 10·0 %

UNEMPLOYMENT

16·0 Average Percentage
Rate, 1983

Great Britain
Rate = 12·7%

15·0

16·0

17·9

14·1

15·8

11·8

16·0   15·7   10·3

9·3

11·2

Source of data: Department of Employment

Fig 6.2 Job losses and unemployment in Britain in the early 1980s
Source: Martin (1986) Fig. 8.1, p. 241

of the entrants to the US workforce take up traditional blue-collar jobs as labourers, operatives and fabricators, and the rate of increase in these occupational categories is expected to be significantly lower than in other categories (Table 6.2). It is also evident that white-collar employment itself has become increasingly polarized between professional and managerial jobs on the one hand and routine clerical jobs on the other. Furthermore, advances in technology and automation within the manufacturing sector have begun to polarize employment opportunities between those for engineers and technicians and those for unskilled or semi-skilled operatives (Cyert and Mowery, 1987). The differential growth of different kinds of service activity has also altered the composition of labour markets. Retailing and consumer services, for example, have been dominated by *part-time* jobs and *secondary* jobs: jobs

Table 6.2: Occupational distribution of labour force entrants in the US

Occupation	1983 Employment ages 16–24 (%)	1984–1995 Forecast employment change (%)
Executive, administrative and managerial workers	3.5	22.1
Professional workers	5.3	21.7
Technicians and related support workers	2.9	28.7
Sales workers	14.2	19.9
Administrative support workers, including clerical	17.6	9.5
Private household workers	1.7	– 18.3
Service workers, except private household	19.2	21.3
Precision production, craft and repair workers	8.9	11.7
Operators, fabricators and labourers	18.3	7.3
Farming, forestry and fishing workers	3.2	– 3.0
Active duty military	5.3	n.a.

Source: Cyert and Mowery (1987) Table 5.2, p. 120

in small firms or the small shops and offices run by large firms, where few skills are required, levels of pay are low, and there is little opportunity for advancement (Gordon, 1979; Townsend, 1986). This trend has been accentuated by the penetration of 'big' capital in areas once dominated by small, family businesses: the expansion of fast-food chains, for example, which has resulted in a marked lowering of skill requirements. Government services, on the other hand, have increased the pool of *primary* jobs (jobs with better levels of pay and security). It should also be recognized that the composition of local labour markets has been profoundly affected by the interaction of all these trends with the steadily increasing – but spatially variable – participation of women in the labour force. As McNabb (1980), Wainwright (1978) and others have pointed out, the economic emancipation of women and the extra incomes associated with increases in female activity rates have to be set against the retrenchment and reorganization of male employment opportunities, the continued sexual division of labour (in which the range and quality of female employment opportunities is generally inferior), and the repercussive effects on culture and family organization.

The aggregate effect of all these changes, according to many observers, is a tendency towards the erosion of the intermediate segment of labour markets, with increasing numbers of higher-qualified, higher-paid employees on the one hand and of employees in part-time and secondary jobs on the other (Edwards *et al.*, 1975; Stanback and Noyelle, 1982). Evidence on earnings seems to support this. In the United States, for example, 54 per cent of the jobs created between 1960 and 1974 were in the lower-earning (i.e. less than 80 per cent of the average for all workers) segment and 35 per cent were in the upper-earning (more than 120 per cent of the average) segment. As a result, the proportion of low-paid workers rose from 32 to 38 per cent of the work-force and the proportion of high-paid workers rose from 32 to 34 per cent. The proportion of workers with intermediate earnings thus fell from 36 to 28 per cent. These developments, in turn, will inevitably feed back to affect the whole process of structural change: altered income patterns will be reflected in altered patterns of consumer demand and, consequently, the expansion or contraction of different kinds of economic activity.

Reorganization and Redeployment

In terms of the evolution of the world's economic landscapes, the most important aspect of the transition to advanced capitalism has been the reorganization and redeployment of business activity. In response to world economic destabilization and intense competition in stagnating markets, private businesses have had to develop new strategies in order to survive; strategies that have significantly altered the fortunes of different kinds of cities, regions and nations. The dominant outcomes have involved the *concentration* and *centralization* of economic activity. The former involves the elimination of small, weak firms in particular spheres of economic activity: partly through competition, and partly through mergers and takeovers. Centralization involves the merging of the resultant large enterprises from different spheres of economic activity to form giant 'conglomerate' companies with a diversified range of activities. Such companies are often transnational in their operations, having established overseas subsidiaries, taken over foreign competitors, or bought into profitable foreign businesses (Dunning, 1981). As these new corporate structures have evolved, they have rationalized their operations in a variety of ways, reorganizing and redeploying their resources between different economic activities *and between different places*. As a result, a complex and often contradictory set of processes has begun to recast many of the world's economic landscapes (Castells, 1988; Blackbourn, 1982; Henderson and Castells, 1987; Holland, 1976; Fröbel *et al.*, 1980; Taylor and Thrift, 1981; Thrift, 1986,).

The Internationalization of Economic Activity

In every industry, there are limits both to the extent to which productivity can be increased and to which consumers can be induced to purchase more. As competition to maintain profit levels becomes more intense, some firms will be driven out of business while others will be taken over by stronger competitors in a process of *horizontal integration*. Furthermore, the chances of new firms being successful tend to be retarded as the larger corporations draw on economies of scale to edge out smaller competitors by price cutting. But even giant corporations cannot forestall market saturation indefinitely; and they are in any case always vulnerable to unforeseen shifts in demand. A common corporate strategy has therefore been to indulge in *vertical integration* (taking over the firms which provide their inputs and/or those which purchase their output) in an attempt to capture for themselves a greater proportion of the final selling price. The net result is the *concentration* of production, within most industries, in the hands of a diminishing number of increasingly large companies. Alternatively – or in addition – *diagonal integration* (taking over firms whose activities are completely unrelated to their own) offers the chance of gaining access to more profitable markets and/or less expensive factors of production. The net result in this case is the *centralization* of assets, jobs, production and decisions about economic life in the hands of an even smaller number of even larger companies (Watts, 1980).

The extent of these trends can be illustrated in relation to the US economy during the postwar period. Spearheaded by the large corporations that had established themselves through early flurries of horizontal integration in the 1900s (e.g. US Steel, International Harvester, American Tobacco, General Electric) and vertical integration in the 1920s (e.g. General Foods, B.F. Goodrich and the major petroleum companies), 'Big Business' began to exert an increasing influence on economic life. Although the incidence of horizontal mergers was greatly reduced by anti-trust legislation (the Celler Kefauver Act, 1950), vertical and diagonal integration proceeded at unprecedented rates, generating around 3,000 mergers per year in the peak years of the late 1960s. By the early 1970s, concentration ratios (the percentage of total sales attributable to the four largest firms) had increased significantly across a broad spectrum of industries, with several industries (e.g. motor vehicles, batteries, telephone equipment, turbines, cereal breakfast foods) each being almost completely dominated by four (or fewer) firms (Table 6.3). Meanwhile, giant conglomerates had begun to emerge as a result of diagonal integration. The first of these was Textron Incorporated, established only in 1943 when it sold blankets and other textile products to the US Army. By 1980 it had been involved in buying or selling over 100 different companies in industries as diverse as textiles, aerospace, machinery, watch bracelets and pens (Bluestone and Harrison, 1982). Textron was by no means an isolated example, however. As early as 1955, the majority of mergers taking place in the US were diagonal, conglomerate mergers. By the early 1980s, nine out of every ten mergers involved conglomerate companies.

As a result of all this merger activity, the US economy is increasingly influenced by the 'monopoly' capital of giant conglomerates. Between 1950 and 1980, the 50 largest US corporations increased their share of the total value added in *all* manufacturing from less than 20 per cent to nearly 30 per cent; and the largest 200 increased their share from 30 per cent to 50 per cent. Similar trends have occurred in the service sector (where the control of variety stores, department stores, car rental firms, motion picture distribution and data processing had become particularly centralized), and in the agricultural sector (where the largest 10 per cent of all farms, in terms of sales, now account for roughly two-thirds of the total market value of all agricultural

Table 6.3: Percentage of sales accounted for by the four largest US producers in selected manufacturing industries, 1947–1982

Industry	Percentage of sales		
	1947	1972	1982
Cereal breakfast foods	79	90	86
Confectioners' products	17	32	40
Chewing gum	70	87	95
Malt beverages	21	52	60
Weaving mills, cotton	18[1]	31	41
Knit underwear mills	21	46	46
Men's and boys' suits and coats	9	19	25
Women's and Misses' suits and coats	31	13	19
Sawmills and planing mills	11[1]	18	17
Greeting card publishing	39	70	84
Cutlery	41	55	49
Turbines and turbine generators	90[2]	93	84
Printing trades machinery	31	42	40
Refrigeration and heating equipment	25	40	34
Household laundry equipment	40	83	91
Sewing machines	77	84	72
Electric lamps	92	90	91
Telephone and telegraph apparatus	90	94[3]	76
Electronic components	13	36	31
Primary batteries, dry and wet	76	92	89
Motor vehicles and car bodies	92[4]	93	92
Aircraft engines and engine parts	72	77	72
Photographic equipment and supplies	61	74	74
Hard surface floor covering	80	91	99

commodities). Because of their size, the larger elements of US monopoly capital have also come to exert an increasing influence in the international economy. As Figure 6.3 shows, the annual sales of the very largest business enterprises are of comparable magnitude to the GNP of nation-states such as Sweden and Portugal. Perhaps more significant is the fact that the combined *overseas* output of US-based multinational companies is now larger than the GNP of every country in the world except the US itself and the Soviet Union (Dunning and Pearce, 1985). As we shall see (Chapter 11), this new dimension of the international economy has come to represent a serious economic threat to small nations, prompting a variety of supranational organizations. It also provides the context for much of the spatial reorganization described in this chapter.

It will be noted from Figure 6.3, however, that the US has by no means been the only core nation to generate giant conglomerates (UN Center on Transnational Corporations, 1983). Major multinational companies have been bred in Australasia, Canada, Japan and Western Europe in response to the same logic that has applied to the US; and even some NICs and peripheral countries now have large home-based MNEs. Indeed, these companies have

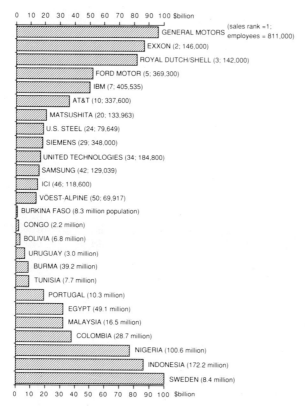

Fig 6.3   A comparison of nation states (GNP) and multinational corporations (sales). Figures in parentheses indicate corporate rank order (by sales) and number of employees; and national population

been increasing their share of world markets at the expense of US-based companies (Franko, 1978); and some of them have extended their operations to the US itself (McConnel, 1980). It is important to recognize, however, that MNEs do not always operate or compete independently. Rather, the complex permutations of functional linkages within and between companies and countries often makes them *interdependent*. The major multinational tyre companies provide a good example (Fig. 6.4), each dependent on some of the others for certain aspects of research, technology, marketing and manufacturing.

International Redeployment

The international activities of major conglomerates – and of many smaller firms – are the product of what is virtually a 'global scan' for investment opportunities (Vernon, 1977). This has been made possible by the availability of 'permissive' technology of two kinds:

Interlocking Relationships Between Major Tire Companies

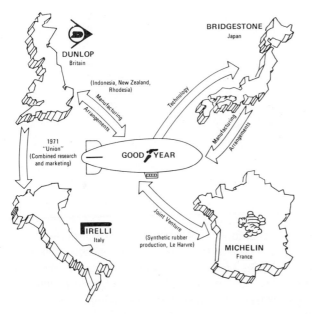

Fig 6.4   Interlocking relationships between major tyre companies
Source: Bluestone and Harrison (1982) Fig. 6.1

1 *Circulation*: improvement in transport and communications technologies (wide-bodied cargo jets, telex, computerized business systems, communications satellites, etc.) that have reduced the time and costs of circulation, bringing a wider geographic market within the range of an increasing range of business activities. This 'global reach' has also been advanced through the economic development of peripheral areas and the standardization of products across cultures (the latter itself being a function of the development of communications media). As Storper and Walker observe, 'These developments not only create new opportunities; they also mean increased competition through the breakdown of protected markets, introduction of new producers, and opening up of new input costs advantages. This forces firms to look farther for new markets and lower cost inputs' (1984, p. 21).

2 *Production*: improvements in production technologies (electronically controlled assembly lines, automated machine tools, computerized sewing systems, robotics, etc.) have *deskilled* many production systems while at the same time increasing the *separability* of their constituent parts. This has made it easier for managers to take advantage of new sources of cheaper and less militant labour. Advances in the manufacture and use of synthetic materials have also extended the locational capability of many industries, since raw materials have traditionally been the most restrictive of all factors of production.

As these permissive technologies have been developed, the international redeployment of capital has not only *increased* in pace and intensity but also *changed* in terms of objectives and outcomes (Cohen, 1981). Taking the example of the international redeployment of US capital, we can identify three main phases. The first, beginning in the nineteenth century and extending to 1940, was dominated by investment directed at obtaining raw materials – mainly oil and minerals – for domestic manufacturing operations. The second began directly after the Second World War, when some of the leading corporations began to use direct foreign investment as a means of penetrating foreign consumer markets through local production operations. Initially, the focus of this investment was Western Europe, where the Marshall Aid programme, NATO rearmament and the US military presence in West Germany provided useful information feedback and points of entry to an expanding consumer market. But with the establishment of the US dollar as the world's principal reserve currency at the 1944 Bretton Woods Conference, the take-over of foreign industries by US companies had been greatly facilitated, so that many US firms soon began to penetrate the expanding markets of parts of the periphery, particularly in Latin America. Mergers and acquisitions were an important part of this process, but before long the evolution of permissive technologies enabled companies to restructure their production processes.

> Bulova Watch provides a clear example. Bulova now manufactures watch movements in Switzerland and ships them to Pago Pago, in American Samoa, where they are assembled and then shipped to the United States to be sold. Corporation President Harry B. Henshel said about this arrangement: 'We are able to beat the foreign competition because we *are* the foreign competition' (Bluestone and Harrison, 1982, p. 114)

Between 1957 and 1967, 20 per cent of all new US machinery plants, 25 per cent of new chemical plants, and over 30 per cent of new transport equipment plants were located abroad. By 1970, almost 75 per cent of US exports and 50 per cent of US imports were transactions between the domestic and foreign subsidiaries of multinational conglomerates. By the end of the 1970s, overseas profits accounted for a third or more of the overall profits of the hundred largest multinational producers and banks.

During the 1970s, however, the new context of crisis and destabilization brought growing competition from goods produced in the NICs with cheap labour. In addition the collapse of the Bretton Woods accord in 1971 allowed the penetration of European and Japanese multinationals into US markets. In response, US multinational companies began to restructure their production processes once again, eliminating the duplication of activities between domestic and foreign-based facilities and reorganizing the division of tasks between them. Effectively, this third phase has meant (a) the further redeployment of capital, bringing peripheral nations into the production space of US companies in order to benefit from lower labour costs (Dixon *et al.*, 1986) (in 1986, the costs of hourly compensation for production workers in manufacturing industries in Austria, Denmark, France and Italy were about 80 per cent of those for US workers; in Australia, Ireland and the United Kingdom, they were about 60 per cent; and in Brazil, Hong Kong, South Korea, Mexico and Taiwan they were between 10 and 15 per cent), (b) withdrawing from locations where unskilled and semi-skilled labour is more expensive (i.e. North America and northwestern Europe), and (c) retaining existing facilities which require high inputs of technology and/or skilled labour (Barnet and Muller, 1974; Fröbel *et al* 1980; Graham *et al.*, 1988; Peet, 1983). Thus, for example, General Electric added 30,000 foreign jobs to its payroll during the 1970s while reducing its US employment by 25,000. Similarly, the RCA Corporation increased its foreign workforce by 19,000 while reducing its US payroll by 14,000 (Bluestone and Harrison, 1982).

It should be acknowledged that not all firms or industries are equal in their need or their capability to engage in international redeployment of this kind. 'Global scan' is more of a tendency than accomplished fact. It is clear, though, that it is the *largest* companies – the multinational conglomerates – that are in the best position to take advantage of the advances in circulation and production technology. Probably the best-developed example – and the most-researched – is provided by the automobile industry, where the clearly defined national markets of the early postwar period have been almost entirely replaced by production and marketing on a global scale. The few companies that have survived to inherit the industry are all giant multinationals, with redeployed production and assembly facilities controlled from headquarters offices that have been retained in the likes of Detroit, Tokyo, Munich and Paris. Parts for the Ford Motor Company's European *Escort*, for example, are made in 16 different countries on three continents (Fig. 6.5). The redeployment of production on this scale not only allows companies to seek out least-cost locations for specific products but also allows them to take advantage of economies of scale, to gain access to new markets through their presence as manufacturers, and to maintain alternative lines of supply by 'dual sourcing'. The same advantages hold for the assembly plants operated by the major automobile companies. The introduction of 'world car' designs (e.g. the Ford Fiesta and Volkswagen Golf/Rabbit) means that the benefits of interchangeable components, economies of scale, multiple sourcing and parallel assembly are potentially greater still, thus inducing further rounds of reorganization and redeployment (Bloomfield, 1981; Cohen, 1983; Dankbarr, 1984; Hill, 1987; Law, 1985; Krumme, 1981; Ward, 1982).

There has been a tendency for industries with 'mature' technologies (such as textiles, clothing, woodworking, leather, footwear, plastics and certain electrical equipment such as televisions and radios) to have been most affected by international redeployment. This tendency is often cited in support of the *product-cycle model* of industrial location, which postulates that products evolve through three distinct stages, each successively requiring fewer inputs of skilled labour as production techniques become standardized, so that the comparative advantage shifts from core locations to peripheral locations. As we saw in Chapter 3 (Fig. 3.5), the first, or 'innovation' stage tends to occur in

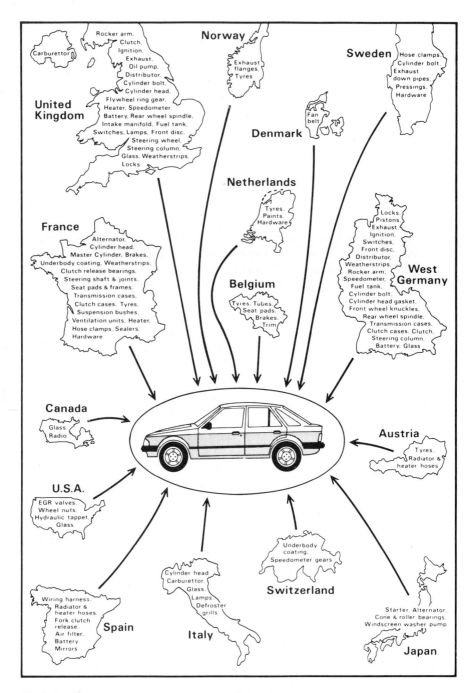

Fig 6.5   The component sourcing network for the *Escort* in Europe
Source: Dicken (1986) Fig. 9.9 p. 304

established industrial/metropolitan regions, with the new product being introduced to other areas through exports. A 'growth' stage follows, during which demand expands to a point where it becomes feasible to invest in production facilities in these other areas. Finally, as manufacture of the product becomes routine, there begins a phase of 'standardized production' in which firms expand their production in branch plants in low-cost locations while closing down the original plants in the industrial/metropolitan regions where the costs of land and labour are high (Taylor and Thrift, 1985; Watts, 1981; see also Markusen, 1985).

Ascent Via Redeployment: The NICs

It will be clear, however, that while 'global reach' may encompass many regions and nations with comparative cost advantages, *only some* will be selected to share in the process of redeployment and make the transition from periphery to semi-periphery. In practice, these have been those with the greatest political stability, the best access to international transport, the most supportive government policies and, hence, the best reputation among international bankers (Browett, 1986; Linge and Hamilton, 1981). Moreover, as with previous phases of industrialization, the places that established an initial advantage have been able to consolidate their position through the operation of cumulative causation of multiplier processes. This is what has happened to the NICs. In broad terms, they have passed chronologically through three stages (Hamilton, 1984):

1 The import-substitution of simple manufactures (mainly textiles and metal products), thus reducing overseas debts and dependency
2 The export of manufactures with a high content either of cheap labour (e.g. clothing, footwear) or of local materials (e.g. non-ferrous metals)
3 The development of industries requiring more skills and capital and relatively modern techniques, largely through the redeployment of activity by multinational conglomerates.

The net result has been the creation of 'offshore industrial nodes' in which a large proportion of activity is controlled from overseas. São Paulo, for example, has become West Germany's biggest industrial city. We examine the implications of these global interconnections in Chapter 10.

Decline Via Redeployment? The Core Nations

The ascent of the NICs within the world system, then, clearly owes much to the selective redeployment of capital from the core nations (much as the ascent of the US and selected parts of Western Europe was stimulated by the redeployment of capital from Britain in the wake of the climacteric of the late nineteenth century). But does this imply the relative decline of the core nations (as Britain came to be overtaken during the early twentieth century)? The answer must be that it is too soon to be certain, but it is unlikely to occur for some time, if at all. There are several reasons for believing this (Hamilton, 1984):

1   The industrial core nations are likely to retain major advantages in knowledge- and skill-intensive activities.

2   Increased protectionism (e.g. European Community quotas) can be introduced to reduce or restrict import penetration for a significant period.

3   The industrial core nations have been able to attract a significant amount of redeployed capital to their own peripheral regions, where relatively cheap land, cheaper and less militant labour, and regional policy incentives are all available within a stable political environment.

4   Some sectors of the West European economy have been able to sustain levels of profitability by obtaining components and intermediate products from Eastern Europe. This integration of socialist and capitalist economies is likely to intensify (Chase-Dunn, 1982).

5   Political instability – real or perceived – and uncertain business climates remain a deterrent to the scale of capital redeployment from the core nations to the NICs.

6   The colonialism, neo-colonialism and dependency experienced by NICs in the past has left a legacy of economic dualism and socio-political polarization that severely constrains the development of their home market – as, for example, in Brazil.

7   The core nations are able to continue to benefit from their dominant trading relationship with peripheral countries. In addition, import penetration by manufactures from peripheral nations, in aggregate, has grown more slowly than the export of manufactures to the periphery. Between 1960 and 1976, for example, LDC import penetration of manufactures cost 370,000 jobs in the US while the growth in US exports of manufactures to the LDCs generated around 520,000 new jobs. Over the same period, the European Community lost 290,000 jobs and gained one million, and Japan lost 70,000 and gained 570,000 (Balassa, 1979).

But while the core nations do not seem likely to be caught up or eclipsed by the NICs in the foreseeable future, it is clear that that there are marked differences in the degree to which they have been able to reorganize their economies to cope with the crisis and destabilization of the post-1973 era. At one extreme is the UK – at the wrong end of climacteric change for the second time – where deindustrialization has been exacerbated by an over-valued currency and, since 1979, a monetarist economic policy. The net effect was an average *net* loss of 1,000 jobs per day between 1979 and 1982, cumulatively leading to well over 3.5 million unemployed. At the other extreme is Japan, where high levels of investment in R & D, energy-saving technologies and new production technologies (Fig. 6.6) have helped to sustain *ascent* within the world-system.

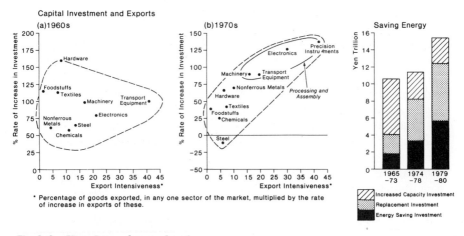

Fig 6.6   How Japan keeps ahead
Source: Hamilton (1984) Fig. 7, p. 362

The Internal Reorganization of the Core

Just as crisis and destabilization have precipitated an international
redeployment of capital and rearrangement of economic activity, so they have
precipitated change *within* countries. We shall examine the nature and implications of this change for the economic landscapes of the NICs and LDCs in
Chapter 10. In the present section, we focus our attention on urban and
regional change in the core nations, emphasizing the overall impact of corporate reorganization on aggregate levels of local economic well-being. As at the
international scale, the major components of change have hinged on the
redeployment of routine production capacity from high-cost to low-cost locations and the retention/localization of facilities requiring high inputs of technology and/or skilled labour in key locations with appropriate resources and
amenities. As a result, two countervailing trends characterize the 'new' economic geographies of Western Europe, North America, Australasia and
Japan: *decentralization* and *consolidation*. The former has been broadly associated with an attenuation of regional and inter-urban gradients in economic
well-being; the latter with an increased spatial differentiation in terms of the
conditions of production and exchange and the hierarchical structure of
control.

Decentralization
Decentralization operates at both metropolitan and regional scales in
response to a variety of complex and often cross-cutting processes of reorganization and adjustment. *Metropolitan* decentralization (the exodus of industry and employment from inner-city areas to suburbs) can in fact be traced to
the inter-war years; but since the early 1970s the process has begun to dominate patterns of urban development in a number of countries (Berry, 1984;

Drewett and Rossi, 1981). Historically, the major impetus for metropolitan decentralization has been employers' desire to sidestep the increasing militancy of labour in inner-city neighbourhoods (Gordon, 1984). Suburban locations have also been attractive to many industries because of the availability of larger tracts of relatively cheap land, so that improvements in transport and communications have greatly accelerated the process of decentralization (Nelson, 1986). Residential suburbanization, meanwhile, has provided labour supplies – including cheap, non-unionized, female labour – that have encouraged the suburbanization of more firms, thus creating a mutually reinforcing process. This, in turn, has been intensified by certain locational disadvantages of inner-city areas: higher taxes, congestion, restricted sites, and so on (Bassett, 1984; Estall, 1983; Fothergill and Gudgin, 1983). The cumulative effect of all these factors was intensified, for many firms, as profits began to be squeezed in the adverse economic climate of the 1970s. What was most pronounced was the 'shake-out' of routine and labour-intensive inner-city areas – some of it destined for relocation in the suburbs, but much more destined for relocation in rural areas, peripheral regions, peripheral countries, or the bankruptcy courts. The net result was a sharp acceleration in the relative rate of growth of employment in the suburbs and a sudden intensification of the 'inner city problem' (Keeble, 1978; Kirby, 1979; Massey and Meegan, 1978).

While metropolitan decentralization is largely a product of the migration of some firms and 'births' and 'deaths' of others, *regional decentralization* involves an additional component: the transfer of productive capacity by plant shutdowns in core, metropolitan regions and the opening of new branch plants (or the expansion of existing ones) in declining or peripheral cities and regions (Camagni and Cappelin, 1981; Cooke and da Rosa Pires, 1985; Howland, 1988; Keeble *et al.*, 1983; Molotch and Logan, 1985; Norton and Rees, 1979; Watts, 1981). The result has been the creation of what have been called 'branch plant economies' and 'module production places' in the peripheral regions of several countries. Hudson (1983) makes the distinction between *branch-plant industrialization* and *diffuse industrialization*. The former is directed towards the skilled manual-labour reserves of declining industrial regions, while the latter is directed towards the reserves of unskilled labour in peripheral rural regions. Central and northeastern Italy provide classic examples of diffuse industrialization, much of it resulting from the decentralization of companies from the Milan–Turin area in response to the increasing shortage, cost and militancy of labour there (Arcangeli *et al.*, 1980). Typically, diffuse industrialization involves activities in which labour costs are an important part of overall production costs *and* in which there has been little scope for reducing labour costs through technological change: it has thus been seen as an expression of the product-cycle model of industrial location (De Smidt, 1983). Empirical studies have shown that the main attractions of rural locations for such activities have been the availability of relatively low-cost labour, inexpensive supplies of easily developed land, lower levels of taxation, and low levels of unionization (Haren and Halling, 1979; Kale and Lonsdale,

1979). Branch-plant industrialization proper, on the other hand, typically involves activities which require significant inputs of technology and of skilled (or at least experienced) labour and which also require a certain degree of centrality in order to assemble and distribute raw materials and finished products. Good examples are provided by many former textile cities – Dundee and Rochdale in the United Kingdom, for example, and Amiens in France – where branch plants in a variety of 'light' industries (from car batteries, cash registers and cameras to tyres, watches and light engineering) have moved in to take advantage of 'surplus' labour, cheap factory space and an established infrastructure. It is not only manufacturing activities that are being decentralized, however. While many places have developed branch-plant economies on the basis of assembly-line activities, some have attracted white-collar information-processing or wholesaling functions. Omaha, Nebraska, for example, has become the '800' telephone exchange centre of the United States; Sioux Falls, South Dakota, is now Citicorp's credit operations centre; and Roanoke, Virginia, has become the centre for a number of mail order and TV shopping companies.

The twin processes of diffuse and branch-plant industrialization, combined with the process of mergers and acquisitions, has meant that regional decentralization has come to be characterized by increasing levels of *external control*. In the Northern region of England, for example, 78 per cent of manufacturing employment in 1973 was controlled by companies with headquarters outside the region, compared with 57 per cent in 1963 (I. Smith, 1979). In the southern states of the US, fewer than one third of the new jobs created in manufacturing plants between 1969 and 1976 belonged to southern-based corporations (Birch, 1979). As at the international level, it has been the large multinational conglomerates that have been particularly important in influencing the extent and spatial pattern of external control. In detail, however, these patterns are highly complex. Not only do the branch plants controlled by companies from different countries reflect different preferences in the allocation of foreign investment between other core countries (Hamilton, 1978; Dicken, 1980); they also reflect different locational preferences for settings *within* each country. Blackbourn (1972), for example, found that while British-owned factories in Ireland tend to be heavily concentrated around Dublin, American-owned factories tend to be localized in government-sponsored industrial estates in development areas and German-owned factories tend to have been attracted to more peripheral locations in the small, remote towns of the southwest (see also Dicken and Lloyd, 1980; Kemper and De Smidt, 1980; McConnell, 1983).

Because of the degree of external control involved in regional economic decentralization, it has become a moot point as to how much long-term benefit will accrue to the regions involved. On the positive side, it can be argued that branch-plant economies and module production places benefit by having access to the financial resources and technological and administrative innovations of the parent firm. Conversely, it has been suggested that the absence of 'higher-order' corporate functions limits the profile of local employment opportunities, leading to a deskilling of the local workforce (Massey and Meegan, 1978), to the suppression of entrepreneurial drive and enthusiasm (Firn, 1975; McDermott, 1979), and to the retardation of technological innovation (Britton, 1980; Ewers and Wettmann, 1980). A high degree of external control will also result in a very open regional economy, so that international economic fluctuations are transmitted into the region relatively quickly. The corollary of this is that because externally controlled plants are poorly integrated with the local economy, their own potential multiplier effects are limited. Finally, it is clear that branch-plant economies are very vulnerable to the further redeployment of capital: branch-plant economies in the core nations are now in direct competition with those of the NICs (Gaffkin and Nickson, 1984; Peck and Townsend, 1985).

Consolidation

The structural and functional reorganization of economic activity under advanced capitalism has also made for counter-trends that have consolidated the economic well-being of many of the strongest and most central components of the core nations' space-economies. One of the effects of the overarching processes of centralization and concentration, for example, has been the consolidation of larger cities at the expense of small ones. The reason for this, as Johnston observes (1980a, pp. 110–11), is that

> Large towns offer larger local markets, with the associated internal economies of scale, plus greater external economies than are available in smaller places, and together these allow production costs which are often significantly lower than those in smaller towns: once transport costs began to fall substantially, so that they were less than the production cost differential between the large-town and the small-town firm, the former could begin the invasion of the latter's market.

The sectoral shifts of advanced capitalism have also worked in favour of many large cities and metropolitan regions. Many of the sophisticated new high value-added products (e.g. computer games, laser discs, household fittings, electronic musical instruments) that manufacturers have turned to in search of higher profits have been drawn to such locations because of their complex links with established industries, their dependence on risk capital in the early stages of development, and the need for access to a large, affluent and sophisticated market during the early stages of marketing. Similarly, large parts of the rapidly expanding service sectors have been channelled towards metropolitan locations because of the kind of environment and workforce required by information-processing, co-ordinating, controlling and marketing activities (Damesick, 1986; Daniels, 1985b; Thrift, 1987; Wheeler, 1986). Moreover, the increasing internationalization of capital means that it has been able to attract and retain a disproportionate amount of key jobs in management and administration. In general, this tends to consolidate centre–periphery patterns, and has led to the emergence of 'world cities' that dominate the global space-economy (Cohen, 1981; Friedmann, 1986). The point is clearly illustrated by Erlandsson's work (1979) on the European 'contact landscape'. Measuring the average amount of time that can be spent in other cities within a 24-hour round trip from a given point of origin, Erlandsson was able to identify what he called the Primary European Centre – the region delimited by lines drawn between Paris-London-Hamburg-Munich-Milan-Lyon-Paris – where accessibility is significantly higher than elsewhere in Europe. It is no coincidence that this pattern is mirrored by the localization of European corporate headquarters offices. Such patterns, once established, are self-perpetuating. Originally the result of relative location, they are intensified by the evolution of air- and rail-passenger timetables which reinforce the initial advantage of the most favoured locations.

The national and international redeployment of activities by large conglomerate companies has also contributed to the consolidation of certain activities in the central regions and metropolitan areas of the developed nations. In particular, there has been a marked localization of two key functions: headquarters offices and R & D establishments. Indeed, the distribution of these two functions has come to represent an important dimension of the 'new' economic geography of advanced capitalism. We can illustrate the changing geography of both functions with reference to the United States. Historically, the most striking feature of the geography of *corporate headquarters* in the US has been the dominance of the Manufacturing Belt in general and of New York and Chicago in particular. Elsewhere, the pattern of headquarters offices has tended to reflect the geography of urbanization, so that the more important 'control centres', in terms of business corporations, have been the major entrepôts and central places which developed under earlier phases of economic development as points of optimal accessibility to regional economies (Borchert, 1978; Harper, 1987; Stephens and Holly, 1980).

With the arrival of advanced capitalism the relative importance of the control centres of the Manufacturing Belt has decreased somewhat, with cities in the Midwest, the South and the West increasing their share of major company headquarters offices (Armstrong, 1979). Atlanta, Denver, Houston, Minneapolis and Seattle have been the major beneficiaries of this shift, though no new control centres have emerged to counter the dominance of New York, Chicago and the other major cities of the northeast. One interpretation of this shift is that it is simply a reflection of changes in the urban system: high-order urban areas tend to be higher-order business control centres because of their reserves of entrepreneurial talent, the array of support services that they can offer, their accessibility in both a regional and a national context. The shift away from the northeast is also related to regional variations in economic specialization. Recent growth in headquarters office employment has been most rapid in trade and service industries rather than manufacturing, and it has been the growing cities of the South and West – Atlanta, Dallas, Los

Angeles and San Francisco, in particular – which have been most successful in attracting headquarters offices in these sectors. In contrast, Manufacturing Belt cities such as Detroit, Cincinnati, Philadelphia and Pittsburgh have missed out almost entirely in attracting new jobs in the headquarters of service-and trade-based corporations (US Department of Housing and Urban Development, 1980). It should also be noted that there has been a significant amount of decentralization within the Manufacturing Belt. Thus, for example, of the 40 actual departures of large headquarters office complexes from New York City between 1968 and 1974, 32 moved to suburban Connecticut, New Jersey or New York (Stephens and Holly, 1980).

In overall terms, however, 'there has been a process of *cumulative and mutual reinforcement* between relatively accessible locations and relatively effective entrepreneurship' (Borchert, 1978, p. 230, emphasis added; see also Dunning and Norman, 1987). This has made for a high degree of inertia in the geography of economic control centres and this, in turn, has consolidated the economic position of the metropolitan areas of the northeast through the multiplier effects of concentrations of corporate headquarters. Pred (1974) points out that these multiplier effects operate in two ways: a general process of 'cumulative causation' related to the increased activity in ancillary services, infrastructural provision, and so on; and a more specific effect whereby the vitality of the corporate administrative sector contributes to the growth and circulation of specialized information concerning business activity, thus generating further employment in a relatively well-paid sector and sustaining the area's attractiveness for headquarters offices.

The geography of R & D activities also has important implications for urban and regional development. Malecki, who has examined the geography of R & D activity in the US in detail (Malecki, 1979a, 1979b, 1980) suggests that the overall pattern can be interpreted in terms of (i) the availability of highly qualified personnel and (ii) corporate organization. In relation to the former, he suggests that amenity-rich locations (cities with a wide range of cultural facilities, well-established universities and pleasant environments) which are attractive to highly-qualified personnel tend to be favoured as locations for R & D activity. Malecki also notes that existing concentrations of R & D activity tend to be attractive because of the potential for 'raiding' other firms. In relation to corporate organization, Malecki observes that corporate-level or long-range R & D is best performed in or near headquarters complexes in a central laboratory where intra-organizational interaction can be fostered. In firms with independent divisions producing quite different product lines, however, R & D activity tends to be located in separate divisional laboratories. Such a pattern is particularly common for conglomerates which have acquired firms with active R & D programmes in existing laboratories. Finally, some industries, whatever the organizational structure of the firms involved, require R & D laboratories to have close links with production facilities, resulting in a relatively dispersed locational pattern corresponding to the pattern of plant location. The net result of these locational forces is in fact a marked agglomeration of R & D laboratories in major control centres and manufacturing regions. It is the metropolitan areas of the Manufacturing Belt which dominate the geography of corporate R & D activity. As Malecki (1980) points out, most of these are either major control centres with concentrations of headquarters offices or major manufacturing centres with a significant element of headquarters office activity. Elsewhere, R & D tends to be concentrated in 'innovation centres' – university cities with diversified economies, some high-technology activity and a strong federal scientific presence (e.g. Austin, Huntsville, Lincoln). In terms of locational *trends*, Malecki has shown that:

> Although industrial R & D appears to be evolving away from a dependence on some large city regions, especially New York, it remains, at the same time, a *very markedly large-city activity.* . . . The comparative advantage of city size, particularly in centres of corporate headquarters location, manufacturing activity and university and government research, shows little sign of reversing. . . .
> (Malecki, 1979a, p. 321, emphasis added)

In short, R & D laboratories, like headquarters offices, exhibit a strong tendency for consolidation overlain by a certain amount of decentralization. This pattern has important implications for regional economic development, for the urban areas in which concentrations of R & D activity exist will be able to consolidate their comparative advantage over other areas in the generation of new products and new businesses. They will also benefit from the short-term multiplier effects of employment generation in a particularly well-paid sector. Conversely, cities and regions with little R & D activity will be at a disadvantage in keeping up with the new economic content of advanced capitalism.

A final example of consolidation within the space-economy of advanced capitalism can be drawn from the *agricultural* sector, where structural change has involved five major trends:

- an increase in large-scale, specialized farm units;

- increased mechanization (and therefore decreased levels of demand for labour);

- increased use of biochemical inputs;

- increased regional specialization;

- increased level of food processing and inter-regional marketing. (Buttel, 1980)

These trends have steadily increased the 'viability threshold' of farms, resulting in a widespread movement toward farm amalgamation. It has been the larger farm units in the more productive agricultural regions which have been most successful in raising the capital necessary to take advantage of increased specialization, mechanization and biochemical inputs. As a result there has been a polarization within the agricultural sector, reflecting what Commins (1980) describes as the 'dualism' of contemporary agriculture: big units in prosperous regions on the one hand; small, residual units in increasingly marginal regions on the other. (Nevertheless, there remain a considerable number of small farm units: even in the highly rationalized and economically efficient agricultural sector of England and Wales more than 60 per cent of the farm units are so small as to be economically marginal.) Implicit in these changes has been a general shift from 'farming as a way of life' to 'farming as a business'. It is clear that, especially since about 1970, there has been a large increase in corporate involvement in agriculture. Direct corporate involvement in agriculture – agribusiness – has been an inevitable outcome of the logic of specialization and economies of scale (Mottura and Pugliese, 1980). With greater specialization, farms become less autonomous and self-contained as productive units, making for the penetration of an integrated, corporate system of food processing and distribution:

> Agriculture has become increasingly drawn into a food-producing complex whose limits lie well beyond farming itself, a complex of agro-chemical, engineering, processing, marketing and distribution industries which are involved both in the supply of farming inputs and in the forward marketing of farm produce. (Newby, 1980, p. 61)

It is in the actions of food-processing conglomerates like Associated British Foods, Nestlé and Rank-Hovis-Macdougall, Newby suggests, 'that the shape of agriculture and ultimately of rural society in virtually all advanced industrial societies is decided' (p. 62). The most common form of corporate involvement in agriculture centres on the forward contracting of produce at a fixed price. This not only weakens the independence of farmers, but also tends to transfer income from farmers and rural communities to the processing industry. Forward-contracting arrangements also reinforce the overall structural changes affecting agriculture:

> They encourage both fewer, larger holdings and increased specialization so that the size of individual enterprises can be enlarged to fully achieve the prevailing scale economies. This trend . . . is likely to lead to both a reduction in the numbers employed in agriculture, and a decline in the managerial role of those farmers remaining . . . leaving them caretaker functions. (Metcalf, 1969, p. 104)

Rural landscapes have also been affected as the logic of industrial production and centralization has been applied to agriculture. In northwestern Europe, for example, field systems have been rationalized, hedgerows and dykes removed, and mechanization has virtually eliminated the need for gang labour, leaving the fields of most farms devoid of human life for most of the year. Factory farming has brought poultry and pigs indoors permanently, while many cattle spend their winter months indoors, and there are now 'zero grazing' techniques which may see them inside the year round. Only sheep steadfastly refuse to acknowledge the laws of industrial production, stubbornly refusing to prosper in regimented and sanitized conditions.

High-Tech Industries: A New Economic Geography?

Advanced capitalism has not only seen the evolution and alignment of the 'old' economy, it has also seen the emergence of *new* industries based on entirely new technologies: semiconductors and computer software, for example; and more recently, biotechnology, photovolatics and robotics. These are the precursors of the fifth Kondratieff upswing (p. 173). Because they are so new, relatively little is known about their spatial implications, though they are widely believed to consist of highly competitive, innovative firms whose activities collectively will not only create substantial numbers of new jobs but also serve a 'seedbed' function for whole economies. The possibility thus emerges of an entirely new dimension to the economic landscapes of the developed nations, with concentrations of high-tech ('sunrise') industries initiating new patterns of urban and regional growth through new 'production ensembles' with new multipliers of cumulative causation.

Studies of high-tech industries in the United States confirm that job creation has been significant and is likely to continue to expand. By 1981, over 5.3 million (about 5 per cent of total US employment) were employed in high-tech industries (defined as those with significantly high ratios of R & D expenditures to net sales), including nearly 1.4 million in service industries such as data processing and commercial testing laboratories.

The growth of some of these industries has been explosive. Employment in computer software, for example, doubled to 250,000 in the 1970s, and is expected to have grown to 450,000 by 1990; while employment in robotics is expected to rise from around 10,000 in 1980 to around 100,000 in 1990 (though a much greater number of jobs in other industries will of course have been *displaced* by the application of robotics). Altogether, it is anticipated that four of the emergent high-tech industries – computer software, photovoltaics, biogenetics and robotics – will have generated about 3 million jobs, directly and indirectly, by 1990 (Hall *et al.*, 1983; Malecki, 1984b). Whether such growth will be sufficient to cancel out the effects of deindustrialization and international redeployment is by no means certain. By the mid 1980s, many US high-tech companies were experiencing acute problems as a result of the combination of the sluggishness of the overall economy, overproduction, and the persistence of Japanese non-tariff trade barriers. Some companies – including Texas Instruments, National Semiconductor, Intel, and Micron Technology – laid off workers; others went out of business altogether. Nevertheless, it should be recalled that, according to Mensch (1983), 1989 is expected to be the year of peak innovation for the next Kondratieff upswing, and the effect on the economies of the developed nations is unlikely to be fully developed for a decade or more after that. It should also be noted that in terms of occupational structure the expansion of high-tech employment is a microcosm of the trends which have dominated advanced capitalism. Studies in California, for example, 'suggest that the occupational, ethnic and gender composition of new jobs in high-tech sectors will tend to worsen the current trend toward the 'disappearing middle', that is toward a labour force bifurcated between high-paid professionals and low-paid service workers' (Markusen, 1983, p. 19). In relation to corporate structure, high-tech industry is distinctive for its tendency towards the proliferation of small breakaway companies set up by key employees; but at the same time the larger and more established firms have soon been drawn into the process of mergers and acquisitions, either as the dominant element (in horizontal and vertical integration) or as a subsidiary element (in diagonal integration).

Technology-Oriented Complexes

The locational impact of these expanding high-tech activities is already emerging, however (Breheny and McQuaid, 1987; Hall *et al.*, 1987; Markusen *et al.*, 1986; Scott, 1986; Scott and Storper, 1987). The phenomenon that has received most attention has been the emergence of 'technology-oriented complexes', and the archetype has been in Santa Clara county – 'Silicon Valley' – in California. In the 1950s, Santa Clara was a quiet agricultural county with a population of about 300,000. By 1980, it had been transformed into the world's most intensive complex of high tech activity, with a population of 1.25 million (Saxenian, 1983a). During the 1970s, the high-tech industries of Santa Clara county generated over 40,000 jobs a year, each new job creating at least two or three additional jobs in other sectors – an extremely high multiplier in comparison with the figure of about one new job created for every new manufacturing job in buoyant (by national standards) metropolitan economies such as San Francisco's.

The development of Silicon Valley in the first instance is generally attributed to the work of Frederick Terman, a professor (and, later, Vice President) of Stanford University at Palo Alto, in the northwestern corner of Santa Clara county. As early as the 1930s, Terman began to encourage his graduates in electrical engineering to stay in the area and establish their own companies (one of the first was founded by William Hewlett and David Packard in a garage near the campus; it is now one of the world's largest electronics firms). By the end of the 1950s, Terman had persuaded Stanford University to develop a special industrial park for such fledgling high-tech firms, creating a hothouse of innovation and generating significant external economies – including a specialized workforce and a specialized array of producer services – which have not only sustained the continued agglomeration of high-tech electronics enterprises but also attracted other high-tech industries. Nearly a third of all employment in biotechnology, for example, is located in California, and of this over 90 per cent is located in the San Francisco Bay area (Feldman, 1983). Stanford University, meanwhile, found itself in receipt of an increasing flood of donations from grateful companies. In 1955, these amounted to around $500,000 annually; by 1965 they exceeded around $2 million, and in 1976 they had reached $6.9 million.

This kind of linkage between university research and high-tech activity is seen by many to be the key to the emerging geography of the fifth Kondratieff cycle (Rees, 1986). Not only do the new industries thrive on a symbiotic relationship with one another and university research departments, but key workers tend to favour technology complexes associated with top-flight universities since they provide abundant social and cultural activities and a job market that allows individuals (and spouses) to switch jobs without relocating. Such areas soon acquire a reputation as 'the right place to be', and this often counts for more than cost-of-living or quality-of-life factors (Oakey, 1984). Where, as in Silicon Valley, the 'right place to be' happens to offer the additional bonus of an attractive environment and climate, the result is explosive growth. An important point in this context, as Hall (1981) observes, is that 'university systems, even in a country as dynamic as the United States, have a great deal of built-in inertia' (p. 536). Large, top-drawer universities like Harvard, MIT, Berkeley and Stanford are secure in their status, but few other institutions seem destined to join them. The result is that, outside these potential areas, there are few places in the US where a high-tech industrial base is likely to be developed – apart, perhaps from the Research Triangle (Raleigh–Durham–Chapel Hill) that has already been established in North Carolina around Duke University and the University of North Carolina.

Similarly, there are few environments in other developed countries that are likely to attract a critical mass of high-tech activity, despite the proliferation of 'technology parks' – or, to be more accurate, *designated* technology parks. Nevertheless, not all technology-oriented complexes need be dependent on proximity to large, first-class universities. A comparative study of existing technology-oriented complexes in Europe and North America has suggested that it is possible to recognize four different types of high-tech complex (Sirbu *et al.*, 1976):

1 Complexes where growth is the product of firms spawned by major research institutions, e.g. Silicon Valley and Boston's 'Route 128' area focused on the Harvard/MIT complex
2 Complexes focused on a park site, e.g. Toronto's Sheridan Park and North Carolina's Research Triangle Park
3 Complexes where growth has been initiated as a result of diffuse industrialization/branch-plant industrialization by large corporations in the high-tech sector, e.g. the Phoenix metropolitan area in Arizona and 'Silicon Glen' in central Scotland
4 Complexes resulting from very large expenditures of government funds at a particular facility, e.g. Houston, Texas and Huntsville, Alabama

It is clear, however, that these categories are by no means mutually exclusive. Thus, for example, Britain's main technology-oriented complex, the 'western crescent' around London (from Portsmouth through Bracknell and Reading to Hemel Hempstead) is a hybrid of types 1 and 4. Similarly, the North Carolina Research Triangle, having started as a type 2 complex, has attracted large new IBM manufacturing facilities, and so has come to contain elements of type 3; while Ottawa's rapidly growing complex has already evolved from

an early stage as a research-oriented park complex to a second stage dominated by the input of government funds for R & D work, a third stage
involving the addition of private-sector research labs and manufacturing
plant, and a fourth stage characterized by the birth of local high-tech firms
(Steed and De Genova, 1983).

The Decentralization of High-Tech Employment
Almost all of the existing high-technology complexes are very much a suburban phenomenon. As Markusen (1983, p. 26) notes in relation to the Silicon
Valley and Route 128 complexes, they are 'newly developed, auto-based,
suburban areas whose jobs and tax base do not overlay the inner-city poor nor
the central city jurisdiction'. But, because high-tech firms have tended to be
very self-conscious about their 'address', these suburban complexes have
become crowded and expensive. The outcome has been the familiar combination of corporate functional and spatial reorganization. More routine production tasks and downstream marketing and service functions are beginning to
be dispersed, while managerial and developmental activities are retained in
order to maximize the external economies of the 'right address'. Research by
Hekman (1980), for example, suggests that American computer firms have
kept their R & D and administrative activities in places like California and
Massachusetts while moving their production facilities to southeastern states
to take advantage of lower labour costs. Furthermore, some of the larger
corporations in the computer and semiconductor fields have already begun to
redeploy at the international scale, partly to acquire foreign technology and
expertise and partly in search of cheaper labour, both highly qualified and
semi-skilled (Saxenian, 1983b). In this way, the central belt of Scotland –
'Silicon Glen' – came, by 1983, to account for 79 per cent of all British and 21
per cent of all European integrated-circuit ('silicon chip') production, almost
all of which came from factories owned by Hughes Aircraft Corporation,
Motorola, National Semiconductor, Nippon Electric (NEC) and General
Instrument (Haug, 1986; Henderson, 1987). As with the local branch-plant
economies generated by the decentralization of traditional manufacturing
industries, these regional concentrations of decentralized high-tech industry
do not seem to generate many local linkages or multiplier effects (Hagey and
Malecki, 1986). It should be emphasized, however, that the products and
processes of high-technology industries continue to change rapidly; and that
they are doing so in the context of corporate emphasis on flexible forms of
production and organization. This has led to the suggestion that corporate
strategies themselves have begun to define the division of labour and market
structures (Malecki, 1986; Schoenberger, 1987; Storper, 1987b).

Urban and Regional Outcomes

Given the various elements of decentralization, consolidation and new activity that we have described, it is logical to ask what the outcome has been in

terms of the *overall* performance of cities and regions. In order to maintain continuity, we shall stay with the example of the United States.

The American urban system provides a very clear reflection of the shift to an advanced economy (Dunn, 1980, 1983; Molotch and Logan, 1985). Until the 1950s it was characterized by the dominance of large manufacturing centres and major gateway cities. Since 1960, however, it has come to be influenced more and more by metropolitan areas specialized in key service industries, particularly producer services:

> In this new urban system, dominance is defined increasingly by the capacity of these service centres to organize and expand production on a system-wide basis – more and more international in dimension – and increasingly less by their ability to get the goods out locally, as was the case in the past. (Noyelle, 1983, p. 126)

What is remarkable about this transformation is that many of these new service-oriented centres are the large manufacturing centres of the previous epoch which have been fundamentally transformed in terms of economic structure; while only a limited number of 'Sunbelt' cities (i.e. cities in the South, Southwest and West) seem to be reaching a dominant status. This conclusion is based on the results of an analysis of the employment structure and functional characteristics of the 140 largest US cities in the mid-1970s (Noyelle and Stanback, 1981). Their analysis suggested the emergence of a three-tiered urban hierarchy, consisting of

1 *First-tier* cities, characterized by large concentrations of national and regional headquarters of large corporations, well-developed banking facilities, dense networks of producer-service firms (insurance, accounting, advertising, legal counsel, public relations, R & D, etc.), and concentrations of important educational, medical and public-sector institutions; and they also tend to be important centres for the wholesale distribution of manufactured goods. They include the 'national nodal centres' of New York, Los Angeles, Chicago and San Francisco, together with 'regional nodal centres' (e.g. Philadelphia, Boston, Baltimore, Minneapolis, Denver and Seattle), and 'subregional nodal centres' (e.g. Memphis, Oklahoma City, Richmond and Charlotte).

2 *Second-tier* cities tend to have a narrower range of service activities. Most are specialized in management and technical production for well-defined industries (e.g. steel in Pittsburgh, office equipment in Rochester, semiconductors in San Jose) and are therefore characterized by concentrations of the headquarters offices, R & D facilities and technically-oriented production establishments of large firms in those industries. These 'functional nodal centres' are heavily concentrated within the old Manufacturing Belt. Noyelle and Stanback also recognize 'government/education centres' as a distinctive sub-group of second-tier cities. In addition to Washington, DC, these include

Albany, Austin, Madison and Raleigh-Durham. In general, companies headquartered in second-tier cities must obtain high-order producer-services such as banking and advertising from firms based in first-tier cities.

3   *Third-tier* cities, generally much smaller in size (though there are several important exceptions – including San Diego, Buffalo, Albuquerque and Tampa). Four subcategories are recognized:

   (a) 'resort/retirement/residential centres', such as Anaheim, Santa Barbara, Las Vegas and Orlando; most of them in the South and West,

   (b) 'manufacturing centres', such as Gary, Binghampton, Buffalo and Youngstown; nearly all of them located in the old Manufacturing Belt,

   (c) 'industrial/military centres' such as Charleston (SC), Norfolk, San Diego, and Huntsville; most of them in the South and West, and

   (d) 'mining/industrial centres' such as Bakersfield, Duluth and Charleston (WV)

What these sub-categories have in common is that they are largely subordinate to the decisions taken in upper-tier cities, with their industrial base biased heavily towards direct production and assembly work and their service base containing a disproportionate number of 'secondary' jobs. Further analysis (Stanback and Noyelle, 1982) has suggested that the basic structure of this new urban system is likely to develop in directions that will intensify these differences. Thus, key services are likely to continue to grow almost exclusively in cities of the first two tiers, while the 'dependent' centres of the third tier are likely to remain highly specialized (and therefore more vulnerable to the fluctuations of business cycles) either in production activities or consumer services.

In terms of *regional* outcomes, the shift to an advanced economy has meant that the 'Manufacturing Belt' – now also known as the 'Rust Belt' – has generally lost ground while the 'Sunbelt' states – especially Arizona, California, the Carolinas and Texas – have gained (Ballard and James, 1983; Beyers, 1979; Rees, 1983a). In very general terms, it appears that Sunbelt states have been able to benefit from relative advantages in terms of labour costs, labour unionization, land costs, energy costs, local taxation, local government boosterism and federal expenditure patterns (Luckingham, 1982; Peet, 1983; Perry and Watkins, 1977; Sawers and Tabb, 1984). In addition, Sunbelt cities have proved attractive to industries because they did not have a legacy of inefficient layout and infrastructure. As Gordon puts it (1979, p. 78):

> They could be constructed from scratch to fit the needs of a new period of accumulation in which factory plant and equipment were themselves increasingly predicated upon a decentralized model. . . . There was consequently no identifiable downtown factory district . . . . Automobiles and trucks provided the connecting links, threading together the separate pieces. The corporate city became . . . The Fragmented Metropolis.

In a sense, therefore, Sunbelt growth can be interpreted as the combined product of diffuse industrialization and metropolitan decentralization. Such an interpretation is supported by the types of employment growth which characterize the rise of the Sunbelt: (a) production jobs in branch plants in industries such as textiles, clothing and electronics; (b) production jobs in branch plants and in locally-based firms in high-growth industries' – mainly in computer hardware, scientific instruments, aerospace, and chemicals and plastics; and (c) service jobs catering both to these industries and to the increased population attracted to the retirement and leisure communities.

The corollary of these gains in the Sunbelt has been the relative – and in some aspects, absolute – decline of economic activity in the old economic core of the Manufacturing Belt. For some communities, the consequences of plant shutdowns have been disastrous. In Youngstown, which has become the symbol of American industrial decline, the closure of the Campbell Steel Works in 1977 eliminated over 10,000 jobs at a stroke (Buss and Redburn, 1983). In overall terms, it has been estimated that the Mid-Atlantic region (New Jersey, New York, Pennsylvania) experienced a net loss of over 175,000 jobs during the period 1969–76 whereas the South Atlantic Region (Delaware, DC, Florida, Georgia, Maryland, North Carolina, South Carolina, Virginia, West Virginia) experienced a net gain of over 2 million jobs in the same period (Bluestone and Harrison, 1982). This represents a job loss of 1.5 per cent in the Mid-Atlantic region and a gain of 24.4 per cent in the South Atlantic region, compared with a net gain of some 15 per cent in the US as a whole (Table 6.4).

Deindustrialization on this scale brings with it a number of *downward spiralling multiplier effects* (Hamilton and Linge, 1983):

1   The substantial contraction of major segments of intra-regional, vertically integrated production chains (e.g. ore-mining, coalmining, steel production, marine engineering and shipbuilding)
2   The creation of selective feedback effects on some small sub-contracting firms and the stranding of many footloose industrial firms which must rapidly restructure product lines and production processes or find new buyers for their existing output in other regions
3   The disappearance of inefficient, more labour-intensive firms and sections of production chains (e.g. in textiles), leaving the region only finishing, specialized and high-quality product lines (e.g. in clothing) which now become dependent on supply linkages that are often 'stretched' overseas
4   The lateral effects of rising unemployment and falling incomes on regional demand, which may 'despoil' the business environment sufficiently to jeopardize the operations of further activities

It would be misleading, however, to place too much emphasis on the rise of the Sunbelt and the demise of the Manufacturing Belt. As we have seen, many of the larger cities of the Manufacturing Belt have been successful in making the transition to an advanced economy. Moreover, the process of deindustrialization

Table 6.4: Jobs created and destroyed as a result of openings, closings, relocations, expansions and contractions of private business establishments in the United States 1969–76 (in thousands of jobs).

Region	Number of jobs in 1969	Employment change 1969–76					
		Jobs created		Jobs destroyed		Net job change	
		By openings & Immigrations	Expansion	By closures & outmigrations	Contractions	Number	Per cent
US as a whole	57936.1	25281.3	19056.1	22302.3	13183.2	8851.9	15.2
Frostbelt:	32701.2	11321.5	9470.4	11351.7	7212.1	2228.1	6.8
Northeast	15824.6	4940.4	4347.5	5881.5	3589.0	–182.6	–1.2
New England	3905.3	1251.2	1131.0	1437.2	952.1	–7.1	–2.6
Mid-Atlantic	11919.3	3689.2	3216.5	4444.3	2636.9	–175.5	–1.5
Midwest	16876.6	6381.1	5123.0	5470.2	3623.2	24107	14.3
East North Central	12563.6	4670.6	3581.8	3962.6	1651.7	1638.1	13.0
West North Central	4313.0	1710.6	1541.2	1507.6	971.5	772.7	17.9
Sunbelt:	25234.9	13959.8	9585.7	10950.5	5971.0	6624.0	26.2
South	16044.5	8934.2	5964.6	6824.3	3803.3	4272.2	26.6
South Atlantic	8204.1	4651.2	2013.0	3547.9	2014.2	2002.1	24.4
East South Central	3065.2	1518.2	1089.9	1211.0	631.9	765.2	24.9
West South Central	4775.2	1764.8	1916.7	2065.4	1157.2	2503.9	31.4
West	9190.4	5025.6	3621.1	4126.2	2167.8	2352.7	25.6
Mountain	1914.9	1226.1	953.6	977.9	481.0	720.8	48.3
Pacific	7248.5	3799.6	2667.6	3148.3	1686.8	1632.1	22.5

Source: Based on Bluestone and Harrison (1982), Table 2.1. p. 30.

(i.e. the *relative* decline of manufacturing jobs), while localized within the third-tier manufacturing centres of the northeast, has affected every region (Table 6.4). Even California, the archetypal Sunbelt state, has been seriously affected by shutdowns. In Los Angeles alone, almost 18,000 manufacturing jobs were lost between 1978 and 1982, many of them the result of plant closures by large corporations like Ford, Pabst Brewing, Max Factor, Uniroyal and US Steel. In the state as a whole in the single year of 1980, more than 150 large plants closed down, displacing more than 37,000 workers (Bluestone and Harrison, 1982). In short, the gains of the Sunbelt and the losses of the Manufacturing Belt conceal a complex and uneven pattern of ebbs and flows (Browning and Gessler, 1979; Fisher, 1981).

The public economy

As we saw in Chapter 5, the onset of industrial capitalism brought an expansion of the role of the state to the point where the public economy had come to exert a pervasive influence on the economic life of the core nations. With advanced capitalism, the public economy has expanded still further, channelling a vast amount of resources into everything from defence, health, education and income security to transport, infrastructural development and industrial investment; and conditioning the whole of the private economy through everything from price guarantees and labour laws to tax structures and import tariffs. Indeed, the sheer magnitude of the public economy has come to blur the boundary between the public and the private sectors. In addition to the state ownership of key industries that is common in much of Western Europe, many governments have been impelled to intervene – for a variety of reasons – to prevent the collapse of private business corporations (examples have included the US government's efforts to rescue Lockheed and Chrysler in the 1970s, and the UK government's continuing efforts to sustain British Leyland). Most important of all, governments everywhere have become the largest single consumer of the goods produced by private sector enterprise. In short, the public economy is pervasive in its effects on economic well-being. What is important in the present context is that nearly all of this activity has a geographical expression. One of the most obvious examples is the deliberate bias of regional policy and planning, which we examine in Chapter 12. In this section, we emphasize the spatial bias – often unintentional – that results from other aspects of the public economy.

Government Spending and Taxation

The geography of public finance is a complex subject, and it is hazardous to attempt detailed comparisons between nations (Bennett, 1980, 1983). It is possible, however, to identify major categories of activity and to illustrate their spatial implications with specific examples. In this context, it is convenient to recognize four major categories of government *expenditure*:

1   The salaries of central government employees, including clerks, bureaucrats and other workers in the armed forces, education, public health, the nationalized industries, the police and the courts. Expenditure on these salaries is of course localized in capital cities. In Washington, DC, for example, almost one third of all earnings come from federal employment. In addition, government salaries can have an important impact in small- or medium-sized cities that have been selected for specific functions – defence installations, for example, or decentralized branches of the bureaucracy (as in the UK government's relocation of social security offices from London to Newcastle upon Tyne).

2   Transfer payments to particular population groups (e.g. the elderly, the unemployed, families with dependent children) and particular industries (e.g. agricultural subsidies and guaranteed prices). These expenditures involve complex flows of monies and are geographically localized only in as much as the 'target' populations and industries are localized (though the *effectiveness* of the payments may vary considerably from one area to another – see, for example, Wohlenberg, 1976).

3   Purchasing and sub-contracting from businesses in the private sector. This includes a wide range of items – buildings, roads, dams, power stations, military equipment, office equipment and publishing, for example – which can make for highly localized impacts. Defence expenditure has been researched in some detail, and it provides good examples of the kind of bias that can result from government purchasing. It seems that the employment generated by defence expenditure generally tends to be sufficiently localized (because it is concentrated in the hands of just a few giant corporations – e.g. General Dynamics, McDonnel Douglas, United Technologies, Boeing, General Electric, Lockheed and Hughes Aircraft in the US) as to create significant multiplier effects. But the resultant spatial bias seems to bear no consistent relationship to centre–periphery patterns or to dimensions of economic geography. In the UK, defence expenditure sustains around 1.25 million jobs – about 5 per cent of all employment – and pays for around 25 per cent of all the R & D activity undertaken in the country. Both the direct spinoff from the employment and the indirect 'seed bed' effects of R & D have reinforced the centre–periphery structure of the UK economy, with the South East, the South West and the East Midlands benefiting most while the likes of Yorkshire and Northern Ireland are under-represented both in terms of job creation and R & D activity (Law, 1983; Short, 1981). In the US, on the other hand, defence procurements have tended to be biased away from the industrial core. Taking R & D activity as well as prime defence contracts into account, and allowing for the effects of subcontracting, it has been California that has benefited most from Department of Defense spending,

together with Washington (state), Massachussetts, Maryland, Arizona and Connecticut (Malecki, 1984a; Rees, 1981).

4   Local government expenditure. In many countries, this now approaches the levels of expenditure by central governments (though a large portion of local expenditure is dependent on revenues provided by central governments in the form of grants and revenue-sharing funds). What is most striking about local government expenditure is that, after fulfilling their statutory obligations, local authorities vary a great deal both in the amount they spend and the categories of their expenditure. This reflects a complex interaction between local resources, local needs, and the local political climate (Kirby, 1982).

In order to gauge the net impact of these expenditures, we have to set them against the geography of *taxation*. Such an exercise is very difficult to achieve at any level of detail, but we can illustrate the kind of biases that can emerge by reference to federal taxes in the US. Around 40 per cent of all federal revenues are derived from personal income taxes, with another 25 per cent coming from taxes on pension trusts and a further 15 per cent from taxes on corporate profits. To a large extent, therefore, the geography of federal revenues reflects the geography of income and economic health. Yet the *structure* of the tax system can have less straightforward geographical implications. Indeed, the *President's National Urban Policy Report* for 1980 concluded that 'the tax system is perhaps the most pervasive federal influence on patterns of economic development. Taxes influence the relative cost to businesses of new capital versus existing machinery, of low-wage or lower-skilled workers versus others, and of land in growing areas which is rising in value as opposed to land whose value may be falling' (US Department of Housing and Urban Development, 1960, p. 3.18). The tax breaks offered under the Investment Tax Credits scheme (which are geared to encourage business investment in new equipment and machinery), for example, tend to benefit growth industries in growth areas; as do the more generous rates of depreciation allowed for new industrial and commercial plants. On the other hand it should be acknowledged that studies of industrial location have established fairly clearly that tax differences between states are not a significant factor in inducing industrial *relocation* (Rees, 1983b; Waslyenko, 1981).

Although it is not possible to quantify the local effect of these structural characteristics of the tax system, it is possible to specify the magnitude of the *net* flows of monies between the federal government and individual states. Labovitz (1978) points out that inter-state differentials in such flows have tended to diminish during the postwar period as the federal tax system has become more uniformly progressive and as state variations in per capita incomes have narrowed. Differences between states remain substantial, however, with a marked disadvantage of states in the Manufacturing Belt and the northeast. This has been interpreted by some as a product of the manipulation of the political 'pork barrel' (Fainstein and Fainstein, 1978). Certainly the dominance of the Democrats in the Deep South has ensured the seniority of its federal senators and thus the chairmanship of committees of Congress controlling the allocation and distribution of federal funds. Moreover, Congressmen do seek membership on the committees of Congress controlling the allocation and distribution of federal funds, they do seek membership on the committees and sub-committees most relevant to the needs of their constituents; and many decisions are blatantly taken for electoral reasons. But political and electoral variables are weak predictors of the overall geography of federal outlays (Archer, 1980, 1983; Brunn, 1975; Hoggart, 1981; Johnston, 1980b).

What is important about patterns of federal expenditure in the present context is that the *marginal* impact of the flow of federal funds seems to have been much greater in the South and West. By improving the infrastructure of communications, transportation, sewage and facilities and energy, the federal government helped to establish the *preconditions* for the development of new industries in the Sunbelt. By direct and indirect investment in electronics research, semiconductors, computers, aeronautics and scientific instruments in the South and West, the federal government enabled the Sunbelt to capture some of the most dynamic activities of the advanced capitalist economy (Markusen, 1984).

Crisis and Retrenchment in the Public Economy

Finally, we must note that the effects of the international economic crisis and destabilization that have characterized the post-1973 period have carried over into the public sector of most economies. This has prompted a certain amount of retrenchment and restructuring, particularly on the welfare state side of the public economy. The dilemma facing most governments has been that deepening economic recession has accentuated the vulnerability of more and more people while making it increasingly difficult – politically as well as economically – to finance existing programmes. As a result, a 'new conservatism' in the orientation of central and local governments has emerged. Electoral victories by right-of-centre parties in Australia, the Netherlands, New Zealand, the United Kingdom and the United States were associated with an ideological stance based on the belief that the welfare state had not only generated unreasonably high levels of taxation, budget deficits, disincentives to work and save, and a bloated class of unproductive workers, but also that it may have fostered 'soft' attitudes towards 'problem' groups in society. Ironically, the electoral appeal of this ideology can be attributed to the very success of welfare states in banishing from the minds of the electorate the immediate spectre of material deprivation. Consequently, the priority accorded to welfare expenditure has receded (though the logic and, critically, the costs of maintaining it has not).

The restructuring of the welfare state has been most pronounced in the United Kingdom and the United States, where the Thatcher and Reagan administrations respectively embarked on programmes of privatization in health, housing and education, accompanied by cuts (some absolute, some relative) in higher education, in programmes for the unemployed, the disabled and the elderly, and in regional policy budgets. In the United Kingdom, closer controls on local government expenditure by the central government have precipitated corresponding cuts at the local level, particularly in depressed towns and cities where the incidence of need for welfare services is high but local fiscal resources are low (Knox and Kirby, 1984).

Table 6.5: Economic performance and policy outcomes in 23 OECD nations 1974–80

	Rank-order of economic performance 1979–80[a]	Labour-market performance and rates of unemployment 1973–80[b]	Growth of social security expenditure in percentage points of GDP 1973–9	Public debt as % GDP 1973	1979
Australia	8	average (4.5)	2.6		—
Austria	5	good (1.8)	2.7	17	31
Canada	6	average (7.2)	0.8		—
Denmark	15	average (6.0)	4.7	16	36
Finland	12	average (4.6)	1.6	6	15
France	11	bad (4.8)	4.9	13	16
Germany (West)	4	bad (3.2)	2.7	18	29
Greece	14	good (1.9)	2.1		—
Iceland	22	good (0.5)	− 1.5		—
Ireland	13	bad (7.0)	2.1	60	91
Italy	18	bad (6.7)	0.3	33	69
Japan	1	good (1.9)	5.8	13	36
Luxembourg	—	good (0.5)	7.5	28	25
Netherlands	9	average (4.1)	7.1	43	44
New Zealand	19	good (1.9)	—		—
Norway	3	good (1.8)	1.6	33	53
Portugal	21	bad (7.0)	5.4		—
Spain	20	bad (6.1)	2.5		—
Sweden	16	good (1.9)	5.7	36	50
Switzerland	7	average (0.5)	2.5	25	30
United Kingdom	17	bad (5.4)	2.5	73	62
USA	2	average (6.7)	1.6	49	45

Notes: a. Rank 1 = 'best performance'; rank 22 = 'worse performance'.
b. Data in parentheses are rates of unemployment (average 1974 to 1980). 'Bad' means a rate of unemployment which is greater than 2% and a decline in the level of employment between 1973 and 1980. 'Good' means a low rate of unemployment (less than 2%) and an increase in the level of employment. 'Average' means either a low rate of unemployment and a decrease in the level of employment (for example, the Swiss case) or a high rate of unemployment and an increase in the level of employment (for example, USA).
Source: Schmidt (1983).

Other countries have responded in different ways to the post-1973 economic recession. Indeed, there appear to have been no systematic relationships between economic performance, political control, policy orientation and policy output. As Table 6.5 shows, Ireland, Italy, Spain and the United Kingdom all turned in an unstable economic performance, with low growth rates and high rates of inflation, declining competitiveness, high rates of unemployment and small increases in welfare expenditure. At the other end of the spectrum, Austria, Japan and Norway enjoyed relatively high growth rates, low rates of inflation, stable or increasing competitiveness, low unemployment and at least a moderate expansion in welfare expenditure. Yet in terms of policy orientation over the same period the pattern is quite different (OECD, 1981; Schmidt, 1983). The UK, the US and Canada gave priority to economic accumulation and the control of inflation at the expense of full employment and welfare expenditure. In contrast, Denmark, Luxembourg and Sweden gave priority to full employment and welfare provision at the expense of economic growth and competitiveness. Schmidt (1983) attributes this to the strength of welfare state bureaucracies and their clientele in these countries, but concedes that such strength does not always result in an expansive welfare policy. In Finland, the Netherlands and West Germany, for example, the main thrust of central government policy during economic recession has been towards the modernization of the economy, coupled with a modest growth in welfare expenditure through a corresponding expansion of public debt. In these circumstances, the net result has been a marked increase in unemployment, relieved by relatively generous but increasingly restrictive unemployment benefits. In other countries, other factors have had a decisive influence. In Switzerland, for example, the good economic performance and low rate of unemployment were the result of a big reduction in the labour force, mainly at the expense of foreign workers.

Overview

In this chapter we have seen how the crisis of industrial capitalism and the sectoral shifts and changing business structures of the emerging era of advanced capitalism have begun to reshape both the international economic order and the economic landscapes of the industrial core regions. Among the salient features of this reshaping are:

- The emergence of production hierarchies within the large companies that have come to dominate most industries. These hierarchies have tended to result in separate locational settings for (a) high-level corporate control, (b) production requiring high inputs of skilled labour and new technology; intermediate administration and R & D activities; and (c) routine production.

- An increase in the external control of regional economies, with the result that the industrial systems of established industrial regions have become fragmented while those of newly-industrializing regions have become segmented or truncated. As a result, 'cities and regions are being used increasingly as entrepôts or 'conveyor belts' in the various stages of the corporate production chain (Hamilton and Linge, 1983, p. 23).

- The organization of the world-economy into three broad international regions (Hamilton and Linge, 1983):

1 the highly integrated and very diversified industrial *cores* and control centres of the 'North'
2 the recently industrialized and newly industrializing *semi-peripheries*, mostly in the world's 'middle regions' (eastwards from Mexico, through the Mediterranean to South East and East Asia) and in parts of the southern hemisphere
3 the relatively thinly industrialized *periphery* that makes up most of the 'South' and is highly dependent on the 'North'

- The persistence within each of these broad regions of nested hierarchies of nations and regions at different levels of economic development. Thus the periphery contains core regions and semi-peripheral regions (as, for example, the Lagos/Ibadan region and Abidjan region respectively in West Africa), the semi-periphery contains core regions and peripheral regions (e.g. the Calcutta–Hooghly–Howra conurbation and Uttar Pradesh respectively in India), and the core contains regions which are, relatively, peripheral and semi-peripheral (e.g. northern Scandinavia and southern Italy respectively in Western Europe).

- Within the core nations of the north the diverse mixes of industry, workers and infrastructure inherited from the industrial era have mediated the broader processes of structural change and reorganization, so that different settings have evolved in different ways. There have been four broad trajectories of change. In the first, restructuring in response to a legacy of declining industry has been the dominant process. Examples include the old manufacturing heartlands of northern England, South Wales, central Scotland and the US manufacturing belt. In some rural areas and peripheral regions, on the other hand, the dominant process has been one of decentralization of footloose, labour-intensive industries from the metropolitan areas and core regions. Examples include parts of the southern US and central and northeastern Italy. A third trajectory is characterized by regions whose industry has developed at or just above the national average, sustained by a consistent supply of new investment. Examples include most of South East England and the Boston–New York–Washington, DC–Richmond corridor. Finally, there have been some regions where there has been rapid growth in most activities (the exceptions being those in serious decline nationally). Examples include California, Texas and the Tokyo-centred Keihin region of Japan.

- Overlying these categories there has been a general accentuation of the importance and prosperity of large metropolitan areas, while many smaller towns and, in particular, many of the specialized new towns spawned by industrial capitalism (mining towns, heavy manufacturing towns, and so on) have declined (Johnston, 1980a).

- Cutting across the effects of sectoral shifts and changing business structures have been the effects of various kinds of government activity. Though often unintentional, the operation of the public economy often exhibits significant spatial biases which have tended to reinforce existing centre–periphery relationships (as with UK defence expenditures); in others, they have tended to modify or reduce centre–periphery relationships (as with US defence expenditures).

Part Three

Spatial Transformation at the Periphery

In the next four chapters we examine the world outside the core of the world-economy, paying special attention to the changing historical relationships between core and periphery outlined in Chapters 2 and 3. In Chapter 7 we briefly describe the historical systems that the modern world-economy has now incorporated within its orbit but which were once relatively autonomous. We also survey the range of impacts and differential responses to the world-economy as it expanded from its European base. In Chapter 8 we examine the spatial transformations that have occurred as a consequence of both an older colonialism and a more recent interdependent global capitalism. However, attention is also paid to how the consequences have varied depending on local reactions and institutional responses. In Chapters 9 and 10 two major economic activities, agriculture and manufacturing industry, are examined both with respect to their roles in economic development and their changing geographical patterns. The emphasis throughout this section is upon the impacts of and responses to the evolving modern world-economy in the 'dependent' world.

7

Independent Systems: Principles of Economic Integration and the Rise of the Modern World-Economy

The term 'independent systems' is potentially misleading in that it can be taken to imply a history of *isolated* local development prior to incorporation into the world-economy. Thus, one eminent economist, W.A. Lewis, can state that 'Economic growth entails the slow penetration and eventual absorption of the subsistence sector' (Lewis, 1955, p. 15). This implies that capitalism (the modern world-economy) spread into the countryside from the cities. In fact, in many parts of the dependent world it was in the countryside that much economic growth was concentrated prior to European contact and conquest (Hill, 1986). Indeed, there are many examples of extensive trading networks based on *rural* periodic market places. Consequently, local isolation or autonomy was rarely complete and development was rarely totally independent.

We would wish to disassociate ourselves, therefore, from those 'stage theories' of development that are based on a linear sequence of economic growth from simpler to more complex within an *isolated* economic system. Todaro (1977), for example, bases his account of agricultural production and circulation around three sequential stages of development: subsistence farming, mixed farming, and specialized farming, and concludes that today 'Most Third World nations are in the process of transition from subsistence to mixed farming' (p. 245). This is dangerously misleading. Not only does it imply a static peasant economy in the first stage (an intellectual construct at considerable variance to the reality of extensive trade in staple crops), it also implies the recency of cash crops, when as Hill (1986, p. 57) puts it 'there is no reason to doubt that most market trade, in the past couple of centuries *at least*, involved cash transactions; among the countless forms of indigenous currency, perhaps gold, gold dust and cowry shells had the widest circulation, the two former types having been very ancient'. It is important, though, to acknowledge that different spheres of exchange (staples, prestige, bridewealth) often involved different forms of currency rather than a single 'general-purpose money' (Bohannan, 1959). Nevertheless, stage accounts suggest an equation of tradition with stasis, thus denying 'societies marked off as traditional any significant history of their own' (Wolf, 1982, p. 13).

By 'independent systems', therefore, we mean socio-economic systems of limited geographical extent rather than isolated 'primitive', 'backward', or 'traditional' societies at an early stage of development in a linear sequence whose final stage is consonant with contemporary Europe or America. In particular, there is absolutely no point in viewing these independent systems as *closed* systems. With but few exceptions they have been *open* systems 'inextricably involved with other aggregates, near and far, in weblike, netlike connections' (Lesser, 1961, p. 42). The purpose of this chapter is to identify the key political-economic principles that differentiate independent systems, describe the geographical attributes of the various types of system, survey the impacts of and responses to the world-economy in different systems, and, finally, describe how the experiences of some independent systems and their early responses to the world-economy have provided the 'seedbeds' for their unique contemporary adaptations to the world-economy (e.g. China and Japan).

Principles of Independent Systems: Reciprocity, Redistribution and Exchange

Approach to the study of the economic geography of independent systems is hampered, as Karl Polanyi (1957, p. 239) put it in a more general context, by

> an intellectual heritage of man as an entity with an innate propensity to truck, barter and exchange one thing for another. This remains so in spite of all the protestations against 'economic man' and the intermittent attempts to provide a social framework for the economy.

In looking for an alternative perspective, however, there is no need to deny the reality of times and places in which a market-based society – market centres, trade for gain, and price-fixing mechanisms together – has been predominant. In particular, the modern world-economy, and its progressive expansion over the globe, represents the spread and penetration of market-exchange into systems where it was previously absent or where one or more of the elements of a market-based *society* were missing. But there is a need to deny the universality of market-exchange as *the* basic principle of production and circulation. In different social settings economic transactions involving production, circulation and consumption are enmeshed in different economic and non-economic institutions that condition the *nature* of the economic transactions.

Polanyi (1957) distinguished three specific principles underlying economic transactions: reciprocity, redistribution and market-exchange. He called these 'forms of economic integration.' Any particular independent system is seen as integrated through the predominance of one specific principle that gives unity and stability to a more complex and 'mixed' set of economic transactions. Thus, while one principle would be dominant this does not preclude the presence of the others, at least in prototype or degenerate form.

Reciprocity denotes the interaction between groupings on the basis of symmetry and mutuality. Kinship, neighbourhood and religious orders are examples of groupings largely organized around reciprocity. But other voluntary associations of a social, religious or vocational character also create situations in which, at least for periods of time and in given localities, members of the associations practice some sort of mutuality.

Redistribution refers to 'appropriational movements toward a centre and out of it again' (Polanyi, 1957, p. 253) or centralized allocation of goods by virtue of custom, law or *ad hoc* central decision. Sometimes collection and allocation are not physical but involve the distribution of rights of disposal of goods at other locations. Redistribution is present whenever there is collecting into and distribution from a centre as is the case in most societies from a hunting tribe to the modern welfare state. The causes of redistribution differ, however. In hunting bands a division of labour is necessary to ensure success, whereas in the modern welfare state a redistribution of purchasing power both stimulates economic activity and serves social ideals.

Exchange, as a form of integration, requires a system of price-making markets. But exchange can exist in three forms: locational movement between places (geographical or operational exchange); and two forms of appropriational movements of exchange, either at a set or fixed-price rate (decisional exchange) or at a bargained rate (integrative or market-exchange). The last of these is integrative *only* if linked in a system that spreads the effects of prices beyond the immediate market-*place*. Such a system involves antagonistic relationships between parties to a transaction in that each is attempting to obtain a price that is solely self-serving. In this case, integration is served by competition rather than by reciprocity or redistribution.

The dominance of any one of these forms of integration is identified by Polanyi with certain distinct patterns of land–labour relationships. So-called 'savage society' is characterized by the integration of land and labour through ties of kinship. By way of contrast 'feudal society' was integrated through ties of fealty. In empires based upon irrigation works, land and labour were distributed by the imperial authorities. Finally, market-exchange under capitalism mobilizes land and labour by making them into commodities to be bought and sold.

However, these forms of integration should not be seen as 'stages' of development. Several subordinate forms can be present and any one can re-emerge as dominant after periods of eclipse. Polanyi (1957, p. 256) makes this argument by way of example:

> Tribal societies practice reciprocity and redistribution, while archaic societies are predominantly redistributive, though to some extent they may allow for exchange. Reciprocity, which plays a dominant part in some Melanesian communities, occurs as a not-unimportant although subordinate trait in the redistributive archaic empires, where foreign trade (carried on by gift and counter-gift) is still largely organized on the principle of reciprocity. . . . Redistribution, the ruling method in tribal and archaic society beside which exchange plays only a minor part, grew to great importance in the later Roman Empire and is actually gaining ground in some modern industrial states. . . . Conversely, more than once before in the course of human history markets have played a part in the economy, although never on a territorial scale, or with an institutional comprehensiveness comparable to that of the nineteenth century.

There is no need to assume, therefore, a progression from primitive to complex or from traditional to modern. In particular, there is no necessary association between the concepts of primitive and subsistence economy. The term subsistence economy is acceptable only if it is *not* taken to mean an inherent incapacity to produce and circulate, 'but the contrary: the refusal of a useless *excess*, the determination to make productive activity agree with the satisfaction of needs' (Clastres, 1977, p. 165). This can involve reciprocity and certain (limited) types of exchange but does *not* include redistribution to non-working élites.

There is also no need to assume a timeless immobility in those independent systems without the dominance of market exchange. For example, contrary to the widespread image of sub-Saharan Africa as a continent mired in stasis prior to European colonialism 'its history has emerged to be one of ceaseless flux among populations that, in comparison to other continents, are relatively recent occupants of their present habitat' (Kopytoff, 1987 p. 7). Modern ethnography suggests that rather than a simple evolution of more complex from more simple independent systems 'what we see are building-blocks of different sizes, and chips off the blocks, and the moving kaleidoscope of their grouping and regrouping' (Kopytoff, 1987, p. 78). In other words,

> bands do not grow into chiefdoms, nor do most chiefdoms grow out of bands. The African societies we know were all born not 'in the beginning' but as part of a continuous and variegated process of interaction and social formation – a process that involved a local political ecology that included these forms as part of the conditions in which they were created and re-created. It was an ecology that made for the fact that 'states and stateless societies have existed side by side for over nearly two millenia' (Curtin *et al.*, 1978, p. 82. Kopytoff, 1987, p. 78)

Types of Independent System

Even if often coexisting and re-emerging rather than invariably sequential in time, the principles of integration do enable us to identify types of independent system that exhibit distinctive political-economic and geographical attributes. The typology of Johnson and Earle (1987) provides us with one categorization, although we would disavow their evolutionism. They identify three 'levels' of integration: the Family-level Group, the Local Group, and the Regional Polity. Reciprocity dominates in the first of these, whereas redistribution and elements of market exchange predominate in the latter two.

The three basic types can be subdivided according to the nature of their socio-cultural organization and geographical attributes into a set of sub-types (Table 7.1). In the family-level society under the dominance of reciprocity one finds a spatial diffuseness and minimal degree of geographical organization and integration. The foraging groups especially must adjust to wide geographical variations in the productivity of the natural ecosystems upon which they rely. Their patterns of movement, settlement, and seasonal activity reflect the strategies they adopt to meet the challenge of dependence on the natural world.

Table 7.1: Types of independent system, with examples

Type	Example	Size of community	Size of polity
FAMILY GROUP			
Camp	Shoshone, N. America	30	30
(without domestication)	!Kung San, Africa	20	20
Hamlet	Machiguenga, S. America	25	25
(with domestication)	Nganasan, Siberia	30	30
LOCAL GROUP			
Acephalous local group	Yanomano, S. America	150–250	150–500
	Eskimos, N. America	150–300	150–300
	Turkana, Africa	20–25	100–200
Big Man collectivity	Indians of NW, N. America	500–800	500–800
	Central Enga, New Guinea	350	350
	Kirghiz, Asia	20–35	1,800
REGIONAL POLITY			
Chiefdom	Trobriand Islanders, Pacific	200–400	1,000
	Basseri, Iran	200–500	16,000
	Hawaii Islanders, Pacific	300–400	100,000
Early state	Inka, S. America	± 400	14,000,000
Nation-state	Northeast China	± 300	600,000,000
	Central Java	± 300	100,000,000
	Northeast Brazil	± 300	80,000,000

Source: Johnson and Earle 1987, Table 1 (p. 23) and Table 10 (p. 314).

With the threat of force or famine, family groups can coalesce into larger groupings. This occurs when population densities threaten resource stocks and food sharing becomes necessary. But within local groups of lower densities the economy remains largely in the hands of the family. Such groups are unstable, however, because of the constant threat of fission and regrouping. When faced by hostile neighbouring groups the tendency is for acephalous local groups to form alliances under the tutelage of Big Men. A Big Man represents the political unity of a local group and serves as a manager of its food production. But his political power is contingent and transitory, depending upon his ability to manage complex flows of debts and credits among family and, perhaps, previously acephalous local groups.

The local group, therefore, shows the beginnings of a switch from reciprocity to redistribution as the dominant principle of integration. This, however, is especially marked in the case of regional polities. Through the centralization of power in the hands of chiefs and bureaucratic hierarchies, the landscape acquires a characteristic nodality. This in turn leads to an ordering of space in core–periphery terms. Territory is accorded primacy over kinship (Fig. 4.2).

In a chiefdom, for example, local groups of a given region are united within one political institution dominated by an aristocratic leader or chief. 'Descended from gods and invested with special powers, the chief has the final say in all matters involving the group, including ceremonies, adjudications, war and diplomacy. The chief is much like the Big Man in status and duties, but his domain is larger and more stable' (Johnson and Earle, 1987, p. 318). However, the stability of the chiefdom depends upon the economic benefits that the chiefdom provides rather than simply myth and mystification.

The state differs from the chiefdom in terms of a larger scale, a larger population, and much more rigid stratificaton. Integration tends to be beyond the personal control of an hereditary élite. It requires a state bureaucracy, a state religion, a judicial apparatus and a police force. The state organizes society through space such that spatial structure is ancillary to the administrative needs of the state.

With the nation-state, trade and markets begin to define the institutional basis for the economy. The state provides military protection, risk management and investment in large-scale technologies. But most economic transactions are determined by market exchange in the form of market centres and trade for gain. Only with the addition of competitive ('price-fixing') mechanisms are economic transactions drawn increasingly outside the control of the state. Even then, however, the state can and does, through its monopoly over a rigidly defined territory, regulate and protect 'its' economy from external competition.

As we saw in Chapter 4, the increased scope of competitive, price-fixing markets emerged slowly in seventeenth and eighteenth-century Europe. 'While we can talk of price-fixing or supply-demand-price markets being established locally or sectorally by the close of the medieval period, it was not until the nineteenth century that we can speak of societies and their spatial order being widely and securely embedded in economic processes' (Dodgshon, 1987, p. 293).

The expansion of trade was a vital precursor to the growth of the competitive markets from which the modern world-economy emerged. As Dodgshon (1987, pp. 293–4) puts it:

> The opportunities presented by the opening-up of the New World, the establishment of sea routes to the Orient and the quickening of flow between Western Europe and the Baltic played a crucial part in this energizing of trade. They injected a wider, more diverse range of goods, afforded scope for new forms of trading organization and agreements and tapped distant areas of supply whose forceful exploitation posed no threat to the social order of the European states. In fact, from the very outset, the colonies were seen as a source of exchange, not of use-values. . . . State-systems responded to the new opportunities opened up by this growth in overseas trade by evolving mercantilist policies that were designed to secure the trading interests of the state as a whole.

Eventually, however, state regulation proved incompatible with expanding trade and industrial development. In these circumstances, nodality and core–periphery relations were transformed in meaning. Space was contoured into locations of differing accessibility and profitability (Fig. 4.4). This loosened the controls exerted by redistributive élites and gave rise to patterns of economic activity determined by the shifting loci of investment. The expansiveness of the European states then was given further impetus by the intrinsic expansiveness of price-fixing markets. This was what turned the earlier expansion of states into empires into the making of the modern world-economy.

The operation of the three principles of economic integration, therefore, has given rise to a variety of types of independent system. The principle of market-exchange, however, contained within it the seeds of wider influence and dispersal. In the form of the modern world-economy it could not easily be restricted or confined geographically.

The Coming of the World-Economy: Impacts and Responses

The problematic nature of geographical incorporation into the modern world-economy has been stressed by many writers (e.g. Arrighi, 1979; Sokolovsky, 1985; Hall, 1986). The process of incorporation is often viewed as a continuum which ranges from weak to strong. But referring to regions along this continuum as 'peripheral areas' without distinguishing the relative impact of market exchange masks important variation. Hall (1986) provides a useful typology of world-economy impacts (Table 7.2). At the weak pole of the continuum are areas external to the world-economy (external arenas). Next come areas where contact has been slight (contact peripheries). In the

Table 7.2: The continuum of geographical incorporation

The continuum of incorporation	None	Weak	Moderate	Strong
Type of periphery	External arena	Contact periphery	Marginal periphery	Dependent periphery
Market articulation	None	Weak	Moderate	Strong
Impact of core on periphery	None	Strong	Stronger	Strongest
Impact of periphery on core	None	Low	Moderate	Significant

Source: Hall (1986, p. 392).

middle-range are marginal peripheries. Finally, at the strong pole are fully fledged dependent peripheries.

The processes involved as a region shifts from the status of an external arena to a dependent periphery are also indicated in Table 7.2. Market articulation refers to the extent of capital and product flows between the expanding world-economy and an absorbed region. At the weak pole of the continuum of incorporation are regions which are only slightly connected to the world-economy, with the primary flow of influence from core to periphery. By way of example, the North American fur industry in the eighteenth century was not vital to European economic development, but the fur trade produced massive social and economic change among the native societies which became tied into it. At the strong pole of the continuum, market exchange is important to core development. Though influence flows in both directions, net product and capital flows favour the core.

It seems clear that the 'motor' of incorporation is not simply profitable trade and capital accumulation in the interest of the 'core', as dependency theory would have it (see Chapter 3). Contact and marginal peripheries do not contribute much to the accumulation of capital, either for the core or any class in it. Consequently, religious zeal, pre-emptive colonization, state expansion for its own sake, and entrepreneurial exploration must be seen as important elements in the expansion of the modern world-economy.

Moreover, movement along the continuum is contingent rather than necessary, both in terms of pace and eventual degree of dependence. A number of conditions can be suggested. First, geographical integration into the world-economy is more or less complete when early contact leads to the complete subjugation or liquidation of indigenous groups. Later, new settlement becomes dominated by market exchange as, for example, in the US and Australian cases. In time, of course, the emergence of independent settler political forces also favoured the pursuit of independent capitalist industrial development (Agnew, 1987; McMichael, 1984).

Second, the pace of movement towards strong incorporation and an eventual degree of political-economic dependence within the world-economy depend upon the strength of the state engaged in expansion and the nature of the world-economy at the time. For example, the late eighteenth and early nineteenth century was a period of expansion and profound change in the world-economy. Indeed, it is in this period that both global self-regulating markets and British hegemony within the world-economy arose. The expansion of market exchange was served by *raison d'état*. Contact in this period, in particular if precipitated by the British, led to rapid incorporation into the world-economy on terms disadvantageous to the incorporated. In a previous period, for instance the sixteenth century, and with a different state, for example Spain, contact led less immediately to effective incorporation and the spread of market exchange. Plunder and religious zeal were more important than 'bringing to market.' This was of course also true of other states at that time, including Britain.

In the nineteenth century, market exchange was effectively globalized under British dominance as production *for* the market everywhere replaced the mere exchange of commodities (Table 7.3). The British national economy became the 'locomotive' of the world-economy. But as its markets in Europe became more competitive it was pushed into a widening of its markets elsewhere. The British Empire was a particularly important part of this 'internationalization', although, as Table 7.3 shows, Latin America and China, regions outside formal British control, were also important. The internationalization of the British economy in the nineteenth century was a crucial

Table 7.3: The geographical development of the world-economy in the nineteenth century

Stage: Factor intensity:	Developed Capital	Developing Labour	Land	Undeveloped Land	Labour
1800	Britain	Europe		US	India
1840	Britain	Europe	US	Latin America Australia Canada	India China
1870	Britain, Europe		US	Australia Latin America Canada Africa	China
1900	Britain Europe US		Australia Canada Argentina Mexico S. Africa	Latin America Africa	India China

Source: Hansson (1952, pp 59–82).

element in the quickening pace and increased strength of incorporation world-wide. But as Doyle (1986, p. 273) puts it

> The extensive internationalization (and imperialization) of the British economy in the nineteenth century was crucial to integrating the disparate societies of the empire. It provided incentives for collaboration in the colonial periphery, and in the British metropole it offered motives for bearing the administrative costs that empire entails. But it could also lead to conflicts of interest. The contrasting experiences of the two centres of the first British empire – the British Caribbean and what would become the United States – are instructive. The first became economically more dependent while the second became economically independent and fractious, *suggesting that circumstances special to each colony are decisive.* (our emphasis)

This leads us to the third condition affecting the incorporation process: the abilities and behaviour of the various indigenous groups and states as they encountered the technologically superior force of Europe (and its 'off-shoots' such as the United States). Skocpol (1976) suggests that the key to whether an indigenous agrarian-order (she excludes more primitive groups) could preserve itself or resist incorporation lay in the degree of state autonomy from the short-run interests of the local economic élite. However, self-preservation often involved adapting or organizing a response to the world-economy rather than long-term resistance to it. Success was variable:

> The Ottoman empire disintegrated while Japan modernized successfully; Africa was partitioned while Latin American governments were more effectively expanding and consolidating their rule (T. Smith, 1979, p. 276).

The responses to European expansion and the penetration of market exchange, therefore, have been diverse. Not only political organization but also the history of previous contact was important. In Africa, for example,

> Some societies accepted colonial rule; others resisted. Some chose to cooperate with the new rulers in order to manipulate them to their purposes; others tried to opt out of the imperial system by force or by stealth . . .
> Generalizations regarding the African response are therefore difficult to make. East Africa lacked that long period of commercial and missionary contact with the West experienced by the societies on the West African coast. When East Africa finally came under European control, the great majority of the indigenous communities in the interior were almost unaffected by Western civilizations. People like the Kamba, the Kikuyu, and the Masai of Kenya continued to live in small-scale societies, preliterate and acephalous, subsisting on rudimentary forms of farming and cattle keeping, dependent on simple technologies, and devoid of general-purpose currencies. (Gann and Duignan, 1978, pp. 361–2)

Even after long exposure of equivalent intensity, responses still differed. In Africa again,

> After a period of initial revulsion, the Kikuyu took easily to education and wage employment; the Kamba and the Masai, on the other hand, for long ignored schools. (Gann and Duignan, 1978, p. 362)

The market economy, therefore, was met with quite different reactions, some of an extremely subtle kind:

> Kamba men, for instance, would not work on white farms, but they accepted employment as askaris or labourers on railway construction projects. (Gann and Duignan, 1978, p. 361)

With the exception of the special case of European settler colonies, areas with special physical characteristics as well as subjugated or liquidated indigenous populations, the process of geographical incorporation into the modern world-economy depended on the intersection between the interests and power of the 'expanders', on the one hand, and the interests and power of the 'incorporated', on the other. Though writing more specifically about what he terms 'imperial authority', Low (1973, p. 28) succinctly summarizes the major factors involved in determining the course of incorporation and the creation of dependence that often followed (at least for a time):

> (1) the gathering in of the threads of legitimacy where these existed; (2) the support for it [imperial authority] of traditionally legitimate, if newly established, indigenous political authorities; (3) force, and a monopoly of coercive powers; (4) the establishment of a *Pax*, and the establishment of a new order offering a larger-scale existence; (5) (very often) upon the slow extension and remoteness of imperial authority, which prevented the colonial people from understanding what was happening until it was too late; (6) the vested interest that a number, sometimes a very large number, of local peoples had, for one reason or another, in the maintenance of the imperial regime; (7) the considerable strength and effectiveness of the imperial bureaucracy; and (8) the charismatic qualities which, at all events in the early years, imperial rulers possessed for many colonial peoples.

The geographical expansion of the modern world-economy, therefore, has had differential impacts and produced different reactions in different places. Indeed, it is largely to this variety of impacts and responses that we can trace the shifts of power and challenges to the global political-economic status quo that have changed the world-economy over the past 200 years, e.g. the American Revolution, the Russian Revolution, the Chinese Revolution, the rise of Japan, and the growth of the NICs. We turn now to two examples in which *contemporary* adaptations to the modern world-economy were 'seeded' in earlier experience as independent systems and in the incorporation process itself.

Seedbeds for Alternative Adaptations to the World-Economy: Independent Systems and the Incorporation Process

The history of independent systems and the incorporation process are not only important in themselves and for what they say about the geographical expansion of the modern world-economy but also because they suggest the possibility in different places of resistance, adaptation, challenge and reformulation of the world-economy itself. At one extreme, as pointed out in Chapter 3, lies an amalgam of adoption and adaptation, as with the United States and Japan. At another extreme, as with contemporary Iran (see Chapter 3) and, intermittently, with China and the Soviet Union, lies resistance, challenge and attempted reformulation. We pursue here the examples of China and Japan.

At the time of initial contact with Europeans, China had a long history of political unity as an independent system. China was thought by its élites to be the centre of all civilization and the Chinese emperor had the *de jure* right to rule over all human affairs. The emperor ruled by virtue in order to preserve harmony among men and in the natural world. The geographical setting of China both inspired and reinforced the sense of China's unique place under heaven. As Kim (1979, pp. 22–23) notes:

> China is guarded on the west by almost endless deserts, on the southwest by the Himalaya Mountains, and on the east by vast oceans. Admired but often attacked by the 'barbarians' of the semi-arid plateau lands on the north and west, and cut off from other centres of civilization by oceans, deserts and mountains, China gradually developed a unique sense of her place under heaven.

China's cosmic centrality was reflected in the model of geopolitical relationships adopted by traditional élites. This was a system of hierarchical harmony promoted and preserved by the preponderance of power and virtue located in China. Ginsburg (1968, p. 80) describes it as follows:

> For centuries upon centuries, the perceived political spatial system remained Sinocentric, zonal, roughly concentric, without formal boundaries, characterized by a distance–intensity relationship between power and territorial control, almost exclusively Asia-oriented, and separated from the rest of the world by indifference or ignorance.

The pattern of relationships between the Chinese centre and the barbarian periphery took a definite and, until the onslaught of the West in the nineteenth century, fixed form – the tribute system. The tribute system provided the dynamic for Chinese relations with the barbarians. The emperor was a receiver of tribute to whom the bearers of tribute from alien states had to come. He was *in situ* and never sent ambassadors to other states. Tribute flowed from the periphery to the centre. There was never any question of reciprocity.

By the mid-nineteenth century, and as a result of increasing Western involvement in Chinese affairs, two separate 'worlds' came into contact and conflict. As a result of the defeat suffered by China in the Opium War (1839–42) a new 'treaty system' imposed by the British displaced the tribute system. Chinese officials at first resisted this imposition, but a series of humiliating military defeats in 1856–57 led to new treaties that 'opened a Pandora's box for the traditional Chinese image of world order' (Kim 1979, p. 36). Military action by the Chinese intended to prevent the exchange of treaty ratification prompted a strong Anglo-French counteraction and the imposition of the

1860 Peking Conventions. In these, foreign states were accorded equal rights with China. This was, according to one authority, 'a decisive violation of Chinese principles (*t'i-chih*) and was probably the greatest loss of prestige which the ruling dynasty had hitherto suffered' (Franke, 1967, p. 13).

Faced with internal disruption in the Taiping Rebellion (1850–64) and the continuing encroachments of the Western powers, the central government began a campaign of 'self-strengthening' (*tzu-ch'iang*) in the early 1860s. The slogan of this campaign was 'Chinese learning for the base, Western learning for practical application' (*Chung-hsueh wei t'i hsi hsueh wei yung*) (Franke, 1967, p. 102). The intention was to borrow Western technology in order to preserve the traditional Chinese order. It met with considerable opposition from conservative elements within the *shen-shih* (ruling bureaucratic) class (Teng and Fairbank, 1979). But in the end it failed because technological thought required a thorough reform of Chinese education and the traditional order required a perpetuation of the existing educational system.

The overthrow of the traditional political structure in 1911 was the outcome of a long period of decline on the part of the Chinese central government. Unable to deal with internal unrest or cope with external threats, universal kingship could not be rescued through 'self-strengthening'. Out of the military defeats and humiliations of the nineteenth century, a rising generation of intellectuals inferred that China had failed to respond to the West because of the 'dead hand' of Confucian thought (Franke, 1967, pp. 75–6). The response was characteristically Chinese. In rejecting the 'totalism' of the Confucian order they perpetuated its totalistic perspective. Lin, (1979, p. x–xi) contends that:

> in spite of the conflicting tendencies within [Chinese] culture, the notion of integral wholeness of culture, the notion that every aspect of society and culture could somehow be controlled through the political order, and the notion that conscious ideas could play a decisive role in transforming human life formed a powerful, widely shared syndrome of ideas within the cultural tradition . . . in many subtle ways these cultural propensities have shaped even those who most decisively rejected the past.

In particular, the anti-traditionalists accepted the basic 'cultural-intellectualistic' approach of previous generations that *ideology* was the foundation for social change.

The history of China since this time has followed the 'totalistic iconoclasm' of those rejecting the substance of Confucian thought without discarding the form. In modern post-1949 China, political thought and the policies of the Chinese government have been dominated by Mao Tse-Dong. Mao's repeated stress on the importance of remoulding the *image* of the world in order to change it clearly reflects an intellectualistic and voluntaristic view of change. In sinicizing Marxism-Leninism, therefore, Mao gave a primacy to consciousness and will rather than to the materialistic factors stressed by others in this Western intellectual tradition. This accounts for Mao's stress on 'cultural revolution.'

But Mao extended his radical anti-traditionalism beyond China as 'a total-istic attack on the culture of the bourgeois West, in which at a certain point he included Soviet Russia' (Lin, 1979, p. 158). This critique of the West marks a break with the earlier anti-traditionalists. Yet in Mao's thought and actions there is still a *tension* between his Chinese revolutionary nationalism and the traditional Chinese ordering of the world in a totalistic and hierarchical way.

Since Mao's death in 1976 China has 'opened up' to more overt dealing with the rest of the world. The ambivalence about trading with barbarians remains, even if China cannot without great cost continue to challenge the new world it came into contact and conflict with in the nineteenth century. But a national ideology, whatever Mao's claims on its behalf, is never enough to build an alternative global order in the face of a world-market in which uneven development is endemic (Harris, 1979). 'To end one's victimization . . . one tries literally to change places' (Friedman, 1979 p. 217). This is the choice, after one hundred years of resistance and challenge, that China may have finally made.

Japan, like China, has a population that is highly homogeneous, at least compared to the United States and many other countries. But Japan in the mid-nineteenth century was if anything less unified politically than China. It consisted of a number of semi-autonomous fiefdoms rather than a single cul-turally unified nation. Although there was a common core of cultural attri-butes, up until the 1930s there were many mutually unintelligible dialects of Japanese and much regional variation in social and economic life. The mod-ern homogeneity of Japan has been created and is maintained through national social policy.

However, the amazing national mobilization characteristic of modern Japan is not based on coercion. Rather, it exploits a peculiar cultural inheritance:

> In the pre-modern Japanese village hardly any household specialized in any occupation other than agriculture, the only exceptions being the blacksmith, for instance, the general store and the local priest . . . This is completely the oppo-site of caste ideology, in which division of labour and the interdependence of groups are the basic principles of social organization. . . . These characteristics of Japanese society assist the development of the state political organization. Competition and hostile relations between the civil powers facilitate the accep-tance of state power, (Nakane, 1970, pp. 105–6)

The ability of the Japanese state, therefore, to organize a positive response to the challenge of the modern world-economy was rooted in the Japanese cul-tural order. It was the state, as we saw in Chapter 5, that undertook the reorganization of the Japanese government and economy after the Meiji Res-toration in 1868. As T. Smith (1979, pp. 270–1) insists:

> It was the state that insisted on agrarian reform in order to accelerate industrial development; it was the state that invested in a whole range of industrial enter-prises where merchant capital at first feared to enter; it was the state that absorbed as many samurai as it could into its bureaucracies and broke the

resistance of the rest; it was the state that began modern systems of banking, taxation and education in Japan.

Of course, these dramatic reactions cannot be separated from the threat that the world-economy was seen by Japanese élites as posing to Japan. The state-enforced isolation of Japan from the rest of the world in the Tokugawa Period (1636–1868) was ended when isolation was seen as an insufficient defence against foreign incursions. Before the mid-nineteenth century Japan escaped colonial rule in part because it was perceived as poor in markets and resources. But when faced by a dramatic increase in foreign interest it was the ability of the state to mobilize people and resources to ensure continued Japanese control over the Japanese economy that enabled Japan to join the modern world-economy on *its* terms rather than those of a colonial power.

Indeed, since World War II and the defeat of Japan's attempt to turn its successful early industrialization into a territorial empire, the institutions developed in the early Meiji period – central government planning, close government business cooperation, and centralized capital accumulation and formal training programmes – have turned out to be better adapted to the contemporary world-economy than those of either Europe or the United States. Vogel (1980, pp. 255–6) summarizes admirably:

> Unlike other nations inundated by Western dominance, the Japanese beginning in the late nineteenth century moved with eagerness and speed to bring in foreign patterns rather than have them brought in; thus they became the masters of change rather than the victims. Other countries were devastated by foreign influence, but Japan was invigorated.

Summary

In this chapter we have described the historical systems that the modern world-economy has progressively incorporated since expanding from its European base. We have stressed the following points:

- Local isolation or autonomy was rarely complete even before the arrival of the world-economy

- Stage or evolutionary theories of development are dangerously misleading accounts of economic growth and social change

- Three principles can underlie economic transactions: reciprocity, redistribution, and market-exchange

- Market-exchange is pre-eminently *the* principle of the modern world economy

- Different principles are associated with different types of independent system that have distinctive political-economic and geographical attributes

- Incorporation into the modern world-economy took a variety of different forms

- Some independent systems have contributed to the world-economy in the form of distinctive adaptations and challenges

The next chapter is directed towards understanding the spatial transformation consequent to the expansion of the modern world-economy.

8

The Dynamics of
Interdependence:
Transformation at the
Periphery

If local isolation was rarely complete and development was rarely totally independent, the coming of the modern world-economy led to greater and greater interaction between different parts of the world. In this chapter we focus on the cumulative consequences of this increased interdependence for those regions incorporated into the world-economy on terms initially and decisively disadvantageous to them. This is *not* to say that the terms of inter-dependence have always remained absolutely disadvantageous, although this is true, for example, in the case of Central America and large parts of Sub-Saharan Africa. Particularly since the late 1960s, the major oil-producing countries (e.g. Saudi-Arabia, Iran, Venezuela, Nigeria, Indonesia) and the NICs have challenged the static picture of a 'fixed' industrial core and a 'fixed' non-industrial periphery. The world-economy has a vibrant semi-periphery.

This chapter begins with a discussion of how existing economies were transformed into colonial ones. A second section identifies the major ways in which these colonial economies were enmeshed and maintained within the world-economy. A third section identifies the importance of frameworks of administration introduced by Europeans. A fourth section discusses the cultural mechanisms that facilitated integration into the world-economy. The final two sections explore the contexts of change in the nature of interdependence since the 1960s, respectively the global context (New International Division of Labour, decolonization, and the Cold War) and new political-economic strategies that challenge the dominant world order.

Colonial Economies and the Transformation of Space

The modern world-economy began with the global expansion of trade and conquest by European merchants, adventurers and statesmen (Fig. 8.1). But a distinction should be drawn between pre-capitalist colonial rule, notably that of Spain and Portugal in Latin America, and the new colonialism that was associated with the growth and global expansion of West European capitalism, beginning in the sixteenth century and itself undergoing successive shifts in development. The major purpose of pre-capitalist colonialism was the extraction of tribute from subject peoples and its major mechanisms involved political-territorial control. In contrast, the 'new colonialism' was associated primarily with economic objectives and mechanisms. Direct political-territorial control, though often advantageous, was not essential. The emphasis initially was upon the exploitation of raw materials. After the industrial revolution in Britain, however, markets became an equally important objective. Realizing both these objectives required a restructuring of the economic landscapes of the colonized societies.

Territorial conquest, with or without the elimination of indigenous peoples, and the planting of either settler enclaves or slave plantations and mining enterprises were the major features of European expansion through the eighteenth century. For much of the nineteenth century, however, many societies that remained or became formally independent were under the economic domination of European and, increasingly, American capitalists. With the 'German challenge' to British hegemony in the 1870s, there was a new 'scramble' for territorial conquest as rival colonial powers attempted to pre-empt one another, especially in Africa. This coincided with the emergence of capital export as a major stimulus to intervention and domination.

In both territorial and interactional forms, capitalist expansion entailed a forcible transformation of pre-capitalist societies whereby their economies were internally disarticulated and integrated externally with the world-economy. They were no longer locally oriented but had now to focus on the production of raw materials and foodstuffs for the 'core' economies. Often

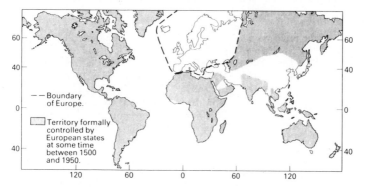

Fig 8.1   The geographical extent of European political control of the periphery
Source: Taylor (1985) Fig. 5, p. 67

they became extremely dependent on monoculture in order to confer the blessings of 'comparative advantage' (the purported benefits of specializing in commodities that a country can produce at a lower *relative* cost while import- ing commodities for which its own production costs are *relatively* higher) on the developed world. At the same time they also provided markets for the manufactured goods exchanged in return. For many parts of the world this relationship still holds true today.

As time wore on, plantations and extractive industries were sometimes supplemented by labour-intensive manufacturing that took advantage of cheap colonial labour. By the mid-twentieth century, Latin America, Asia and Africa were organically linked to and financially dependent upon West- ern Europe and the United States. The emergence of the United States as a dominant force and the growth of the Soviet bloc, however, undermined the monopoly of political control exercised by the European powers over large parts of the world. A process of decolonization began with the independence of the South Asian countries in 1947. This brought the *possibility*, however constrained (as the experience of Latin America, 'independent' since 1820, shows), of more autonomous development.

The late nineteenth century was an especially critical period in the creation of colonial economies (Fig. 8.2). Whole regions became specialized in the production of a specific raw material, food crop or 'stimulant'. Many of these had a prior history, such as the sugar-producing areas of the Caribbean or the cotton-growing regions of the United States, India, and Egypt. But the Great Depression (1883–96), a major downturn in the world-economy (the IIB phase of Kondratieff's long-cycle) – due, among other things, to decreased profitability in manufacturing – ushered in a major spurt in the global expan- sion of capitalism and intensified regional specialization. During this time- period more and more resources and labour were drawn into an increasingly differentiated world-economy (Wolf, 1982).

Adam Smith and David Ricardo, writing well before this period, had envis- aged a global division of labour in which each country would freely choose the commodities it was most suited to produce and freely exchange its optimal commodity for the optimal commodities of others. Unfortunately, this eco- nomic vision ignores the historical-political conditions under which commodities are selected and the costs faced by a specialized economy in terms of vulnerability to the vagaries of 'world' demand.

In the late nineteenth century, 'choice' of commodity was often imposed by force or through market domination. Moreover, once embroiled in the global system of regional specialization, an economy had to organize its factors of production in order to foster capital growth or fall by the wayside. At the same time, other regions, without some initial advantage in raw material, climate, social organization or accessibility, became providers of labour power to the new outposts of global capitalism.

Three examples, out of a host of possibilities, illustrate how externally- oriented colonial economies were created on the basis of regional specialization:

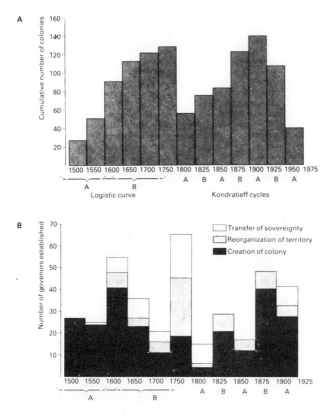

Fig 8.2   Colonies and long waves. A. The two long waves of colonial expansion and contraction; B. Establishment of colonies 1500–1925
Source: Taylor (1985) Figs, 6 and 7, p. 76

bananas in Central America, rubber in Malaya and tea in Sri Lanka (see Wolf, 1982, Chapter 11 for other examples).

Bananas are hardly a major food staple, but the creation of banana plantations in the late nineteenth century affected many areas, especially in Central America. Introduced into the Americas by the Spaniards, the banana became a staple crop among the lowland populations of Central America. In the 1870s it became a plantation crop as an American entrepreneur engaged in railroad construction in Costa Rica experimented with commercial banana production to increase the profitability of his railroad. As a result of this initiative was developed the United Fruit Company, incorporated in 1889 as a corporation engaged in the marketing of bananas from Central America in the United States.

Over the years, the Company produced bananas on plantation-estates in Costa Rica, Panama, Honduras, Colombia and Ecuador. Geographic dispersal had a number of advantages; it enabled the Company to offset political pressures in any one host country. Dispersal also allowed it to take advantage of suitable environments in different locations, thus reducing the chance that floods, hurricanes, soil depletion and plant diseases could bring production to a halt in any one of them. To further reduce these risks, the Company acquired a great deal more land than it could use at any one time, to hold as a reserve against the future. In some areas it formed relationships with local cultivators who grew bananas and then sold them to the Company. (Wolf, 1982, 324)

Much of the labour on the plantations was recruited locally, especially in Colombia and Ecuador, but in parts of Central America workers were brought from the English-speaking islands of the Caribbean. This resulted because of the difficulty the Company faced in obtaining labourers from the populated highlands to work in the lowlands and the preference for a workforce that could be socially isolated and made wholly dependent upon the Company. The role of these foreign workers gradually decreased as host governments limited immigration and encouraged their native populations to engage in wage labour on the plantations. Bananas are still an important export crop, especially for Panama and Costa Rica.

Wild rubber from Brazil dominated the world market for most of the nineteenth century. In 1876, however, Amazonian rubber seeds were smuggled from Brazil to England where they were prepared for planting in Malaya. Malayan rubber plantations grew from 5,000 acres in 1900 to 1,250,000 acres in 1913. During this expansion, an original planter class was supplanted by a class of managers for companies operating from London (Jackson, 1968). Labourers were initially imported from southern India but over time many plantations came to employ local Malays. Although plantation production remained dominant, many Malay cultivators tapped their own rubber trees as a source of cash income. Rubber increasingly replaced irrigated rice as the major commodity produced by small-scale proprietors. It remains so today.

Finally, among the range of commodities destined for consumption in the industrial world, some were neither foodstuffs (such as bananas) nor industrial crops (such as rubber). Such commodities as sugar, tea, coffee, cocoa, tobacco and opium were of fundamental importance in the global expansion of capitalism. Explaining the popularity of these 'stimulants' is not easy. Some accounts suggest that the work behaviour required under industrialization favoured the sale of these stimulants (except opium, a special case) because they provided 'quick energy' and prolonged work activity. Others suggest that some (e.g. sugar and cocoa) provided low-cost substitutes for the traditional and increasingly costly diet of pre-industrial Europe. Whatever the basis to demand, by the late nineteenth century the stimulants were of great and increasing importance in world trade (see Mintz, 1985, for a splendid discussion of sugar and its role in world trade).

Tea had become 'the drink' of English court circles in the late seventeenth century. It came entirely from China. Demand was so great that in the early eighteenth century tea replaced silk as the main item carried by British ships in the Chinese coastal trade. At the time of the American War of Independence, as the 'Boston Tea Party' reminds us, tea was the third largest import, after textiles and iron goods, of the American colonies.

Some tea plantations were established in Assam (NE India) in the 1840s, but until the opening of the Suez Canal Indian tea could not compete with the Chinese tea carried by the famous clipper ships around the Cape of Good Hope. With the opening of the canal and decreasing cost of steamship transportation, Indian 'black' teas became commercially competitive with the green teas of China. In the 1870s tea plantations spread with great speed throughout the uplands of Ceylon (Sri Lanka). This was done by confiscating peasant land through the device of 'royal condemnation' and then selling it to planters. By 1903 over 400,000 acres were planted in tea shrubs.

Tea cultivation is extremely labour intensive. To obtain the necessary labour, the Ceylon tea planters imported Tamil labourers from southern India. These Tamils, not to be confused with the Sri Lankan Tamils of northern and eastern Sri Lanka, now number over 1 million people, in a region in which the upland or Kandyan Sinhalese are about 2 million. As a consequence an ethnic conflict has been imposed on top of an economic conflict between Sinhalese cultivators and Tamil plantation workers. Tea remains an important export crop in the contemporary Sri Lankan economy.

Many other examples could be added to these three to demonstrate the degree to which regional specialization was the classic motif of the colonial economies as they developed at an accelerating rate in the late nineteenth century. The Great Depression of that time stimulated an unprecedented expansion of the world-economy into all parts of the globe as European and American capitalists sought to maintain capital accumulation as industrial production slowed down. Commodity production for a world market was not new but in its late nineteenth century 'explosion' it 'incorporated pre-existing networks of exchange and created new itineraries between continents; it fostered regional specialization and initiated world-wide movements of commodities' (Wolf, 1982, p. 352).

Economic Mechanisms of Enmeshment and Maintenance in the Colonial World-Economy

How was it that the regional specialization that began in the late nineteenth century was possible? And how did it evolve over time? Answering these questions requires us to focus on the means by which an integrated world-economy was created: flows of capital investment, networks of communication and marketing, movements of commodities and people, and transportation – urban networks as channels of diffusion and concentration.

The period 1860–70 inherited from the earlier centuries of colonial expansion two major systems of economic interaction, an Atlantic system built upon the 'Triangular Trade' between Europe, Africa and the Americas (Fig. 8.3),

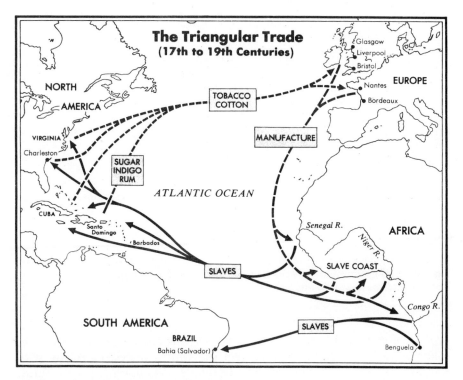

Fig 8.3   The Atlantic system, 1650–1850
Source: Duignan and Gann (1985) Map 1, p. 12

and a Eurasian system built upon trade with India and the Far East. In the mid-nineteenth century the Atlantic system in its classic form collapsed. It was replaced by a system based on a mix of competitive colonialism, regional specialization, and investment in infrastructure (especially railways).

Between 1830 and 1876 there was a vast increase in the number of colonies and the number of people under colonial rule. There was also a tremendous expansion of foreign investment by European states and capitalists in the late nineteenth and early twentieth centuries (Table 8.1). Moreover, there was an important shift in the geographical distribution of both investment and

Table 8.1: Stock of foreign capital investment held by Europe 1825–1915 ($ billion)

	1825	1855	1885	1915
UK	0.5	2.3	7.8	19.5
France	0.1	1.0	3.3	8.6
Germany	0.1	1.0	1.9	6.7
Others	—	—	—	11.4
Total	0.7	4.3	13.0	46.2

Source: Warren (1980) p. 62

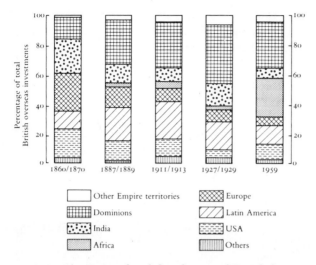

Fig 8.4   The geographical distribution of British foreign investment, 1860–1959
Source: Hobsbawm (1968) p. 303

exports. British trade and investment, to use the most important example, shifted away from India, Europe and the United States, especially with respect to investment in the first two and with respect to exports to the third, from the 1870s on. South America and the Dominions (Australia, New Zealand, Canada and South Africa) became more important, especially with respect to investment. However, the pattern was to fluctuate considerably over the years as some regions/states increased and others decreased in attractiveness to investors (Fig. 8.4).

The geographical switching of investment, however, was not always economic in motivation. In particular, European incorporation of Africa into the world-economy was based largely on competitive colonialism. Local settlers, as in South Africa, sometimes developed their own local imperialisms and when challenged by hostile natives called in the Motherland. The relative weakness of many African polities also invited direct intervention. Once one European state was involved, others were tempted to engage in pre-emptive strikes to limit the damage to their 'interests'. Between 1880 and 1914 Africa was divided into a patchwork of European colonies and protectorates (Fig. 8.5).

At the global scale the colonial system was bound together by a network of steamship and communication (postal, telegraph, and, later, telephone) routes (Latham, 1978, 1981). These became progressively more dense and interconnected from the 1860s onwards. The Suez and Panama Canals were important in providing shorter and less hazardous routes between 'home ports' in Europe and North America and colonial destinations. By 1913 the world-economy was effectively integrated by a system of regularly scheduled

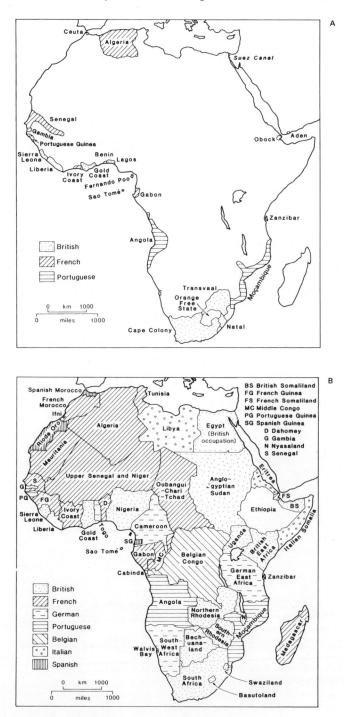

Fig 8.5   The colonization of Africa. A: 1880; B:1914
Source: Christopher (1984) Figs. 2.1 and 2.2, p. 28–29

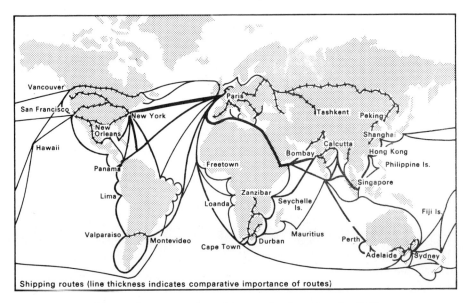

Fig 8.6   World steamship routes, by volume and value of trade, 1913
Source: Latham (1978) Map 2, p. 33

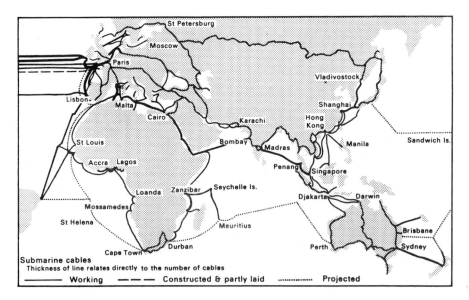

Fig 8.7   The telegraph system in Asia and Africa, 1897
Source: Latham (1978) Map 3, p. 36

steamship routes (Fig. 8.6). A world telegraph system enabled orders to be placed and shipments to be embarked for a large number of ports around the world (Fig. 8.7).

Within colonies, railway building was the major mechanism of spatial transformation. A good idea of how linear port–hinterland transport routes developed, especially in Africa, is provided by Taaffe, Morril and Gould's sequential model of transport development (Fig. 8.8). Only in a few cases, however, did railway networks develop beyond sequence D. In most of Africa and Asia, with the important exceptions of India, South Africa and north China, railways were not mechanisms for creating integrated colonial economies but, rather, means for moving a basic export commodity for shipment to Europe or North America.

However, railways were often an important investment in their own right rather than a burdensome state responsibility. This was especially the case in South America and China, if much less so in India and Africa (Latham, 1978). In Argentina, for example, though the road and railway networks were oriented towards the River Plate estuary and the capital city of Buenos Aires, they provided a progressively dense grid for the rich commercial agriculture of the Argentinian pampas (Fig. 8.9). This produced a transport system considerably more interconnected and integrated than the simple linear systems prevalent in Central America, SE Asia and most of Africa. In short, spatial integration into the colonial world-economy did not take the same form everywhere.

Whatever the precise nature of railway networks, there was a tendency for all networks to focus on one or, at most, several coastal ports. These became 'privileged' locations, often assuming the role of administrative as well as economic centre for the entire colony. Specialization in the export of raw materials and concentration of administrative functions thus had the effect of stimulating the disproportionate growth of these 'links' to the world-economy. This was especially marked in India and Africa.

But the character of the colonial system also put limits on the growth of the dominant or 'primate' settlements. There was only a limited stimulus to the growth of a distinctive *urban* economy. The orientation of urban networks was towards exploitation of hinterlands rather than an industry– and service–based urban economy. It was only with political independence that a new dynamic for urban growth occurred as the primate cities shifted from being mechanisms for colonial control to their contemporary role 'as the corporate representative of the people of the former colony' (Fiala and Kamens, 1986, 28). As Rondinelli (1983, p. 49) points out 'colonial activities often stimulated the growth of secondary cities. In some cases they were encouraged to grow as colonial administrative posts or as transfer and processing centres for the exploitation of mineral and agricultural resources in the interior of a country.'

Regions without a history of urbanization before colonialism were not surprisingly the most easily and strongly reoriented to the colonial

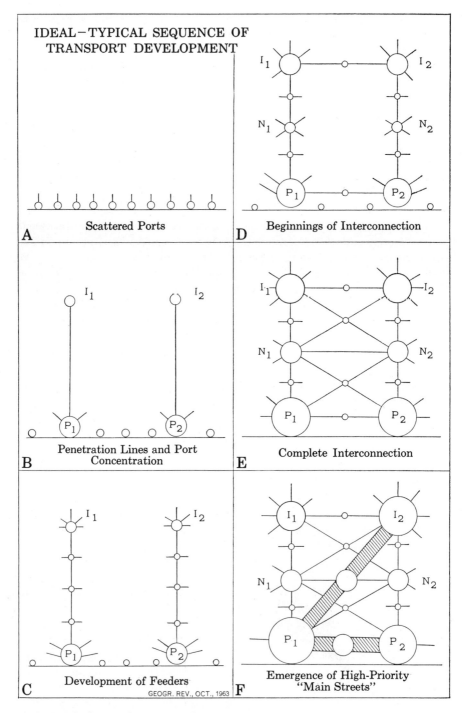

Fig 8.8 Ideal-typical sequence of transport system development
Source: Taaffe *et al.* (1963) p. 504

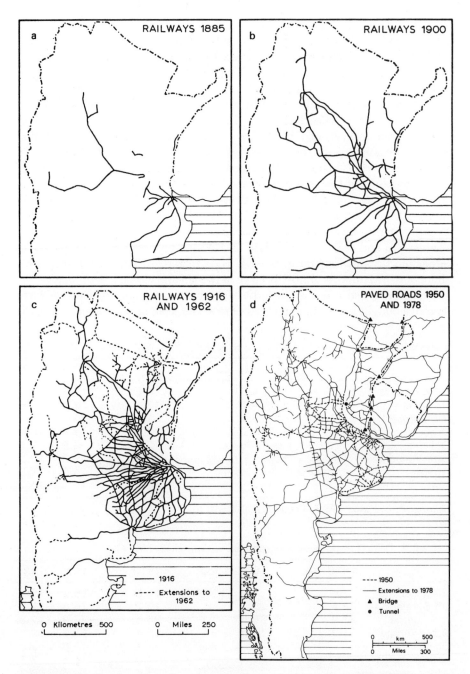

Fig 8.9 The development of roads and railways in Argentina, 1885–1978
Source: Crossley (1983) Fig. 9.3, p. 401

world-economy. In Malaysia, for example, cities grew up where crops were grown for export or where other exportable commodities (tin, especially) were exploited. These cities were connected by railway and road to port cities which grew as processing and transfer points. In western Nigeria, a region with a long pre-colonial history of urbanization, roads and railways were often built to bypass traditional centres of trade such as Ife, Benin City and Sokoto. New, more effectively *colonial* cities grew up at nodes in the transportation network. As one study notes 'fortune rode the trains. [Towns] that received terminals grew, but those that did not stagnated or declined, as did many river ports' (Gugler and Flanagan, 1978, pp. 27–8).

The outcome of the new extension of the world-economy and the intensification of trade within regions already incorporated was a substantial increase in world trade (Latham, 1978). How important was the contribution of Asia, Africa and Latin America? The answer is: of great importance (Tables 8.2 and 8.3). By 1913 Asia and Africa provided more exports than either the US and Canada or the UK and Ireland. In 1913, Asia also had a share of world imports almost as large as the US and Canada combined.

What happened was that the industrializing countries of Europe and North America bought increasing amounts of raw materials and foodstuffs from the

Table 8.2: World exports by geographical region, 1876–1937 (%)

	1876–80	1896–1900	1913	1928	1937
US & Canada	11.7	14.5	14.8	19.8	17.1
UK & Ireland	16.3	14.2	13.1	11.5	10.6
NW Europe	31.9	34.4	33.4	25.1	25.8
Other Europe	16.0	15.2	12.4	11.4	10.6
Oceania			2.5	2.9	3.5
Latin America	24.1	21.7	8.3 — 26.3	9.8	10.2
Africa			3.7	4.0	5.3
Asia			11.8	15.5	16.9

Source: P. L. Yates 1959: Table 6, p. 32

Table 8.3: World imports by geographical region, 1876–1937 (%)

	1876–80	1896–1900	1913	1928	1937
US & Canada	7.4	8.9	11.5	15.2	13.9
UK & Ireland	22.5	20.5	15.2	15.8	17.8
NW Europe	31.9	36.5	36.5	27.9	27.8
Other Europe	11.9	11.0	13.4	12.5	10.2
Oceania			2.4	2.6	2.8
Latin America	26.3	23.0	7.0 — 23.4	7.6	7.2
Africa			3.6	4.6	6.2
Asia			10.4	13.8	14.1

Source: P. L. Yates 1959: Table 7, p. 33

undeveloped economies and ran up large trade deficits with these regions. Britain, however, as a result of its free trade policy, ran up substantial deficits as a result of importing manufactured goods and investing heavily in the industrializing countries (especially the United States and Germany). In turn, Britain financed its deficits through the export of manufactured goods to the undeveloped world. Thus the circle of international trade and dependence was closed (Saul, 1960).

India and China were particularly important to this world pattern of trade and payments. It was Britain's trade with India and China that compensated for a negative balance of payments with the United States, industrial Europe, Canada, South Africa and New Zealand. Without the 'Asian surplus' Britain would not have been able to subsidize the growth of these other economies. So, far from being 'peripheral' to the growth of the world-economy, the undeveloped world, especially India and China, was vital (Latham, 1978, 1981).

Between 1918 and 1939 this system of multilateral trade suffered a number of setbacks. One was the overall decline in trade as the world experienced a major depression. But the worst was the decline in Britain's relative position as the linchpin of the colonial world-economy. This reflected both successful industrialization in India and China displacing British products (especially cotton textiles) and increased competition from Japan in Britain's 'traditional' colonial markets. But another problem was the overproduction of the main export crops and raw materials (Baker, 1981). As a consequence, commodity prices fell and so did demand for manufactured goods. The successful expansion of plantations and mines, therefore, ultimately undermined the system of capital circulation and accumulation that their introduction had brought into existence in the nineteenth century (Latham, 1981).

The onset of the Great Depression of the 1930s effectively ended the expansionist regime of international trade established in the late nineteenth century. The major industrial states reacted to the Depression by raising tariffs and devaluing their currencies. These shifts in economic policy were premised on the assumption that Britain would remain 'open' as the linchpin of the colonial world-economy. But, as Stein (1984, p. 375) puts it: 'Depression left Britain unable and unwilling to accept an increasingly asymmetric bargain.' Not until the 1970s would world trade return to the relative levels that it had achieved in the early 1900s.

The keys to economic recovery in Western Europe and the United States were provided by military spending and massive increases in domestic consumption of domestic manufactures. Although this did lead to increased demand for many of the industrial raw materials and foodstuffs produced in the 'periphery', there was no longer the 'cross-over' system of trading linkages. If anything, the European colonial states and, above all, the United States now came to have *direct* links to specific sites of exploitation in the periphery without the necessity of the infrastructure and administrative investments that had limited short-run payoffs. This approach favoured direct investment and the creation of subsidiaries by multinational firms rather than portfolio investment and conventional trade (Tables 8.4 and 8.5). Advantages hitherto specific to the United States – the cost-effectiveness of large plants, economies of process, product and market integration – had become the proprietary rights of large firms (Dunning,1983). The world was now *their* oyster, rather than that of the colonial states. 'American governments could preach against colonialism while large American [and other] firms colonized the world' (Agnew, 1987, p. 62).

The Influence of Colonial Administration on Interdependence

Many of those who colonized the world from Europe, in both the sixteenth and the nineteenth centuries, saw their activities as part of a historic 'mission' of Western civilization: to bring progress to backward and barbarian peoples (Ranger, 1976; Spence, 1980). Lord Lugard, the famous British colonial administrator, maintained that Britain stood in a kind of apostolic succession of empire – 'as Roman imperialism . . . led the wild barbarians of these islands along the path of progress, so in Africa today we are re-paying the debt, and bringing to the dark places of the earth . . . the torch of culture and progress' (quoted in Ranger, 1976, pp. 115–16). At best the political ideas of the European imperialists were that 'political power tended constantly to deposit itself in the hands of a natural aristocracy, that power so deposited was morally valid, and that it was not to be tamely surrendered before the claims of abstract democratic ideals, but was to be asserted and exercised with justice and mercy' (Stokes,1959, p. 69).

The chief problem was to understand and pacify the indigenous colonized. The Nigerian novelist Chinua Achebe (1975, p. 5) puts this as follows: 'To the colonialist mind it was always of the utmost importance to be able to say: *I know my natives*, a claim which implied two things at once: (a) that the native was really quite simple and (b) that understanding him and controlling him went hand in hand – understanding being a precondition for control and control constituting adequate proof of understanding'. This approach provided the ideology for what Hopkins (1973, p. 189) has called the 'art of light administration', administration without too much expense or explicit violence.

However, the colonial regimes themselves never amounted to more than a thin veneer of European officials and soldiers on top of complex networks of local collaborators. In India in the 1930s, for example, 4,000 British civil servants, 60,000 soldiers and 90,000 civilians ruled a country of 300 million people. The British were able to do this

> by constructing a delicately balanced network through which they gained the support of certain favoured economic groups (the Zamindars acting as landed

Table 8.4: Estimated stock of accumulated foreign direct investment by recipient country or area, 1914–78

	1914 $m	%	1938 $m	%	1960 $bn	%	1971 $bn	%	1978 $bn	%
Developed countries	5,235	37.2	8,346	34.3	37.7	67.3	108.4	65.2	251.7	69.6
North America										
USA	1,450	10.3	1,800	7.4	7.6	13.9	13.9	8.4	42.4	11.7
Canada	800	5.7	2,296	9.4	12.9	23.7	27.9	16.8	43.2	11.9
Western Europe	1,100	7.8	1,800	7.4	12.5	22.9	47.4	28.5	136.2	37.7
Of which UK	(200)	(1.4)	(700)	(2.9)	(5.0)	(9.2)	(13.4)	(8.1)	(32.5)	(9.0)
Other European	1,400	9.9	400	1.6	neg.	neg.	neg.	neg.	neg.	neg.
Of which Russia	(1,000)	(7.1)	—	—	—	—	—	—	—	—
Australasia and South Africa	450	3.2	1,950	8.0	3.6	6.6	16.7	10.0	23.9	6.6
Japan	35	0.2	100	0.4	0.1	0.2	2.5	1.5	6.0	1.7
Developing countries	8,850	62.8	15,969	65.7	17.6	32.3	51.4	30.9	100.4	27.8
Latin America	4,600	32.7	7,481	30.8	8.5	15.6	29.6	17.8	52.5	14.5
Africa	900	6.4	1,799	7.4	3.0	5.5	8.8	5.3	11.1	3.1
Asia	2,950	20.9	6,068	25.0	4.1	7.5	7.8	4.7	25.2	7.0
Of which China	(1,100)	(7.8)	(1,400)	(5.8)	(neg.)	(neg.)	(neg.)	(neg.)	(neg.)	(neg.)
Of which India and Ceylon	(450)	(3.2)	(1,359)	(5.6)	(1.1)	(2.0)	(1.5)	(0.9)	(2.5)	(0.7)
Southern Europe					0.5	0.9	1.7	1.0	3.4	0.9
Middle East	400	2.8	621	2.6	1.5	2.8	3.5	2.1	8.2	2.3
International and unallocated	neg.	neg.	na	na	na	na	6.5	3.9	9.5	2.6
Total	14,085	100.0	24,315	100.0	54.3	100.0	166.3	100.0	361.6	100.0

Source: Dunning (1983) p. 88

Table 8.5: Estimated stock of accumulated foreign direct investment by country of origin, 1914–78

	1914		1938		1960		1971		1978	
	$m	%	$m	%	$bn	%	$bn	%	$bn	%
Developed countries	14,302	100.0	26,350	100.0	66.0	99.0	168.1	97.7	380.3	96.8
North America										
USA	2,652	18.5	7,300	27.7	32.8	49.2	82.8	48.1	162.7	41.4
Canada	150	1.0	700	2.7	2.5	3.8	6.5	3.8	13.6	3.5
Western Europe										
UK	6,500	45.5	10,500	39.8	10.8	16.2	23.7	13.8	50.7	12.9
Germany	1,500	10.5	350	1.3	0.8	1.2	7.3	4.2	28.6	7.3
France	1,750	12.2	2,500	9.5	4.1	6.1	7.3	4.2	14.9	3.8
Belgium					1.3	1.9	2.4	1.4	5.4	1.4
Italy					1.1	1.6	3.0	1.7	5.4	1.4
Netherlands	1,250	8.7	3,500	13.3	7.0	10.5	13.8	8.0	28.4	7.2
Sweden					0.4	0.6	2.4	1.4	6.0	1.5
Switzerland					2.0	3.0	9.5	5.5	27.8	7.1
Others										
Russia	300	2.1	450	1.7	–		–		–	
Japan	20	0.1	750	2.8	0.5	0.7	4.4	2.6	26.8	6.8
Australia										
New Zealand	180	1.3	300	1.1	1.5	2.2	2.5	1.4	4.8	1.2
South Africa										
Others	neg.	neg.	neg.	neg.	1.2	1.8	2.5	1.4	5.2	1.3
Developing countries	neg.	neg.	neg.	neg.	0.7	1.0	4.0	2.3	12.5	3.2
Total	14,302	100.0	26,350	100.0	66.7	100.0	172.1	100.0	392.8	100.0

Source: Dunning (1983) p. 87.

tax collectors in areas such as Bengal, for example), different traditional power holders (especially after the Great Mutiny of 1857, the native princes), warrior tribes (such as the Sikhs of the Punjab), and aroused minority groups such as the Muslims (Smith, 1981, p. 52).

This kind of brokerage system was to be found in every colonial territory without a large European settler population. Sometimes a foreign economic presence was crucial (the Chinese in SE Asia; the Lebanese in W. Africa; European settlers in Algeria and Kenya). Often there were alliances with new or traditional ruling groups (the Princely States in Malaya; the Ottoman bureaucracies in Tunisia and Morocco; the Hashemite family in Mesopotamia and Syria). Above all, local rivalries were exploited to advantage, as in Madagascar, India and China. Even in the face of nominal local political independence, as in China or Latin America, colonial imperatives and administrative models had considerable influence through imported school curricula and business practices.

Alliances and administrative forms were far from static and differed from colony to colony and between colonial powers. But one change was permanent. The new colonies, often vastly bigger than the territorial units they superseded, created markets of unprecedented size. Internal tolls and other restraints on trade disappeared. Sumptuary laws that prevented people of low status from acquiring luxury goods were abolished. All forms of servitude that interfered with the wage economy were outlawed. The great tribal migrations of eastern and southern Africa were brought to a close. New judicial methods were introduced and old ones were eliminated. Schools and hierarchical systems of local administration were established (Christopher, 1984; Overton, 1987).

In Africa the colonial powers operated in different ways. The British administration was more civilian and decentralized than the French and Belgian administrations. Its officials 'prided themselves on being gentlemen and amateurs, rather than on being military, legal or administrative specialists. The British pioneers set up an administrative hybrid based partly on British metropolitan models and partly on models derived from colonial India and Ireland' (Gann and Duignan 1978, p. 355). In particular, there was a dispersal of administrative power.

Any description of the particularities of administration in the various territories would require much more space than is available here (see Gann and Duignan, 1978; and Gifford and Louis, 1971 for some of the details). Suffice it to say that in Nigeria, Britain's most populous colony in Africa, the coastal (Lagos) and northern (Kaduna) regions were administered in completely different ways. The coastal region had a long-standing commercial base and export trade, tied to Liverpool and England's northern industries. Consequently 'Lagos governors . . . tried to please north country British businessmen by emphasizing the needs of trade, communications and public health, by avoiding wars and punitive expeditions, by their reluctance to impose direct taxation, and by their determination to maintain a policy aimed at 'peaceful penetration' and commercial development' (Gann and Duignan, 1978, p. 209). The northern region was a borderland and its international trade was limited. 'In this region the tone of administration was military; the British ruling group was linked to London and the Home Counties rather than to Lancashire; . . . The northern administrative ethos was shaped by Lord Lugard, whose administrative gospel blended muscular Christianity with a military puritanism that exalted the virtues of physical fitness, self-denial and 'character'. Government emphasized prestige instead of profit, hierarchy in place of diversity' (Gann and Duignan, 1978, p. 209).

In all colonies, however, priority was given to communication, transport and medical care. Railways were built both to promote agricultural and mineral exports and to facilitate the movement of police and army detachments. Post offices, telegraphs and telephones gradually tied together the local administrative units. Indicative of the centrality of transportation networks to colonial administration was the fact that public works departments were often the first government units established in a territory. As Gann and Duignan (1978, p. 271) emphasize: 'By 1914 all the British African dependencies possessed a basic infrastructure of specialized services, the most important of which was the creation of a modern transportation network.'

An important cultural import into the colonies, therefore, was the assumption that the state should both encourage development and provide social services – education, agricultural instruction, etc. 'The very notion of the state as a territorial entity independent of ethnic or kinship ties, operating through impersonal rules, was one of the most revolutionary concepts bequeathed by colonialism to post-colonial precedent, . . . All of them have taken over, in some form or other, both the boundaries and the administrative institutions of their erstwhile Western overlords' (Gann and Duignan, 1978, p. 347).

Mechanisms of Cultural Integration

The imposition of colonial rule, and, more generally, Western penetration of societies outside Europe, involved a great deal of violence and war. But, once established, 'law and order' involved the imposition of Western values as much as terminating local conflicts and suppressing practices (witchcraft, infanticide, bride burning) that Europeans regarded as 'barbaric.'

The social effects of Western values were paradoxical. On the one hand, old values were destroyed, as missionaries and schoolteachers attacked animistic creeds, polygamy and other customs. Families often broke up as some members 'converted' and others did not. On the other hand, the new ways were used by some people to establish new bases to authority. In particular, western-educated natives became indispensable to European rule and influence. Interpreters, clerks, foremen and police sergeants were cultural pioneers; they represented the new order and profited from it.

The economic effects were also double-edged. As restraints on trade disappeared, commercial agriculture and trade spread in extent and intensity. Yields increased as agricultural techniques improved, and trade proved more profitable as new communications linked previously isolated interiors with coastal entrepôts. Yet, as a consequence, the certainties and rhythms of local life broke down and traditional skills were devalued. Above all, new types of consumption, while adding to the comforts of life of those with sufficient disposable income, led to the destruction of many local industries and the growth of dependence on manufactured imports from the colonial 'motherland'. In this context, obligations to community and chief began to weaken. Money became the major metric for assessing social status. This was in part because money could help purchase an education. 'Education, in turn, brought power and influence. These new opportunities profoundly affected life in the village, and the village ceased to be an almost self-contained unit, absorbing all the interests of its people. Instead, cash-cropping and wage labour for limited periods gradually came to occupy a much more central position in the cultivator's life' (Gann and Duignan, 1978, p. 367).

The growth of 'free' labour was a process that was 'always uneven and idiosyncratic' (Marks and Rathbone, 1982, p. 13). It depended upon spatial variation in the extent of competition for labour; conflicts of interest between firms and the colonial states; and the availability of alternatives to wage labour (Sender and Smith, 1986). But once national labour and other markets were effectively created, the prospering of commercial enterprises (both foreign and indigenous), such as mines and plantations, depended upon an increasingly efficient and productive labour force to operate new equipment and machinery. This required measures to both increase labour-force stability (housing, minimum wages) and attempts to upgrade the health, literacy and skills of employees. Of course, employee organizations also played a role in pressuring for these changes. Consumption demands, and hence demands for higher incomes, tended to increase in concert with the increase in permanent wage employment (Sender and Smith, 1986).

It is evident that in many colonies there were dramatic improvements in education and health. In Africa in the period 1910–60 the number of children attending school grew much faster than had school enrollments in Europe in the boom years 1840–80. There were also significant increases in life expectancy (e.g. in Ghana in 1921 it was 28 years; in 1980 it was 44.8), and reductions in infant mortality rates.

To the British colonial authorities education was an important means of inculcating both 'modern' work habits and a commitment to the class structure of colonialism. At the centre of colonial education, was

> the idea of work – taught to those who lacked property – emphasizing regularity, the organization of time and human energy around the work routine, and the necessity of discipline. It was a moral and cultural concept . . . Prohibitions against drinking and dancing . . . were as much a part of changing concepts of labour as forced recruitment, vagrancy laws, and the insistence that workers put in regular hours. (Cooper, 1980, pp. 69–70)

But, above all, it was necessary 'to get workers to internalize cultural values and behaviour patterns that would define their role in the economy and society' (Cooper, 1980, p. 70).

This conception of education was particularly characteristic of the British colonies. Other colonies either failed to develop the capitalist labour markets to which it was a reaction (e.g. sections of French Sudan) or were severely underfunded for public activities (e.g. Belgian Congo and Portuguese colonies). But British policy brought a price. It was precisely the educated élite that 'formed the vanguard of the nationalist movements, and the more 'disciplined' African workers became, the more effective were their trade union organizations in pursuing not only economic, but political anti-colonial objectives.' (Sender and Smith, 1986, p. 66). As taught in colonial schools, Western concepts of 'democracy' and 'justice' served to undermine the legitimacy of the Western empires that had introduced them.

The growth of wage labour incorporated women as well as men into the colonial world-economy, although at significantly lower levels of participation. More importantly, however, the spread of wage employment disrupted existing sexual divisions of labour, often to the detriment of women (Joekes, 1987). Women remained powerfully constrained by family, marriage, religion, and so-called 'domestic duties', even while engaged in wage employment. But norms, power and traditional patterns of authority based on gender, as well as age, caste and lineage, were subject to radical challenge because of wage labour, education, migration, and urbanization. Lonsdale (1985, p. 730) quotes from one Zulu chief who in 1905 expressed his opposition to the cultural changes of the time as follows:

> Our sons elbow us away from the boiled mealies in the pot when we reach for a handful to eat, saying, 'we bought these, father', and when remonstrated with, our wives dare to raise their eyes and glare at us. It used not to be thus. If we chide or beat our wives and children for misconduct, they run off to the police and the magistrate fines us.

Cultural change was not always one way, however. Some pre-capitalist and pre-colonial social and religious institutions were strengthened. More accurately, perhaps, 'new' syncretic traditions were invented out of elements of past traditions. Mission-educated élites often invented mythic histories of ancient empires and new nationalist traditions both to legitimize their quests for political power and to protect themselves in the new labour markets (Ranger, 1984; Lonsdale, 1985; Van Onselen, 1982). Adaptation was at least as common as straightforward assimilation in many colonial settings.

Ultimately, however, cultural incorporation, whether by adaptation or assimilation, undermined the socio-political relation of dominance–subordination that colonialism existed to reproduce. Langley's (1983, p. 223) conclusion concerning American colonial adventures in the Caribbean is a fitting epitaph to the cultural contradictions of the entire colonial enterprise:

> Striving to teach by example, they found it necessary to denigrate the cultural

values of those whom they had come to save. . . . Their presence, even when it meant a peaceful society and material advancement, stripped Caribbean peoples of their dignity and constituted an unspoken American judgement of Caribbean inferiority. Little wonder, then, that the occupied were so 'ungrateful' for what Americans considered years of benign tutelage. But, then, Americans do not have in their epigrammatic repertory that old Spanish proverb that Mexicans long ago adopted: 'The wine is bitter, but it's our wine.'

The Changing Global Context of Interdependence

The colonial world-economy began to disintegrate after World War II. The 'cross-over' trading system had effectively ended in the 1930s. World War II's build-up of industrial capacity for military purposes in the United States and the Soviet Union and European decolonization further undermined the colonial world order. In the 1950s and 1960s the so-called Third World (of politically independent but non-aligned and less prosperous nations) was born (Pletsch, 1981). Large parts of Asia and Africa now joined Latin America as a largely non-industrial and ex-colonial but still 'dependent' World (Fig. 8.10).

As new states came into existence, so did attempts to stimulate industrial development and economic growth. From the Depression of the 1930s on, and especially during World War II, stagnation and shipping blockades had encouraged some import substitution in the colonies. Increasingly traders and

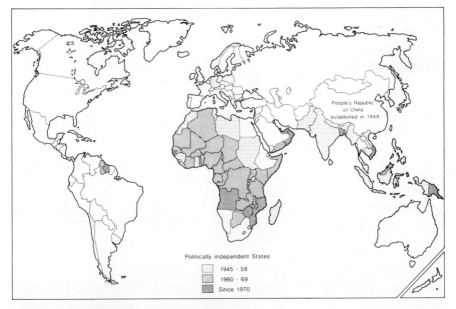

Fig 8.10   Decolonization after World War II
Source: Edwards (1985), p. 210

Table 8.6: A hundred years of the barter terms of trade

	LDCs against DCs		Primaries against manufactures	
	all products	all products (excluding fuels)	LDCs' primaries and DCs' mfrs	World primaries and world mfrs
1880	126	n.a.	130	114
1900	114	n.a.	103	91
1913	177	n.a.	185	106
1928	172	n.a.	178	98
1937	150	n.a.	152	78
1952	115	122	109	118
1962	100	101 (1960)	100	100
1968	101	102 (1965)	97	93
1970	101	105	96	97
1975	143	78	198	156
1980	177	76	309	211

Source: Edwards (1985) Table 4.2, p. 62

merchants in the richer peripheral countries looked to manufacturing industry as a source of capital accumulation. Leading politicians also saw in industrial development both national and personal advantage.

Most importantly, however, the barter terms of trade for many of the basic
commodities exported to the 'core' appeared to have deteriorated, as had the
general barter terms of trade (Table 8.6). This was widely viewed as inevitable, given the low-income elasticity of demand for 'less developed countries' '
(LDCs) primary products, the low wages in the primary production sector in
the LDCs, and the high protective barriers for competing primary production
(mainly agricultural products and largely erected in the 1930s) in the 'developed countries' (DCs) (Spraos, 1980; Edwards, 1985, pp. 209–11).

Pessimism about the future prospects for primary products was reinforced
by the view that the primary sector was inherently backward compared to the
manufacturing sector: because of the latter's multiplier effects and, allegedly,
greater economies of scale. Consequently, the pursuit of industrialization
could be justified 'theoretically' as well as materially.

The promotion of industry came from either protection – from reserving
domestic markets for domestic industry – or, later, establishing export
enclaves. Once established, and/or protected through their early, vulnerable
years, new industries would be able to compete globally. A predilection for
protection, in many cases, reflected both a positive interpretation of the past
practices of such countries as the United States, Japan and Germany, which
had in their day protected 'infant industries'; and the conception of an
'activist' state common to many ex-colonial territories.

During the 1960s exports of manufactures from LDCs grew quickly, from
around $3 billion in 1960 to over $9 billion in 1970 (UNIDO 1981). As a
percentage of total world trade in manufactures this was an increase of from
under 4 per cent to 5 per cent. In the 1970s growth was even more rapid. By

1980 LDC manufactured exports were more than $80 billion, or over 9 per cent of the world total. This growth is part of the New International Division of Labour (NIDL; see also pp. 30–43).

One of the most notable features of the period 1960–80, however, and perhaps even more notable since then, has been the polarization of performance and prospects between different regional groupings of LDCs. More than 80 per cent of the total of LDC manufactured exports comes from ten NICs (Argentina, Brazil, Hong Kong, India, Malaysia, Mexico, Pakistan, Singapore, South Korea and Taiwan). In most of these cases, especially Hong Kong, Malaysia, Mexico, Singapore, South Korea and Taiwan, industrial growth has been export-led (export-enclave) rather than import substitution (protection).

More than 60 per cent of all LDC manufactured exports are now sold to DCs. This market is limited by both high levels of protection in the DCs and the risk of increased protection in the future. Since the early 1970s the level and uncertainty of protective barriers (tariffs, quotas, etc.) to LDC manufactured exports have increased tremendously. This is especially the case for relatively more finished products (Fig. 8.11).

Manufactured goods can be classified into two main product groups: capital goods (machinery and equipment, including transport equipment) and consumer and intermediate goods, of which textiles and clothing are the largest single category in international trade. Capital goods account for about half of all manufactured goods traded in the world-economy (46 per cent in 1984). But different world regions account for different shares of the two product categories. DCs supply 92 per cent of world exports of capital goods and 52 per cent of textiles and clothing. They also supply 81 percent of other miscellaneous manufactures. LDCs are important only as suppliers of textiles and clothing and certain light industrial products, mainly consumer goods (with the important exception of electronics components and automobile components, in the case of Brazil and Mexico). The specialization of trade flow between LDCs and DCs, therefore, extends today beyond the distinction between primary commodities and other goods to apply *within* the category of manufactured goods (World Bank, 1984).

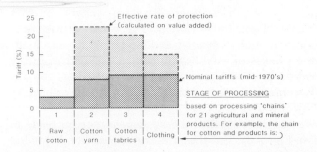

Fig 8.11 Escalating economic protectionism in the North
Source: Edwards (1985) Fig. 8.5, p. 220

The growth of trade in manufactures in the 1970s, after a 40 year period in which manufacturing production was intensively concentrated in the DCs and there was more limited DC–DC as well as DC–LDC trade in manufactures, was influenced by the growing significance of multinational corporations and of contractual cooperation between firms in different countries (DeVroey, 1984). Multinational corporations have long been active in manufacturing in LDCs. As we saw in Chapter 6, they tended at first to duplicate plants around the world in order to gain access to protected markets, or to make use of local raw materials. The production by MNEs of automobiles (e.g. in Brazil), agricultural engineering products (e.g. in S. Africa and Mexico), and pharmaceuticals (e.g. in India) across a range of LDCs are examples. This kind of manufacturing production still exists, especially in countries with large internal markets. In Brazil, for example, in the mid-1970s to take an extreme case, almost 50 per cent of industrial output was produced by MNEs and more than 90 per cent of MNE production was sold locally (Joekes, 1987).

Since the 1960s, however, MNE involvement in LDCs has also involved what is known as 'global sourcing'. As a result of technical change and the appeal of cheap (often female) labour in certain countries, production functions that once were adjacent spatially can now be dispersed widely. Many so-called light industrial processes are especially suited to the separation of various stages of production. In particular, labour-intensive stages can be located to take advantage of both the enormous international spread in wage levels and the exchange-rate fluctuations between currencies that have been a feature of the world-economy since the early 1970s. With respect to wage levels, and as one illustration, the shoe industry faces wage costs of $6 per hour in the United States but only $0.85 to $1.39 in East Asia.

One industry that has engaged in global sourcing on a massive scale (perhaps, and for this reason, somewhat exceptional) is the electronics components and consumer products industry. This industry has two characteristics that have encouraged the shift to global sourcing: discrete production segments, of which some are extremely labour-intensive and require 'flexible response' because of short product-cycles that make automation uneconomic (Eisold, 1984), and compact products (parts and components) that can be shipped relatively cheaply. East Asian locations with cheap, reliable, literate and tractable (largely female) labour forces have been especially attractive to this industry (and some others such as textiles and clothing). Governments have often facilitated the process of establishing component and assembly plants through the provision of export-processing zones, subsidies, and tax advantages and the enforcement of the 'political stability' highly valued by MNEs and their local sub-contractors.

For most LDCs, however, there is still a heavy dependence on trade in primary commodities (see Fig. 2.8). But the primary commodity sector has become extremely heterogeneous with respect to trading conditions since World War II. Four major categories stand out in this regard: fuels (mainly petroleum), non-fuel minerals, grains, and other agricultural products. These product groups have experienced very different price movements and to some extent quantity fluctuations over the past 30 years. The non-food commodity prices have been especially volatile. Generally, manufactures have increased in price to the disadvantage of primary commodity exporters. But there have been two periods, 1949–52 and 1973–80, when demand for primary non-food commodities was extremely strong and commodity prices surged. Since 1973, inflation and uncertain economic conditions in the DCs have also boosted the prices of agricultural raw materials. Since 1980, however, the relative price strength in the fuels and agricultural products groups has largely disappeared and the value of commodity export earnings has sunk precipitously in relation to the prices of manufactures and minerals. Perhaps the most negative price movement from the perspective of most DCs has been in the price of grains. There has been a long-term decline in world grain prices. This reflects tremendous increases in production the world over, but especially in the United States and other DCs. Normal yields per hectare are now twice what they were in 1950. The real price of wheat, however, is now about half what it was 100 years ago (Joekes, 1987).

Across all primary commodities, commodity agreements between producers and consumers (cocoa, tin, sugar and natural rubber) and producer cartels (most famously, OPEC for petroleum) have failed to reduce volatility and raise the prices of primary commodities relative to those of manufactures because of fundamental differences of interest between producers and consumers *and* among producers. Even OPEC, after successfully raising the price of oil from 1973 to 1979, has been driven by conflict and the failure to attract some major oil producers (such as Mexico, UK, Norway) to its ranks (Fieleke, 1986). This failure has encouraged further attempts at industrialization.

Nevertheless, some countries, especially those in sub-Saharan Africa, could probably benefit from increased attention to primary commodities. Sender and Smith (1986) show that the macroeconomic policies of many African governments have worked to undermine their region's shares of world export markets across a range of primary commodities (Table 8.7). Inelasticity of demand cannot explain these declines (see p. 170). Neither can the absence of commodity diversification, since those countries with a relatively diversified structure of agricultural exports – such as Tanzania – have not experienced more favourable trends in export earnings than more specialized ones (see Love, 1983). Sender and Smith (1986, p. 127) explain the absolute decline of Sub-Saharan Africa's contributions to world commodity markets in terms of 'the continued dominance of anti-trade ideologies and export pessimism' that are 'probably explained by the political hegemony of nationalism. It remains expedient for the national bourgeoisie, or for those determining the form and nature of state intervention, to deflect criticism by resort to anti-imperialist rhetoric and to blame foreign scapegoats for economic failure.'

However, this is probably too narrow a perspective. Political agendas and social problems of a more general nature also have played important roles. In

Table 8.7: Sub-Saharan African exports as a percentage of total world exports of selected commodities

	1961–3	1969–71	1980–2
Cocoa	79.9	75.9	69.3
Coffee	25.6	29.3	25.9
Tea	8.7	14.4	9.3
Groundnut oil	53.8	57.6	27.8
Groundnuts	85.5	69.1	18.0
Oilseed cake and meal	9.5	8.3	2.2
Palm kernel oil	55.2	54.8	21.6
Palm kernels	90.4	82.2	75.8
Palm oil	55.0	16.4	3.0
Sesame seed	68.6	75.3	40.7
Bananas	10.9	6.5	3.0
Cotton	10.8	15.5	9.2
Rubber	6.8	6.8	4.4
Tobacco	12.1	8.2	11.8
Maize	2.5	1.4	0.4

Source: World Bank (1984) pp. 80–1

the post-independence period, considerable political energy was expended in diversifying import and export markets rather than building larger ones. This was a direct result of trying to slay 'the colonial dragon' as the newly-independent countries tried to become less dependent on the former colonial power. Governments have also been faced with major ethnic divisions and rivalries, fragile political institutions, and 'superpower' infiltration and manipulation (Jackson, 1986). The Nigerian Civil War, frequent military *coups d'état*, and American or Soviet covert operations in most African countries are symptomatic examples of the diversions from economic policy-making that have faced political élites in Sub-Saharan Africa (and to a lesser extent also in Latin America and Asia) since the 1940s.

The end of colonialism did not usher in an era of 'sustainable' national development in the former colonial world; that much is clear from the preceding discussion. Two features of the world-economy in the recent past have played some role in this. One is the Cold War between the United States and the Soviet Union, that, while encouraging 'aid' programmes of one kind or other, has also encouraged militarization and political instability. After World War II the world was effectively divided into two spheres of influence with large parts of the new 'Third World' as a zone of superpower competition (Figure 8.12). In certain cases, such as, for example, South Korea and Taiwan, superpower aid (American in these cases) has contributed to economic growth (Cumings, 1984). In many African countries aid has helped achieve major improvements in physical and social infrastructure, although much of the most productive aid has not come from the superpowers, who have specialized in military aid and technical assistance (intelligence gathering) rather than direct economic assistance. International agencies (the UN,

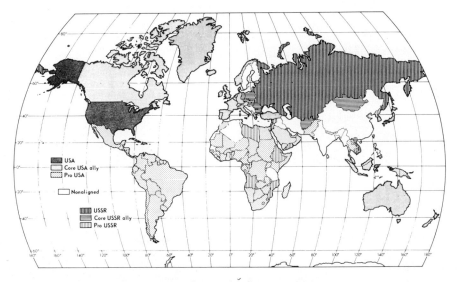

Fig 8.12   Soviet and American spheres of influence, 1982
Source: O'Loughlin (1986), Fig. 10.1, p. 242

World Bank, etc.), and some European countries have provided much of the more 'useful' aid.

In other cases, 'models' of development were imported from either the United States ('free enterprise') or the Soviet Union (central planning) and then supported/undermined from outside by each of the superpowers. This often led to increased militarization both of governments and national budgets as internal opponents were repressed and external patrons satisfied (S.W. Williams, 1986; Black, 1977 on Brazil). Between 1960 and 1982, more than 10,700,000 people were killed in 65 major wars (those with more than 1,000 deaths attributable to them). Most of these wars were fought in the Third World (Sivard, 1982, 1986).

A second change in the global context of interdependence has been the increased pace and internationalization of the world-economy (Fig. 8.13). Capital has become much more mobile, both in time and space. Before 1973, currency exchange-rates changed once every four years on average, interest rates moved twice a year, and companies made price and investment decisions no more than once or twice a year. This has all changed. There is now an almost constant review of prices and investment decisions, a constant instability and disorder (Thrift, 1986). This places an even greater premium on the ability of firms and governments in LDCs to react within some coherent national framework to changes in the global political-economic environment.

Nowhere is this clearer than with respect to the world financial system. As we have seen (p. 39), the growing integration of the world-economy and the loosening of government control over exchange rates when the major industrial governments, led by the United States, abandoned the Bretton Woods

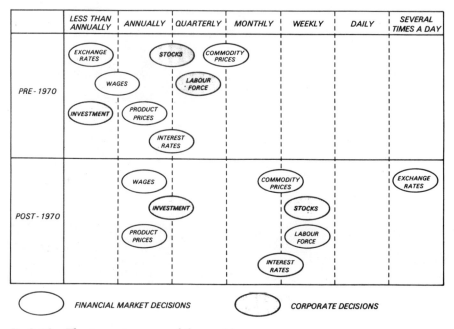

	LESS THAN ANNUALLY	ANNUALLY	QUARTERLY	MONTHLY	WEEKLY	DAILY	SEVERAL TIMES A DAY
PRE-1970	EXCHANGE RATES · WAGES · INVESTMENT	PRODUCT PRICES	STOCKS · LABOUR FORCE · INTEREST RATES	COMMODITY PRICES			
POST-1970		WAGES · INVESTMENT · PRODUCT PRICES		COMMODITY PRICES · STOCKS · LABOUR FORCE · INTEREST RATES			EXCHANGE RATES

◯ FINANCIAL MARKET DECISIONS   ⬭ CORPORATE DECISIONS

Fig 8.13   The increasing pace of the world economy
Source: *Economist*, 24 Sept. 1983, p. 11

system in 1973, triggered the growth of a massive *private* international monetary system (Corbridge,1988). This system was organized around Eurodollars, a term that originally meant US dollar deposits in banks in Europe but now refers to dollars that circulate outside the United States, which are used for world trade, and are not regulated by the US government. This global currency mushroomed between 1974 and 1981 as a result of the enormous dollar surpluses earned by the OPEC countries from oil sales. The large banks which received these funds sought borrowers who

> could be charged enough interest to enable the banks to earn a profit. The banks first moved Eurodollars into Third World countries, saddling them with a $1 trillion debt burden by the end of 1986, compared to less than $100 million in 1973. Instead of supporting new productive investment, however, a large portion of this debt went into luxury consumption. Over $200 billion disappeared through capital flight from the Third World back to the industrial countries. (Wachtel, 1987, p. 786)

Since 1982, when Mexico and certain other major Latin American borrowers effectively defaulted on loan repayments, the Eurodollars have shifted into funding the US budget deficit, into firm mergers and acquisitions, and into the world's stock markets (Lessard and Williamson, 1987). But the burden of debt, in both the form of repayment and inability to borrow fresh capital with outstanding debt, has emerged as a major new barrier to economic development (Lever and Huhne, 1987) (see Fig. 2.9).

From one point of view, the net effect of these changes in the global context for interdependence has been an increased division between the LDCs, on the one hand, and the DCs, on the other. National income and purchasing power statistics support this interpretation (Emmanuel, 1972; McMichael *et al.*, 1974). But, from another point of view, the periphery has in fact developed rapidly. This interpretation is supported by data on output, health and education (Warren, 1980; Schiffer, 1981). One way of reconciling these discordant interpretations is to argue that the post-colonial world-economy has rested on integrated global production but has lacked global consumption. The relatively low incomes in LDC factories and plantations have put a cap on local purchasing power even as local labour forces were made more efficient (through improved health and education) and increased their output.

The problem with this reconciliation and the interpretations upon which it is based is that they are geographically overaggregated. The experience of different groups of LDCs has been different. Some of the Latin American countries, for example, are relatively large and have relatively high levels of per capita national income (e.g. Brazil, Argentina). Some of them did achieve considerable income growth in the 1960s and 1970s on the basis of industrialization to satisfy local markets. Most of them, however, were heavy importers of oil (Mexico and Venezuela were exceptional) and their industrial sectors were generally uncompetitive in world markets. They were hit in the 1970s by the combination of oil price rises and their failure to switch to export-oriented manufacturing in the boom years of the late 1960s. They had to borrow to ease the oil shock adjustment instead of paying for it with export earnings. They are now caught in a 'debt trap' of accumulated loans and compounded by the high interest rates of the early 1980s and the growth of trade barriers to the manufactures they export to the United States and Western Europe (Nogués *et al.*, 1985).

The Sub-Saharan African countries, on the other hand, are much poorer on the average than Latin American countries and their low level of output in all sectors is stressed by their even faster rates of population increase. They are economies with small industrial sectors and a heavy dependence on primary commodities. As commodity prices have dropped in the 1980s they have been forced to borrow to maintain minimal levels of consumption. Their debt burden is similar to that of the most indebted Latin American countries. The consequence, as in Latin America, is a general reduction in the standard of living but in contexts where it is already desperately low.

Finally, Asian countries have, on average, managed the best over the past 20 years. They have been more successful in maintaining economic growth as a secular trend and adjusting to cyclical downturns such as the world recessions of 1974–75 and 1979–82. The East Asian NICs, the most dynamic economies in the region, have been able to expand their export of manufactures. They now account for about three-quarters of LDC total exports of manufactures. Although, like the Latin American countries, they borrowed heavily in 1974–75 to adjust to the oil price increases, their export performance has allowed them to keep relatively good borrowing terms and adjust more easily to the massive interest rate increases of 1980–81.

New Models of Development

In the face of the failure of many LDCs to maintain, let alone increase, the consumption levels of their populations, the models of development upon which national development efforts have been based have been called into question. This coincides with the growing questioning of both American and Soviet models in their homelands. Neither they nor the syncretic versions that have appeared over the past 30 years appear to offer a way out of the 'development impasse.' It is in this context that new models have appeared (and disappeared). Perhaps the three most important ones are based on (1) Japanese experience (2) Chinese experiments in the 1960s and (3) Islamic economic practices. Each of these alternative models is noted briefly. There is no space here for critical evaluation.

Japanese experience is seen as relevant because Japan is the sole case of a country with a non-European population rising from periphery to core within the world-economy (see pp. 148–155). Even other DCs are now exhorted to imitate the Japanese (Vogel, 1980). The Japanese model is seen as involving, among other things, national mobilization around economic objectives; an integration of business and government operations through finance and product targeting; export-orientation; capitalization of agriculture to increase agricultural self-sufficiency; and increased urbanization to profit from external and agglomeration economies of scale. In practice, of course, combining these elements is most difficult since the historical and geographical settings in which Japan developed cannot be reproduced at will.

The Chinese experiments with emphasizing agricultural development and national self-sufficiency have had a greater appeal in many LDCs (Harris, 1978). But, of course, the Chinese have themselves now departed from this road in pursuit of industrialization and world trade (Nolan, 1983). The model remains, however, and is an important part of the philosophy of oppositional and guerilla movements in many parts of Africa, Asia and Latin America (e.g. Peru's 'Shining Path').

Finally, practices and beliefs drawn from the Islamic religion have become important in the Middle East, North Africa and parts of Asia (e.g. Indonesia). The prohibition of usury or 'excessive' interest charged on monetary loans is one of the more concrete and obviously appealing features of Islamic economics. But as yet no *system* of political economy based upon Islamic principles has been established in any country (including Iran). The conclusion of Katouzian (1983, p. 164), one of the leading authorities on Islamic economics, seems appropriate:

While one may empathize with the desire to construct an indigenous ideology that can be identified with the Islamic beliefs and practices of its advocates, particularly in view of the havoc caused by selective application of Western ideas under the late Shah [of Iran], it is no more to be expected that Islam can provide a comprehensive economic system than that the latter could be based on Christianity, Judaism, or any other traditional religio-political system.

Summary

In this chapter we have surveyed the dynamics of interdependence between the core and the periphery of the world-economy from the colonial period to the present day. We have identified the following points as being of critical importance:

- Existing economies were transformed into colonial ones through regional specialization in primary commodity production.

- In the late nineteenth and early twentieth centuries a 'cross-over' multilateral system of trade with Britain as its linchpin integrated the world-economy.

- The 'cross-over' system was progressively displaced by direct investment from multinational firms (MNEs). American firms were especially important.

- Colonialism created the conditions for wage labour and gave priority to improving communications, transportation and medical care. The notion of the state as a territorial entity became widespread.

- Western values had paradoxical effects. On the one hand, values of work and private property were disseminated. On the other hand, new syncretic traditions were invented.

- With decolonization, new states came into existence which attempted to encourage industrialization.

- For many years much manufacturing in the LDCs was import substitution. Since the 1960s, however, MNEs have engaged in 'global sourcing': dispersing some production functions to appropriate sites in LDCs and exporting components/products back to the US, Western Europe or Japan.

- Many LDCs are still heavily dependent on the export of primary commodities, the prices of which are highly volatile.

- Cartels and production agreements have largely failed to stabilize the production or prices of most primary commodities. The success of OPEC in the 1970s is the one exception.

- The Cold War between the United States and the Soviet Union and the increased pace and internationalization of the world-economy have placed serious constraints on development efforts. The global 'debt crisis' is an especially important constraint.

- The integration of production within the world-economy has not been matched by an integration of consumption. However, different regions of the periphery have had different experiences in this regard: the Asian countries (especially the East Asian NICs) have been most successful, the countries of Sub-Saharan Africa least so.

- New models of development, from Japan, China and Islam, have arisen to challenge the dominant Western/Soviet ones (or mixes thereof) because of the failure of the dominant ones to maintain or generate sustainable economic development.

The next two chapters examine the contemporary patterns of agriculture and industry in the periphery.

9

Agriculture: The Primary Concern?

'Development' is often equated with the structural transformation of an economy whereby agriculture's share of the national product and of the labour force declines in relative importance. Agriculture has often been viewed as a 'black box from which people, and food to feed them, and perhaps capital could be released' (Little, 1982, p. 105). This perspective, long dominant among planners and politicians, and common to both American and Soviet models of development, reflected the low income elasticity of food (demand increases very little with higher incomes), the secular global trend towards higher labour productivity in agriculture (same output can be produced by fewer workers), the limited multiplier or stimulative effect of agriculture, and the secular tendency for the terms of trade to turn against countries that export primary products and import manufactured goods (Staatz and Eicher, 1984).

However, it is almost certain that the world's population will rise to at least 6 billion by the end of this century. It is equally certain that about 70 per cent of the growth in population between now and 2000 will take place in the underdeveloped countries. Consequently, these countries in particular will need to increase their food production to supply the additional people and to increase their standard of living. At the same time they face two major constraints: much land is unsuitable for agricultural purposes (Figs. 2.3 and 9.1) and their involvement with the world-economy often reduces their food self-reliance without sufficient compensation in other sectors.

The purpose of this chapter is to describe the contemporary state of agriculture in the 'periphery' of the world-economy. To this end, the chapter is organized as follows: a first section establishes the importance of agriculture as an economic sector and stresses the dual trends of increased commodity production and decreased food self-reliance; a second section discusses the general relationships between land, labour and capital in the periphery; a third section provides a review of efforts at rural land reform; fourth, the capitalization of agriculture in the periphery by multinational enterprises is described; fifth, and finally, the role of science and technology, especially in the form of the so-called Green Revolution, is assessed.

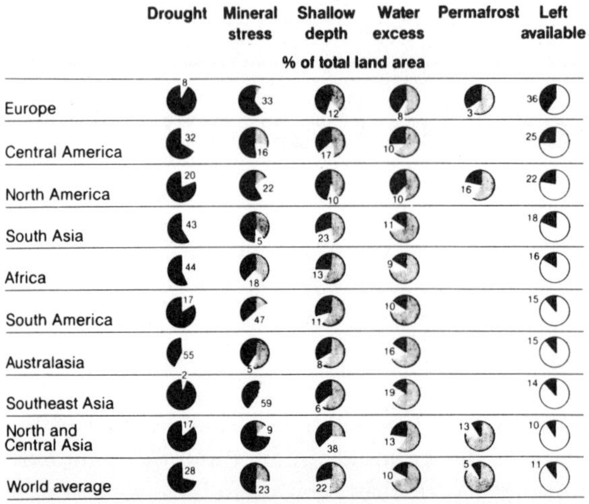

	Drought	Mineral stress	Shallow depth	Water excess	Permafrost	Left available
			% of total land area			
Europe	8	33	12	8	3	36
Central America	32	16	17	10		25
North America	20	22	10	10	16	22
South Asia	43	5	23	11		18
Africa	44	18	13	9		16
South America	17	47	11	10		15
Australasia	55		8	16		15
Southeast Asia	2	59	6	19		14
North and Central Asia	17	9	38	13	13	10
World average	28	23	22	10	5	11

Fig 9.1   Major limitations on agriculture
Source: Warnock (1987), Fig. Vlla, p. 166

Agriculture at the Periphery

The countries of the periphery have all been significantly involved with modern commercial farming since the beginning of Western colonization in the sixteenth century. But subsistence and production for local markets have remained of great, if decreasing, importance. Malassis (1975) identifies four types of agricultural systems in the periphery: (1) the 'customary' farm involving common ownership of land for both cultivation and grazing; (2) the 'feudal or semi-feudal' estate, *hacienda* and *latifundia* (3) 'peasant agriculture', including *minifundia* (small, subsistence farms), commercial farms and share-cropping; and (4) capitalist plantation or mechanized agriculture based on wage labour. These four types of farm organization produce three types of commodity: (i) wage foods, primarily cereals for the domestic market; (ii) peasant foods, primarily for personal use; and (iii) export crops, where the major market is overseas (Crouch and de Janvry, 1980). The historical trend in agriculture in most countries of the periphery has been from (1) and (2) to (3) and, especially, (4) in farm organization and from (i) and (ii) to (iii) in types of agricultural commodity (Crouch and de Janvry, 1980; Rotberg *et al.*, 1983; Grindle, 1986).

However, the three continents of the periphery – Africa, Latin America and Asia – differ in terms of agricultural organization and performance. Above all, Sub-Saharan Africa is, or has been until recently, abundant in land and sparse in population; Asia is largely short of land relative to population; and Latin America contains both areas with heavy populations and areas with few inhabitants. Agriculture is also of much greater relative importance in

Sub-Saharan Africa and Asia than in Latin America, both in terms of employment and contribution to national product (Hopkins, 1983).

It is also important to recognize that agriculture is overwhelmingly more important as a source of employment to women than to men. Indeed, the 'gender dimension' is not a secondary consequence of variations in agricultural organization but 'a fundamental organizing principle of labour use' (Joekes, 1987, p. 63). Regional differences are apparent, however, indicating the contingencies of resource endowment and carrying capacity. There are far more women involved in agriculture in Africa, relatively speaking, than elsewhere. In 1980, 87 per cent of all women in the labour force in Sub-Saharan Africa were involved in agriculture, compared to 70 per cent in India, 74 per cent in China, 66 per cent in other low-income Asian countries and 55 per cent in middle-income Asian countries. In Latin America the comparable figure is a very low 14 per cent. This reflects the greater degree of mechanization (and export crop orientation) in Latin American agriculture and higher levels of female rural to urban migration compared to other regions (Joekes, 1987).

Official figures probably miss many of the subsistence and peasant agriculture activities carried out predominantly by women (Beneria, 1981). Labour force participation data usually involve very narrow definitions of agricultural activity focused on land cultivation and large-scale livestock keeping (Hill, 1986). Bearing this in mind it is nevertheless obvious that agriculture is most important for African women, of lesser but still significant importance for Asian women, and of more limited importance as a source of employment to women in Latin America.

Forms of agricultural employment and organization also tend to differ by world region, as suggested by the Latin American case. 'Mechanized agriculture' and export crops have become of greatest importance in Latin America and in some areas elsewhere. 'Green Revolution' agriculture has become most widespread in producing wage and peasant foods in lowland Asia with pockets in Latin America and North Africa. 'Resource-poor' agriculture producing a range of crops predominates in Sub-Saharan Africa and areas of poor soils and drainage elsewhere. Production differences reflect these organizational and endowment differences.

While per capita food production in the periphery has not matched that of the core, and in many cases has not kept up with population increases, spectacular growth in the production of specific crops for export to the core was characteristic of the 1970s. For example, in Latin America, the production of sugar increased by over 200 per cent in El Salvador, Guatemala and Honduras between 1965 and 1977. Beef production in the Dominican Republic grew at 7.6 per cent per annum between 1970 and 1979. Sorghum, unimportant in Brazil before 1970, averaged 253,000 metric tons per annum in that country by 1979. 'By the late 1970s, it was estimated that commercial agriculture, largely centred in the large-farm sector, accounted for half of all agricultural production, utilized nearly a third of the cultivated area, and employed a fifth of the work force in Latin America as a whole' (Grindle, 1986, p. 81).

The expansion of commodity production and regional specialization has been most characteristic of agriculture in Latin America. In Sub-Saharan Africa, however, export crops have failed to maintain global market shares even as total agricultural production increased (Sender and Smith, 1986). This reflects both declining productivity in the export sector and government attempts to direct investment into industrialization rather than primary commodities. Food production has been dismal, particularly in the context of rapid population increase. In Asia, both productivity and production have increased enormously because of fertilizers and the application of new technologies, but most growth has been in cereals (especially rice and wheat) production rather than 'special' export crops such as those of growing importance in Latin America (e.g. fruits, beef) (Lele, 1984). The problems for the Asian countries are their high land/population ratios and the competition they face from agriculture in the United States and Western Europe in the crops (such as wheat and rice) in which their growth has been concentrated.

Each of the three major regions of the periphery, therefore, faces distinctive problems with respect to its agriculture. For Latin America it is the expansion of export crops at the expense of local food crops. As a consequence, food imports are often necessary (Grindle, 1986). For Sub-Saharan Africa it is the total deterioration of agriculture in the face of population pressure on marginal land, low productivity, government bias against investment in agriculture, and fluctuations in export earnings. Food imports are now an absolute necessity (Lele, 1984; Eicher, 1984). For Asia, production of cereals has increased greatly but prices have been low because of global 'gluts.' Hence, increased agricultural production has not generated the capital necessary for investment in other sectors such as industry. When prices increase local populations must pay the increase or substitute other cereals that are imported, more often than not, from Western Europe or the United States. Even agricultural 'success stories' (such as India) are now faced with food deficits that are likely to grow in the future (Table 9.1).

In large parts of the periphery today agriculture is a vulnerable sector: either oriented externally or subject to the vagaries of the world market without the protection and subsidies enjoyed by agriculture in the core. Yet it is absolutely vital. Vast numbers of people are still employed in or are immediately dependent on agriculture. And, whatever the model of economic development adopted, any hope of improving living standards in general depends upon increasing agricultural production.

Land, Labour and Capital

Agriculture in the contemporary periphery rests upon a foundation of agrarian history, and recent changes can only be understood in this context. Central to agrarian history the world over has been the impact of market forces on landholding patterns and the structure of rural social relationships. Though

Table 9.1: Food deficits for selected countries

	Actual 1975		Projected 1990	
	Million metric tons	% of consumption	Million metric tons	% of consumption
India	1.4	1	17.6–21.9	10–12
Nigeria	0.4	2	17.1–20.5	35–39
Bangladesh	1.0	7	6.4–8.0	30–35
Indonesia	2.1	8	6.0–7.7	14–17
Egypt	3.7	35	4.9	32
Sahel group	0.4	9	3.2–3.5	44–46
Ethiopia	0.1	2	2.1–2.3	26–28
Burma	(0.4)	(7)	1.9–2.4	21–25
Philippines	0.3	4	1.4–1.7	11–13
Afghanistan	...	...	1.3–1.5	19–22
Bolivia and Haiti	0.3	24	0.7–0.8	35–38

Source: Loup (1983) Table 7.6, p. 106

rural areas are often characterized as static and traditional, the historical record shows frequent changes in agricultural practices and labour relationships in response to global and domestic political-economic conditions. But some features of landholding systems and rural life have persisted from the period of incorporation into the world-economy. In this section the mix of 'old' and 'new' in the agricultural organization of different parts of the contemporary periphery (Latin America, Sub-Saharan Africa, Asia) will be examined.

Latin America

In Latin America, conquest and colonial domination created patterns of subsistence and commercial agriculture based on large landholdings (Duncan and Rutledge, 1977). After independence, this characteristic, and its corollary, an exploited and powerless peasantry, became firmly entrenched as the region was firmly tied into the world market as a producer of primary commodities (Keith, 1977; Grindle, 1986). Between the 1850s and 1930s the various countries of Latin America came to depend on the export of one or two primary commodities to the industrial countries – first Britain and later the United States (Cortes Conde, 1974). The older *hacienda* system, though complex and varied in its particulars from place to place, went into decline and was replaced by a plantation system that already had a considerable history in the sugar plantations of NE Brazil and the Caribbean (Table 9.2).

The growth of export-oriented agrarian capitalism was associated with the emergence of a politically powerful landed élite linked to foreign investors and commercial agents dealing in primary commodities. Agriculture for domestic consumption was largely ignored and through control over governments the agricultural élite was able to increase its hold over land, labour and capital. As Grindle (1986, p. 42) puts it

Table 9.2: Land, labour, capital, and markets: haciendas and plantations

	Haciendas	Plantations
Markets	Relatively small and unreliable, regional, with inelasticity of demand; attempt to limit production to keep prices high.	Relatively large and reliable, European, with elasticity of demand; attempt to increase production to maximize profits.
Profits	Relatively low; highly concentrated in small group.	Relatively high; highly concentrated in small group.
Capital and technology	Little access to capital, especially foreign. Operating capital often from Church. Technology simple, often same as that of peasant cultivators.	Availability of foreign capital for equipment and labour. Direct foreign investment late in nineteenth century. Relatively advanced technology, with expensive machinery for processing.
Land	Size determined by passive acceptance of indigenous groups. Attempt to monopolize land to limit alternative sources of income to labour force; much unused land. Relatively cheap. Unclear boundaries.	Size determined by availability of labour. Relatively valuable with carefully fixed boundaries.
Labour	Large labour force required seasonally; generally indigenous; informally bound by debt, provision of subsistence plot, social ties, payment in provisions.	Large labour force required seasonally; generally imported; slavery common; also wage labour.
Organization	Limited need for supervision; generally hired administrators/managers, absentee landlord.	Need for continual supervision and managerial skill. Generally resident owner/manager.

Source: Grindle (1986) Table 3.1, p. 30

At times emerging from the colonial land-holding élite, at times competing with it, this élite was instrumental in discouraging initiatives to tax landholdings or to intrude in the regulation of rural labour relations. It sought instead to encourage public investment in infrastructure to establish official subsidies for agricultural inputs and services, and to facilitate credit. By limiting the availability of these resources to large landowners, the agricultural élite was able to increase its hold on land, labour and capital and to deny these to smallholders, tenants and sharecroppers.

The concentration of land-holding and the marginalization of peasant agriculture did not occur without resistance. Agrarian uprisings and social banditry were widespread. In Mexico the 1910 uprising was a major impetus to the Revolution; strikes were extremely common in the corporate plantations of coastal Peru in the period 1912–28; in Colombia rural violence by agrarian tenant syndicates directed against commercial coffee producers lasted well into the 1930s. The 1930s also was a period of rural unrest in the Brazilian northeast and in El Salvador among dispossessed peasants and unemployed plantation workers (Duncan and Rutledge, 1977; Wolf, 1968; Landsberger, 1969).

When the world-economy collapsed in the 1930s so too did export-oriented agriculture. This spurred the emergence of active nationalists, often in the military, who wanted to increase industrialization and diminish reliance on the export of primary commodities. Between 1930 and 1934 there were 12 forcible takeovers of power – from Argentina to Peru to El Salvador. Mexico, Brazil, Argentina, Colombia, Chile and Uruguay all instituted import-substitution industrial strategies. These led to a massive movement of people off the land. For the region as a whole, in 1920, only 14 per cent of the population lived in urban areas, but by 1940 the proportion had risen to 20 per cent. In Argentina, Chile and Uruguay urban percentages reached 35–45 per cent of the population. One major consequence of this was a decline in the hold of the land-holding élite over national politics in some countries as urban professional and working classes grew in size and influence (Grindle, 1986).

This change, however, can be exaggerated, Many countries continued to rely on the export of one or few primary commodities – the Central American and Caribbean countries, but also Argentina, Colombia, and Chile – and rural land remained concentrated in the hands of the landed élite. What was different was the emergence of nationalist and populist movements committed to industrialization rather than export agriculture.

Pursuing policies of import substitution had important effects on agriculture. For one, manufacturing surpassed agriculture it its contribution to gross domestic product in a number of countries (Argentina, Brazil, Chile, Mexico, Uruguay and Venezuela) in the 1940s. Much of the new capacity was concentrated in or near the capitals of the states which were its major sponsors (Buenos Aires, Rio de Janeiro, Santiago, etc.).

Industrialization required a 'draining' of agriculture for resources (cheap food, raw materials, foreign exchange) and capital (taxation). As a consequence a premium was placed upon efficiency in agricultural production. This was thought to require large holdings, the spread of technological innovation, and capitalization. Between 1940 and 1960 there was a massive migration of people from the country-side to the cities as a consequence of mechanization and the expansion of large landholdings at the expense of small tenants and proprietors.

In the 1960s import-substitution became increasingly expensive as the 'easy phase' emphasizing light consumer goods was played out and the prodigious expense of moving into heavier capital goods became apparent. In a process that accelerated during the 1970s, import substitution was slowly displaced by a new development model based on export promotion. According to this model agriculture had been neglected and, although no substitute for industrialization, more efficient production of domestic food crops and increased agricultural exports were important in both maintaining political stability and obtaining foreign exchange. After 1965 public investment in rural areas and agriculture increased in a large number of Latin American countries (Grindle, 1986).

Government policies have discriminated heavily in favour of the larger land-owners. The geographical distribution of official credit, research and extension, infrastructure mechanization and Green Revolution inputs reflect the geography of landholding. In Peru, for example, about half the credit supplied by the Agricultural Development Bank between 1940 and 1965 went to cotton growers, who were among the wealthiest coastal agricultural exporters. Food crop producers – mainly peasants – were mainly ignored by the bank (Frankman, 1974; Durham, 1977). In Mexico in 1970, mechanization was used on 25.7 per cent of the crop area of farms of more than 5 hectares but was used on only 4.3 per cent of the crop area of farms under 5 hectares in size (Grindle, 1986). In Brazil all government policies have tended to reinforce the emphasis upon commercial agriculture in the south and east regions at the expense of the northeast and small-scale producers everywhere (Gomes and Perez, 1979).

This is not to say that large-scale capitalist agriculture has completely displaced peasant production. Far from it. A large section of the agricultural labour force is still 'part-peasant' in that it supplements its wage-earnings with the produce of its often less-than-subsistence plots. This serves to sustain capitalist agriculture through reducing the costs of reproducing a labour force (Taussig, 1978). In many parts of Latin America, therefore, large-scale capitalist agriculture and small-scale peasant production still uneasily coexist. The past is still present.

Sub-Saharan Africa

In Sub-Saharan Africa, unlike Latin America (or Europe), access to labour not land was always the basis of economic and political power. From 1830 to 1930 agriculture in Sub-Saharan Africa underwent an incredible expansion in the form of small-scale commercial farming. Some commercial farming had existed prior to this period, for example in the Hausa-Fulani and Mandinka states of northwest Africa, but the introduction of new crops and the expansion of existing ones into previously uncultivated areas increased the scale and geographical distribution of commercial agriculture. Of special importance were such crops as cocoa, cotton, coffee, groundnuts and oil palm, which were grown mainly for export markets. They spread along with European traders, the introduction of foreign capital, the shifting objectives of native farmers and traders, and finally colonial rule. This was the 'cash crop revolution' (Tosh, 1980) that brought Africa into the world-economy and capitalism into Africa.

Colonial rule involved massive intervention in existing agriculture through forced labour and taxation. Taxation in particular provided a fresh stimulus to cash-cropping. In some parts of Africa, especially the east and south, taxation also encouraged labour migration to mines, plantations and industries established by European settlers (Berg, 1965). In West Africa, however, labour migration pre-dated colonial rule. It was of a seasonal nature and involved the integration of farming in the interior with migration to more fertile but labour-deficient coastal areas (Swindell, 1979). In West Africa cash cropping by small-scale farmers and long-distance labour migration at harvest time were indigenous phenomena that increased in intensity after the onset of colonial rule. Elsewhere, cash-cropping and labour migration were relatively novel and related much more to either European settlement (as in South Africa, Zimbabwe or Kenya) or European initiatives in mining and plantation agriculture (as in Zambia and Zaire) (Hart, 1982; Swindell, 1985).

Another distinctive feature of West Africa as compared, for example, to Kenya was that the production of food and cash-crops was complementary rather than competitive (Bates, 1983). Even today food crops such as plantains, cocoyams and peppers are grown to provide shade for young cocoa trees. Moreover, the period of peak labour demand for cocoa harvesting (November–February) complements the peak labour demand periods for the cereal-growing areas to the north (May–July and February–March). Cocoa farms, therefore, have rarely faced a maximum price for labour and the commercial cocoa industry can coexist with the market for labour in food-crop production.

In Kenya, however, the European settlers specialized in the production of food crops and their production cycle matched that of subsistence producers. They consequently had to compete for labour with the subsistence sector. In addition, the establishment of estates or plantations in Kenya involved the confiscation of land from subsistence producers and the subsidy of commercial production at the expense of the subsistence sector (Bates, 1983).

The rate of agricultural production slowed markedly during the 1930s and World War II. It was only in the 1950s, when world prices for many export crops increased as the industrial countries entered into their long boom of the 1950s and early 1960s, that there was a rapid expansion in export crop production. But the increase in demand for Africa's export crops was short-lived, peaking as early as 1956. Since then cash cropping and commercialized livestock farming have been concentrated in the districts where they were dominant 30 years ago. With the exception of sugar, most new planting (of cocoa, coffee or tea) has taken place within the areas which were already the major producers in the early 1950s (O'Connor, 1978).

In those districts in which agricultural production has intensified or expanded it has involved different types of farming. For example, in Ivory Coast plantations have been the major agent of growth, whereas in Ghana, Kenya and Sudan it has been small-scale peasant cash crop production that has been responsible for most growth. Indeed, in Kenya the small-scale

Table 9.3: Index of agricultural production (1961–5 = 100), selected African countries

	1974–6	1981–3
Ethiopia	109	134
Ghana	117	94
Ivory Coast	171	236
Kenya	136	162
Malawi	163	214
Mozambique	122	109
Nigeria	116	144
Senegal	130	118
Tanzania	152	175
Zambia	157	140
Zimbabwe	142	145

Source: Sender and Smith (1986) Table 4.25, p. 103

farming sector has largely replaced the plantation sector as the most dynamic in terms of commercial production.

Total agricultural production (cash crops and food staples) increased substantially in Sub-Saharan Africa over the period 1961/5–1981/3 (Table 9.3). However, the rate of population increase over the region as a whole has meant that there has been very little or no increase in per capita terms. Most African governments have adopted policies which seek to depress food prices to feed their burgeoning populations. This often leads them to set higher prices for large-scale producers because of presumed efficiencies (and political influence?). Penalizing the food production sector is meant to both stimulate export-crop production and feed increasingly large urban populations. In fact it has discouraged farmers, especially the mass of small-scale farmers, from increasing their production through investment in increased productivity.

But countries differ in the relative extent to which farmers must bear the brunt of tax and price-setting policies. It all depends upon the political base of governing élites and the origins of marketing organizations (Bates, 1983). In Ghana and Zambia, for example, urban-based politicians have put the burden on small-scale farmers to a much greater extent than the rural-based politicians of Kenya and Ivory Coast. In Ghana the Cocoa Marketing Board is a patronage organization whereas in Kenya marketing organizations are controlled by producers. Interestingly, agricultural production has been much higher in Kenya and Ivory Coast than in Ghana and Zambia (see Table 9.3). In the former this has benefited both food production for domestic consumption and increases in sales of export crops (Sender and Smith, 1986; Bates, 1983; Ravenhill 1986; Rothchild and Gyimah-Boadi, 1986).

Three trends have nevertheless been fairly general over the past 30 years. One has been the increased importance of wage labour, especially with respect to export crops. This has further 'monetized' the rural economy and reduced the degree of reliance on domestic groups as sources of farm labour. This in turn has reinforced the role of long-distance migration in agricultural labour and given some districts the specialized role of 'migrant labour reserve' for other districts in which export agriculture is important. For example, even with restrictions on international migration, Burkina Faso in West Africa has been a major source of temporary and permanent migrants to Ivory Coast and Ghana (Fig. 9.2).

A second trend has been the changing role of women in African agriculture. Women have become central to the production of food crops on small-scale farms such as those which dominate throughout Sub-Saharan Africa (Joekes, 1987). As Swindell (1985, p. 179) puts it:

> As men have become more involved in commercial cropping and non-farm occupations, so women have become increasingly responsible for the cultivation of food staples. This is especially true in those areas where the out-migration of men is persistent, and it could be argued that the expansion of commercial cropping and the industrial labour force has been built on the backs of women farmers.

The third trend has been growth in agricultural production through extending areas under cropping or grazing rather than through raising yields. Green Revolution technologies, mainly addressed to cereal production, have been either inappropriate or not widely adopted in Sub-Saharan Africa. The lack of incentive for investment by farmers was noted earlier. Whatever the cause, however, commercial agriculture has become extensive rather than intensive. This has led to farming on poor soils in areas with unreliable rainfall and the displacement of subsistence agriculture onto ever more marginal terrain. Sen (1981b) implicates this trend as a major factor in the famines that have afflicted many parts of Africa over the past 20 years.

Though much of African agriculture has become increasingly commercialized, it remains largely small-scale and still involves domestic groups. As yet there is still an imperfect specialization of labour in Sub-Saharan Africa between farm and factory, city and countryside. Perhaps a majority of Africans still have 'rights' to farmland (Swindell, 1985). The level of agricultural production, however, has not kept up with the world's highest rates of population increase. In many countries there are now major national food deficits. At the same time government policies in many countries have had the effect of discouraging agricultural production both for food staples and export crops. But in most countries farming must remain the dominant activity for the foreseeable future if only because an increase in agricultural productivity is a prerequisite for industrial development. At present the growth of industry through import substitution is limited by the small size of most domestic markets and these can only grow if the incomes of farmers rise.

Asia

Asian agriculture presents a more complex picture than agriculture in Latin America and Sub-Saharan Africa. On the one hand are the world's highest

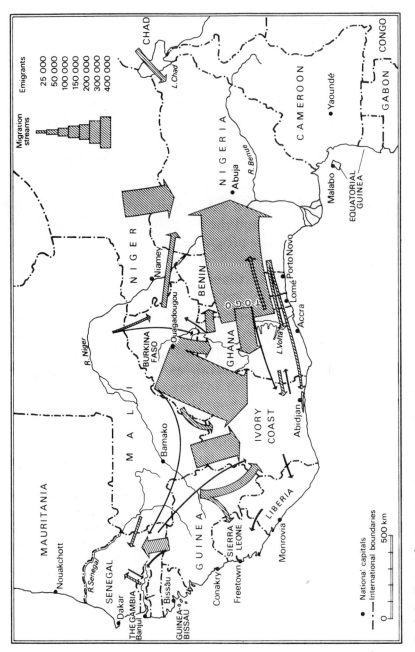

Fig 9.2 External migration streams in West Africa
Source: Swindell (1985) Fig. 4.3

rural population densities but on the other hand the populations are organized in agricultural systems with quite different and distinctive features. The major contrast, at least until recently (Kojima, 1982; Nolan, 1983), was between China, where there is no export agriculture to speak of, and the rural economy has been organized around 'collective' ownership (from 1954 to 1979), and those countries such as Malaysia and the Philippines, where export agriculture (rubber and sugar, respectively) is important and sharecropping tenancy (renting with payment in kind to landlords) predominates outside the plantations. But in general there is a high incidence of tenancy in Asian countries and sharecropping is its major form, especially in those areas where rural population densities are very high such as Bangladesh, Java, Central Luzon (in the Philippines), the West Zone of Sri Lanka, and eastern and southern India (Hossain, 1982).

Along with the preponderance of tenants goes an extreme concentration of landholding, although less on average than in Latin America (Table 9.4). Half the farms in India cover less than one-tenth of the total agricultural area; in Pakistan one-third of the farms account for 3.5 per cent of the total area. Some of the figures in Table 9.4 suggest that the proportion of small farms (less than one hectare) has recently increased in several Asian countries. Other evidence from India suggests two types of change in historical patterns of rural social structure: the growth in some areas of the class of self-employed cultivators or rich peasants, favoured by 1950s land reform (e.g. Gujarat) and the transformation of large landowners into capitalist farmers employing migrant labourers (e.g. Punjab) (Rudolph and Rudolph, 1987). Both of these changes are signs of increasing commercialization of agriculture even as share-cropping tenancy persists in 'marginal' areas to provide labour reserves for seasonal and cyclical purposes at little or no cost to the commercial sector.

In the colonial period, governments concerned themselves either with plantation agriculture or with raising taxes from other forms of agriculture. In India the British created a class of landed aristocrats called *Zamindars* as revenue collectors for the government. The Zamindars, however, did not have any real interest in improving agriculture. Over time they and other intermediaries became an immense burden upon actual cultivators whose rents included not only revenue for the government but also income for the various intermediaries (Hossain, 1982, p. 149). After independence India, Pakistan and other countries in South and Southeast Asia where this system prevailed, abolished intermediary tenures. However, many of the old intermediaries continued to cultivate their holdings through tenants and sharecroppers on the same exploitative terms as before. Only in China, South Korea and Taiwan did land redistribution lead to an effective abolition of the power of large landlords (Loup, 1983; Perkins and Yusuf, 1984).

Since independence, however, total agricultural production has increased at rates at least commensurate with population growth in most Asian countries. Unfortunately, much of the growth has been concentrated in export crops or cereals (wheat, rice) rather than across the board. Moreover, the

Table 9.4: Land distribution in Asia and Latin America
A. Asia

Country	Year	% of farms under 1 hectare	% of total area covered by farms under 1 hectare
Bangladesh	1960	51.6	15.2
	1974	66.0	24.0
India	1961	39.8	6.8
	1970/71	50.6	9.0
Indonesia	1963	70.1	28.7
Korea	1963	73.3	45.0
	1974	67.0	58.3
Philippines	1960	11.5	1.6
	1970	13.6	1.9
Pakistan	1960	32.9	3.5
Malaysia (West)	1960	45.4	15.2
Thailand	1963	18.5	2.5

B. Latin America

Country	Year	Subfamily farms[a] % of total farms	Subfamily farms[a] % of total area	Small holdings[b] Av. size (ha.) 1960	Small holdings[b] Av. size (ha.) 1970	Small holdings[b] % change 1960–70
Argentina	1960	43.2	3.4	...	...	...
Brazil	1950	22.5	0.5	2.46	2.16	− 12.2
Chile	1960	36.9	0.2	1.40	1.67	+ 19.3
Colombia	1955	64.0	4.9	1.64	1.64	0
Ecuador	1954	89.9	16.6	1.72	1.50	− 12.8
Guatemala	1950	88.4	14.3	...	...	...
Peru	...	88.0	7.4	1.70	1.44	− 15.3
Uruguay		...	...	2.64	2.71	+ 2.6
Venezuela		...	...	2.17	2.24	+ 3.2
El Salvador		...	...	1.67	1.56	− 6.6
Nicaragua		...	...	3.10	2.36	− 23.9
Jamaica		...	...	1.54	1.25	− 18.8

[a]'Subfamily farms' were defined as 'farms large enough to provide employment for less than 2 people with the typical incomes, markets and levels of technology now prevailing in each region.'
[b]'Small holdings' were defined as enterprises of less than 5 hectares except in El Salvador (less than 10 hectares) and Jamaica (less than 25 acres).
Source: Loup (1983) Table 3.4, p. 115

unequal social structure of most rural areas has ensured an upward drift of the benefits of increased production. Rural poverty has increased as agricultural production has increased (Jones *et al.*, 1982; Loup, 1983).

A major source of increased production of cereals (especially wheat) since the 1960s has been the Green Revolution. This had its most significant impact in the two Punjabs (in India and Pakistan) and the Indian state of Haryana where irrigation facilities could be utilized. Benefits have accrued disproportionately to large farmers and the technologies involved (new seed varieties, heavy applications of chemical fertilizers) cannot be applied in areas without irrigation facilities: 80 per cent of the cultivated area in India, 90 per cent in Bangladesh (Loup, 1983).

In general over the past 40 years most Asian governments have not favoured agriculture. Many have pursued pricing and credit policies similar to those noted earlier for Sub-Saharan Africa. This seems also to be true at least for considerable periods in the case of China (Hsu, 1982; Lardy, 1984). Indian development plans until the late 1970s were systematically biased against the agricultural sector. Yet there is a direct relationship between agricultural yields and price structure (Table 9.5). The countries with the highest ratios of prices to input costs are also where yields are highest. The three countries with the highest yields also have perhaps the poorest soils of all the countries in Table 9.5. Government policies and difference in rural social structure are the only plausible causes of the differences in yields.

According to the World Bank, three-quarters of the world's 'absolute poor' (unable to maintain a minimum nutritional standard) live in Asia and more than four-fifths of them live in rural areas. Rather than improving, their lot has appeared to worsen. During the 1970s the number of rural unemployed increased and the real wages of agricultural workers stagnated or decreased in most countries of the region. The number of landless workers also increased: from 22 per cent (1961) 38 per cent (1973) in Bangladesh and from 25 per cent (1961) to 38 per cent (1971) in India (Asian Development Bank, 1977). Even in the face of improved production it is hard to avoid the general conclusion of Loup (1983, p. 31) that

> The verdict is disastrous. During recent decades the situation of the rural masses of non-Communist Asia has at best stagnated and at worst has deteriorated.

Table 9.5: Comparative price data for fertilizer and rice

Country	Paddy price to producers (in US cents per kg.)	Price of fertilizer nutrients to producers (in US cents per kg.)	Ratio of paddy price to fertilizer price	Paddy yield in 1970 (in million tons per hectare)
Japan	30.7	21.5	1.428	5.64
Korea	18.4	19.1	0.963	4.55
Taiwan	11.7	26.2	0.447	4.16
Malaysia	8.8	20.3	0.433	2.72
Ceylon (Sri Lanka)	11.3	15.8	0.715	2.64
Indonesia	4.5	15.2	0.296	2.14
Thailand	4.5	14.3–50.0	0.315–0.090	1.97
Philippines	7.0	17.3	0.405	1.72
Burma	3.1	25.1	0.124	1.70

Source: Timmer and Falcon (1975) Table 1, p. 68

Whatever assumptions we retain, there is a striking contrast between the present picture and the euphoria created 15 years ago by the beginnings of the Green Revolution!

Reform

In Latin America and Asia the landholding and tenurial systems have been periodically 'reformed' as a result of pressure from peasant movements, government attempts to make agriculture more efficient and productive, and external pressures from MNEs and international development agencies. Certain models have sometimes been followed depending on whether efficiency or equity has been the overriding goal. In the former case the Taiwanese and South Korean experiences are emphasized, in the latter the Chinese experience is often the model. However, in practice, agricultural reform, especially land reform, is overwhelmingly a socio-political process rather than a technical one of choosing a model and then following it.

At one time or another, but especially between 1960 and the early 1970s, virtually every country in Latin America and Asia passed land reform laws. A wide range of arguments have been proposed to justify a role for land reform in agricultural development. There are perhaps four justifications that have been most common and they have appealed differentially to different social groups. The first of these is a 'conservative' argument: land reform is a minimal concession for political stabilization; second, the 'liberal' argument: land reform is needed to create a class of capitalist farmers and expand the domestic market; third, the 'populist' argument: small farms are more efficient (and equitable) than large ones; and fourth, the 'radical' argument: peasants are rapidly being dispossessed of their status as independent producers and are prisoners of cheap food policies and agro-export policies, consequently land reform towards collective production is necessary, if insufficient, for economic development (de Janvry, 1984).

Most actual land reform policies have been of the 'liberal' type, concerned with creating a reform sector. Thirty-three land reforms are classified in Table 9.6, including those in the same country when a land reform programme was later redefined (e.g. Chile). All the diagonal reforms are redistributive ones in the sense that they either increase the size of the reform sector without changing the non-reform sector (1, 7, 13 in Table 9.6) or involve expansion of the reform sector (25). Reforms 2, 3, and 4 are oriented towards eliminating 'feudal' (or other precapitalist) remnants from agriculture rather than redistributing land. In each case the transition to capitalism is dominated by (2) a landed élite, (3) farmers or (4) peasants.

The only possible reforms once a capitalist agriculture has been established are either shifts in the type of agrarian structure (8, 9, 14) or distributive reforms within a given type (7, 13, 19). All reforms can give way to counter-reforms: Chile essentially switched to (12) from (3) after the 1973 military

Table 9.6: A typology of land reforms

	Post-Land Reform				
Mode of production in whole society	Semifeudal	Capitalist			Socialist
Mode of production in agriculture	Semifeudal	Capitalist			Socialist
Land Tenure	Semifeudal estates and reform sector	Capitalist estates and reform sector	Capitalist farms and reform sector	Peasant farms	Socialist farms
Semifeudal estates	(1) Mexico, 1917–34 Taiwan, 1949–51 Colombia, 1961–67 Chile, 1962–67	(2) Bolivia, 1952– Venezuela, 1959– Philippines, 1963–72 Equador, 1964– Peru, 1964–69 Colombia, 1968–	(3) Mexico, 1934–40 India, 1950– Guatemala, 1952–54 Egypt, 1952–66 Iran, 1962–67 Chile, 1967–73	(4) South Korea, 1950– Taiwan, 1951–63 Iraq, 1958–	(5) China 1949–56
Capitalist estates	(6)	(7) Costa Rica, 1962–76	(8) Peru, 1969–75 Philippines, 1972–79	(9)	(10) Cuba, 1959–63 Algeria, 1961–71
Capitalist farms	(11) Guatemala, 1954–	(12) Chile, 1973–	(13) Mexico, 1940– Dominican Republic, 1963– Egypt, 1961–	(14)	(15)
Peasant farms	(16)	(17)	(18)	(19)	(20)
Socialist farms	(21)	(22)	(23)	(24)	(25) Cuba, 1963– China, 1952– Algeria, 1971–77

(Pre-land-reform row groupings: Semifeudal, Capitalist, Socialist)

Source: De Janvry (1984) Table 1, p. 266

coup, Guatemala returned to (11) from (3) after the military coup of 1954. The Chinese, Cuban and Algerian cases are ones of land reform that were part of more 'radical' social political change.

The most widespread and successful (in the sense of lasting) land reforms have been those facilitating the creation of a capitalist agriculture (1–5 in Table 9.6). In Latin America the combination of anti-feudal land reforms with more spontaneous development of capitalism has both removed most feudal remnants and put an end to reform efforts (Grindle, 1986). A similar conclusion can be drawn for Asia (Jones *et al.*, 1982). Reform efforts generally ended in the early 1970s.

The Capitalization of Agriculture

Spontaneous change, therefore, has now become much more important than reform in agricultural development. Over the past 20 years there has been a substantial increase in direct and indirect investment by multinational enterprises (MNEs) in the agriculture of a number of peripheral countries. In many countries, MNEs, attracted by cheap land and labour, appropriate physical conditions, improved infrastructure, and a decline in the relative profitability of other sorts of investment, have increased their involvement in export-oriented agriculture and the production and distribution of seeds, pesticides and fertilizers (Feder, 1978; Dinham and Hines, 1983; Hawes, 1982). Thailand, for example, which exported no pineapples in the early 1970s had by 1979 become the major world exporter after Hawaii because the US company Castle and Cooke had moved a major part of its pineapple operations out of Hawaii. Similarly, the Philippines, which exported no bananas in 1960s, had become one of the world's major exporters by the mid-1970s. This was again due entirely to new multinational investment (Turton, 1982; Jones *et al.*, 1982).

It is in Latin America that this capitalization of agriculture by MNEs has been both most extensive and intensive. Sometimes control is exercised directly by purchase of land and involvement in production. For example, between 1964 and 1970 US-based MNEs purchased 35 million hectares of agricultural land in Brazil alone (Feder, 1978). Increasingly, however, MNEs and international development agencies (World Bank, US AID, etc.) are encouraging traditional rural élites to become commercial élites practicing mechanized farming of export crops that are processed and marketed by the MNEs. This strategy reflects both fear of the revolutionary potential of peasant movements in traditional agrarian structures and the need for MNEs to keep a low profile lest they become the targets of nationalization drives.

The impact of 'agribusiness' investment in the agriculture of the periphery, therefore, is not restricted to the development of export enclaves or plantation enclaves as was characteristic of an earlier phase in the development of the world-economy. Rather, its most important effect is probably the way in which it channels capital to a class of rural capitalists and thus consolidates MNE control over *entire* national agricultural systems. The penetration of peripheral agriculture by international agribusiness is, in effect, just another aspect of the New International Division of Labour (Burbach and Flynn, 1980).

Between 1966 and 1978 US investment in Latin American agriculture expanded from $365 million to $1.04 billion, growing from 15 per cent to 21 per cent of total US direct foreign investment in Latin America. This investment was heavily concentrated in Argentina, Brazil, Mexico and Venezuela, where the growing urban middle and upper classes provided a domestic supplement to US demand for so-called 'luxury foodstuffs' (meat, fruits and vegetables). As demand grew for the fertilizers, pesticides, herbicides, improved seeds and agricultural machinery needed by the 'new' agriculture, MNEs such as du Pont, W.R. Grace, Monsanto, Exxon and Allied Chemical were increasingly involved in local production.

MNEs and foreign portfolio investment capital were involved in a variety of ways. In the state of Sinaloa in Northern Mexico, for example, 20–40 per cent of the credit for agricultural production in the 1970s came from north of the border. In Argentina the amount of foreign capital in beef production decreased while it increased in the packing and processing industries. In Mexico and Central America contract production now links national producers with MNEs. Foreign banks have become major agricultural lenders. For example, the Bank of America became heavily involved in Guatemala in the 1970s, lending for major development projects, such as converting forest to pasture for beef production, and providing speculative export loans (Nairn, 1981; Grindle, 1986).

The consequences are manifold. At a global level there has been a marked reorientation of Latin American export agriculture from Europe to the United States. Before World War II exports were strongly oriented to Europe. At a national level there has been an extraordinary expansion of some crops at the expense of other crops, especially traditional food staples. Some crops that were not widely produced in the 1960s grew at enormous rates in the 1970s: Sorghum in Brazil (125.5 per cent per annum), Venezuela (68.9 per cent) and Colombia (20.4 per cent); soybeans in Paraguay (83.3 per cent), Argentina (63.9 per cent), and Brazil (59.0 per cent); and palm oil in Ecuador (29.6 per cent) (Grindle, 1986).

Table 9.7 shows the decline in the amount of land devoted to a number of basic crops in a number of Latin American countries in the 1970s. In some cases the decline in area was compensated for by increases in yield. This was the case with corn (maize) in Costa Rica, the Dominican Republic, Guatemala, Mexico and Venezuela. Typically, however, decreased area has meant decreased output. The food staples have been replaced by more profitable products destined for affluent urban and foreign markets. In Chile fruits and livestock have replaced wheat and sugarbeet; sorghum has replaced corn

Table 9.7: Area planted and production of selected staple crops, 1969–80

Crop and country	Area planted (1,000 hectares)		Production (1,000 metric tons)	
	1969–71	1978–80	1969–71	1978–80
Beans				
Costa Rica	22	21	9	11
Ecuador	78	45	36	24
Mexico	1,789	1,523	904	893
Panama	16	14	5	4
Peru	77	73	62	56
Venezuela	97	69	34	40
Cassava				
Argentina	26	21	296	188
Bolivia	18	16	223	219
Ecuador	35	22	382	179
Venezuela	39	38	317	345
Corn				
Argentina	3,880	2,624	8,717	8,203
Colombia	684	637	856	848
Costa Rica	50	39	56	64
Dominican Republic	27	22	46	62
Ecuador	312	204	239	209
Guatemala	671	621	751	968
Mexico	7,412	6,647	9,025	10,045
Nicaragua	260	188	238	217
Panama	77	66	66	64
Peru	373	351	605	565
Uruguay	194	130	161	121
Venezuela	606	494	698	745
Potatoes				
Argentina	190	110	2,212	1,618
Brazil	214	198	1,557	2,032
Ecuador	47	28	560	286
Peru	293	253	1,877	1,636
Uruguay	22	21	135	137

Source: Grindle (1986) Table 5.8, p. 88

in Mexico and Brazil; livestock have replaced the basic crops throughout the region as indicated by statistics showing the vast expansion of permanent pasturelands at the same time croplands have either decreased in area (as in Mexico and Venezuela) or increased only moderately (as in Costa Rica, Colombia, Panama and Honduras). In some places increased livestock production has also stimulated the expansion of feed-grain production, often on land that formerly produced the food staples of middle- and low-income groups. Livestock production has also produced widespread deforestation and erosion of land that could be productive under other uses (R.G. Williams, 1986; Grindle 1986; Brockett; 1987).

Shortfalls in food staple production have necessitated the increased import of basic food items. Until 1973 agricultural exports grew steadily even if they

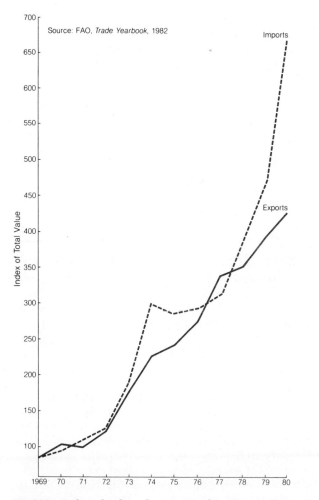

Source: FAO, *Trade Yearbook*, 1982

Fig 9.3 Index of value of exports and imports in Latin America, 1969–1980
Source: Grindle (1986) Fig. 5.1, p. 92

did not keep pace with imports (Fig. 9.3). Since then, however, economic stagnation in the United States and Western Europe has reduced demand for Latin America's exports at the same time the cost of imported food (and other products such as fertilizers and machinery) increased appreciably.

The penetration of foreign agribusiness has also had important effects on rural populations. One effect has been the increased concentration of landholdings in the hands of capitalist farmers and MNEs such that

> Throughout the region, tenants and sharecroppers were replaced by agricultural workers, and permanent workers were displaced by part-time labourers. Given these changes, land-owners could minimize the costs of maintaining a labour force through periods when it was not needed and expand cropping or

> livestocking areas by taking over lands that had been assigned to resident labour-
> ers, tenants, and sharecroppers. Labour costs were thus reduced for the entre-
> preneur, and the available pool of labourers, forced to provide for their own
> maintenance during inactive periods, was enlarged. (Grindle, 1986, p. 98)

Another effect has been to increase the need to borrow and hence the indebtedness of surviving peasant farmers and part-time labourers. Debt is nothing
new for peasant farmers. As the meaning of subsistence changed in a monetized economy to include 'urban goods' and processed foods, so did the
importance of money. In the past, money was obtained through the sale of
labour for cash wages or sale of market crops. Debt arose because of the need
to store and transport crops and pay for inputs before cash was available.
Often yields and cash wages were so low that more debt was incurred merely
to survive. Today debt is also incurred by the necessity of competing against
the capitalist-export sector for land, inputs and water resources (Pearse, 1975;
Warman, 1980).

In order to manage the higher debt load, peasants must farm their land
more intensively. This only exacerbates the problem. Traditional farming
methods such as crop rotation and fallow periods are replaced by monoculture
to grow the most remunerative crop. This process leaches and depletes the
soil, leading to poor harvests and soil erosion. As a consequence, more
fertilizers and new seeds are required, thus deepening the cycle of indebtedness. Warman (1980, p. 238) describes the cycle of indebtedness that has
followed the increased 'capitalization' of agriculture in central Mexico:

> The peasant has to combine several sources of credit, on occasion all of them, in
> order to bring off the miracle of continuing to produce without dying of starva-
> tion. He does it through a set of elaborate and sometimes convoluted strategies.
> Some people plant peanuts only in order to finance the fertilizers for the corn
> crop. Others use official credit to finance planting a cornfield or for buying corn
> for consumption in the months of scarcity, while they resort to the local bour-
> geoisie or the big monopolists in order to finance a field of tomatoes or onions.
> Many turn to usurers to cover the costs of an illness or a fiesta. . . . Given what
> they produce in a year, what is left after paying the debts does not go far enough
> even for food during the dry season, much less for starting a crop on their own.
> For them, obtaining a new loan is a precondition for continuing cultivation, one
> that must be combined with the sale of labour if they are to hold out to the next
> harvest. Each year the effort necessary to maintain the precarious equilibrium
> increases, and it seems to be a spiral that constantly demands more work, as well
> as the daring and inventiveness to find it. Creating employment, inventing ways
> of working harder, is part of peasant leisure.

Peasants, then, are survivors as much as victims. Increasingly, wage labour
has come to provide a major portion of family income even for peasants who
own land. Often this has involved temporary long-distance migration. In
Guatemala, for example, the coffee, cotton and sugar harvests involve the
seasonal migration of more than 300,000 highland Indians (Miro and

Rodriguez, 1982). Temporary wage labour on nearby plantations and capitalist farms, however, is perhaps the major form of adaptation.

In some areas peasants have also supplemented their incomes by switching to the cultivation of drug crops. The market for these crops in the United States has grown exponentially since 1970 and the crops can be grown in remote areas on low-grade soils. Given the illegality of drug crops in world trade, remoteness becomes a virtue rather than the liability it is in more legitimate trade. In Peru, Colombia and Bolivia, cocaine, heroin and marijuana exports are estimated to bring in $600 million per annum. In Bolivia, cocaine exports exceed the total value of all legitimate exports. In Peru, cocaine is the country's largest export earner (Stone, 1988). Of course, much of the proceeds goes to 'drug barons', public officials and intermediaries. But for many peasants the drug traffic is one of the only ways they have of paying their debts and, thus, responding to the disruptions consequent upon the capitalization of agriculture by MNEs and foreign investment.

An interesting case study in the capitalization of Latin American agriculture is the so-called 'beef boom' in Central America in the 1970s and early 1980s (R.G. Williams, 1986). This led to the emergence of Central America as a major supplier of beef to the United States when it had been previously relatively insignificant. It resulted from the tremendous increase in demand for beef in the United States as a result of the emergence of the fast-food franchises such as McDonald's and Burger King catering to a population increasingly given to 'eating out.' The new franchises were not particularly demanding of high quality beef. What they wanted was quantity that could be formed into patties of equal size and weight by sufficient grinding and tenderizing. But the quantity needed was so huge that the fast-food chains (and 'TV dinner' makers) needed to look beyond the US for sources of supply. Sources such as Australia, New Zealand and Canada were subject to severe quota limitations that were part of intensive 'tit-for-tat' trade negotiations. South America was 'out' because of the prevalence of hoof (foot)-and-mouth disease there. Central America was favoured by US government policy to help 'friendly' governments diversify their exports in the face of the 'geostrategic threat' from Cuba and the Soviet Union in the region. By 1979 Central America had acquired 93 per cent of the share of the US beef quota available to underdeveloped countries.

A number of MNEs and individuals found it profitable to respond to the demand for beef from Central America. Some very large US companies became involved through subsidiaries and joint ventures. For example, R.J. Reynolds owns huge grazing ranches in Guatemala and Costa Rica through its Del Monte subsidiary and it directly processes and markets its beef through a variety of outlets: Ortega beef tacos, Chun King beef chow mein and Delmonte Mexican foods. It also sells beef through Zantigo Mexican Restaurants (Kentucky Fried Chicken). One of the largest firms in the Central American beef business is Agrodinamica Holding Company, a company formed in

1971 with 60 per cent of the stock owned by wealthy Latin Americans and 40 per cent of the stock owned by the American ADELA Investment Company. This operation controls thousands of acres of pastures in Central America, owns numerous packing plants, and runs a Miami (Florida) beef-import house and wholesale distributor (Williams, 1986).

Other MNEs have become involved in supplying the beef business with inputs (grass seed, barbed wire, fertilizers, feed grains and veterinary supplies). Pulp and paper companies such as Crown Zellerbach and Weyerhauser invested in cardboard box factories to supply packinghouses with containers for shipping the beef. Finally, fruit companies with access to large blocks of land turned them into money-making properties.

MNEs, however, were not the only beneficiaries. Wealthy families with access to large amounts of 'marginal' and forest land have turned them into profitable pastures. Some very powerful families, for example the Somozas in Nicaragua before 1979, have tapped profits from every stage of the beef-export business. Some urban-based professionals (lawyers, bankers, etc.) have also become involved as 'weekend ranchers' of peripheral areas previously untouched by commercial agriculture (R.G. Williams, 1986; Brockett, 1987).

The massive displacement of peasants by ranchers and cattle, however, has met with tremendous resistance. As R.G. Williams (1986, p. 151) puts it: 'The receding edge of the tropical forest became the setting of a conflict between two incompatible systems of land use, one driven by the logic of the world market, the other driven by the logic of survival.' The contemporary violence and civil war throughout Central America bear no small relationship to the expansion of the beef-export business. As the US government backs the beef business and local revolutionaries organize the peasants, the political consequences of economic change become apparent.

Science and Technology in Agriculture

The beef-export boom in Central America would not have been possible without the importation of techniques of 'scientific agriculture.' In this context this involved creating 'new' breeds of cattle by combining 'beefier' attributes with high resistance to pests and tropical heat, transforming pasture management by sowing higher-yield grasses and fertilizers, enhancing water supplies by digging new wells and ponds, and providing better veterinary care to cattle herds.

The past 30 years have witnessed an intensive drive on the part of international development agencies, some national governments, and agribusiness to introduce scientific farming into agriculture in LDCs. The results have been controversial. From one point of view, yields have been increased and, especially in parts of Asia but to a degree also elsewhere, agricultural productivity and production have been significantly increased. Of particular importance have been the new wheat and rice varieties associated with the so-called 'Green Revolution.' It is generally acknowledged that the gains from these new varieties (and the fertilizers and irrigation they require) have been concentrated in certain districts of India, Pakistan and Sri Lanka, the Central Philippines, Java in Indonesia, peninsular Malaysia, northern Turkey and northern Colombia. In addition to increased yields the new techniques can involve an increase in demand for labour in land preparation, fertilizer application, and harvesting and increases in the wages of agricultural labourers (as in the Indian Punjab). Doubts are sometimes expressed, however, about the sustainability of these trends in yields and labour use (Wortman and Cummings, 1978; Hayami, 1984).

From another point of view, scientific agriculture is largely an instrument of commercialization and capitalization rather than a mechanism for improving agricultural productivity and production *per se*. This is not to say that new seed varieties, fertilizers, etc., are *always* inappropriate; rather that it all depends on the socio-political context in which they are applied. In particular, research efforts in scientific agriculture have been heavily biased towards certain commodities that are either most important in the industrialized countries or significant in world trade (Table 9.8). The very small

Table 9.8: Estimates of international and national research investment by major commodities (1971 constant dollars)

Commodity, in order of value of production	Value of commodity in all developing nations ($ billions)	Estimated research investment		National investment as proportion of product value (percentage)
		International centres (1976) ($ millions)	National centres (1976)[b] ($ millions)	
1 Rice	Over 13	7.9	34.7	0.26
2 Wheat	5–6	3.8	35.9	0.65
3 Sugar cane	5–6	0	30.2	0.50
4 Cassava	5–6	1.9	4.0	0.07
5 Cattle	5–6	7.9	54.8	0.88
6 Maize	3–4	4.1	29.6	0.75
7 Coconuts	3–4	0	2.0	0.06
8 Sweet potatoes	3–4	0.6	3.4	0.09
9 Coffee	2	0	8.5	0.40
10 Grapes	2	0	6.9	0.35
11 Sorghum	1–1½	1.2	12.2	0.77
12 Barley	1–1½	0.5	9.4	0.62
13 Groundnuts	1–1½	0.5	4.0	0.13
14 Cotton	1–1½	0	60.1	3.50
15 Dry beans	1–1½	1.5	4.0	0.25
16 Chick peas	1–1½	1.2	3.0	0.18
17 Chillies and spices	1–1½	0	4.0	0.25
18 Olives	1–1½	0	5.0	0.33
19 Grain legumes	1	1.6	(25.3)	(2.00)
20 Potatoes (white)	1	2.0	8.2	0.68

Source: Evenson (1984) Table 2, p. 352

amount of research on important food staples such as cassava, coconuts, sweet potatoes, groundnuts and chickpeas is especially noteworthy. At present the 'research system' gives high priority to export crops such as cattle, cotton and sorghum and to those such as rice and wheat which have 'wide adaptability': ability to transfer a new variety from one region to others (Evenson, 1984; Eicher, 1984). Wide adaptability can be criticized, however, for its potential in reducing genetic variety and making crops more vulnerable to disease.

A more frequent criticism of scientific agriculture, particularly in its manifestation as the Green Revolution, is that it primarily benefits larger, more prosperous farmers who have readier access to the necessary inputs and credit sources. At the same time it encourages the 'debt cycle' among poorer peasants and part-time labourers discussed earlier (Pearce, 1979; Yapa, 1979; Griffin, 1974). Moreover, the new varieties require increased dependence on the acquisition of energy-intensive inputs (such as fertilizers and agricultural machinery), largely controlled by MNEs.

Evidence from such diverse settings as Mexico, India and Bangladesh suggests that where capital-intensive agriculture is introduced into areas with an uneven distribution of resources it exacerbates the condition of the rural poor by marginalizing subsistence systems, such as sharecropping, and encouraging the polarization of land control between a class of capitalist farmers on the one hand and the mass of the rural population on the other (Schejtman, 1982; Joshi, 1982; Jones, 1982; Hewitt de Alcantara, 1976). The impact of scientific agriculture, therefore, cannot be separated from issues of social structure.

Summary

Since 1960 GNP growth rates have been faster in the underdeveloped countries than in the developed countries (5.5 per cent per annum compared to 4.2 per cent). In addition, despite large rates of population growth, the per capita incomes of the periphery taken as a whole have grown at about 2.5 per cent per annum. Agricultural production has increased at similar rates, in contrast to the stagnation of the colonial period in many Asian and some African countries. Food production per capita in Latin America and Asia grew by 5 and 10 per cent between 1960 and 1980. Only in countries with birth rates of 3 per cent or more, as in parts of Sub-Saharan Africa, or where there were major social upheavals, such as Central America, Bangladesh and Vietnam, is this picture particularly misleading.

At the same time, however, the incidence of rural poverty has increased enormously. This is because increased production in the context of the modern world-economy is no guarantee that the people involved in achieving it will see its fruits. This chapter has attempted to show how this can be the case by detailing the effects of progressive commercialization and capitalization. When subsistence uses and food-staple production are displaced by export crops, increased agricultural production does not necessarily benefit rural populations. Far from it. They often find themselves ensnared in webs of poverty and indebtedness that are the direct product of modern scientific agriculture in contexts where there are few alternatives to agricultural employment.

In reaching this conclusion the argument of this chapter has involved making the following major points:

- Agriculture is often given a subsidiary role in models of development even when it is a vital source of sustenance and employment.

- The three continents of the periphery – America, Africa and Asia – differ significantly in terms of agricultural organization and performance.

- Agriculture is overwhelmingly more important as a source of employment to women than to men, especially in Sub-Saharan Africa.

- There is a long history of commercial agriculture in the periphery. Until recently, however, it was a plantation or export-enclave sector surrounded by a largely subsistence sector.

- Governments have not tended to favour agriculture. For a variety of reasons, their pricing and credit policies have tended to drain agriculture in favour of the industrial-urban sector.

- Land reform has tended to encourage the development of capitalist agriculture rather than benefit the interests of peasant farmers.

- Land reform and the recent activities of governments and multinational enterprises have produced a much more widespread commercialization and capitalization (increasingly capital-intensive) of agriculture. This has been most marked in Latin America but can also be seen elsewhere.

- 'Scientific' agriculture has tended to reflect and reinforce the capitalization of agriculture even as it has increased yields for a limited number of agricultural products.

10

Industrialization: The Path to Progress?

In the 1950s and 1960s the development strategies of many underdeveloped countries placed considerable emphasis upon industry, which was considered to be the 'noble' or leading sector of economic development. More recently, as the industrialized countries have 'lost' some branches of manufacturing to some locations in the global periphery and some peripheral countries have embarked on aggressive export-oriented development strategies, it seems that efforts at industrialization can pay off. Indeed, an earlier complacency about the *immobility* of capital at a global scale has now given way in some quarters to predictions about 'the end of the third world' (Harris, 1986). But what exactly has been the result of several decades of industrialization in the periphery?

In the periphery over the past 30 years value added in manufacturing (MVA) has risen at a rapid pace. The increase is relative, however. The LDCs supplied 8.2 per cent of world MVA in 1960 and still only 10.9 per cent in 1980 and 11.6 per cent in 1984 (UNIDO, 1981, 1985). Moreover, industrialization is highly concentrated. From 1966 to 1975, four countries, representing 11 per cent of the population of the LDCs, accounted for over half the increase of the LDCs' MVA. Eight countries (Brazil, Mexico, Argentina, South Korea, India, Turkey, Iran, Indonesia) with 17 per cent of the total population produced about two-thirds of the increase. At the same time, growth rates of MVA have been lowest in the poorest countries. In Sub-Saharan Africa the growth of manufacturing has been particularly slow. In 1975 manufactured production represented 5 per cent of the GDP of the African LDCs as opposed to 16 per cent for the Asian ones and 25 per cent of those in Latin America and the Caribbean (Loup, 1983).

In all LDCs, irrespective of their growth rates, industrial production has been characterized by a particular expansion of heavy industries: iron and steel, machinery and chemicals. Over the entire period 1950–80 this expansion was more rapid than the growth of food processing or textile, clothing and shoe industries. This point needs emphasizing because of the tendency to assume, because of increasing exports of clothing and shoes to Europe and the United States, that *light* and consumer goods industries have grown the most in the LDCs.

However, since the 1960s the industrial *mix* of many underdeveloped countries has undergone significant change. After World War II, industrialization, even if involving foreign investment by MNEs, was largely concerned with import-substitution. Since the early 1960s the possibilities of substitution have dwindled in the face of mounting costs of establishing heavy industries and as new subcontracting and global sourcing strategies of MNEs have replaced the older strategy of direct establishment of subsidiaries. In this new global context a fundamental reorientation has taken place in the most industrialized LDCs in East Asia and Latin America. In these countries an increasing proportion of industry is oriented towards exporting manufactured goods, mostly to the developed countries of the core (Jenkins, 1988).

The shift towards an export-orientation was facilitated by rapid economic growth (and increasing consumer incomes) in the developed countries (especially in Western Europe and Japan) and the liberalization of world trade in the 1960s. Above all, however, it reflects a change in national industrialization strategy. The role of the state remains central. Like import-substitution, export-promotion involves a strong managerial role for the state in adjusting to new global pressures. The states that have been most successful in doing so, such as South Korea and Taiwan, are now the leading industrializers (Tyler, 1981).

In this chapter the progress of industrialization in the LDCs is examined in four complementary ways. First, the national and global stimuli to industrialization are described. Particular attention is directed towards the role of industrialization in national ideologies of modernization, the practical basis to the demand for industrialization, and the global context for the shift from import-substitution to export-orientation. Second, the problems facing industrialization in the periphery are reviewed, paying special attention to the limits on industrialization posed by certain national and global constraints. Third, the geographical pattern of industrialization is surveyed at global, regional and urban scales. Fourth, and finally, Brazil and Cuba are profiled for their particular experiences of industrialization over the recent past.

National and Global Stimuli to Industrialization

The central attention given by many peripheral countries to industry is partly a result of the *prestige* of this sector, which is widely considered the hallmark of development. Although the notion of 'industrialization-in-general' can be criticized on grounds of vagueness and lack of attention to the specific mix of industries and their relation to the needs of the mass of the population (e.g. Corbridge, 1982), industrialization figures prominently in most national ideologies of modernization. Perhaps Maoist China, at least in theory (see Murphey, 1980) was the exception that only proves the rule is otherwise everywhere else!

Three ideas of mythic proportions are at the centre of the claim that national industrialization is the path to modernity, even though they are of questionable empirical validity. Interestingly, they all involve negative views of agriculture as much as positive endorsements of industry and they all imply a simple sectoral logic of development as movement *from* agriculture *to* industry (Loup, 1983, pp. 155–8).

First, agriculture is viewed as having more limited stimulus effects on other economic activities than industry. In other words, industry is seen as providing *multiplier effects* that agriculture cannot provide. The best refutation of this particular idea is the key role that agriculture played in the early industrialization of Europe and the continued importance of agriculture in the economies of the developed world. Of course, in each case investment was required to develop forward linkages to consumer industry (food processing, etc.) and backward linkages to input providers (fertilizers, etc.). In each case farmers were also important as consumers of industrial products, when not penalized by low prices for their products, and significant financers of industrial investment, through savings and taxation. Adelman (1984) has proposed that precisely these stimulative features of agriculture can be used to substitute 'agriculture-demand-led-industrialization' (ADLI) for import-substitution and export-led models.

Second, farmers have a reputation for *conservatism* whereas industrialists (and workers) are viewed as agents of modernization. Imprisoned in ancient and traditional cultures, farmers, especially peasant farmers, are without dynamism and rationality. Yet, again, this idea is easily refuted by evidence from all over the world. For example, as shown in Chapter 9 there is a strong link between producer prices and yields of rice in different Asian countries. Corn (maize) production in Thailand, bean production in the Sudan, and wheat production in India and Pakistan have all increased as prices have increased and decreased when prices have declined. These are hardly indications of conservatism and lack of responsiveness to commercial incentives.

Third, for many governments industry is seen as the only *productive* sector. Only in industry, the argument goes, are there increasing marginal returns through economies of scale in production. Moreover, the average productivity of workers in industry is higher than that of those in agriculture. However, the productivity of other factors, capital in particular, is probably higher in agriculture. In most of the countries for which data exist, the gross marginal capital/output ratio is lower and hence productivity is higher in agriculture than in other sectors (Szcezepanik, 1969). In the United States, the only country with a sufficiently long statistical series, the total productivity of *all* factors has increased faster in agriculture than in other sectors (Samuelson, 1964).

But whatever the empirical merit of the three ideas they have become firmly entrenched and associated with modernization through industrialization. Manufacturing industry is widely viewed as the path to progress and it figures prominently in most national development ideologies and plans. These ideologies, whatever precise roles they reserve for 'private' business and state direction, have been reinforced by certain practical problems facing most governments. There are perhaps three that appear most important. One of them concerns the terms of trade in exchanging primary commodities for manufactured goods. As suggested in Chapter 8 there are good grounds for pessimism about the growth potential *in general* of primary production (also see Delacroix, 1977; Stokes and Jaffee, 1982). However, for specific primary commodities and specific countries investment in primary production can be preferable (Ray, 1977; Spraos, 1983; Love, 1983; Sender and Smith, 1986). Nevertheless, by and large, governments have not been persuaded of this. They can even point to the case of the OPEC cartel, the most successful attempt in the history of the world-economy to bolster the price of a primary commodity, to illustrate the limitations of primary production. From its dominant position in 1973–74, OPEC has become less and less able to govern the world price of oil. This reflects both adjustment strategies in consumer countries (energy conservation, shifts to non-OPEC suppliers) and the emergence of conflicts of interest among member countries (Iran–Iraq war; conservation vs. rapid production e.g. Saudi Arabia vs. Nigeria). It is easy to infer from the experience of OPEC the long-run limitations of a development strategy based upon primary production for world markets.

Second, many LDCs have massive unemployed and underemployed populations concentrated increasingly in urban areas. Deteriorating living conditions in the countryside (see Chapter 9) and the availability of better public services in urban areas have encouraged large-scale rural–urban migration, often in the absence of industrialization. To survive, people engage in a wide range of 'informal' economic activities as street vendors, shoeshine boys, stall keepers, public letter writers, auto mechanics, taxi drivers, subcontractors, tailors, drug dealers and prostitutes (Mattera, 1985; Sanders, 1987). Sometimes these activities can be linked to industrialization of a formal variety through subcontracting, but often they cannot. It is in this context that expansion of employment in manufacturing industry can often become an important national imperative.

A third incentive for industrialization comes from the state-building activities of national élites. National industrialization can be a 'prestige' goal around which national populations can be mobilized. All governments are also under pressure to industrialize in order to compete with other countries. Pressure comes from both domestic élites, especially the military, and from foreign allies and patrons. Some of the emphasis on heavy industries undoubtedly derives from this pressure. The significant growth of military industries in the periphery is directly related to it (Neuman, 1984). Industry is also an important instrument of political favouritism and patronage. Governments can reward 'loyal' social and ethnic groups and punish 'disloyal' ones by directing industrial activities towards some places and away from others. Industrialization, therefore, often involves political stimulation, of both 'noble' and 'ignoble' varieties.

The national industrialization drives that took place in the aftermath of decolonization had limited effects until the late 1960s, except in those

Fig 10.1   Twenty-five years of falling profits in OECD countries, 1955–1980
Source: Edwards (1985) p. 155

countries with large domestic markets and long-sustained import substitution policies (e.g. Brazil, Mexico). The spread and intensification of industrialization since the late 1960s coincides with the declining rate of profit in the industrialized countries (Fig. 10.1) and the consequent shift in strategy by MNEs from high-wage/high-consumption forms of production in the industrialized countries (Fordism) towards spatially decentralized forms of production in which low-wage labour forces are important in certain phases (see Table 10.1). This suggests that the global context has been fundamentally important in stimulating the recent expansion of manufacturing industry in some underdeveloped countries (Schmitz, 1984; Lipietz, 1986; Peet, 1987). In other words, the New International Division of Labour in manufacturing and its associated spatial decentralization of many production activities are closely related to the 'crisis' of capital accumulation in the industrialized countries. A new geography of manufacturing employment has been the result (Table 10.2).

Nevertheless, export-oriented industrialization did not take root everywhere. It has been concentrated in certain countries. The most successful ones, the East Asian NICs of South Korea, Taiwan, Singapore and Hong Kong, were ones in which the state and local industrial capital were closely interlocked and receptive to massive foreign investment (Evans and Alizadeh, 1984). Moreover, they are the ones in which much of the foreign investment was bank credit rather than direct investment by MNEs (Goldsbrough, 1985). They thus maintained more local control over investment decisions. In addition, the privileged geopolitical arrangements of South Korea and Taiwan with the United States were important in opening American markets and making available American aid and investment in return for the East Asian countries' forward role in 'containment' of mainland China and the Soviet Union (Hamilton, 1983). The global context may well trigger the *possibility* for industrialization, especially of the export-oriented type, therefore, but it never guarantees the realization. Various contingencies – political, economic, social – intervene.

Table 10.1: Labour conditions in global manufacturing

Country	Average hourly earnings in manufacturing	Industrial disputes 1974–83*
United States	8.83	312
United Kingdom	5.25	470 (1974–82)
Germany, Fed. Rep. of	5.94	26
Japan	6.91	59
Venezuela	3.63 (1981)	45
Mexico	1.59	n.a.
Hong Kong	1.26	10
Korea, Rep. of	1.35	2
Singapore	1.43	2 (1974–82)
Taiwan	1.67	n.a.
India	0.40 (1981)	1,696
Sri Lanka	0.17	383

*Average annual working days lost from disputes per 1,000 non-agricultural workers.
Source: Peet (1987) p. 780

Table 10.2: The changing geography of manufacturing employment: Paid employment in manufacturing (millions)

Region/country	1974	1981–84	Change
North America	22.0	21.4	−0.6
Japan	12.0	12.1	+0.1
Western Europe*	35.2	28.2	−7.0
'Centre'	69.2	61.7	−7.5
South Asia+	5.6	6.9	+1.3
Southeast and East Asia†	6.3	9.6	+3.3
Latin America§	7.0	8.7	+1.7
'Periphery'	18.9	25.2	+6.3

*Austria, Belgium, France, Fed. Rep. of Germany, Italy, Netherlands, Spain, Sweden, Portugal, United Kingdom.
+Bangladesh, India, Sri Lanka.
†Hong Kong, Republic of Korea, Malaysia, Philippines, Singapore, Thailand, Taiwan.
§Brazil, Venezuela, Mexico.
Source: Peet (1987) p. 781

The Limits to Industrialization in the Periphery

There are a number of constraints that will probably limit the spread and intensification of the export-oriented industrialization that has lain behind the impressive growth of the NICs in the 1970s. In the first place, the declining rate of profit in the industrialized countries may well have been cyclical rather than secular. There is some evidence that corporate profitability in the US, for example, has begun to rebound after a 15-year downturn (Uchitelle, 1987). This may mean that there will be less incentive to locate production facilities or engage in subcontracting in the underdeveloped countries. However, the figures (4.9 per cent average return in manufacturing in the US in 1986 compared to 3.5 per cent in the late 1970s and 8 per cent in the early 1960s) may reflect the falling dollar helping American manufacturers and the increased return on *foreign* investments rather than improving domestic profitability.

Second, there are inherent limits to the generalization to other LDCs of the export successes of the NICs. To begin with, the period 1950–80 was one of unusually high growth in world trade. Whereas global trade expanded only at 1 per cent per annum during 1910–40, the period 1953–73 saw an increase of total trade of 8 per cent per annum, and of 11 per cent per annum for manufactures (Tuong and Yates, 1981). The consequence was an increased interdependence in the world-economy as trade barriers were lowered. Since the late 1970s, however, protectionism has been a major response in the industrialized countries to their declining rates of economic growth and increased unemployment, inflation and balance of payments deficits (Yoffie, 1983). Cline (1982) estimated that if all the LDCs had the same export-intensity as South Korea, Taiwan, Singapore and Hong Kong, there would be a shift from 16.4 to 60.4 per cent of aggregate DC manufactured imports originating in the LDCs. Given the reliance of the NICs on DC markets, the likelihood of this expansion without protectionist responses seems extremely unlikely. As Cline (1982, p. 89) concludes: 'It is seriously misleading to hold up the East Asian G4 (Gang of Four, i.e. Hong Kong, Taiwan, South Korea, Singapore) as a model of development because that model almost certainly cannot be generalized without provoking protectionist response ruling out its implementation.'

Of course, Cline's generalization from the current NICs to *all* LDCs represents an extreme scenario. There is still considerable scope for building up export-markets in both DCs and other LDCs (Hughes and Walbroek, 1981; Loup, 1983). In particular, there is evidence that the established NICs are now transferring some of their more labour-intensive industries to countries that have a short-run comparative advantage. For example, Taiwanese firms have subsidiaries in Malaysia, and Hong Kong firms have subsidiaries in the Peoples Republic of China. Among the LDCs, consequently, newcomers are not necessarily condemned to see initially advantaged neighbours permanently monopolize the positions they have won in world markets.

Third, the MNEs that have been involved in setting up subsidiaries or engaging subcontractors in the NICs must now respond to protectionist pressures in the DCs where their final markets are concentrated. This will involve substituting radical new automation technologies for low-wage labour (Jones and Anderson, 1983; Radar, 1982; Hoffman and Rush, 1983). Even if the technology diffuses evenly at a global scale, production costs will decline more steeply in the DCs than in the NICs (Rada, 1984). In addition, new scale economies associated with batch-production for stratified as opposed to mass markets (Sabel, 1982) and new external economies associated with a close geographical integration of component suppliers and final assembly in 'last-minute,' 'just-in-time' and 'zero-inventory' production systems will reduce the attractiveness of global sourcing (Ayres and Miller, 1983; Baillie and Felix, 1983; Kaplinsky, 1984a; Hershey, 1988). There is already evidence that the assembly of electronics circuits is being brought back to DCs from LDCs and the introduction of new technologies and new production systems may further reduce the need for cheap, unskilled labour (Rada, 1982; Ernst, 1982; Kaplinsky, 1984b).

It is important to note, however, that the growth of the NICs is not uniquely due to the activities of MNEs. Domestic firms have played important roles, particularly in such export sectors as textiles, clothing and shoes. This is especially the case in the East Asian countries where the share of manufactured exports attributable to MNEs is in the range of only 5 to 15 per cent (Loup, 1983). Only in Latin America are the expansion of MNEs and the growth of exports closely related (Evans, 1987). But the control of MNEs over most of the new automation technologies will limit their transfer even when the MNEs are not locally dominant (Kaplinsky, 1984b).

Fourth, the success of export-oriented industrialization has been tied to the growth of enormous debt loads underwritten by foreign direct investment, official aid agencies and multinational banks. One of the most problematic features of the world-economy in the 1980s is the absence of any new actor willing to finance industrialization in underdeveloped countries. The institutions which did play such a role in the past are largely unwilling to do so now. Perhaps the only institution that has substantially increased its lending and encouraged others to do likewise is the International Monetary Fund (IMF). But the IMF still lends relatively little compared to the size of LDCs' current account deficits and attaches conditions to loans that many countries with strong state direction find undesirable (Griffith-Jones and Rodriguez, 1984; Lewis, 1988). Even in the 1970s, lending, especially private bank lending, was concentrated in the LDCs with relatively high per capita incomes and those with already impressive growth records. The four largest borrowers (Mexico, Brazil, South Korea, and the Philippines) accounted for over 60 per cent of total accumulated non-OPEC LDCs' debt to international banks in December 1982. Much of the money lent came from recycled 'petrodollars' in the context of declines in credit demand from traditional clients in the DCs in the wake of the 1974–75 recession. This situation is not likely to repeat itself (Griffith-Jones, 1980; Seiber, 1982).

Fifth, the new leading sectors of industrial growth in the world-economy are the so-called 'information technologies'. The US, Japan and three European countries (France, West Germany and the United Kingdom) account for nearly 85 per cent of the world demand for these technologies and their products. Consequently, success in the global information processing and electronics industries requires a research and development, production, marketing and political lobbying base *inside* all three of the regions of demand. Given the importance of politics – especially in the form of lobbying against protectionist threats – established MNEs and countries with large public sector investments in information technologies are at a distinct advantage. Those companies and countries struggling to gain entry beyond the labour-intensive, assembly level will be faced with formidable barriers, not least the absence of local protection in the face of US-led attempts at 'deregulation' of peripheral domestic markets over the past 10 years (Tunstall, 1986; Schiller and Schiller, 1982; Kirchner, 1983).

Sixth, the non city-state NICs with the highest growth rates – South Korea and Taiwan – have enjoyed a unique set of circumstances that are not generalizable to other peripheral settings (Lim and Yang, 1987; Corbridge, 1986). In particular, they inherited the transport and education infrastructure imposed by Japanese colonialism. Later, massive US aid in the 1950s – for geopolitical purposes – stabilized their economies and tight controls on imports plus government allocation of foreign exchange and capital promoted export-led growth (Cumings, 1984). In addition to land reform (see Chapter 9) in both South Korea and Taiwan, state enterprises were a key part of national growth strategies in the 1970s, accounting for 25 per cent to 35 per cent of total fixed investment (Bradford, 1987). In South Korea – following the practice of Japan – interest subsidies and other incentives were employed to induce private companies to develop major industries and focus on exports.

Finally, relatively equal income distributions in Taiwan, South Korea and Japan – where the richest 20 per cent receive, respectively, 4.3, 7.9 and 3.7 times the incomes of the poorest 20 per cent – allow governments to adopt policies pursuing efficiency and growth with limited social and political unrest. By contrast, Latin American countries such as Brazil, where the comparable income differential exceeds a factor of 33, run larger budget deficits to avoid political unrest while yielding to the demands of the rich to limit taxation (Fishlow, 1972; Menzel and Senghaas, 1987). In such circumstances the extreme inequality of incomes, stimulated according to some accounts by the greater degree of penetration by MNEs and their stimulus to service rather than manufacturing jobs (Evans and Timberlake, 1980; Rau and Roncek, 1987), limits government fiscal flexibility (Table 10.3).

Seventh, and finally, it seems that export-oriented industries can make and have already made an important contribution to the creation of new employment in certain *small* countries. However, it would probably be mistaken to believe that these industries can make anything other than a marginal contribution to employment in the periphery as a whole. As of 1980, the World Bank estimated the total number of *direct* jobs created by export industries in the LDCs as between 2 and 3 million, about 10 per cent of total industrial employment in these countries, or, in other terms, less than one half of one per cent of the total labour force of some 850 million people (World Bank, 1979). Even

Table 10.3: International variations in the concentration of income

	Year	Income of lower fifth/ Income of upper fifth	Gini-coefficient
Low income countries:			
Sri Lanka	1969–70	5.79	0.4090
India	1964–65	7.30	0.4675
Middle income countries			
Taiwan	1980	4.17	0.3242
	1971	4.51	0.3505
Yugoslavia	1973	6.15	0.3955
Spain	1974	7.03	0.4185
South Korea	1976	7.95	0.4520
Argentina	1970	11.43	0.5180
Philippines	1970–71	14.57	0.5660
Costa Rica	1971	16.61	0.5710
Venezuela	1970	18.00	0.5875
Mexico	1977	18.76	0.5886
Turkey	1973	16.62	0.5891
Malaysia	1970	17.15	0.5994
Peru	1972	32.11	0.6705
Brazil	1972	33.30	0.7060
Honduras	1967	29.48	0.7145
High income countries:			
Japan	1977	4.10	0.3223
Sweden	1972	5.61	0.3625
Norway	1970	5.92	0.3690
Australia	1966–67	5.88	0.3711
Great Britain	1973	6.16	0.3815
Canada	1969	8.20	0.4225
USA	1972	9.51	0.4530
West Germany	1973	7.11	0.4555
Italy	1969	9.12	0.4700
France	1970	10.91	0.4905

Source: Menzel and Senghaas (1987) p. 70

considering multiplier effects, the total number of direct and indirect jobs created came to 5 to 10 million, around 1 per cent of the total labour force. As this labour force is growing today at an annual rate of 2.2 per cent, the number of workers added every year is more than twice as large as the *total* labour force employed in jobs created by export-oriented manufacturing. Across all underdeveloped countries, therefore, export industries cannot possibly absorb the additional labour force arriving each year or even reabsorb those unemployed due to cyclical shifts in demand for export products. Even restricting attention to eight NICs (Brazil, Mexico, Egypt, India, the Philippines, South Korea, Taiwan, and Yugoslavia), *total* jobs created during the 1960s by the export of manufactured goods represented only 3 per cent of total employment (Tyler, 1976).

However, for small countries with high levels of industrial exports the picture is somewhat different. Thus in Taiwan in 1969 one job in six was created by manufactured exports and in South Korea in 1970 one job in 10 was created by exports of all kinds (Tyler, 1976; Westphal, 1978). In all likelihood these figures are higher today because of the surge in these two countries' exports in the 1970s and middle 1980s. Moreover, for the city-states such as Hong Kong and Singapore, with their dynamic producer-service (finance, organization, research) sectors as well as large concentrations of export-oriented manufacturing industries, the figures would probably be even higher.

But it is not only the absence of large *dependent* peasant and urban populations that gives the small states of East Asia distinct advantages in relative job creation from export-oriented manufacturing. These countries have concentrated on labour-intensive export industries, such as textiles, clothing and electrical and mechanical assemblage. These industries use a great deal of labour per unit of production and this labour is unskilled. They also employ disproportionately large numbers of women whose social position can be exploited to suppress wages and limit union organization. As Joekes (1987, p. 90) puts it 'Women's lesser education and their expectation (born of past experience) of receiving little training make them apparently suited to unskilled occupations and, most importantly, prepared to stay at such unskilled jobs, however monotonous they may be.'

Moreover, these countries have managed to limit capital-intensive production in order to maximize the return on their higher labour/capital ratios in export-oriented manufacturing (Krueger, 1978). This sets them apart from other NICs that have much lower capital/labour ratios in export industries and higher levels of capital intensive production for domestic markets (e.g. Brazil). It also leads to an improvement in income distribution as well as employment creation, since the heavy reliance on unskilled labour implies that relatively more of the incomes generated by export industries will go to the poorest segments of the population and less to those classes rich in capital or technical skills. The peculiar historical development of the East Asian NICs in job creation by export industries, therefore, is not readily duplicated by larger countries (or some smaller ones e.g. Puerto Rico (Santiago, 1987)) in which incomes and wealth are divided unequally and in which powerful classes have a vested interest in maintaining the status quo.

The Geography of Industrialization in the Periphery

As stated earlier, during the late 1960s and 1970s a number of LDCs underwent a rapid process of industrialization, financed in part by the export of capital from the developed world. These countries, the NICs, were the ones where growth was fastest. But growth was not limited to them. What is most important is to grasp the dynamics of industrialization in the late 1960s and

1970s. Figure 10.2 illustrates one way of doing this. This shows the groupings of countries resulting from applying Sutcliffe's (1971) three 'tests' of industrialization: Test One, at least 25 per cent of GDP in industry; Test Two, at least 60 per cent of industrial output in manufacturing; Test Three, at least 10 per cent of the total population employed in industry. This last test measures the impact of the industrial sector on the population as a whole. Seven groupings and two paths to industrialization result from applying the three tests.

The groupings are:

A Fully industrialized countries that pass all three tests.

B Countries which pass the first two tests but with limited 'penetration' into the population or the economy as a whole. These are semi-industrialized countries.

A/B Borderline cases (e.g Greece, Chile).

C Countries which pass the first and third tests. A large industrial sector (in mining or oil) affects the population widely, but manufacturing is weak.

D Countries which pass the second test only. A small industrial sector dominated by manufacturing.

E Countries which pass the first test only. A substantial industrial, but non-manufacturing, sector has limited impacts on the population.

O Other countries i.e. non-industrialized countries failing all three tests.

There are two possible paths to industrialization given this categorization. They are E → C→ A, where a mining enclave expands to involve the total population and manufacturing develops later; and D → B → A where manufacturing leads to increases in industrial output and later towards a more industrial labour force. A third path, perhaps from labour-intensive rural industry towards manufacturing and an increasing industrial labour force, is possible but without any real-world examples.

If data for 1985 are used as well as data for 1975 a number of shifts are discernible (Fig. 10.3). A number of D → B → A moves are clearly visible; most of the NICs (see below) fit this model. The E → C → A path, characteristic in the past of the US, Australia and South Africa, and the expected route, perhaps, the OPEC members, is also of importance, but as yet at an early stage. There are also a number of D → B → C moves; a new phenomenon since 1975 (Crow and Thomas, 1985).

Figure 10.3 shows the industrialization process in terms of Sutcliffe's groupings and 1975–85 changes, across the entire world, including estimates where firm figures are not available. It is clear that, although there are some important examples of industrialization in the periphery, most LDCs are either not industrializing or are industrializing quite slowly.

This conclusion is reinforced by focusing more directly on rates of growth in manufacturing output. Figure 10.4 shows that the high rates of growth in the 1970s (1973–83) were relatively concentrated. There is no exclusive list of

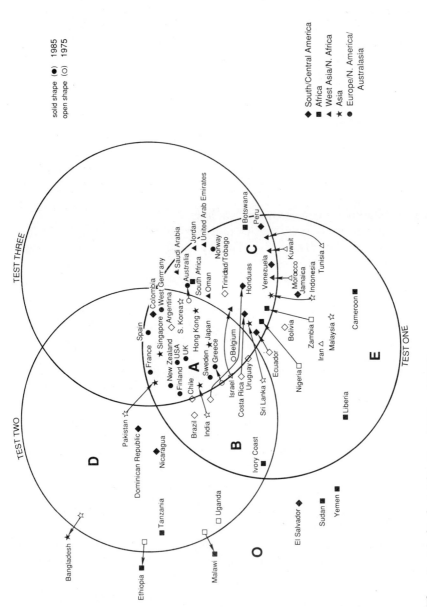

Fig 10.2 Three 'tests' of industrialization, 1975 and 1985
Source: Adapted from Sutcliffe (1971); World Bank (1987)

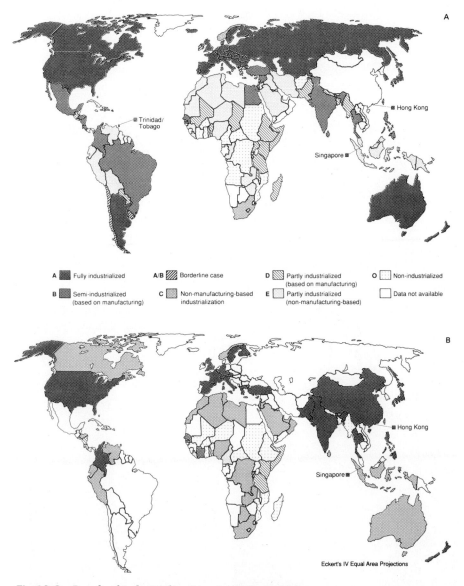

Fig 10.3 Levels of industrialization. A. 1975; B.1985

NICs as different indicators lead to the inclusion of different countries (see Menzel and Senghaas, 1987). The Organization for Economic Cooperation and Development (OECD) recognizes 10 countries as NICs (Brazil, Mexico, S. Korea, Taiwan, Hong Kong, Singapore, Spain, Portugal, Greece and Yugoslavia) on the grounds of 'fast growth of the level and share of industrial employment, an enlargement of export market shares in manufactures, and a rapid relative reduction in the per capita income gap separating them from

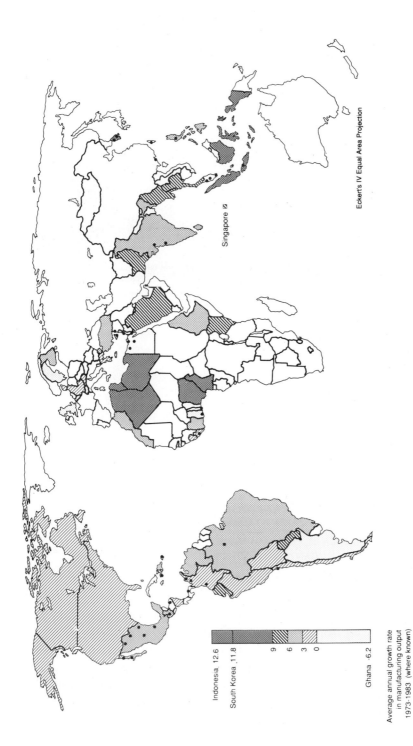

Fig 10.4 The Newly Industrializing Countries (NICs), 1973–1983
Source: World Bank (1987)

Average annual growth rate
in manufacturing output
1973-1983 (where known)

Indonesia 12.6

South Korea 11.8

9

6

3

0

Ghana -6.2

• EPZ

Singapore ▨

Eckert's IV Equal Area Projection

the advanced industrial countries' (OECD, 1979). In Figure 10.4, one of these NICs has a growth rate exceeding 10 per cent per year (South Korea) one exceeds 7·per cent (Singapore), two exceed 4 per cent (Brazil, Mexico), and five are unknown. Of the other countries with high growth rates, some are major oil exporters (Libya, Algeria, Saudi Arabia, Nigeria, Ecuador, Indonesia) or starting from tiny industrial sectors (Haiti, Burma). Some are 'potential' NICs (e.g. Thailand, India).

The NICs have been especially active in export-oriented industrialization (Fig. 10.5). As we have noted previously, some of this industry has been attracted to and is concentrated geographically in 'export-processing zones' (EPZs) or 'free trade zones' (see p. 34). These are limited areas in which special advantages accrue to investors. These include duty-free entry of goods for assembly, limited restrictions on profit repatriation, lower taxation, reduced pollution controls, and constraints on labour organization (strikes banned, etc.). The intention of EPZs is to attract local and international capital to set up factories oriented to export production. By 1984 there were 68 zones in 40 LDCs (Thrift, 1986). As of 1987 most of the EPZs were still clustered around major markets as they had been in 1979 (Fig. 10.4): North America, Western Europe and Japan. South Korea, Taiwan, Mexico, Malaysia, Haiti and Brazil have the largest employment in EPZs. EPZ production is concentrated in textiles and clothing, micro-electronic assembly, and the assembly of cars and bicycles. More specifically, it is the labour-intensive stages of production that are characteristic of the EPZs, (Fig. 10.6).

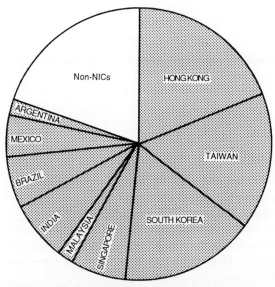

NICs' share of Third World exports 1976 (by value)

Fig 10.5 The NICs' share of Third World exports, 1976 (by value)
Source: Crow and Thomas (1985), p. 49

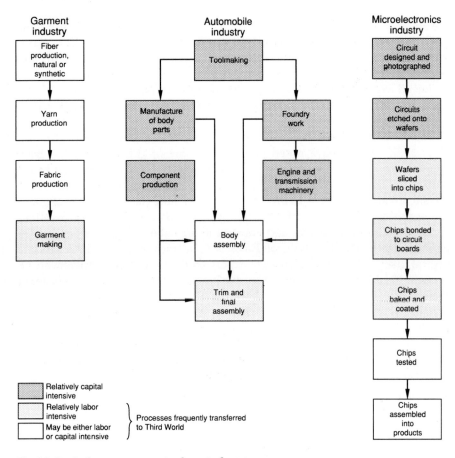

Fig 10.6   Labour processes in three industries
Source: Crow and Thomas (1985) p. 49

Much of the industry in EPZs is owned by MNEs and most of the employment is in microelectronics and textiles and clothing. In Mexico in 1978, 60 per cent of the *maquiladoras*, the assembly plants located in EPZs along the US border, were engaged in electrical and electronic assembly and 30 per cent were involved in textiles and clothing (Hansen, 1981). In the Asian EPZs, over 60 per cent of the employment is in electronics with the clothing and footwear industries second. The build-up in electronics has been especially marked since the early 1970s (Scott, 1987).

The total amount of employment in EPZs, however, is relatively small. In Mexico *maquiladora* employment in 1980 was only around 110,000. There are perhaps 500,000 workers directly employed in EPZs in Asia. Most of the workers are unmarried women between the ages of 17 and 23. About 85 per cent of employment in Mexican EPZs is of such young women. Within Asia, young women account for 88 per cent of zone employment in Sri Lanka, 85 per cent in Taiwan and Malaysia, 75 per cent in South Korea, and 74 per cent in the Philippines (Morello, 1983). Young women are preferred as workers because their wages tend to be lower than men's and because they are considered 'nimble fingered' and 'more able to cope with repetitive work' (Armstrong and McGee, 1986). Certainly, very little training is required and wages are very low. Often an exploitative trainee system is used in which 'trainees' are paid only 60 per cent of the local minimum wage and are repeatedly fired and rehired so as to obtain a permanent 40 per cent reduction in the wage bill (Thrift, 1986).

Many of the EPZs also do not appear to have had major stimulative effects outside their boundaries. Links to local economies are generally limited,

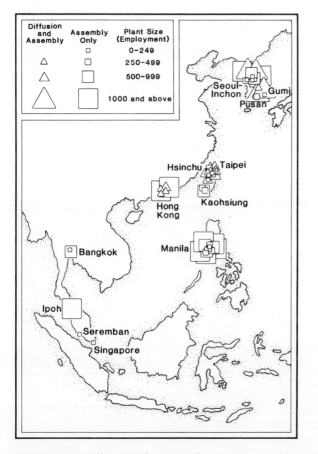

Fig 10.7 Locally-owned semiconductor plants in South-East Asia, 1985
Source: Scott (1987) Fig. 3, p. 150

Table 10.4: Corporate affiliation of US-owned assembly plants in South-East Asia, 1985

	Hong Kong	Indonesia	Korea	Malaysia	Philippines	Singapore	Taiwan	Thailand	Sub-total
Advanced Micro Devices				1	1	1		1[1]	3
Ampex							1		1
Analog Devices					1		1		1
ATT						1		1	2
Commodore	1								1
Data General	1							1	1
Fairchild	1	1	1		1	1			5
General Electric						1			1
General Instrument				1			1		2
Gould[2]			2	1					3
GTE							1		1
Harris Semiconductor				1					1
Hewlett Packard				1		1			2
Intel				1	1				2
Intersil						1			1
Microsemiconductor	1								1
Monolithic Memories				1					1
Mostek				1					1
Motorola	1		1	2	1		1		6
National Semiconductor	1	1		2	1	2		1	8
Raytheon					1				1
RCA				1			1		2
Signetics			1					1	2
Siliconix	1						1		2
Silicon Systems						1			1
Sprague	1				1		1		3
Teledyne	1								1
Texas Instruments				1	1	2	1		5
Western Digital				1					1
Zilog					1				1
Sub-total	8	2	5	14	11	11	8	4	63

Notes: 1. Plant under construction
2. American Microsystems and Korean Microsystems
Source: Scott (1987) Table 6, p. 151

especially in Latin America (Thrift, 1986). However, Scott (1987) shows that in some cases the activities of MNEs have led to the growth of both 'diffusion facilities' owned by local firms engaged in higher-level (not solely assembly) operations and locally owned subcontract assembly houses. The former are concentrated in South Korea, Taiwan and Hong Kong, the latter are found in Thailand, Malaysia, Singapore, the Philippines, Hong Kong, Taiwan and South Korea (Fig. 10.7).

Direct investment by American MNEs has shifted dramatically over time. In 1969, most investment in electronic assembly was in Hong Kong, South Korea, Taiwan and Singapore. By 1983 the Philippines and Malaysia had become relatively more important. Direct foreign investment, therefore, is extremely footloose and sensitive to marginal shifts in wage rates, local fiscal conditions, and political 'instability.' To spread their risks, many of the 30 US MNEs engaged in electronic assembly operations in Asia have plants in a number of different locations in different countries (Table 10.4). Motorola, for example, has seven different manufacturing facilities in six Asian countries (including Japan).

In textiles and clothing there has also been a tendency for the most labour–intensive activities to move away from Hong Kong, Taiwan and South Korea to other parts of Asia. China, Bangladesh, Sri Lanka, and Indonesia have become especially important. 'The clothing industry uses little capital and is very mobile. All you need is a shed, some sewing machines, and lots of cheap nimble fingers' (*Economist*, 27 June 1987, p. 67). Perhaps of greatest importance in this geographical shift has been the imposition of quotas by the US and European countries on imports from established producers. This has set businessmen from Hong Kong and South Korea, the major figures in this industry, searching for countries with higher quotas and low production. For example, Hong Kong is allowed only a 0.6 per cent annual increase in its shirt exports to the EEC, while Sri Lanka is allowed 7 per cent. China has been allowed a large expansion simply because the rich countries are keen to expand their exports of capital goods to such a large market and do not want to invite retaliatory action in the face of a clothing quota decrease.

Although the EPZs and the geographical division of labour within Asia are symptomatic of the importance of 'off-shore production' for final markets in the developed countries, it would be mistaken to see peripheral industrialization solely in these terms. For one thing, as Scott (1987), for example, shows, *local* markets for electronic components and semiconductor devices have grown rapidly in East Asia over the past decade. Even US-owned branch plants now ship about 18 per cent of their production to consumers in East Asia. This has encouraged the establishment of marketing, sales and after-sales service facilities in the region, especially in Hong Kong and Singapore. These two centres now function as nodes in a global system of producer services located in major world cities (Daniels, 1985b; Cohen, 1981; see Fig. 2.18). They have also become important global banking and financial centres as a result of their coordinating roles in East Asia manufacturing industry (Forbes and Thrift, 1987). One factor facilitating this has been the international networks between 'ethnic Chinese' groups in East Asia and North America (Goldberg, 1987).

Also of great importance, however, local firms have developed a wide range of industries oriented towards producing *final* products for exports. Since the early 1960s, for example, South Korea has pursued an aggressive export-oriented industrial policy. In the early 1960s, familiarity with manufacturing acquired during the earlier import-substitution period was used to develop a number of 'infant' export industries by obtaining manufacturing licenses, loan capital and imported business 'know-how' (Table 10.5). These are mainly labour-intensive activities. But even with low-wages it was not until the late 1960s that productivity and quality were high enough to make these industries, textiles, clothing and footwear, internationally competitive. The South Korean government subsidized this process by using currency deprecia-tions to boost exports, making tax concessions and providing cheap loans.

During a second stage, 1966–71, other 'infant' industries were encouraged as the initial group achieved international competitiveness. These were more technologically advanced industries such as electronic assembly and ship-building. In shipbuilding, production went from 25,000 gross tons in 1970 to 996,000 gross tons in 1975; the ships built were also increasingly large and simple (such as supertankers and bulk carriers) with greater potential for automated production. By 1976 the Korean shipbuilding industry was glob-ally competitive (Linge and Hamilton, 1981).

In the early 1970s a third 'wave' of industries was in the process of creation. For instance, the automobile industry, which began in South Korea in 1967, produced 83,000 units in 1977 and 3.5 million units in 1985. By the mid-1980s, therefore, South Korea had acquired a wide range of inter-nationally competitive and self-sustaining industries. And, despite the increasing technological sophistication of each wave of innovation, consider-able emphasis is still placed on the original labour-intensive industries; although some of these are increasingly decentralized to other Asian locations.

The South Korean policy of widening its manufacturing base is the most successful model of the kind of development policy being pursued by all the NICs. Peripheral industrialization, therefore, is not just the off-shore pro-cessing or assembly work for MNEs that a single-minded focus on EPZs would imply.

Peripheral industrialization is organized at the intra-national and urban levels as well. Coastal and metropolitan areas have been favoured locations, because of infrastructural advantages and ease of external access. Even in countries with little export-oriented industry this pattern is evident. In Nigeria, for example, nearly 65 per cent of the country's industrial employ-ment is concentrated in Lagos and five other coastal states, leaving the remaining 35 per cent to the 13 hinterland states (Ayeni, 1981; Abumere, 1982).

In East Asia and Latin America much of the new manufacturing industry of

Table 10.5: Stages in South Korea's export-orientated industrial development

	1961–66	1966–71	1971–76	1976–81	1981
Infant industries	Textiles Clothing Footwear	Electronic assemblies Shipbuilding Fertilizers Steel	Motor vehicle assembly Consumer electronics Special steels Precision goods (watches, cameras) Turn-key plant building Metal products	Automotive components Machine tools Machinery assembly Simple instruments Assembly of heavy electrical machinery Semiconductors	Automotive components Machine tools Machinery assembly Simple instruments Assembly of heavy electric machinery Semiconductors
Industries becoming competitive		Textiles clothing Footwear	Electronic assemblies Shipbuilding Fertilizers Steel	Motor vehicle assembly Consumer electronics Special steels Precision goods Turn-key plant building Metal products	Motor vehicle assembly Consumer electronics Special steels Precision goods Turn-key plant building Metal products
Self-sustaining industries			Textiles Clothing Footwear	Electronic assemblies Shipbuilding Fertilizers Steel	

Source: Linge and Hamilton (1981) Table 1.9, p. 33

the past 30 years is found in the major metropolitan areas. Both foreign and indigenous investment tends to be attracted by the amenities, basic infrastructure and political access characteristic of the larger urban areas. When urban growth is already concentrated in a primate city, such as in Bangkok in Thailand, recent growth has tended to reinforce primacy. This seems to be especially true of foreign direct investment (Forbes, 1986).

The case of Japanese direct investment in East Asia is illustrative. It is highly concentrated in the national capitals and their immediate vicinity (Figure 10.8). This is the case whether investment is measured by number of firms, employment or capital, although capital concentration is most pronounced (Table 10.6). Metropolitan concentration ranges from nearly 100 per cent in Thailand to 62 per cent in Malaysia with respect to capital; and from 99 per cent in Thailand to around 30 per cent in Malaysia with respect to firms and employment. In Taiwan and South Korea there is a relatively high proportion of Japanese investment in regional centres. What distinguishes Malaysia is that even its rural periphery has some share of Japanese direct investment (Fuchs and Pernia, 1987). So there is some variation even if metropolitan concentration is the norm.

In a number of urban areas there are also incipient industrial complexes redolent of Silicon Valley in California and other high-technology complexes in developed countries. They are made up of both foreign (US and Japanese) owned and locally owned assembly plants and a surrounding constellation of linked activities. Hong Kong, Manila, Seoul, Singapore, Penang, and Taipei all have such complexes. Scott (1987) uses the Manila case to illustrate how a complex can arise in a context of low general economic development. The Manila complex consists of a core of nine major US-owned semiconductor branch plants. These are served by 14 locally owned subcontract assembly houses and three specialized capital-intensive 'test and burn' facilities. Lastly, the Manila complex has a number of specialized tool and die and metal shops serving the semiconductor industry. Some of these are 'captive' to or totally dependent on the US-owned assembly plants but most are independent, local operations. All of these units cluster together to minimize transactional costs and gain joint access to the Manila International Airport. They are also at the centre of a metropolitan labour market that provides production workers who have considerable experience with the norms and rhythms of assembly work and a pool of technicians and engineers with the necessary skills (Scott, 1987).

Attempts have been made in many underdeveloped countries to decentralize manufacturing activities to growth centres. For example, beginning in 1967 the government of Indonesia established a set of tax incentives for 'priority sectors' that were to be located in eleven industrial zones. The idea was to decentralize suitable industries away from Java in general and Jakarta in particular. The policy has failed. At a time when Indonesia's MVA growth rate was the highest in the world (1973–81) – 14.6 per cent per annum – more than half of both domestic and foreign investment was in Java (56.8 per cent of foreign and 64.6 per cent of domestic investment). Only resource-based

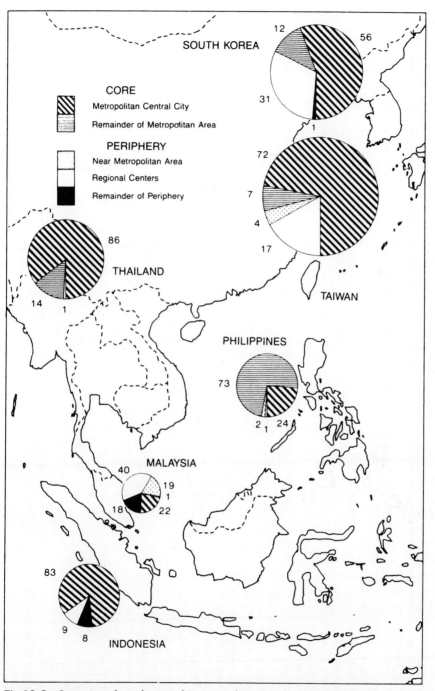

Fig 10.8   Location of employees of Japanese firms in selected Asian countries (percentages)
Source: Fuchs and Pernia (1987), p. 99

Table 10.6: Spatial distribution of Japanese investments, by size: Pacific Asia, 1978

Size of investment and location	Taiwan	South Korea	Malaysia	Philippines	Thailand	Indonesia
Number of firms (%)						
Metro centre	53	51	37	44	81	83
Rest of metro	9	14	1	50	18	0
Metro periphery	7	1	25	3	0	1
Regional centre	30	33	21	3	1	8
Rural periphery	1	1	16	0	0	8
All locations	100	100	100	100	100	100
Number of employees (%)						
Metro centre	72	56	22	24	86	83
Rest of metro	7	12	1	73	14	0
Metro periphery	4	0	19	2	0	0
Regional centres	17	31	40	1	1	9
Rural periphery	0	1	18	0	0	8
All locations	100	100	100	100	100	100
Estimated capital (%)						
Metro centre	81	90	61	24	99	98
Rest of metro	4	3	1	76	1	0
Metro periphery	4	0	12	0	0	0
Regional centres	11	7	23	0	0	1
Rural periphery	0	0	4	0	0	1
All locations	100	100	100	100	100	100
Firms (N)	175	154	126	97	184	158
Employees (N)	114	64	25	45	51	44
Estimated capital (US million dollars)	$592.3	$37.8	$7.2	$3.1	$1.4	$129.3

Source: Fuchs and Pernia (1987) Table 5.3, p. 98

industries have pulled some investment away from the centre even in the presence of significant tax incentives (Noer, 1985; Suhartono, 1987). Similar failures are reported from Latin America (Conroy, 1973; Gore, 1984), Africa (Moudoud, 1986; Dewar et al., 1986), and other parts of Asia (Lo and Salih, 1978; Lavrov and Sdasynk, 1980).

Paralleling the concentration of manufacturing in coastal regions and metropolitan areas has been the growth of a proportionate 'service' sector. Within this sector there are essentially two groups: a minority employed in commercial and bureaucratic activities and a huge 'army' of unemployed and underemployed street vendors, day labourers, domestic workers, and other low-wage workers. While one-quarter or more of the labour force in the NICs and 'middle income' countries is involved in industrial activity, over one-third is engaged in 'services.' In poorer countries the proportions are almost even. This suggests that rather than resolving the problem of urban unemployment and underemployment, recent industrialization has been unable to employ rural–urban migrants at a rate commensurate with their rate of movement from the countryside (Petras, 1984).

The only countries in which the labour force categorized in services has declined relative to that employed in manufacturing are the so-called socialist or collectivist ones (Petras, 1984). If the countries listed in Table 10.7 can be regarded as cases of collectivist industrialization in the periphery, they indicate a distinctive pattern relative to that of industrialization based on an export-orientation or the advanced capitalist countries. Above all, the pattern probably reflects restrictions placed on rural–urban migration and government import-substitution policies. It is important to note, however, that governments in some of the collectivist countries, especially China, have recently begun to encourage the growth of the service sector (Shunzan, 1987) and to engage in export-oriented industrialization through the creation of EPZs and joint ventures with MNEs (Leung and Chin, 1983; Wong, 1987).

The possibility of industrialization throughout the periphery under present global conditions is limited. The process of industrial growth is not a linear

Table 10.7: Growth of industrial to service labour in collectivist countries

	Services		Industry		Service: Industry Ratio	Service: Industry Ratio
	1960	1979	1960	1979	1960	1979
China	—	12	—	17	—	.71
Democratic Rep. of Korea	25	34	9	30	2.77	1.13
Cuba	39	45	22	31	1.77	1.45
Mozambique	11	16	8	17	1.37	.94
Albania	11	14	18	25	.61	.56
Mongolia	17	22	13	22	1.23	1.00
Vietnam	14	19	5	10	2.80	1.90

Source: Petras (1984) Table 7, p. 195

Table 10.8: Declining or stagnant industrial labour force among middle income countries: per cent of labour force in industry

	1960	1979
Yemen PDR	15	15
Nicaragua	16	14
Ecuador	19	18
Paraguay	19	19
Jordan	26	19
Jamaica	25	25
Chile	20	20
South Africa	30	29
Argentina	36	28

Source: Petras (1984), Table 12, p. 197

diffusion process spreading throughout the globe. Indeed there are a number of cases not only of a lack of any growth at all (largely, but not entirely, in sub-Saharan Africa) but also of stagnation and even (as in Argentina) of deindustrialization (Table 10.8). The causes of stagnation are numerous: for example the migration of labour from Yemen to the oil-rich states of the Persian Gulf; the civil war during the late 1970s in Nicaragua; the pursuit of extreme 'free-market' monetarist policies by governments in Argentina and Chile. Consistent industrialization in the face of global downturns and increasingly competitive world markets seems to require at a minimum, in Petras's (1984, p. 199) words, 'a cohesive industrializing class linked to a coherent policy, promoting an internal market and selective insertion in the international market.'

Profiles of Peripheral Industrialization

Brazil

Brazil was incorporated into the world-economy as an exporter of primary commodities. Today the country is characterized by a large land area; 170 years of political independence; a large population (141.3 million in 1987); and a large and diversified industrial economy that has grown mainly since World War II.

Several stages in Brazil's industrialization can be distinguished (Cavalcanti *et al.* 1981; Baer *et al.*, 1987):

1   Until World War II there was an emphasis on import-substitution of non-durable goods for the domestic market and raw materials processing for export.

2   During World War II Brazil accumulated large foreign exchange

reserves by exporting raw materials without a corresponding increase in imports.

3 After the war (1950–62) these reserves combined with pent-up demand led to a substantial increase in the import of consumer durables. The rapid rise in imports depleted exchange reserves, leading the government to place restrictions on imports. The import restrictions coincided with the global expansion of MNEs which, attracted by the potential of Brazil's domestic market, began to establish branch plants in order to avoid limitations on their sales. A major example would be the large automobile manufacturers (General Motors, Volkswagen, etc.) which all established subsidiaries in Brazil.

4 Although the markets for Brazilian-produced consumer durables expanded beyond the national boundary, by the late 1960s the Brazilian government was keen to expand them further because of its ambitious industrialization plans and, later, because of the need to pay for vastly more expensive oil imports. This coincided with the massive restructuring of MNE operations (especially in the automobile industry response to Japanese competition. In Brazil, government underwriting of new plant and technology encouraged the MNEs to become more export-oriented. For example, Volkswagen embarked on the manufacture and export of specifically 'developing country' models. In other cases the strategy of international production has led to world-wide sourcing of components such that Brazil now exports parts for assembly elsewhere: Brazilian four-cylinder engines are shipped by Ford to Canada for installation in vehicles that are then sold in the United States (Mericle, 1984); Fiat uses Brazilian engines in its 127 model, and Volkswagen exports Brazilian engines and transmissions to its German factories (Jenkins, 1987).

Within this changing political-economic context there have been two major spurts of economic growth: the first between 1948 and 1961, when average growth was around 7 per cent per annum; and the second between 1968 and 1981, when growth averaged 8.9 per cent per annum. Since 1984 growth rates have again gone up after three successive years of decline (Tyler, 1986). This boom-and-bust picture represents in modern form the old image of Brazil that originated in the sixteenth century. Sugar boomed first in the Northeast but it dwindled as an export earner when faced with competition from the Caribbean. Gold came next in the southern state of Minas Gerais in the eighteenth century. As the gold ran out, coffee took over. By the mid-nineteenth century coffee accounted for half of Brazil's export earnings.

The difference today is that Brazil is a major industrial power with an infrastructure and internal markets on a par with most DCs and an ability to export that compares to the East Asian NICs. Brazil is the fifth largest country in area in the world. It is sixth largest in population. With a GDP of $280 billion in 1986 Brazil is the eighth largest market economy. Among LDCs, Brazil produces more than India. East Asia's NICs are export-oriented states with a total GDP that is a fraction of what Brazil produces for its internal market. Mexico is the only challenger to Brazil among LDCs in size of GDP – but then only with a GDP of around $130 billion (Harvey, 1987). More specifically, Brazil's steel production is the seventh largest in the world, about one-quarter that of the United States; Brazil is the world's ninth largest producer of cars; the second largest producer of iron ore and the eighth largest producer of aluminum. In other words, by virtue of its position in the international production league table, Brazil is a colossus.

But Brazilian industrialization has a number of features associated with it that severely tarnish the image of miraculous growth. In the first place, the current productive structure of the Brazilian economy reflects an incredibly inegalitarian consumption structure. In a simulation exercise Locatelli (1985) has shown that a more egalitarian distribution of income (similar to that of Britain) would result in a 16 per cent growth in industrial employment. This would happen because the purchasing power of poorer groups would increase the demand for goods with greater labour-intensity in production (also see Baer, 1983; Baer *et al.*, 1987). However, labour policies adopted in the late 1960s to make industries more internationally competitive have reduced worker incomes relative to productivity. The share of wages in final prices has been in steady decline since the 1960s. This has led to large-scale labour unrest. In the motor vehicle industry, for example, workers 'face unstable employment, harsh supervision, limited promotion prospects and intensive work' (Humphrey, 1984 p. 109). Outside of manufacturing industry working and living conditions are even more precarious and marginal.

Second, the Brazilian economy is dominated by MNEs (Table 10.9). Multinational penetration has affected most industrial sectors but it is especially concentrated in the more dynamic ones (Table 10.10). There is some evidence that the falling cost of labour in the period 1968–81 and the restructuring of MNEs were particular incentives for expanded MNE operations (Cunningham, 1986). This has led to considerable debate over the future 'survival' of Brazilian private enterprise. Yet there is evidence that Brazilian private concerns can be successful both alone and in 'triple alliance' with multinational and public sector interests (Evans, 1979; Baer *et al.*, 1987). What is clear is that the Brazilian state has played a major role in encouraging MNE investment, especially since the early 1970s (Cunningham, 1986).

Third, Brazil is massively indebted to multinational banks. In the aftermath of the 1973-74 oil price shock, Brazil's international indebtedness increased markedly. Between 1975 and 1980 external debt grew at an annual rate of 18.4 per cent (Tyler 1986). The borrowing this reflected, though it went primarily to finance balance of payments deficits, was also channelled into major industrial and infrastructural projects, especially in the Amazon basin and elsewhere in the interior. Contracting such indebtedness was possible because of the high dollar liquidity of the large US and European banks associated with the 1975 recession and massive petrodollar deposits from oil exporters. Much of the borrowing involved variable interest rates linked to the

Table 10.9: Foreign firms' percentage share of Brazilian industry in 1970 and 1977.

Industry/Products	Fixed assets 1970	Fixed assets 1977	Sales 1970	Sales 1977	Equity 1970	Equity 1977	Employment 1977
I Highest foreign penetration:							
Automobiles	100	100	100	100	100	100	100
Auto components	58	57	63	54	63	50	46
Chemicals	54	57	55	57	55	42	61
Domestic appliances	76	74	73	76	73	74	64
Drugs	83	82	30	84	80	74	64
Electrical products	81	86	81	79	81	84	83
Glass	53	69	49	76	73	74	79
Industrial machinery	66	51	67	59	67	47	54
Office equipment	96	91	93	73	93	76	65
Plastics	73	42	68	57	68	43	49
Rubber	67	62	71	81	71	68	70
Tobacco	91	99	95	99	95	98	96
Tractors	83	83	80	84	80	61	69
II Marked increase from low base:							
Footwear	—	26	—	32	—	28	26
Furniture	9	24	9	13	9	19	23
Non metallic materials	3	25	5	42	5	23	32
Vegetableoils	5	52	4	59	4	52	45
III Other (Trend + or − m = mixed)							
Aircraft (−)	36	7	46	20	46	13	26
Beverages (+)	16	23	13	24	13	17	17
Cement (+)	26	41	25	33	25	25	27
Metallic minerals (+)	18	36	17	21	17	21	15
Metallurgical products (−)	38	29	36	32	36	33	33
Paper (m)	33	20	23	24	23	33	33
Petroleum (m)	10	9	14	36	14	9	14
Shipbuilding (−)	45	34	30	16	30	17	30
Spinning and weaving −	39	37	39	34	39	29	26
All sectors	34	33	37	44	37	31	38

Source: Cunningham (1986), Table 3.8, p. 53

US prime rate, which was low in the mid-1970s but much higher by the end of the decade. Tyler (1986) is optimistic that the Brazilian debt load can be rescheduled (because of its sheer size) without lasting damage to Brazil's economy. Others (e.g. Cunningham, 1986), however, suggest that the 1970s was a decade that provided a unique 'one-time' opportunity for the industrial restructuring that did take place but that it cannot probably continue. 'The superimposition of multinational bank finance upon an existing nexus of

Table 10.10: Brazil: Multinationals and employment in dynamic sectors of manufacturing, 1980

Sectors	Quem é Quem[1] 1980 Employment in multinationals	Total employment	Industrial Census[2] 1980 Total employment
Machinery	79,558	211,520	515,237
Electrical equipment	88,997	199,542	242,017
Transport equipment	178,053	327,845	264,853
(1) Sub-total	346,608	738,907	1,022,107
Chemicals, etc	94,958	262,046	222,688
Plastics	8,987	57,076	117,379
(2) Sub-total	103,945	319,122	340,067
(1) and (2)	450,553	1,058,029	1,362,174

1. *Quem é Quem* does not cover all establishments, but is confined to the large corporate sector enterprises.
2. The Industrial Census covers establishments of all sizes. Sectoral classification differences between the two sources and *Quem é Quem's* estimating procedures where necessary, also account for discrepancies in employment totals.
Source: Cunningham (1986), Table 3.11, p. 57

foreign direct investment established by other multinational corporations (especially in manufacturing)' (Cunningham, 1986 p. 61) may not return, especially with so many other countries vying for loans and investment.

Fourth, and finally, industrialization in Brazil is extremely concentrated geographically. In 1977 70.9 per cent of all factories were in the South-east 'core' region with 58.4 per cent of these in the São Paulo and Rio de Janeiro metropolitan areas (Cavalcanti *et al.*, 1981). The Northeast region with about 29 per cent of the population has only 9.6 per cent of the factories but 50 per cent of the country's poor (Thomas, 1987). Industrialization has thus deepened historic spatial inequalities in living standards. This has been especially true since the late 1960s as MNEs and export-orientation have conspired to encourage industrial development in the coastal-metropolitan regions of the South and Southeast.

Cuba

At the same time in the 1980s that Latin America in general had been experiencing negative or low growth rates, public austerity programmes and declining industrial wage rates, Cuba increased spending on social welfare, widened the availability of consumer goods and maintained robust growth rates (Table 10.11). In 1972 the future prospect had looked bleaker. The terms of trade for sugar exports (Cuba's major primary commodity) had deterio-

Table 10.11: Cuban growth rates (in constant prices)

Year	GDP	GDP per capita	GSP†
1959	5.0	2.9	
1960	1.4	−0.4	
1961	4.0	2.5	
1962	−1.4	−3.0	
1963	1.7	−0.6	
1964	9.5	6.7	
1965	0.9	−1.6	
1966	−1.9	−4.1	
1967	2.2	0.2	
1968	6.3	4.4	
1969	−2.7	−4.3	
1970	−0.5	−1.9	
1971	−0.7	−2.3	
1972	8.4	6.4	
1973	12.8	10.5	
1974	8.7	6.9	
1975	10.5	8.7	
1976	8.3	6.7	
1977	8.9	7.5	
1978	6.1	5.0	
1979	2.3	1.6	
1980	2.3	2.7	3.3
1981	9.3	8.5	13.9
1982		1.3	2.5
1983			5.2
1984			7.4
1985			4.8

† Global Social Product. GSP doublecounts intermediate inputs and excludes non-material services (primarily education and health). This is the official national income statistic.
Source Turits (1987) Table 2, p. 165

rated badly and the country's hard currency debt of $3 billion was roughly three-and-a-half times the value of exports that generated hard currencies. The constraints facing Cuba seemed remarkably similar to those of the rest of Latin America. Despite its socialist political system and incorporation into the Soviet trade bloc (CMEA) Cuba still seemed to be subject to the vagaries of the world-economy and dependent upon capital from the 'capitalist world' (Turits, 1987).

The question raised by Cuba's surprising resilience – it has reduced its debt as well as met its rescheduled debt repayments on time – is whether this is due to the nature of its political economy, increased dependence on Soviet aid, or some of each. From one point of view, Cuba remains in an almost classic mode of dependency having exchanged one dominant partner (the United States) after the 1959 Revolution for another (the Soviet Union). Certainly, Cuba's choice of a development strategy based on sugar has maintained a high level of structural dependence and a high degree of vulnerability. Yet there is only limited evidence to suggest that dependence on the Soviet Union shapes and limits the Cuban economy in any way analogous to Cuba's former dependence on the US. For example, Cuba is not subject to long-term capital outflows, foreign ownership of the means of production nor increasing economic inequality; all features of prerevolutionary Cuba and much of Latin America today. But Cuba is fortunate that the Soviet Union takes so much of its sugar and provides considerable aid.

Though sugar exports remain the engine for surplus-generation and foreign exchange, the Cuban economy from 1970 onwards was increasingly driven by a growing industrial sector. In the 1970s import-substitution, sugar-processing and agricultural machinery industries were built up by so-called 'debt-led' growth. By 1981 34.9 per cent of investment was in industry compared to 16.7 per cent in 1966 (Brundenius, 1984). A radical reallocation of labour from agriculture to industry and services followed. The percentage of agriculture in GDP declined from 18.1 per cent in 1961 to 12.9 per cent in 1981 (Brundenius, 1984; Zimbalist, 1987).

Debt-led growth was possible for Cuba because, even though blockaded and ostracized by the United States, credit and capital were increasingly available in the 1970s and this coincided with a dramatic climb in world sugar prices, which improved Cuba's credit rating. Western imports increased four-fold in the years 1973–75. Trade with capitalist countries reached over 40 per cent of total trade in 1975, compared to 20 per cent in 1967, and less than 14 per cent as of 1983 (Turits, 1987). The four years 1975–78 culminated in a trade deficit with capitalist countries of 2.1 billion pesos, compensated for by increased foreign borrowing.

The burden of debt service impelled renewed attention to import reduction and export production. But the investment of the 1970s had paid off in terms of new and growing industries such as capital goods, consumer durables, chemicals, medicines (Cuba produces 83 per cent of its needs), electronics, computers and steel. For example, where engineering and capital goods industries accounted for 1.4 per cent of total industrial production in 1959, this sector accounted for 13.2 per cent of industrial output in 1983 (Zimbalist and Eckstein, 1987), due to an annual average growth rate of 16.6 per cent from 1970 onwards. Cuba also currently produces a large share of its new sugar cane harvesters, buses, refrigerators and other durables (Edquist, 1985). From 1976 to 1980 Cuba also introduced 115 new export products that sell mainly in other LDCs.

Since 1980 debts have been met by rescheduling payments, increased hard currency earnings and large-scale Soviet aid. Nevertheless, it is important to note, Soviet aid to Cuba is considerably less per capita, and of more immediate benefit in terms of the conditions of existence of the population, than American aid to Israel or Puerto Rico (Turits, 1987). Cuban planners have tended to reduce investment in industry and agriculture in order to maintain

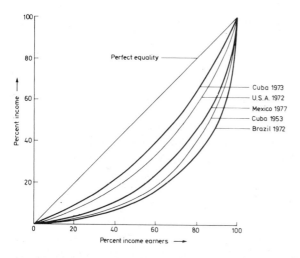

Fig 10.9 Income distribution in Cuba (1959 and 1973), Brazil, Mexico and the US
Source: Reitsma and Kelinpenning (1985), 3.7, p. 354

high levels of employment and provision of social services. The income distribution in Cuba is extremely egalitarian by world standards (Fig. 10.9).

The decision in the 1960s to emphasize agricultural development in general and sugar in particular, led to a focus on industries that would have favourable effects in rural areas. As a result there was considerable investment in sugar mills. Much of this type of industry was located in small and medium-sized cities. In an effort to spread economic development throughout the country much of the new industry was given to Oriente province at the eastern end of the island. As a consequence urban growth has been more rapid there than elsewhere (Gugler, 1980). The chief objective throughout the 1960s was to weaken the urban primacy of Havana and slow down its growth. After 1970, however, and with the switch towards an industrializing strategy, Havana again experienced growth. This is because of its advantages in infrastructure, skilled labour, port facilities and market potential. Some 70 per cent of all industrial activities other than sugar processsing are now located in the Havana metropolitan area (Reitsma and Kleinpenning, 1985).

The major problem now facing Cuba is that non-sugar exports will have to increase if the country is to have sustained growth and a more independent political economy. In particular, it is unclear how much more sugar the Soviet Union can absorb! (Turits, 1987). It is also unlikely that debt-led growth will work again (as for Brazil). Some research suggests that an internal decentralization of planning controls and an external decentralization of export markets might jointly produce more sustained industrial development in the future (White, 1987; Zimbalist and Eckstein, 1987). But this might be at the expense of the truly impressive levels of social services enjoyed by its 10 million people if expenditures on production are increased without foreign borrowing or increases in Soviet aid.

Summary

According to the World Bank (1983), the aggregate rate of growth of both industrial (mineral resources plus manufacturing) and manufacturing output have been over 3 per cent per annum for 34 low-income countries and over 6 per cent per annum for 59 middle-income countries over the period 1960–81. These rates have been higher than those for the industrialized countries and consequently the share of the LDCs in the world's manufacturing output has risen somewhat – from 17.6 per cent in 1960 to 18.9 per cent in 1981 (World Bank, 1983). Their combined share of world exports of manufactures rose from 3.9 per cent to 8.2 per cent in the same period. Or, from a slightly different perspective, the LDCs' share of the manufactured imports of all industrial countries rose from 5.3 per cent in 1962 to 13.1 per cent in 1978 (World Bank, 1982). At the same time the share of the GDP of the poorest (low-income) countries coming from the industrial sector rose from 25 per cent in 1960 to 34 per cent in 1981. For manufacturing the rise was only from 11 to 16 per cent. In the middle-income group the changes were from 30 to 38 per cent for industry, and from 20 to 22 per cent for manufacturing alone (World Bank, 1983). Much of this growth has been concentrated in the small group of NICs (Sutcliffe, 1984).

These figures call into question the optimistic conclusion of Warren (1980) and others (see Chapter 8) that a massive industrialization of the periphery is under way. Indeed, this chapter has suggested that there are significant constraints upon the industrialization of the periphery and the 1970s provided a time period uniquely favourable to the type of development that did take place. Indeed, even in that time period a number of economies stagnated or deindustrialized. The economic problems of the industrial core have not created inevitable advantages for industrialization in the global periphery. Some of the major conclusions are:

- Industrialization plays a major role in national ideologies of modernization and is seen as a solution to various major practical economic and social problems.

- The spread and intensification of industrialization since the late 1960s coincides with the declining rate of profit in the industrial core.

- Much of the new industrialization is export-oriented rather than directed (as in import-substitution) to domestic markets.

- There are limits to the development of this industrialization: such as improving profit rates in the industrial core, protectionist measures in export markets, technological changes that reduce the attractiveness of low-wage locations, incredible debt loads, and relatively limited employment effects.

- Most LDCs are either not industrializing or industrializing only very slowly.

- Export-processing zones represent one geographical form taken by the New International Division of Labour but 'offshore production' of components or assembly is not the only feature of peripheral industrialization. There are now important industries engaged in the production of locally-created final products.

- The new industrialization has favoured existing metropolitan areas and coastal regions. Attempts at decentralization to growth centres have not met with much success.

- Two profiles, of Brazil and Cuba, illustrate two different paths to industrialization. Although obviously dissimilar in many respects (size of economy, role of foreign MNEs, form of government, etc.) there is a remarkable similarity in their reliance in the recent past on debt-led growth. Both now face problems precisely because of this previous emphasis.

Part Four

Adjusting to a New Global Economy

In the final two chapters we examine some of the reactions to the emergence of ever-larger and more-powerful economic forces and the time-space compress-ion that have come to characterize the world-economy. In Chapter 11, we explore the changing role of nation states within the world-economy, empha-sizing the relationships between economic change and the new geopolitics and, in particular, the spatial consequences of transnational political and economic integration that has occurred in response to the increased scale, sophistication and interdependence of the modern world-economy. In Chapter 12, we examine the other side of the coin: decentralist reactions to the changing world-economy. Here, the focus is on regionalism and regional policy, nationalism and separatism, and grassroots movements towards eco-nomic democracy.

11

Transnational Integration

In this chapter we return to the theme of the close relationship between economic development and the role of the state. As Parts II and III have shown, nation states have been pivotal, both in the struggle for domination within the core and as peripheral and semi-peripheral economies have struggled to reduce their dependency on core economies. As the world-economy has become more and more internationalized, however, nation states throughout the world-economy have had to explore cooperative strategies: transnational political and economic integration of various kinds. This chapter outlines the rationale for these strategies, describes the scope of the major transnational organizations, and illustrates some of the more important spatial implications of transnational integration.

Economic Change and the New Geopolitics

In order to understand the emergence of transnational organizations we must first remind ourselves of the shifting economic and geopolitical foundations of the world-economy since the Second World War. In the aftermath of the war, the capitalist economy was reordered as a more open system: one without the economic barriers of the 'trading empires' that had been set up in the 1930s but, rather, based on free-market capitalism with stable monetary relations and minimal barriers to trade. This required, first of all, an orderly world, internally peaceful and secure from outside threats. Second, it required leadership in providing and furthering mechanisms for establishing a stable reserve standard for international currency exchange rates and for ensuring access to world trade markets. The one state that could provide military order – the United States – was also the only state economically strong enough to impose order on the economic system. Socialist states, meanwhile, turned inward in their attempt to restructure economy and society along different ideological lines; and their existence, in turn, mobilized an ideological reaction – anti-communism – that provided both economic stimulus and political solidarity within the core economies.

In short, the world-economy was characterized by the *hegemony* of the United States. While clearly a desirable condition for the hegemonic power, hegemony need not necessarily be seen as a bad thing for other nation states. Kindleberger (1981), for example, argues that a prosperous world-economy needs a leader and a stabilizer; while Deutsch (1978) has suggested that security, the precondition for prosperity, requires a strong core area with the capacity not only to bully others but also to make short-term sacrifices that will in the long run make for economic growth in the system as a whole.

Under US hegemony, the world-economy came to be characterized by 'Fordism', the socio-economic system that links mass production with mass consumption. A tense but durable relationship between big business, big labour and big government enabled Fordism to provide the basis for the long postwar boom and unprecedented rise in living standards throughout much of the capitalist world. This boom was also crucially dependent on the massive expansion of world trade and international investment flows made possible by the hegemonic umbrella of US financial and military power. Following the Bretton Woods agreement that made the US dollar the world's reserve currency (see p. 39), Fordism was implanted in Europe and Japan, either directly during the occupation phase or indirectly through the Marshall Plan and foreign direct investment by US companies. The consequent opening-up of foreign trade, observes Harvey (1987, p. 4):

> permitted surplus productive capacity (and potentially surplus labour reserves) to be absorbed in the United States, while the progress of Fordism internationally meant the formation of global mass markets and the absorption of the mass of the world's population, outside the communist world, into the global dynamics of a new kind of capitalism. . . . At the input end, the opening up of foreign trade meant the globalization of supply and often ever cheaper raw material. This new internationalism also brought a host of other activities in its wake – banking, insurance, hotels, airports, and, ultimately, tourism. It also meant a new international culture and a new global system of gathering and evaluating information.
>
> The postwar period saw, therefore, the rise of a series of industries – such as autos, steel, petro-chemicals, rubber, etc. – that acted as the propulsive engines of economic growth, coordinated through the collective powers of big labour, big business and big government. And out of this there arose a series of grand production regions in the world-economy – the Mid-West of the United States, the West Midlands of Britain, the Ruhr and the Tokyo–Yokohama production region, built around a series of world financial and governmental centres, and reaching out to dominate an increasingly homogeneous world market.

The imperatives of Fordist production also fostered, as we have seen (Chapter 6), the emergence of MNEs with the capacity to move capital and technology rapidly from place to place, drawing opportunistically on resources, labour markets and consumer markets in different parts of the world. Multinational corporations, moreover, have gone far beyond the point where they can be seen simply as extensions of a specific national economy; and even some small firms have now acquired both the capability and the propensity to operate globally. Although private companies are by no means absolute masters of their own fate, they do have a great advantage in the ability to redefine their commitments and objectives in response to the changing opportunities presented by the globalization of the economy (Branscomb, 1987). This in turn, intensified the political and economic *interdependency* of the world-economy (Kafkalas, 1987). Even without the activities of multinational companies the widespread adoption of Keynesian economic management had reached the stage where domestic economics were exerting a significant influence on international politics. For example the British resistance to a devaluation of the pound in the 1960s had direct consequences on patterns of European trade and politics. Conversely, domestic economics were increasingly sensitive to international politics. A good example here is the way that the arms race associated with the Cold War affected regional and national economies through the multiplier effects of defence industries. The emergence of MNEs served both to intensify these interdependencies and to make them more complex. Perhaps the most striking example of this complexity was the emergence in the 1970s of joint ventures, licensing and non-equity resource flows between multinational conglomerates (mostly European or European subsidiaries of US corporations) and enterprises in Eastern Europe and the Soviet Union. Levinson (1980) found that the 40 largest multinational corporations all have agreements of some sort with one or more East European states, and that 34 of them had agreements with the Soviet Union. The best-known of these agreements is the Pepsi Cola Corporation's deal to sell soft drinks in the Soviet Union and to market vodka in the West. Less well known, perhaps, is that by 1977 one third of Soviet imports and one quarter of Soviet exports were with Western countries. As Taylor observes:

> The motives for all this activity are very traditional. For the corporations there is an extension of the geographical range of their profit-making. . . . The Eastern European states provide a source of relatively cheap, yet skilled, disciplined and healthy labour. And of course there is the vast raw material potential of the Soviet Union. For the latter, the motive is equally straightforward. Cooperation with Western corporations was the only solution to a technology lag which the Soviet Union has suffered in the wake of the rise of electronics industries in the West. Increasing integration into the world-economy is the price the USSR has to pay for keeping up with its ideological competitors. (1985, p. 60)

A further layer of global interdependence, meanwhile, is represented by the 'East–South' trade that is used by the Eastern bloc to finance 'East–West' trade (Frank, 1977; Gutman and Arkwright, 1981).

Within this new context of political and economic interdependence, regional and international shifts in economic and political power began to occur, as we saw in Chapter 6: shifts that the policies of particular governments seemed powerless to prevent by normal means. Moreover, the ascent of the NICs brought a new dimension to the world-economy in the form of second-order economic powers that effectively created a *hierarchical* geopolitical system (Cohen, 1982). As the regional influence of such states has grown, so they have come to exert an independent effect on the landscapes of the world's core economies:

> None has had a greater political/psychological effect on the major powers than the omnipresence of persons, symbols and signs in Europe's great cities, and in such American cities as New York, Miami, New Orleans and Los Angeles. In Europe, billboards advertising Asian, African and Latin American Airlines, store signs in Arabic script, national airline offices and ethnic food restaurants from three continents, a plethora of Arabic-language newspapers displayed prominently in kiosks and, above all, the businessman, tourist, shopper, student and adolescent youth from these newly-powerful countries demonstrate that the world has changed. They have joined the overseas symbols of American power – the Hilton, the Holiday Inn, Hertz, Avis, ESSO, Mobil, IBM, the English-language newspaper, the American bar and restaurant, and the tourist, student and businessman – to share the landscape of sight, sound and taste with Americans. (Cohen, 1982, p. 227)

Meanwhile, the prosperity associated with Fordist regime in the core economies had been replaced by the uncertainty, destabilization and crisis resulting from the 1973 OPEC oil embargo and the conjunction of slowed productivity and increasing public expenditures which created national economic management problems that could not be solved except at the price of accelerating the inflation that, ultimately, undermined the role of the US dollar as the international reserve currency.

At the same time, the role and relative power of nation states changed significantly. Economic circumstances reduced the ability of governments to deliver full employment *and* a full range of welfare services, and the growth of the global financial system blunted the power of individual nation states to pursue independent fiscal and monetary policies with any degree of success. In particular, the United States has had to struggle hard to maintain its hegemony (Corbridge, 1984; Keohane, 1984), running a mounting trade deficit and a very large public debt; facing dissent from other core economies over East–West trade issues; being pushed towards protectionism by domestic interest groups; and having persistently to devalue the dollar in order to maintain competitiveness with Japan and West Germany.

In the decentralized, restructured and consolidated world-economy that emerged in the 1980s, new communications technologies, new forms of corporate organization, and new business services have intensified 'time–space compression', decreasing the time horizons of both public and private decision-making and making it easier to spread those decisions over an ever-wider space (Doz, 1987; D.W. Harvey, 1987). As we saw in Chapter 6, one result has been the acceleration of shifts in the patterning of uneven development on the basis of particular local mixes of skills and resources. Another outcome is that local governments are being forced to be much more competitive with one another as they attempt not only to protect their economic base during a time of upheaval and transition but also to identify and exploit some comparative edge with which to lure the newly flexible flows of finance and production. This inter-governmental competition has bred so-called 'entre-preneurial' cities, whose governments have been drawn beyond questions of tax policies, infrastructure provision and service delivery to the exploration of public–private partnerships, the fostering of a favourable 'business climate' and the initiation of labour control through contract negotiations with municipal workers (Davis, 1987; Judd and Ready, 1986).

These conditions of change and uncertainty, though not necessarily the prelude to 'the disintegrating West' (Kaldor, 1978), have inevitably made for a state of geopolitical flux. Even NATO, the geopolitical centrepiece of postwar capitalism, 'is threatened by internal economic rivalries and disaffection. The Pentagon may seek to enhance NATO's solidarity but the Federal Reserve just as surely undermines it by monetary policies judged appropriate to control inflation but which also force unacceptable levels of devaluation on Western Europe. Policies directed overtly at the Soviet bloc by the United States affect adversely those countries, such as West Germany, which sought outlets for surplus capital in East–West trade (squabbles over credit to the Soviet Union, the gas pipeline, and the Polish debt are recent cases in point)' (Harvey, 1985, p. 159).

Transnational Integration

It within this changing economic and geopolitical context that we have to see the various attempts to adjust to the modern world-economy through strategies of transnational economic and political integration. We should nevertheless remember that, as Parts II and III have shown, the dominant processes in both intra-core rivalry and in the struggle by the periphery to escape from dependency have been dominated by conflict and competition. Indeed, economic nationalism, drawing on practical examples (e.g. eighteenth-century Britain and nineteenth and twentieth-century Japan – Chapter 5), political ideology (e.g. Juan Péron in Argentina and Getúlio Vargas in Brazil in the 1940s and 1950s) and development theory (e.g. the import-substituting industrialization espoused by Raoul Prebisch) continues to dominate global economics and geopolitics (Corbridge, 1986; Burnell, 1986).

Having acknowledged this, however, we must also recognize the long-term trend among the world's space-economies towards the progressive integration and interdependence of local, regional and national economic systems. What has happened is that the logic of the world-economy has in many ways transcended the scale of nation states. The logic and apparatus of statehood is not conducive to transnational integration, economic or political; but the contingencies of advanced capitalism, first under US hegemony and more recently in less stable circumstances, have forced many states to explore co-operative strategies of various kinds. As a result, the world's economic landscapes now bear the imprint, in a variety of ways, of transnational economic and political integration.

Imperatives of Integration

The increased scale, sophistication and interdependence of the modern world-economy would not have been feasible if it were not for the fact that new technologies and new forms of organization gradually made it possible to conquer several of the *frictions* that tend to operate against hierarchical flows of production and consumption. In addition to the obvious – for geographers – friction of distance itself, these include the frictions associated with spatial variations in social organization and culture. As railroads, the telegraph, automobiles, aircraft, computer networks, satellite communications systems and fibre optics have successfully 'shrunk' the globe, Fordist principles of mass production have brought about a convergence of patterns of social organization, and radio and television have undermined local and regional cultures and replaced them with an international culture characterized by the language and artifacts of consumerism: American Express, Benetton, Burger King, Coca Cola, Gucci, Guerlain, Laura Ashley, Marlboro, Mercedes-Benz, Rolex, Shiseido, Sony, Visa, and so on.

The framework of nation states, however, is a source of friction that has persisted, not least because the functional logic of statehood hinges on reinforcing *differences between* nations while reinforcing *similarities within* nations. In order to establish the required feelings of common identity, even the oldest states have had to engage in creating and diffusing a distinctive identity. Much of the ideology and symbolism of nation states in Europe, for example, has centred around the systematic mythologizing of history, reinforced by the stereotyping of outsiders.

One important outcome of this was the jingoism and xenophobia that set the context for the First World War, nurtured the ambitions of the Third Reich, and hampered postwar attempts to establish common economic and legal ground. Among the more explicit functions of nation states that have contributed to the frictions affecting the world-economy are those relating to national security and the promotion of homogeneous internal standards and conditions. The latter include controlling fiscal and monetary policy, upholding labour contracts, establishing standards for everything from education to ballbearings, and overseeing key industries such as telecommunications.

Once a significant amount of economic activity had transcended the scope of national boundaries, however, nation states had to confront the need to rethink these activities in order not to become isolated or to become even more vulnerable to underdevelopment. In short, it was the international trade system that provided the major impetus for nation states to be drawn into various forms of institutionalized integration. For core nations, the objective was primarily to protect and consolidate existing advantages through increased international security, access to wider markets, investment opportunities and labour markets. For peripheral nations, the objective was primarily to minimize or reduce dependency through harnessing more resources and more investment potential. In addition, most nations were able to subscribe, in public at least, to the more lofty ideals of good international relations and a more equitable international economic order. In theory, the particular *advantages* of formalized transnational integration include:

1 the potential for economies of scale, particularly for the smallest nation states and the weakest national economies,
2 the potential for creating multiplier effects from the existence of enlarged markets, and
3 the potential for strengthening regional interaction by easing the movement of labour, goods and capital.

On the other hand, the particular *disadvantages* of formalized transnational integration include:

1 the potential loss of sovereignty over a broad spectrum of issues, and
2 the potential for the intensification of internal inequalities as a wider geographical context makes for more pronounced processes of uneven development.

Types and Levels of Integration

Figure 11.1 and Table 11.1 summarize the 'where' and 'when' of transnational economic integration since 1945. In practice, integration can be pursued in a variety of ways and at different levels. It can be *formal*, involving

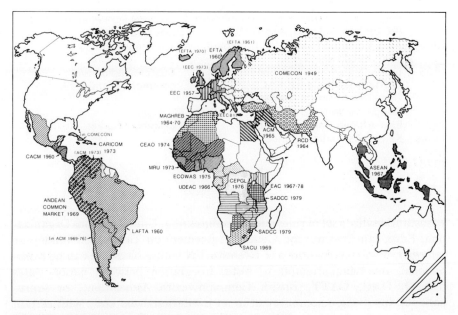

Fig 11.1   Regional integration in the world-economy
Source: Edwards (1985) Fig. 8.6

Table 11.1: The where and when of regional integration since 1945

Year	Grouping	Main provisions
1949	Council for Mutual Economic Assistance (Comecon): USSR, Bulgaria, Czechoslovakia, GDR, Hungary, Poland, Romania, Mongolia and Cuba	Trade and development agreements and contracts
1957	European Economic Community (EEC): France, West Germany, Italy Belgium, the Netherlands and Luxemburg	Common Market (common internal and external tariffs and common agricultural and industrial policies)
	(1973: plus UK, Ireland, Denmark)	
	(1981: plus Greece)	
1960	European Free Trade Association (EFTA): UK, Switzerland, Austria, Denmark, Norway and Sweden	Common internal tariffs but not common external tariffs
	(1961: plus Finland as an associate member)	
	(1970: plus Iceland)	
	(1973: minus UK and Denmark)	
1960	Latin American Free Trade Association (LAFTA): includes Mexico and all of South America, except the Guyanas	Free trade area (no common external tariff) and sectoral agreements
1960	Central American Common Market (CACM): Costa Rica, El Salvador, Guatemala, Honduras, Nicaragua	Common market (but note that Honduras has reimposed some tariffs)
1964 (broke up in 1970)	Maghreb Permanent Consultative Committee: Algeria, Morocco and Tunisia	Co-operative agreement
1964	Regional Cooperation for Development (RCD): Iran, Pakistan and Turkey	Sectoral agreements (not a free trade area)
1965	Arab Common Market (ACM): Egypt, Iraq, Jordan and Syria	Trade agreements
1966	Union Douanière et Economique de l'Afrique Centrale (UDEAC): Cameroon, Central African Republic, Congo, Gabon	Customs union with common central bank
1967 (broke up in 1978)	East African Community (EAC): Kenya, Tanzania, Uganda	Common market

an institutionalized set of rules and procedures (e.g. United Nations Organization, European Community, General Agreement on Tariffs and Trade); or *informal*, involving coalitions of interests (UN voting blocs). It can be *transnational*, involving attempts to foster integration between nation states (NATO, OAU, GATT, British Commonwealth Association); or *supranational*, involving a commitment to an institutionalized body with certain powers over member states (EC). It can be *economically* oriented (GATT, the European Free Trade Association), *strategic* (NATO, the Warsaw Pact), *poli-*

Table 11.1: *continued*

Year	Grouping	Main provisions
1967	Association of South-East Asian Nations (ASEAN): Indonesia, Malaysia, Philippines, Singapore and Thailand	Some regional trade preferences and sectoral agreements
1969	Southern African Customs Union (SACU): Botswana, Lesotho, Swaziland and the Republic of South Africa	Customs union
1969	Andean Common Market (ACM): Bolivia, Chile, Colombia, Ecuador and Peru	Common market envisaged, common policy on foreign investment
(1973: plus Venezuela)		
(1976: minus Chile)		
1973	Caribbean Community (Caricom): Antigua, Barbados, Belize, Dominica, Grenada, Guyana, Jamaica, Montserrat, St Kitts-Nevis-Anguilla, St Lucia, St Vincent, Trinidad and Tobago	Common market (Caricom) succeeded free trade association—Carifta—in 1969 with agricultural and industrial integration
1973	Mano River Union (MRU): Liberia and Sierra Leone	Customs union
1974	Communauté Economique de l'Afrique de l'Ouest (CEAO): Ivory Coast, Mali, Mauritania, Niger, Senegal, Upper Volta (a re-formed West African Customs Union)	Customs union; joint sectoral policies
1975	Economic Community of West African States (ECOWAS): Benin, Gambia, Ghana, Guinea, Guinea-Bissau, Ivory Coast, Liberia, Mali, Mauritania, Niger, Nigeria, Senegal, Sierra Leone, Togo, Upper Volta	Common external tariff envisaged by 1990—free movement of labour
1976	Economic Community of the countries of the Great Lakes (CEPGL): Zaire, Rwanda and Burundi	Trade agreements
1979	Southern Africa Development Coordination Conference (SADCC): Angola, Botswana, Lesotho, Malawi, Mozambique, Swaziland, Tanzania, Zambia, Zimbabwe	Sectoral integration

Source: Edwards (1985) Table 8.3, p. 226–7.

tical (UN voting blocs), *socio-cultural* (UNESCO), or *mixed* (EC, OAU) in orientation.

Our immediate concern here is with economically oriented integration schemes. Within the capitalist world, these have had to conform to the rules of the General Agreement on Tariffs and Trade (GATT), a transnational association of most of the world's trading nations formed in the aftermath of the Second World War to promote world-wide free trade and to untangle the complex trade restrictions that had accumulated. Article 1 of GATT provides that each member state shall extend most-favoured status to all other member countries. (Thus if, say, the US were to lower its import duty on textile products from Canada, it would immediately have to extend that same reduced rate to every other GATT member.) Article 24, however, provides an exception to this principle for free trade associations and customs unions, members of which may reduce their tariffs against each other without extending such concessions to remaining GATT members.

In a *free trade association*, member countries eliminate tariff and quota barriers against trade from other member states, but each individual member continues to charge its regular duties on materials and products coming from outside the association. The only free trade association of any real significance at present is the European Free Trade Association (EFTA), whose membership comprises Austria, Finland, Iceland, Norway, Sweden and Switzerland.

A *customs union* also involves the elimination of tariffs between member states, but has a common protective wall against non-members. Where, in addition, internal restrictions on the movement of capital, labour and enterprise are removed, the result is a *common market*. Most customs unions have gone at least some way towards common market status. Examples include the European Community or EC (Belgium, Denmark, France, Greece, Ireland, Italy, Luxembourg, Netherlands, Portugal, Spain, West Germany and the United Kingdom), the Central American Common Market or CACM (Costa Rica, El Salvador, Guatemala, Honduras, Nicaragua), the Arab Common Market (Egypt, Iraq, Syria, Jordan), the Andean Common Market (Bolivia, Colombia, Ecuador, Peru, Venezuela), the Eastern Caribbean Common Market, The Economic Community of the States of Central Africa, and the Economic Community of West African States (for a full listing see Carl, 1986).

A still higher form of integration is the *economic union*, which, in addition to the characteristics of a common market, provides for integrated economic policies among member states. The highest form of integration possible would have to involve some form of *supranational political union*, with a single monetary system and a central bank, a unified fiscal system, a common foreign economic policy, and a supranational authority with executive, judicial and legislative branches. The EC has gone a long way towards becoming an economic union, and it contains significant elements of a supranational political union, to which it formally aspires.

Beyond the EC, however, many free trade associations and common markets have found it difficult to overcome the obstacles imposed by memberships that include nations at very different levels of development, and that involve enormous distances and poorly developed transportation networks. In response to such problems, the GATT authorized, in 1971, the waiver of the Article 1 most-favoured nation provision for developing nations offering concessions to other developing nations. As a result, Mexico, for example, could offer to reduce its duty on a product from Bolivia without having to extend the same lower rate to the United States. The GATT decision meant that developing countries were free to experiment with a variety of integration models without incorporating internal free trade as a legally binding obligation. The result has been the emergence of a series of *trade preference associations* such as the Association of Southeast Asian Nations or ASEAN (Brunei, Indonesia, Malaysia, the Philippines, Singapore, Thailand) and the Latin American Integration Association, formerly the Latin American Free Trade Association (Argentina, Bolivia, Brazil, Chile, Colombia, Ecuador, Mexico, Paraguay, Peru, Uruguay, Venezuela).

Finally, we come to the integration of socialist economies. Because the international movement of goods and capital is controlled by state trading organizations (foreign trade associations, or FTOs), economic integration between socialist countries has centred on the coordination of economic plans and the rationalization of resource allocation and production rather than the manipulation of tariffs and quotas. The formal manifestation of this integration is the Council for Mutual Economic Assistance, CMEA or COMECON (Bulgaria, Cuba, Czechoslovakia, East Germany, Hungary, Mongolia, Poland, Romania, Soviet Union, Vietnam), which is second only to the EC in terms of its collective economic power. At heart, the CMEA is an 'international protection system'; that is, its primary function is to provide a stable arena for the development of centrally planned economies, sheltered from the pressures and imperatives of the rest of the world-economy. Although the CMEA has been able to achieve certain economies of scale through the centrally planned integration of production (particularly in terms of energy, iron and steel, chemicals, automobiles and computers), cooperation on macroeconomic plans has been significantly restricted by the smaller members' fears over national sovereignty, and there has been very little integration with respect to internal market mechanisms (Pinder, 1986). A recent study of the CMEA, noting that the most significant undertakings seem to have been motivated by the desire to acquire convertible currency and Western technology, concludes that 'cooperation and specialization in Comecon is a collective response to alleviate the disadvantages associated with participation in the grouping. Seen in this light integration in Comecon appears as "integration upside down" ' (Sobell, 1984, p. 248). In other words, CMEA economic integration is largely an *ex post* response to the political decision to create an international protection system.

Spatial Outcomes

It follows from the basic principles of distance and movement outlined in Chapter 3 that the enlargement of markets and the removal of artificial barriers to trade will result in a realignment of patterns of economic activity. Two main sets of effects can in fact be anticipated. The first relates to patterns of trade. With transnational integration, the removal of trade barriers should lead to a more pronounced regional division of labour, with each region in the larger association tending to specialize in those activities in which it has the greatest comparative advantage. In effect, production is thereby reallocated from high-cost to low-cost settings, and a great deal of trade is generated within the association. At the same time, lower costs can, theoretically, be passed on to consumers, thus contributing to improved levels of living. These effects of integration are generally referred to as *trade creation* effects. Countries that do not belong to the association, however, tend to lose trade: the external tariff wall prevents them from competing effectively with higher-cost internal producers whose output is able to circulate duty-free within the association. To the extent that the old sources of supply were more efficient producers than the new ones, *trade diversion* will have taken place, with the result that consumption is shifted away from lower cost external sources to higher-cost internal sources, consumers have to pay more for certain goods, and levels of living may be depressed.

The extent to which trade creation might outweigh trade diversion depends on several factors, including the degree to which the range of goods produced in member states overlap and the degree of pre-integration reliance on trade with countries outside the association. If integration *is* successful in the long run in creating trade and accelerating economic growth, it is possible that consequent increases in demand for goods and raw materials will generate 'spread effects' (see p. 77), thus creating a positive spillover effect for other economies.

The second set of effects relates to patterns of regional development. Because of the need to exploit new patterns of comparative advantage, a certain amount of relocation of production must take place, with related activities tending to cluster together in the most efficient settings. The corollary is the disinvestment that takes place as production is withdrawn from less efficient locations. Given the logic of cumulative causation (see p. 77), the net effect in terms of regional development within the association will clearly be a tendency for *spatial polarization* as a result of 'backwash effects' (see p. 78). Because of the political dimension inherent to integration, this in turn provides a powerful case for a strong *regional policy*. Meanwhile, integration can also be expected to precipitate other changes in patterns of regional development. Reorganization of patterns of production may occur where changes in patterns of comparative advantage are not sufficient to write off past investments or to prompt relocation, but are sufficient to justify intra-industry specialization. Steel-producing regions, for example, may come to specialize in certain kinds of steel products rather than producing a broad spectrum of steel products for a domestic national market; or agricultural regions may move from mixed farming to a more specialized set of outputs. Another important consequence of integration is the stimulus that is provided for foreign direct investment. Excluded by high external tariff walls, foreign suppliers are likely to seek to open branch plants inside the association in order to get access to its market. If successful, this not only makes for a drain of capital as profits are repatriated; it also makes for a degree of *external control* of some local labour markets (see p. 199). We must also consider the implications of integration for patterns of regional development outside the association. The most striking effects in this context will be those related to the dislocations experienced by specialized regions whose exports are no longer competitive within the protected market of the association.

These same principles and tendencies mean that we should expect integration to reinforce the dominant core–periphery patterns in the world's economic landscapes at the macro scale. Patterns of trade between core economies, for instance, are already so strong that integration is able to draw on a good deal of momentum. At the same time, it is relatively easy for core states to meet the political, social and cultural prerequisites for successful economic integration. These include:

- similarity in power of units joining the association

- complementarity of élite value systems

- the existence of pluralistic power structures in member countries

- positive perceptions concerning (a) the expected equity of the distribution of benefits from integration, and (b) the magnitude of the costs of integration

- the compatability of states' decision-making styles

- the adaptability, administrative capacity and flexibility of member states' governments and bureaucracies (Alger, 1977; Haas and Schmitter, 1964; Nye, 1970).

The success of the European Community has dramatized how effective integration between core states can be. Between 1959 and 1971, trade among the six original member countries increased nearly sixfold; by 1979 the expanded Community of nine nations accounted for nearly 20 per cent of all world trade; and by 1987 the Community of 12 accounted for nearly 24 per cent of all world trade.

In the case of peripheral economies, on the other hand, patterns of trade offer little realistic scope for the reallocation of output following the removal of trade barriers in trade preference organizations, common markets or free trade associations. As we have seen (Chapter 2, Chapter 9), most peripheral nations produce primary commodities which are exported to the core economies rather than to each other, and most are so short of capital that even pooled resources are likely to be insufficient to trigger economies of scale of sufficient magnitude to be able to break free from their functional dependency on trade with core economies. Experience has shown, moreover, that it is difficult for peripheral states to meet the political, social and cultural preconditions for successful economic integration. ASEAN, for example, despite having generated a growing sense of regional identity, has been unable to progress beyond a preliminary stage of economic regionalism. Regional projects such as the Asian Highway and the Mekong River Project have been discussed and tentative national responsibilities and commitments planned; but it has not proved possible to foster a significant increase in inter-ASEAN trade. Indeed, inter-ASEAN trade actually fell, as a proportion of total ASEAN trade with the world, during the 1970s. Moreover, a large proportion of inter-ASEAN trade is accounted for by exports that are transshipped through Singapore with only marginal value added by processing or packaging (Golay, 1977; Leng, 1983). Quite simply, the ASEAN economies are more complementary to those of Japan, the United States and Western Europe than they are to one another: ASEAN itself cannot absorb all the primary products it produces, and it is still dependent on these core economies for capital, technology, and many consumer goods. Even less successful is the Andean Common Market, where integration has been truly half-hearted. Members have been unwilling to build integration into their own economic planning and policymaking and unable to reach agreement about the harmonization of policies with regard to foreign trade, industrial development or fiscal affairs. Although some progress has been made at diplomatic levels (on pronouncements in favour of human rights in Nicaragua, for instance) and some increase has been achieved in absolute levels of intra-market trade, the negative effects of spatial and socio-economic polarization, particularly in Bolivia and Ecuador, have led to new tensions. Meanwhile, there have been virtually no positive effects in terms of the promotion of new sectors of production or the strengthening of existing regions of production (Puyana de Palacios, 1982).

One important response to such problems has been the so-called 'North–South dialogue'. The most important platform for this dialogue has been the United Nations Conference on Trade and Development (UNCTAD), launched in Geneva in 1964. By the end of the Geneva meetings, a degree of political solidarity had emerged among developing countries. Under the banner of the 'Group of 77' they issued a declaration:

> The unity [of the developing countries in UNCTAD] has sprung out of the fact that facing the basic problems of development they have a common interest in a new policy for international trade and development. The developing countries have a strong conviction that there is a vital need to maintain, and further strengthen, this unity in the years ahead. It is an indispensable instrument for securing the adoption of new attitudes and new approaches in the international economic field.

By 1987, the Group of 77 had nearly 130 members and had succeeded in articulating demands for a 'New International Economic Order' (not to be confused with the New International Division of Labour). Central to the new order envisioned by the Group of 77 are demands for fundamental changes in the marketing conditions of world trade in primary commodities. These changes would require a variety of measures, including price and production agreements among producer countries, the creation of international buffer stocks of commodities financed by a common fund, multilateral long-term supply contracts, and the indexing of prices of primary commodities against the price of manufactured goods. Such changes have been at the centre of discussions in a series of UNCTAD conferences, special sessions of the United Nations General Assembly, meetings of a specially convened Conference on International Economic Cooperation, and successive meetings of the heads of state of the British Commonwealth (G. Williams, 1981). Throughout these discussions, however, the core countries in general and the United States in particular have been reluctant to do more than agree to general statements about the desirability of a new international economic order. As a result, observes Williams, 'It is clear to everyone that so far the North–South dialogue has failed, and the New International Economic Order is still a dream' (1981, p. 99).

In practice, therefore, there have been two dominant sets of spatial outcomes of transnational economic integration. One has simply been the reinforcement of the dominant core–periphery structure of the world-economy because of the relative success of economic integration between core states. The second has been the imprint of this success on particular regions. This imprint can be discerned: (a) in terms of the effects of trade creation, trade diversion, spatial polarization, regional policy and socio-spatial tensions within core associations, and (b) in terms of the dislocations experienced within non-member states. In the remainder of this chapter we illustrate the importance and complexity of the second of these sets of spatial outcomes – the consequences of the success of economic integration between core states – using the example of the European Community.

The Imprint of the European Community

The European Community has its origins in pragmatic responses to the changed economic climate of postwar Europe. It was formed in 1967 by an amalgamation of three institutions which had been set up in the 1950s in order to promote progressive economic integration along particular lines: Euratom, the European Coal and Steel Community (ECSC) and the European Economic Community (EEC). The ultimate aim of the EC is economic and political harmonization within a single supranational government. Having expanded from its six original members – Belgium, France, Italy, Luxembourg, the Netherlands and West Germany – to include Denmark, the Republic of Ireland and the United Kingdom in 1972, Greece in 1981 and Portugal and Spain in 1984, it now boasts a population of over 320 million, with a combined GNP two-thirds that of the United States. It has developed into a sophisticated and powerful institution with a pervasive influence on patterns of economic and social well-being within its member states and a significant impact on certain aspects of economic development within some non-member countries.

The cornerstone of the Community is the compromise worked out between the strongest two of the original six members. West Germany wanted a larger but protected market for its industrial goods; France wanted to continue to protect its highly inefficient (but large and politically important) agricultural sector from overseas competition. The result was the creation of a tariff-free market within the Community, a common external tariff, and a Common Agricultural Policy (CAP) to bolster the Community's agricultural sector. Given the nature of this compromise, it should be no surprise that the European Community has performed very unevenly (Pryce, 1986).

Trade Creation

In overall terms, it has been estimated that trade between member countries in 1970 was 40–50 per cent more and in 1980 100–125 per cent more than it would have been if the Community had not been formed (Balassa, 1975; Williamson and Bottrill, 1971; Owen, 1983). The net benefits of this increase are far from clear, however, since it is generally acknowledged that the overall increase in intra-Community trade has been the product of a high degree both of trade *creation* and of trade *diversion*. Although it may seem somewhat surprising that there is little hard evidence as to the actual magnitude of these effects, given that the putative benefits of trade creation are fundamental to the Community's existence, it must be acknowledged that it is very difficult to isolate the effects of Community membership from other effects, such as transnational corporate activity (El-Agraa, 1985). What does seem clear, however, is that overall increases in intra-Community trade have generated scale economies for EC producers that have in turn stimulated further trade, accelerated changes in industrial structure and corporate organization, and brought about efficiency gains in both importing and exporting countries. Owen (1983) has estimated that these economic benefits could be more than half as great as the value of trade itself.

Spatial Polarization

It is also clear that these benefits have been associated with a significant amount of regional change within the Community, although once again it is difficult to isolate the effects of the common market from others. In overall terms, the removal of internal barriers to labour, capital and trade has worked to the clear disadvantage of peripheral regions within member states and in particular to the disadvantage of those furthest from the 'Golden Triangle' (between Amsterdam, Brussels and Cologne) that is increasingly the 'centre of gravity' in terms of both production and consumption (Keeble, Owens and Thompson, 1982). At the same time, integration has accelerated and extended the processes of concentration and centralization (see p. 187), creating structural as well as spatial inequalities (Lee, 1976; Knox, 1984). As Holland puts it:

> the market of the Community is essentially a capitalist market, uncommon and

unequal in the record of who gains what, where, why and when. Its mechanisms have already disintegrated major industries and regions in the Community and threaten to realize an inner and outer Europe of rich and poor countries. (1980, p. 8)

Slower-growing states with economies dominated by inefficient primary or manufacturing industries are, in short, in danger of becoming backward problem regions within a prosperous Community (Kiljunen, 1980). Evidence on trends in personal incomes supports this prognosis. Although the overall range of incomes has remained more or less constant, there is clear evidence of a steady convergence of per capita income at the top end of the range in Belgium, Denmark, France, Luxembourg, the Netherlands and West Germany. This has led in effect to a two-tier Community as far as income levels are concerned, with the lower tier consisting of Greece, Ireland, Italy, Portugal, Spain and the United Kingdom (Hallett, 1981).

The Effects of the CAP
The most striking changes in the regional geography of the EC, however, are those related to the operation of the CAP. It is the CAP which dominates the Community budget, accounting for over 70 per cent of the total expenditure. Its operation has had a significant impact on rural economies, rural landscapes and rural levels of living; and has even influenced urban living through its effects on food prices. The basis of the CAP is a system of support for farmers' incomes that is operated, in the main, through the artificial support of wholesale prices for agricultural produce. While motivated mainly by political considerations, the CAP has also been an instrument of farm modernization. By setting stable institutional prices above those prevailing on world markets, the CAP has provided a relatively risk-free environment in which investment for farm modernization has been encouraged. At the same time, stable, guaranteed prices have provided security and continuity of food supplies for consumers. Assured markets have also allowed trends in product specialization and concentration by farm, region and country to proceed at a faster rate than might otherwise have occurred, as Bowler (1985) has shown in his survey of the geography of agriculture under the CAP. Not all products are subject to CAP support, however, so that while regions specializing in crops and livestock subject to price guarantees, intervention and market regulation have been able to intensify their specialization, other regions have been subject to Community-wide competition. The net result has been a realignment of production patterns, with a general withdrawal from mixed farming. Ireland, the United Kingdom and Denmark, for example, have increased their specialization in the production of wheat, barley, poultry and milk; while France and West Germany have increased their specialization in the production of barley, maize and sugar beet. It is at regional and sub-regional scales that these changes have been most striking. CAP support for oilseeds, for example, has made rapeseed a profitable break-crop in cereal-producing regions of the United Kingdom, with the bright yellow flowers of the crop bringing a remarkable change to the summer landscapes of the countryside.

The reorganization of Europe's agricultural geography under the CAP has also brought some unwanted side effects, however. Environmental problems have occurred because of the speed and scale of modernization, combined with farmers' desire to capitalize on generous levels of guaranteed prices for arable crops. In particular, moorlands, woodlands, wetlands and hedgerows have come under threat, and some 'vernacular' landscapes have been replaced by the prairie-style settings of specialized agribusiness. Another serious problem with geographical implications concerns the large surpluses fostered by the price support system. Prices set to give a reasonable return to producers on small farms have been so favourable to the modernized sector of European agriculture that 'mountains' of beef, butter, wheat, sugar and milk powder and 'lakes' of olive oil and wine have had to be sold off at a loss to Eastern European countries, dumped on world markets, or 'denatured' (rendered unfit for human consumption) at considerable cost.

A third set of problems results from the the income transfers caused by CAP policies. Price support mechanisms involve a transfer of income from taxpayers to producers and from consumers to producers. There is plenty of evidence to show that these transfers are regressive within member countries and inequitable between them. Expenditure on food generally accounts for a larger proportion of disposable income in poorer households than in better-off households. Producers, on the other hand, benefit from price support policies in proportion to their total production, so that the larger and more prosperous farmers receive a disproportionate share of the benefits. Spatial inequity arises because countries or regions that are major producers of price-supported products receive the major share of the benefits while the costs of price support are shared among member nations according to the overall size of their agricultural sector. Furthermore, the CAP pricing system made no concessions for a long time to the variety of agricultural systems practised on farms of different sizes and in different regions. As a result, areas with particularly large and/or intensive or specialized farm units (such as northern France and the Netherlands) benefitted most, together with regions specializing in the most strongly supported crops (cereals, sugar beet and dairy products). Effectively, this has meant that the most prosperous agricultural regions have benefited most from the CAP, so that farm income differentials within member countries have been maintained, if not reinforced (Cuddy, 1981; UK Select Committee on the European Communities, 1980).

In addition to all this, the budgetary cost of the CAP has escalated. By 1983, budgetary problems had become acute; but reform of the CAP has been hampered by domestic political considerations in member countries that have been the biggest beneficiaries of the CAP (Bowler, 1985). The CAP has now become a source of serious disharmony, particularly in the United Kingdom, where, before EC membership, food policies had been progressive, subsidizing lower-income households. Embracing the CAP meant a higher and regressive system of food prices without any compensatory benefits: peasant farming and inefficient agricultural practices had been purged from the UK economy long before.

Regional Policy

The United Kingdom's position in the Community highlighted the lop-sidedness of Community policy in favour of rural interests compared with those of industrial areas. As a result, the Community was persuaded to launch the European Regional Development Fund (ERDF). Although the Community had effectively operated 'regional' policies through the ECSC and the European Investment Bank (EIB) for some time, there had been no comprehensive, coordinated framework within which to operate (Klein, 1981; Molle and Paelinck, 1979; Pinder, 1983). The ECSC was limited to the 'readaptation' of workers and the 'conversion' of local economies in depressed coalmining and steel-producing regions. The EIB is a Community banking system designed to reduce intra-Community disparities in economic development by disbursing loans to selected projects in priority regions (Pinder, 1978); but although it has been particularly influential in sponsoring projects in marginal, trans-frontier regions, it is simply not equipped to deal with the casualties of regional economic restructuring within an expanding common market. The entry of the United Kingdom to the Community in 1972 not only made for a significant increase in the scope and intensity of regional restructuring processes but also brought a legacy of chronic regional problems and, with them, a certain political resolve. Following an examination of the issues (Thompson Report, 1973), the Community launched the ERDF in 1975 with a relatively modest budget (1,300 million European Units of Account, compared with the 2,250 million recommended by the Thompson Report).

Following the principle of 'additionality', projects must qualify for national funding in order to receive Community support: the ERDF thus claims to complement rather than replace national policies and strategies. The bulk of ERDF funds (> 85 per cent) are allocated to member nations on a quota basis. In the 1980s, about a third of this has been allocated to Italy, with the United Kingdom receiving a further 25 per cent and France, Greece and, latterly, Portugal and Spain receiving most of the rest. Because preference is given to projects in nationally-defined priority regions, this effectively channels a large proportion of ERDF funds to the Mezzogiorno, Sardinia, Scotland, Northern Ireland, northern England, and Brittany (Martins and Mawson, 1980). Although encompassing most of the Community's most acute problem areas, this distribution is generally regarded as being poorly targeted. While the local impact of Community-funded development projects has often been significant, little headway seems to have been made in redressing the regional restructuring and spatial polarization that has accompanied the creation and enlargement of the common market. It is, if course, debatable whether regional policies could in fact do so, particularly since the new reach and flexibility of multinational corporations can exploit cost advantages elsewhere in the world that EC incentives could never hope to match (Holland, 1976; Yuill et al., 1980).

External Effects of the EC

Meanwhile, the scale of the EC and its maintenance of a strongly protectionist agricultural policy as well as a protected common market has inevitably had a significant impact on non-member countries: diverting trade and creating complex new layers of interdependence. Much of this complexity relates to the 'pyramid of privilege' that has arisen from the Community's trade agreements with different groups of non-member countries. At the base of the pyramid is a Generalized System of Preferences negotiated through UNCTAD (Mishalani *et al.*, 1981). This allows access to the Community market for a broad range of products from developing countries. Bilateral trade agreements also exist with some countries as a result of attempts by the EC to extend and diversify its trading patterns. The most favourable trading privileges are extended to a large group of countries in Africa, the Caribbean and the Pacific (the 'ACP states'), most of them former Colonial territories of member states. Originally established at the Youndé Convention in 1963 and later extended at Lomé Conventions in 1975 and 1979, these privileges allow access to the Community market for tropical agricultural products without having to provide reciprocal privileges to EC members or abandon trading agreements with other developing countries. They also involve an export revenue stabilization scheme – STABEX – that covers nearly 50 key primary products and raw materials (Hewitt and Stevens, 1981; Huddleston *et al.*, 1982).

In detail, the mechanics of these privileges are complex, and it is very difficult to assess their impact on patterns of trade and development. It is clear, however, that the 'privileges' extended to non-members are essentially designed to enhance the position of the EC rather than to contribute to a New International Economic Order. 'Sensitive' products (i.e. those that compete directly with EC agricultural and industrial products), for example, are excluded from preferential treatment, or are subject to seasonal restrictions. Moreover, the net effect of the Lomé 'privileges' has been to increase the dependency of many countries on exports of a narrow range of primary produce to the EC market. Particular examples include Burundi (coffee), Uganda (coffee), Chad (cotton), Ghana (cocoa), Ivory Coast (groundnuts), Senegal (wood, groundnuts), Sudan (coffee), and Tonga (copra) (Bowler, 1985). As a result, EC relations with ACP countries have been interpreted as neo-imperialist, effectively extending the core–periphery structure of the world-economy (Hewitt and Stevens, 1981; Koester and Bale, 1984; Verreydt and Waelbroeck, 1982).

It is not only peripheral countries that have been affected by the EC, however. The EC represents an outcome of the struggle for economic power within the core and to preserve power in relation to the semi-periphery as much as it is an attempt to consolidate power in relation to the periphery. EC trade relations with the United States have been described as 'stormy' (Ginsberg, 1983), while the EC has been forced to mount a 'diplomatic assault' on Japan in an attempt to stem the impact of Japanese direct investment in sophisticated manufacturing industries (automobiles, electronics, etc.) within the EC (Daniels and Gow, 1983). Core and semi-periphery countries have also been directly affected by the trade-diverting effects of the EC's protection of 'temperate' agricultural products. Trade diversion effects are particularly evident where EC subsidies have produced large surpluses for export. EC exports of beef, for example, rose from 5 per cent of world trade in 1977 to over 20 per cent in 1980 and in so doing displaced Australian and Argentinian exports to Egypt and Uruguayan exports to ·Ghana (Bowler, 1985). Other striking cases of trade diversion have occurred as specialist producers of 'temperate' products with strong traditional ties to European markets found themselves largely excluded by the EC's external tariff wall. New Zealand is a good example. The United Kingdom used to take nearly all of New Zealand's butter, cheese and sheepmeat, so that after the United Kingdom joined the EC, New Zealand agriculture had to he restructured, new products had to be developed (a notable success here being the kiwi fruit) and new markets had to be penetrated in Latin America, India and Japan – in the face of competition from the subsidized surpluses of dairy produce from the EC (Lodge, 1982; Willis, 1984).

Summary

In this chapter we have shown how the imprint of transnational economic and political integration has begun to affect the world's economic landscapes as nation states have responded to the changing economic and geopolitical context of the world-economy. This response has resulted in a variety of forms and levels of integration, but in practice the basic principles of distance and movement outlined in Chapter 3 have resulted in three main outcomes:

- the reinforcement of the dominant core–periphery structure of the world-economy

- the spatial reorganization of production as trade creation and trade diversion affect both member and non-member states

- the creation and intensification of regional polarization as the economies of scale and multiplier effects in regions most favoured by integration create backwash effects elsewhere.

Yet, while it is important to acknowledge transnational integration as a response to the globalization of the world-economy, it would be unwise to overstate its effects. Transnational and supranational organizations are not about to replace nation states, and we must recognize their limits as contributors to the constant rewriting of the world's economic landscapes. The further integration of the EC, for example, is seriously hampered by a number of issues that transcend its territory and jurisdiction, including its inability to curb inflation, to reduce unemployment, or to stem the 'brain drain' (Albert and Ball, 1983; Pinder, 1986). Moreover, as Nairn has pointed out, spatial polarization within the EC has 'sought out and found the buried fault lines of the area. . . . Nationalism in the real sense is never a historical accident, or a mere invention. It reflects the latent fracture lines of human society under strain' (1977, p. 69). Indeed, nationalism and localism can be seen to be intensifying, not only in response to the backwash effects of transnational integration but also in response to the overall globalization of the economy, the internationalization of culture and society, and the insecurity and instability generated by the transition to advanced capitalism (Harvey, 1987). In the next, final chapter of the book, therefore, we turn to an examination of decentralist reactions to the changing world-economy.

12

Decentralist Reactions

Trends towards ever more powerful states and growing economic monopolies have often appeared to be inexorable and irreversible features of the modern world-economy. The emergence into prominence of supranational institutions (such as the EC) and multinational enterprises would suggest a pervasive bureaucratization of modern life under the control of fewer and fewer organizations and individuals. However, though manifestations of centralization, homogenization and standardization are real enough, there is also evidence for persisting and even increasing differentiation and decentralization. They are related. For example, the centralization of economic power in MNEs has recently led to a decentralization of their productive activities (as noted in Chapters 6 and 10). Attempted political and cultural homogenization often generates resistance to and rejection of efforts at state unification (as noted in Chapter 8).

In fact, all over the world the increased integration of the world-economy has increasingly produced differentiation and decentralist reactions of one kind or another. Three kinds of reaction have been especially common. First, national governments must satisfy local and regional constituencies that they represent their best interests. When faced by geographically differentiated patterns of economic growth and decline, regional policies and regional devolution have been important responses. Second, many modern national states are divided culturally along regional/geographical lines. This has sometimes led to national separatist movements directed towards achieving autonomy or independence for disaffected regions. Third, and most generally, the growing internationalization of the world-economy has encouraged decentralization rather than centralization of economic activities. In particular, small-scale production has become of increasing importance (the 'batch production,' etc. noted in Chapters 6 and 10) and 'basic needs', 'appropriate technology' and local control have become the basic demands of new political movements calling for economic as well as political democracy.

Regionalism and Regional Policy

Processes of economic growth and decline are not geographically neutral in their impact. In particular, the locational requirements of new profitable manufacturing production are likely to differ from those of existing production (see Chapters 6 and 10). If left to firm decision-making alone there is no guarantee of compensating investment. It is in this context that appeals for governmental action arise to 'help' a particular region or set of regions either 'adjust' to a new economic situation or encourage compensating investment by means of fiscal measures such as tax breaks or relocation allowances (Agnew, 1984).

In the 1950s and 1960s there was widespread acceptance in many countries of the need to encourage regional 'balance' in economic growth. In some countries this took the form of revitalizing or establishing lower 'regional' tiers of government. Regional governments were viewed as agents for maintaining or attracting private investment. In the United States this took an extremely competitive form as the states began to compete with another in establishing the most attractive 'business climates'. In some countries, such as Italy, Norway, and, to a lesser degree, Britain, regional authorities were introduced to encourage regional economic planning and foster local industrial regeneration.

In many countries, especially those with federal political systems (such as the United States, Canada, Australia, Switzerland and West Germany), lower-tier governments have traditionally played an important role in stimulating economic growth within their territories. In the downturn of the world-economy in the 1970s and especially in the face of the 1974–75 and 1979–83 recessions, local governments became even more involved in economic development efforts. What they are able to do, however, is constrained by their relative autonomy (compare American states with British local authorities) and the macroeconomic imperatives of national governments to curb public spending and reduce taxation.

However, direct central government intervention has always been more widespread than regionalism. Substantial regional variations in unemployment rates and prospects for economic development have been widely viewed as creating a national *political* problem, threatening the social and economic cohesion of the state itself. As a result, national governments have felt it necessary to intervene in the economic geography of their territories by manipulating the costs of production.

The policies adopted have varied over time and by country. Some have sought to reduce the costs of fixed capital in declining regions, through government investment in infrastructure, subsidies for private investment, etc. Others have sought to reduce the costs of variable capital in declining regions through subsidies for labour costs in those regions and making costs higher in growing regions. In other words, 'The goal has been both to direct employment-generating activities into the depressed regions and to stimulate growth generally. Conventional wisdom suggested that the former should occur in any case, that the geographical disparities in wages should stimulate the migration of workers to the higher-wage areas and the migration of employers to low-wage areas. However, the problems of the immobility of labour, of abandoning expensive fixed investments, and of inertia prevented a new equilibrium situation occurring naturally – and quickly' (Johnston, 1986, p. 270). Regional policies have been intended to stimulate a new equilibrium for purposes of political legitimation without harming capital accumulation.

The increased globalization of the world-economy, however, has challenged the relevance of conventional regional policies. In the first place, the largest firms no longer choose sites from among a single national set. There is no longer much identity between the scale of economic-locational decision making and the spatial scale over which governments can exert their fiscal powers. Indeed, in this context 'the difficulties of guaranteeing full employment nationally mean that the state has increasingly to focus its attention on the national rather than the regional crisis; regional policy is in large part irrelevant' (Johnston, 1986, p. 274).

In the second place, the cost of subsidies raises government spending and produces a macroeconomic environment that is unattractive to global capital. Regional policy is then viewed as both an expensive luxury and an increasing liability. This is very much the view adopted by the Thatcher government in Britain and the Reagan administration in the United States. Reducing state spending on regional policy and other 'welfare' programmes is seen as a necessity for improving *national* competitiveness in a global economy. In Britain between 1979 and 1985, for example, regional aid was cut from £842 million to £560 million; a cut in real terms of exactly one-third. Moreover, the areas eligible for aid were 'rolled back' considerably (Martin, 1986, p. 271) (Fig. 12.1).

Third, and finally, as Doreen Massey (1984, p. 298) has pointed out: 'No longer is there really a 'regional' problem in the old sense. No longer is there a fairly straightforward twofold division between central prosperous areas and a decaying periphery.' Rather, because 'it is not regions which interrelate, but the social relations of production which take place over space' (p. 122) a new spatial division of labour based upon spatial division of firm activities has given rise to a new and more *localized* pattern of spatial inequality. Her summary argument is as follows (p. 295):

> The old spatial division of labour based on sector, on contrasts between industries, has gone into accelerated decline and in its place has arisen to dominance a spatial division of labour in which a more important component is the inter-regional spatial structuring of production within individual industries. Relations between economic activity in different parts of the country are now a function less of market relations between firms and rather more of planned relations within them.

From this perspective regional policy no longer engages with economic reality. Rather than discrete regional economies in competition with one another,

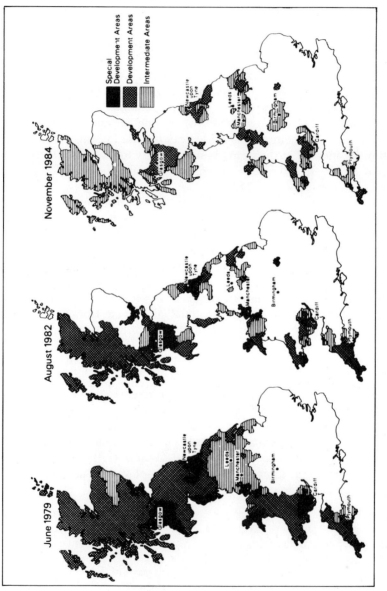

Fig 12.1 The Thatcher government's rolling back of the map of regional aid
Source: Martin (1986) Fig. 8.4, p. 273

'a new spatial division of labour *made possible* by new information and communication technologies and new non-spatial scale economies has created a localized pattern of restructuring' (Agnew, 1988, p. 131; also see Chapter 6 and Gertler, 1986).

As decentralist reactions, therefore, regionalism and, especially, regional policy appear increasingly problematic. As Martin and Hodge (1983, p. 319) argue

> however much regional policies of the conventional type are strengthened, if they are pursued against a background of continued unfavourable macro-economic conditions, their 'social' role will be largely limited to simply spreading the misery of mass unemployment more 'fairly' around the country while providing little boost to total economic activity or employment.

Nationalist Separatism

The growth of industrial capitalism in the nineteenth century was accompanied by promotion of the nation state and the growth of nationalism. The conviction grew among élites and populations at large that each state should be clearly bounded geographically; it should be organized as an economy; and it should be as linguistically and culturally homogeneous as possible. To many, the blessings of material abundance and personal freedom became associated with the interrelated development of capitalism and the nation state.

In the twentieth century, however, nationalism has regularly been perverted into fascism. Dreadful wars have been fought. National independence has been no guarantee of national prosperity. Even in the original or 'founding' states of Europe such as Spain, France, and Britain, political movements rejecting established national claims and asserting political and economic rights for regional and ethnic populations have become widespread.

This last trend ·reflects the fact that state making and nationalism have never rebounded equally to the benefit of all the nominal citizens of a country. In particular, since the formation of modern national states a diversity of cultural groups can be found within one political boundary. In the social science literature the term ethnicity has come to signify the organization of cultural diversity within modern states. Thus, an ethnic group can be defined as

> a collectivity of people who share some pattern of normative behaviour, or culture, and who form a part of a larger population, interacting within the framework of a common social system. (Cohen, 1974, p. 92)

But ethnic groups are not simply primordial groupings. They are differentiated and integrated through such mechanisms as a cultural division of labour, political favouritism and historically created economic roles. Indeed, ethnicity can be viewed as a mechanism for allocating wealth and power.

A clear example of the use of ethnicity in this way would be Northern Ireland where a dominant élite of Protestant landowners and businessmen maintained their hegemony through a web of mutual obligations, customs, duties and economic favours that bound Protestant workers and small farmers to them while excluding the Catholic population (MacLaughlin and Agnew, 1986). This process of ethnic competition for control over the fruits of economic growth and government policy is extremely widespread the world over; the more so the greater the number of ethnic groups and the weaker the alternative means of political mobilization (e.g. social class).

Students of ethnicity have noted that in recent years the level and intensity of conflicts between ethnic groups have been on the increase. Writing of Indonesia, Clifford Geertz (1973, pp. 244-5) provides a particularly vivid description:

> Up until the third decade of this century, the several ingredient traditions – Indic, Sinitic, Islamic, Christian, Polynesian – were suspended in a kind of half-solution in which contrasting, even opposed styles of life and world outlook managed to coexist, if not wholly without tension, or even without violence, at least in some sort of workable, to-each-his-own sort of arrangement. This *modus vivendi* began to show signs of strain as early as the mid nineteenth century, but its dissolution got genuinely under way only with the rise, from 1912 on, of nationalism; its collapse, which is still not complete, only in the revolutionary and post-revolutionary periods [1945 on]. For then what had been parallel traditionalisms became competing definitions of the essence of the New Indonesia. What was once, to employ a term I have used elsewhere, a kind of 'cultural balance of power' became an ideological war of a peculiarly implacable sort.

Some, for example Kedourie (1960), have seen this ethnic 'schismogenesis' as a world-wide process associated with the diffusion of the idea of nationalism from Europe. Others have emphasized modernization or industrialization (e.g. Gellner, 1964). In fact, ethnic nationalism seems to have developed in different ways and with different causes in different parts of the world. Rokkan and Urwin (1983) argue that processes of economic, military-administrative, and cultural 'system building' have combined in different ways to produce different effects in different European localities (Fig. 12.2). In turn, ethnic nationalism has been both encouraged in some settings (such as the Celtic fringe of the British Isles and the Basque provinces of Spain) and discouraged elsewhere (for example in Alsace and the South Tyrol).

Whatever its precise origins in particular cases, however, ethnic conflict and nationalist separatism have become increasingly marked features of the contemporary world. From Ireland to Yugoslavia to Lebanon to India to Sri Lanka to Canada, to name only a few of the best known cases, ethnic groups and ethnic conflict have become major elements in national political life. Three factors seem to be especially important in this trend. One of these is the increased geographical-economic differentiation within states and its relationship to ethnic divisions. It is not that ethnic conflict always involves poor

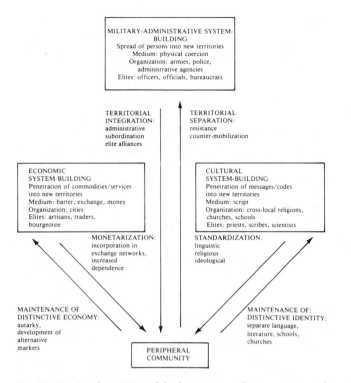

MILITARY-ADMINISTRATIVE SYSTEM-
BUILDING
Spread of persons into new territories
Medium: physical coercion
Organization: armies, police,
administrative agencies
Elites: officers, officials, bureaucrats

TERRITORIAL
INTEGRATION:
administrative
subordination
elite alliances

TERRITORIAL
SEPARATION:
resistance
counter-mobilization

ECONOMIC
SYSTEM-BUILDING
Penetration of commodities/services
into new territories
Medium: barter, exchange, money
Organization: cities
Elites: artisans, traders,
bourgeoisie

CULTURAL
SYSTEM-BUILDING
Penetration of messages/codes
into new territories
Medium: script
Organization: cross-local religions,
churches, schools
Elites: priests, scribes, scientists

MONETARIZATION:
incorporation in
exchange networks,
increased
dependence

STANDARDIZATION.
linguistic
religious
ideological

MAINTENANCE OF
DISTINCTIVE ECONOMY:
autarky,
development of
alternative
markets

MAINTENANCE OF:
DISTINCTIVE IDENTITY:
separate language,
literature, schools,
churches

PERIPHERAL
COMMUNITY

Fig 12.2 An abstract model of processes of interaction and resistance within large-scale territorial systems
Source: Rokkan and Urwin Fig. 1.3, p. 15

regions rebelling against more affluent ones. It is difference *per se*. In Spain, for example, it is the Basque and Catalan regions, the most prosperous in the country, that are the most rebellious (Greenwood, 1977). Likewise in Yugoslavia, where the relatively well-off Slovenians and Croatians periodically demonstrate their impatience with 'subsidizing' the ethnic groups (Serbs, Albanians, etc.) which occupy other regions (Bridge, 1977).

A second factor is the increased bureaucratization of the state and the growth of the welfare state. Ethnic identity can be a basis for collective action against the intrusiveness of the modern state and its destruction of particularity. Fox *et al.* (1981) note, for example, how political mobilization in Europe increasingly takes regional and cultural rather than social class forms. But the welfare state in its increased provision of social services also reduces the appeal of class-based politics.

The third factor is the growing globalization of political and economic activity. The shift of power and control over local economies to ever more distant locations provides an incentive for regional counter-mobilization. The development of the EC in Europe may have been one stimulus, the growing importance of MNEs may have been another. At the same time the increase in the flow of international migrants, especially into Europe, has introduced new ethnic groups, such as Indians in Britain, Turks in West Germany, and Algerians in France (Thrift, 1986), which both stimulate indigenous ethnic groups and provide new 'out-groups' for new rounds of ethnic conflict.

With few exceptions, outright separatist movements have not met with success. In both Europe and peripheral countries the ethnic-territorial status quo has been largely maintained (Williams, 1982). The world super-powers have generally refused to back separatist movements, perhaps for fear of stimulating them at home. Often political changes short of outright independence have proved satisfactory responses to regional-ethnic revolt. These include federalism, regional devolution, and consociationalism (cartelization among ethnic groups as in Switzerland and Belgium) (Esman, 1977; Williams, 1986). What is clear, however, irrespective of the prospects for nationalist separatism as such, is that 'there is little likelihood of an abatement of ethnic nationalism in the near future' (Williams, 1982, p. 36).

Grassroots Reactions

A peculiar paradox of the growing internationalization of the world-economy has been the stimulus it has provided to the destruction of regional-sectoral economies and the decentralization/localization of production facilities. New information and transportation technologies have made it possible to decentralize production operations to 'cheaper' locations (lower wage bills, etc.) at the same time that central corporate control is maintained or enhanced (Teece, 1980). This process has been brought about by increased competitive pressures upon large firms from the appearance of foreign competitors. Many large firms, especially in Europe and the United States, now face a marketplace far more competitive than the one they had known for the previous 40 years (Agnew, 1987; Noyelle, 1987).

Coincidentally, union–management conflicts in established production facilities and changes in market conditions, especially the increased demand in many developed countries for customized rather than mass-produced goods, have also encouraged decentralization (Sabel, 1982; Brusco and Sabel, 1981). In Italy, for example, one can see evidence of both causes. Large firms in Piemonte (Turin) and Lombardia (Milan) have increasingly contracted-out to small firms for parts and services that used to be provided on-site at large factories. Moving production in this way both undermines the power of workers in large factories, where solidarity is more easily achieved than in scattered small factories, and protects the large firm from the need to shed labour cyclically. In Emilia-Romagna (Bologna) and elsewhere in Central Italy many small firms provide customized products (both industrial and consumer goods) to domestic and export markets (Brusco and Sabel, 1981; Mattera, 1985).

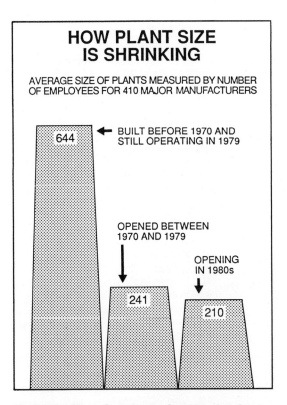

Fig 12.3 How plant size in the US is shrinking
Source: Business Week, 22 October 1984, p. 156

In the United States both types of decentralization are also increasingly common, although the small firm as supplier to a large firm is most characteristic (Sabel, 1982; Hershey 1988). Companies with fewer than 500 workers added 1.2 million jobs in the United States between 1976 and 1984, while larger companies lost 300,000 jobs. There are estimates that companies with fewer than 250 employees could account for more than half of the US's manufacturing jobs by the early 1990s, up from 42 percent today (Hershey, 1988) (Fig. 12.3).

The new 'decentralized economy', however, is incredibly volatile (Table 12.1). Patterns of new firm creation/destruction are extremely sensitive to minor cyclical fluctuations. Many firms have tiny inventories and limited equity. Though advantageous financially this introduces major limitations in terms of employee security and long-term commitment to local economies (Agnew, 1988). In this context local rather than aggregate national conditions are of increased significance for the welfare of populations. Political parties such as the Labour and Social Democratic parties in Britain have proposed decentralization of governmental powers as, at least in part, a reaction to the

Table 12.1: The volatility of US states in new business growth, 1986–1987

Rank/State (1987)	Change in rank (1986–1987)	Rank/State (1987)	Change in rank (1986–1987)
1 Arizona	0	26 Maine	0
2 New Hampshire	+ 2	27 Rhode Island	− 5
3 Maryland	+ 3	28 New York	− 5
4 Georgia	+ 1	29 Minnesota	+ 1
5 Virginia	+ 5	30 New Mexico	− 13
6 Florida	+ 1	31 Missouri	0
7 Delaware	− 1	32 Pennsylvania	0
8 California	+ 3	33 Oregon	+ 7
9 Massachusetts	0	34 Kentucky	+ 3
10 Nevada	+ 10	35 Wisconsin	+ 4
11 Tennessee	+ 5	36 Illinois	+ 2
12 Texas	− 9	37 Arkansas	− 4
13 N. Carolina	+ 2	38 Kansas	− 2
14 S. Carolina	0	39 Alaska	− 37
15 Utah	− 3	40 Mississippi	+ 1
16 Connecticut	+ 3	41 West Virginia	+ 5
17 New Jersey	+ 1	42 Idaho	0
18 Vermont	+ 3	43 Nebraska	+ 1
19 Michigan	+ 5	44 Louisiana	− 9
20 Hawaii	+ 14	45 South Dakota	0
21 Alabama	+ 7	46 Iowa	+ 2
22 Colorado	− 9	47 Oklahoma	− 4
23 Ohio	+ 6	48 Montana	− 1
24 Washington	+ 3	49 North Dakota	0
25 Indiana	0	50 Wyoming	0

Source: Agnew (1988) p. 136. From *Inc.* October 1986, pp. 58–9 and October 1987, pp. 76–7

increased localization of economic activities. In Italy the Communist party is a major sponsor of both economic and political decentralization.

From another point of view, however, local control or 'small is beautiful' can only work when decision-making power is no longer vested in giant MNEs, as it still is even when small firms proliferate to serve them (Mattera, 1985). The theme of 'economic democracy' is especially strong in recent writing on the US economy. Economic democracy refers to an egalitarian form of political-economic structure in which a serious attempt is made to democratize the economic sphere in general and workplaces in particular. The major point is to challenge the political and economic position of global capital and the commitment to it and its international role by the major capitalist states (the US, Britain, etc.). It builds on the view characteristic of movements for participatory democracy that, to be more than a sham, democracy should be extended to the economic sphere (Boyte, 1980).

Economic democracy differs from democratic capitalism (in both *laissez-faire* and welfare state manifestations), in which democracy is limited to periodic involvement in electoral politics and the means of production are largely privately owned. It also differs from conventional state socialism, especially of the Soviet variety, in which markets are prohibited (in public), there is little meaningful electoral politics and the means of production are owned by the state (Agnew, 1987).

There are a number of reasons why interest in both the theory and practice of economic democracy has increased in recent years. First, as the heavy 'smokestack' industries in the United States and other developed countries have become less profitable there have been numerous attempts by their employees to save their jobs by buying failing factories. Changes in tax laws have also made employee stock option plans (ESOPs) more attractive to businesses. Between 1976 and 1983 the number of ESOPs grew in the United States from less than 300 to over 5,000 (English, 1983). While owning stock is hardly the same as control, ESOPs do raise the question of where employees' participation should stop. But it is probably the competitive environment for businesses and the prospect for bankruptcy that do most to encourage talk about and proposals for producer cooperatives and worker self-management.

Second, interest in economic democracy reflects consideration of actual practices in a number of countries which have high levels of economic growth and high standards of living. In West Germany, 'co-determination' allocates positions on corporate boards to employees. In Sweden, after much controversy, a tax on corporate profits will be used to purchase corporate assets. In addition, the success of several large-scale prototypes has given advocates of economic democracy a ready reply to those who assert that self-management by employees is inherently utopian. The Yugoslavian economy, which gives employees considerable self-management through elections, has performed relatively well over the past 30 years, if World Bank statistics are any guide, when compared to other middle-income, developing countries (Tyson, 1980). The extensive network of Basque producer cooperatives in Spain, 'Mondragon,' employs over 10,000 workers and is more efficient than its more conventional competitors (Thomas and Logan, 1982).

Third, and finally, especially in the LDCs, economic democracy is frequently seen as an alternative to both American-style corporate capitalism and Soviet-style central planning. Under nationalistic pressure to avoid becoming satellites of either superpower, the rhetoric and sometimes the substance of economic democracy arise (Seibel and Damachi, 1982). But the pressure is also immediately practical. Considerable evidence suggests that rapid economic growth in LDCs does not necessarily improve the welfare of large numbers of their people. Directing attention to local production for 'basic needs' has been one, if yet only weakly sponsored, response. Discussion of 'appropriate technology' and 'alternative' development strategies, however, are both inspired by similar concerns.

There are of course a range of possible 'grassroots reactions' within the general confines of economic democracy. Among advocates of economic democracy are some who are committed to a vision of large firms with powerful, central councils, while others look to smaller, decentralized firms. Ellen

Comisso (1979) has compared this difference to that between federalists and Jeffersonians at the time of the founding of the United States.

An important objection to economic democracy of all types, but especially the more decentralized ones, is that they are utopian dreams since those in power will not hear of them. The world is now bureaucratized; bureaucracies will not seriously consider participatory democracy (see, for example, Ross, 1982). In particular, many LDCs are run by oligarchies determined to fix the best deals for themselves from MNEs and the superpowers.

Williams (1981), however, has defended the need for utopias. He argues (p. 98) that 'the purpose of a radical utopia is to create a tension in our souls . . . We must imagine something better. That defines us as people who offer our fellow citizens a meaningful choice about how we can define and live our lives . . . (p. 95). Radicals must confront centralized nationalism and internationalism and begin to shake it apart, break it down, and imagine a humane and socially responsible alternative. It simply will not do to define radicalism as changing the guard of the existing system' (also see Hodgson, 1984). In essence this is what grassroots reactions are really all about.

Conclusion

In this chapter three types of decentralist reaction to the impact of the world-economy have been described. Regionalism and regional policy were common in the 1950s and 1960s but may well be increasingly irrelevant in the face of the changed relationship between national and world economies. Nationalist separatism does challenge both existing states and supranational organizations. But most separatist movements will usually settle for something less than complete independence. Finally, recent trends in the world-economy have generated renewed interest in the possibility of economic democracy. Disillusionment with both American-style corporate capitalism and Soviet-style socialism in the face of an increasingly volatile world-economy has directed attention to the possibility of people taking control of their economic activities and putting them to work for them.

Whether or not decentralist reactions persist in importance depends in part on whether the world-economy recovers from its present problems, especially the debt crisis and the lack of congruence between global production and global consumption, and whether or not the 'free market' ideologies associated with the Reagan administration in the US, and the Thatcher government in Britain continue to find support (Toye, 1987).

The basic issue concerning the future geography of the world-economy is that the old international division of labour, of a static core and periphery, has been revealed as being less rigid than was once thought. But this does not necessarily point to an inevitable extension of the recent experience of the NICs to all other LDCs. Far from it. As Lipietz (1986) reminds us: 'Beware . . . of labels, beware of the "international division of labour"; or rather, let us see how every country functions, what it produces, for whom, how, what the forms of wage relations are' (pp. 24–5) . . . 'no exterior destiny, no general law of capitalism dictates to any nation its place within an implacable division of labour. Unless, that is, "exterior destiny" means simply the weight of the past, inscribed in social structure . . .' (p. 39). The future is made, not predicted.

References

AAREBROT, F.H. 1982. On the structural basis of regional mobilisation in Europe. In B. De Marchi and A.M. Boileau (eds) *Boundaries and Minorities in Western Europe*. Milan: Franco Angeli, pp. 33–92.

ABlODUN, J.O. 1967. Urban hierarchy in a developing country. *Economic Geography*, 43, 347–67.

ABLER, R., ADAMS, J. and GOULD, P. 1971. *Spatial Organization: The Geographer's View of the World*. Englewood Cliffs, NJ: Prentice-Hall.

ABUMERE, S.I. 1982. Multinationals and industrialisation in a developing economy: the case of Nigeria, in M. Taylor and N. Thrift (eds.) *The Geography of Multinationals: Studies in the Spatial Development and Economic Consequences of Multinational Corporations*. New York: St Martins Press.

ACHEBE, C. 1975. *Morning Yet on Creation Day*. London: Faber.

ADELMAN, I. 1984. Beyond export-led growth. *World Development*, 12, 937–49.

AGLIETTA, M. 1979. *A Theory of Economic Regulation: The US Experience*. London: New Left Books.

AGNEW, J.A. 1982. Sociologizing the geographical imagination: spatial concepts in the world-system perspective. *Political Geography Quarterly*, 1, 159–66.

—— 1984. Devaluing place: 'place prosperity' versus 'people prosperity' and regional planning. *Society and Space*. 2, 35–45.

—— 1987. *The United States in the World-Economy: A Regional Geography*. Cambridge: Cambridge University Press.

—— 1988. Beyond core and periphery: the myth of *regional*, political–economic restructuring and a new sectionalism in American politics. *Political Geography Quarterly*, 7, 127–39.

ALBERT, M. and BALL, R.J. 1983. *Towards European Recovery in the 1980s*. Luxembourg: European Parliament.

ALDCROFT, D.H. 1987. *The European Economy 1914–1970*. Beckenham: Croom Helm.

ALGER, C.F. 1977. Functionalism and integration. *International Social Science Journal*, 29, 71–93.

ALONSO, W. 1964. *Location and Land Use: Toward a General Theory of Land Rent*. Cambridge, Mass.: Harvard University Press.

AMEDEO, D. and GOLLEDGE, R.G. 1975. *An Introduction to Scientific Reasoning in Geography*. New York: J. Wiley.

AMIN, S. 1973. *Neo-Colonialism in West Africa*. Harmondsworth: Penguin.

AMSDEN, A.H. 1980. *The Economics of Women and Work*. New York: Penguin.

ANDERSON, P. 1974. *Passages from Antiquity to Feudalism*. London: New Left Books.

ARCANGELI, F. BORZAGA, C. and GOGLIO, S. 1980. Patterns of peripheral development in Italian regions. *Papers and Proceedings of the Regional Science Association*, 44, 19–34.

ARCHER, J.C. 1980. Congressional incumbent re-election success and federal outlays distribution: a test of the electoral-connection hypothesis. *Environment and Planning A*, 12, 263–77.

—— 1983. The geography of federal fiscal politics in the USA: An explanation. *Government and Policy*, 1, 377–400.

ARMSTRONG, P., GLYN, A. and HARRISON, A. 1984. *Capitalism Since World War II*. London: Fontana.

ARMSTRONG, R.B. 1979. National trends in office construction, employment and headquarter location in US Metropolitan Areas, in P.W. Daniels (ed.) *Spatial Patterns of Office Growth and Location*, London: Wiley, 61–94.

ARMSTRONG, W. and McGEE, T. 1986. *Theatres of Accumulation: Studies in Asian and Latin American Urbanization*. London: Methuen.

ARRIGHI, G. 1977. *The Geometry of Imperialism*. London: New Left Books.

—— 1979. Peripheralization of Southern Africa, I: Changes in Production Processes. *Review*, 3, 161–91.

—— and DRANGEL, J. 1986. The stratification of the world-economy: an exploration of the semi-peripheral zone. *Review*, 10, 9–74.

ASIAN DEVELOPMENT BANK. 1977. *Rural Asia: Challenge and Opportunity*. New York: Praeger.

AYENI, B. 1981. Spatial dimensions of manufacturing activities in Nigeria. Unpublished paper, Department of Geography, University of Ibadan, Nigeria.

AYRES, R.U. and MILLER, S. 1983. Robotics, CAM and industrial productivity. *National Productivity Review*, 1, 452–60.

BAER, W. 1983. *The Brazilian Economy: Growth and Development*. New York: Praeger (2nd edition).

—— *et al.* 1987. Structural changes in Brazil's industrial economy, 1960–80. *World Development*, 15, 275–86.

BAILLIE, A.S. and FELIX, D. 1983. *Kanban*: a fundamental solution to production problems. Paper presented at second US-Japan Business Conference, Tokyo, 5 April.

BAIROCH, P. 1979. Ecarts internationaux des niveaux de vie avant la Révolution industrielle. *Annales: economies, sociétés, civilisations*, 34, 20–63.

BAKER, C. 1981. Economic reorganization and the slump in South and Southeast Asia. *Comparative Studies in Society and History*, 23, 325–49.

BAKIS, H. 1987. Telecommunications and the global firm. In F.E.I. Hamilton (ed.) *Industrial Change in Advanced Economies*. Beckenham: Croom Helm, 130–60.

BALASSA, B. 1975. *European Economic Integration*. Amsterdam: North Holland, Elsevier.

—— 1979. *The Changing International Division of Labor in Manufactured Goods*. Washington DC: The World Bank. Working Paper 329.

BALLARD, S.C. and JAMES, T.E. (eds.) 1983. *The Future of the Sunbelt*. New York: Praeger.

BARNET, R. and MÜLLER, R. 1974. *Global Reach*. New York: Simon & Schuster.

BASSETT, K. 1984. Corporate structure and corporate change in a local economy: the case of Bristol. *Environment & Planning A*, 16, 879–900.

BATES, R.H. 1983. *Essays on the Political Economy of Rural Africa*. Cambridge: Cambridge University Press.

BEEMAN, W.O. 1983. Images of the Great Satan: Representations of the United States in the Iranian Revolution, in N. Keddie (ed.) *Religion and Politics in Iran*. New Haven, CT: Yale University Press.

BEENSTOCK, M. 1983. *The World Economy in Transition*. London: Allen & Unwin.

BEESON, P. 1987. Total factor productivity growth and agglomeration economies in manufacturing, 1959–1973. *Journal of Regional Science*, 27 183–200.

BENERIÁ, L. 1981. Conceptualizing the Labour Force: The Underestimation of Women's Activities. *Journal of Development Studies*, 17, 10–27.

BENNETT, R.J. 1980. *The Geography of Public Finance* New York: Methuen.

BENSEL, R.F. 1984. *Sectionalism and American Political Development 1880–1980*. Madison: University of Wisconsin Press.

BERARDI, G.M. 1985. *World Food Population and Development*. Totowa, NJ: Rowman & Allanheld.

BERG, E.J. 1965. The development of a labor force in sub-Saharan Africa. *Economic Development and Cultural Change*, 13, 394–412.

BERRY, B.J.L. 1961. City-size distributions and economic development. *Economic Development and Cultural Change*, 9, 573–87.

—— 1967. *Geography of Market Centers and Retail Distribution*. Englewood Cliffs, NJ: Prentice-Hall.

——, CONKLING, E.C., and RAY, D.M. 1976. *The Geography of Economic Systems*. Englewood Cliffs, NJ: Prentice-Hall.

—— *et al.* 1987. *Economic Geography*. Englewood Cliffs, NJ: Prentice-Hall.

BERRY, M. 1984. The political economy of Australian urbanization, *Progress in Planning*, 22, 1–83.

BEYERS, W.B. 1979. Contemporary trends in the regional economic development of the United States, *Professional Geographer*, 31, 34–44.

BINNS, P. and HAYNES, M. 1980. New theories of European class societies. *International Socialism*, 2, 18–50.

BIRCH, D.L. 1979: *The Job Generation Process*. Cambridge, Mass.: MIT Program on Neighborhood and Regional Change.

BIRNBAUM, P. and BADIE, B. 1983. *The Sociology of the State*. Chicago: University of Chicago Press.

BLACK, J.K. 1977. *United States Penetration of Brazil*. Philadelphia: University of Pennsylvania Press.

BLACKBOURN, A. 1972. The location of foreign-owned manufacturing plants in the Republic of Ireland. *Tijdschrift voor Economische en Sociale Geografie*, 63, 438–43.

—— 1982. The impact of multinational corporations on the spatial organization of developed nations. In M.J. Taylor and N.J. Thrift (eds.) *The Geography of Multinationals* London: Croom Helm 147–59.

—— and PUTNAM, R.G. 1984. *Canada: An Industrial Geography*. Beckenham: Croom Helm.

BLAIKIE, P. 1986. Natural resource use in developing countries. In R.J. Johnston and P.J. Taylor (eds.) *A World in Crisis?* Oxford: Blackwell, 107–26.

BLOOMFIELD, 1981. The changing spatial organization of multinational corporations in the world automotive industry. In F.E.I. Hamilton and G.J.R. Linge (eds.) *International Industrial Systems* Chichester: Wiley, 357–94.

BLUESTONE, B. and HARRISON, B. 1982. *The Deindustrialization of America*. New York: Basic Books.

BODDY, M. 1987. High Technology industry, regional development and defence manufacturing: a case study of the UK sunbelt. In B. Robson (ed.) *Managing the City*. Beckenham: Croom Helm, 60–83.

BOHANNAN, P. 1959. The impact of money on an African subsistence economy. *Journal of Economic History*, 19, 491–503.

BORCHERT, J.R. 1967. American Metropolitan Evolution. *Geographical Review*, 57, 301–32.

—— 1978. Major control points in American Economic Geography. *Annals, Association of American Geographers*, 68, 214–32.

BORTS, G.H. and STEIN, J.L. 1964. *Economic Growth in a Free Market*. New York: Free Press.

BOSERUP, E. 1981. *Population and Technology*. Oxford: Blackwell.

BOUSQUET, N. 1980. From hegemony to competition: cycles of the core. In T.K. Hopkins and I. Wallerstein (eds.) *Processes of the World-System*. Beverly Hills: Sage.

BOWLER, I.R. 1985. *Agriculture Under the Common Agricultural Policy.* Manchester: Manchester University Press.

BOYTE, H. 1980. *The Backyard Revolution: Understanding the New Citizen Movement.* Philadelphia: Temple University Press.

BRADFORD, C.I. 1987. Trade and structural change: NIC and next tier NICs as transitional economies. *World Development,* 15, 299–316.

BRADLEY, P.N. 1986. Food production and distribution – and hunger, In R.J. Johnston and P.J. Taylor (eds.) *A World in Crisis?* Oxford: Blackwell, 89–106.

BRANSCOMB, L.M., 1987. National and corporate technology strategies in an interdependent world economy. In B.R. Guile and H. Brooks (eds.) *Technology and Global Industry Companies and Nations in the World Economy,* Washington, DC; National Academy Press, 246–56.

BRAUDEL, F. 1972. *The Mediterranean and the Mediterranean World in the Age of Phillip II.* Translated by S. Reynolds. New York: Harper & Row.

BREHENY, M. and McQUAID, R.W. (eds.) 1987. *The Development of High-Technology Industries: An International Survey.* Beckenham: Croom Helm.

BRENNER, R. 1976. Agrarian class structure and economic development in preindustrial Europe. *Past and Present,* 70, 30–75.

—— 1977. The origins of capitalist development: a critique of neo-Smithian marxism. *New Left Review,* 104, 25–91.

BRIDGE, S. 1977. Some causes of political change in modern Yugoslavia. In M.J. Esman (ed.), *Ethnic Conflict in the Western World.* Ithaca, NY: Cornell University Press.

BRITTON, J.N.H. 1980. Industrial dependence and technological underdevelopment. *Regional Studies,* 14, 181–200.

BROCKETT, C.D. 1987. The commercialization of agriculture and rural economic insecurity: the case of Honduras. *Studies in Comparative International Development,* 22, 82–102.

BROMLEY, R.J. 1974. *Periodic Markets, Daily Markets, and Fairs: A Bibliograhy.* Clayton, Australia: Monash Publications in Geography No. 10.

BROWETT, J.G. 1986. Industrialization in the global periphery: the significance of the newly industrializing countries of East and Southeast Asia. *Environment and Planning* A, 4, 401–18.

BROWNING, C.E. and GESSLER, W. 1979. The Sunbelt-Snowbelt: a case of sloppy regionalizing. *Professional Geographer,* 31, 66–74.

BRUNDENIUS, C. 1984. Revolutionary Cuba: *The Challenge of Economic Growth with Equity.* Boulder, Co: Westview Press.

BRUNN, S.D, 1975. Vietnam war defense contracts and the House Armed Services Committee. *East Lakes Geographer,* 10, 17–32.

BRUSCO, S. and SABEL, C. 1981. Artisan production and economic growth, in F. Wilkinson (ed.) *The Dynamics of Labour Market Segmentation.* London: Academic Press.

BUCHANAN, K. 1972. *The Geography of Empire.* London: Spokesman Books.

BURBACH, R. and FLYNN, P. 1980. *Agribusiness in the Americas.* New York: Monthly Review Press.

BURNELL, P.J., 1986. *Economic Nationalism in the Third World.* Brighton: Wheatsheaf Books.

BUSS, T. and REDBURN, F.S. 1983. *Shutdown at Youngstown.* Albany: SUNY Press.

BUTLIN, R.A. 1986. Early Industrialization in Europe: Concepts and Problems. *Geographical Journal,* 152, 1–8.

BUTTEL, F.H. 1980. Agricultural structure and rural ecology: toward a political economy of rural development, *Sociologia Ruralis,* 20, 44–62.

CAMAGNI, R. and CAPPELIN, R. 1981. European regional growth and policy issues for the 1980s. *Built Environment,* 7, 162–71.

CAMERON, R. 1973. The logistics of European economic growth: A note on historical periodization. *Journal of European Economic History*, 2, 145–58.

CARL, B.M., 1986. *Economic Integration Among Developing Nations*, New York: Praeger.

CARNEIRO, R.L. 1970. A theory of the origin of the state. *Scientific American*, 169, 733–8.

CARTER, H. 1983. *An Introduction to Urban Historical Geography*. London: Edward Arnold.

CARROTHERS, G.A. 1956. An historical review of the gravity and potential concepts of human interaction. *Journal of the American Institute of Planners*, 22, 94–102.

CASTELLS, M. 1988. High technology and urban dynamics in the United States. In M. Dogan and J. Kasarda (eds.) *The Metropolis Era, Vol. 1: A World of Giant Cities*. Newbury Park, CA: Sage, 85–110.

CAVALCANTI, L. *et al.*. 1981. Multinationals, the new international economic order and the spatial industrial structure of Brazil. In F.E.I. Hamilton and G.J.R. Linge (eds.) *International Industrial Systems*. Chichester: Wiley.

CELL, J.W. 1982. *The Highest Stage of White Supremacy: The Origins of Segregation in South Africa and the American Southwest*. New York: Cambridge University Press

CHAMPION, A., GREEN, A.E., OWEN, D.W., ELLIN, D.J. and COOMBES, M.G. 1987. *Changing Places: Britain's Demographic, Economic and Social Complexion*. London: Edward Arnold.

CHASE-DUNN, C. (ed.) 1982. *Socialist States in the World-Economy*. Beverly Hills: Sage.

CHAUNU, P. 1959. *Seville et l'Atlantique 1504-1650*, VIII (1): Les structures géographiques. Paris: SEVPEN.

—— *L'expression europeénne du XIIIe au XVe siècle*, Collection Nouvelle Clio 26. Paris: Presses Universitaires de France.

CHILDE, V.G. 1950. The urban revolution. *Town Planning Review*, 21, 3–17.

CHISHOLM, M. 1962. *Rural Settlement and Land Use: An Essay in Location*. London: Hutchinson.

—— 1982. *Modern World Development*, Totowa, NJ: Barnes & Noble.

CHORLEY, R.J. 1972. Geography and analogue theory, in W.K.D. Davies (ed.) *The Conceptual Revolution in Geography*. London: University of London Press.

CHRISTALLER, W. 1933. *Die Zentralen Orte in Suddeutschland*. Jena: Fischer.

—— 1966. *Central Places in Southern Germany*. Trans. C.W. Baskin. Englewood Cliffs, NJ: Prentice-Hall.

CHRISTOPHER, A.J. 1984. *Colonial Africa*. London: Croom Helm.

CIPOLLA, C. 1965. *Guns and Sails in the Early Phase of European Expansion, 1400-1700*. London: Collins.

—— 1976. *Before the Industrial Revolution: European Society and Economy 1000-1700*. New York: Norton (1st edition).

—— 1981. *Before the Industrial Revolution: European Society and Economy 1000-1700*. London: Methuen. 2nd edition.

CLARK, C. 1977. *World Prehistory in New Perspective*. Cambridge: Cambridge University Press.

CLARK, G.L. 1981. The employment relation and the spatial division of labor: a hypothesis. *Annals of the Association of American Geographers*, 71, 412–24.

CLASTRES, P. 1977. *Society Against the State*. New York: Urizen.

CLINE, W.R. 1982. Can the East Asian model of development be generalized? *World Development*, 10, 81-90.

COATES, B.E., JOHNSTON, R.J. and KNOX, P.L. 1977. *Geography and Inequality*. Oxford: Oxford University Press.

—— and RAWSTRON, E.M. *Regional Variations in Britain*, Batsford, London.

COHEN, A. 1974. *Two-Dimensional man: An Essay on the Anthropology of Power and Symbolism in Complex Society*. Berkeley, CA: University of California Press.

COHEN, R.B. 1981. The new international division of labor, multinational corporations and the urban hierarchy. In M. Dear and A. Scott (eds.) *Urbanization and Urban Planning in Capitalist Society*. London: Methuen, 287–315.

—— 1983. The new spatial organization of the European and American automotive industries. In F. Moulaert and P. Salinas (eds.) *Regional Analysis and the New International Division of Labour*. Boston: Kluwer Nijhoff, 135–44.

COHEN, S.B. 1982. A new map of global geopolitical equilibrium: a developmental approach. *Political Geography Quarterly*, 1, 233–41.

COLE, J.P. 1984. *Geography of the Soviet Union*. London: Butterworth.

—— and HARRISON, M.E. 1978. Regional inequality in services and purchasing power in the USSR, 1940–1976. *occasional Paper*, 14. London: Department of Geography, Queen Mary College.

COLMAN, D. 1986. *Economics of Change in Less Developed Countries*, 2nd edition. Totowa, N.J.: Barnes and Noble.

COMISSO, E.T. 1979. *Workers' Control Under Plan and Market*. New Haven: Yale University Press.

COMMINS, P. 1980. Imbalances in agricultural modernisation – with illustrations from Ireland, *Sociologia Ruralis*, 20, 63–81.

CONKLING, E.C. and M. YEATES 1976. *Man's Economic Environment*. New York: McGraw–Hill.

CONROY, M.F. 1973. Rejection of growth center strategy in Latin American development planning. *Land Economics*, 49, 371–80.

CONZEN, M.P. 1977. The maturing urban system in the United States, 1840–1910. *Annals, Association of American Geographers*, 67, 88–108.

—— 1981. The American urban system in the nineteenth century. In D. Herbert and R.J. Johnston (eds.) *Geography and the Urban Environment*, Vol. 4, 295–347. Chichester: Wiley.

COOKE, P. 1988. Flexible Integration, scope economies ands strategic alliances: social and spatial variations, *Society and Space*, 6, 281–300.

—— and A. DA ROSA PIRES. 1985. Productive decentralisation in three European regions. *Environment and Planning A*, 17, 527–54.

COOPER, F. 1980. *From Slaves to Squatters: Plantation Labour and Agriculture in Zanzibar and Coastal Kenya, 1890–1925*. New Haven, CT: Yale University Press.

CORBRIDGE, S. 1982. Urban bias, rural bias, and industrialization: an appraisal of the work of Michael Lipton and Terry Byres, in J. Harriss (ed.) *Rural Development: Theories of Peasant Economic and Agrarian Change*. London: Hutchinson.

—— 1984, Crisis, What Crisis? Monetarism, Brandt II and the politics of debt. *Political Geography Quarterly*, 3, 331–45.

—— 1986. *Capitalist World Development: A Critique of Radical Development Geography*. London: Macmillan.

—— 1988. The debt crisis and the crisis of global regulation. *Geoforum*, 19, 105–27.

CORTÉS CONDE, R. 1974. *The First States of Modernization in Spanish America*. New York: Harper & Row.

CROSSLEY, J.C. 1983. The River Plate countries. In H. Blakemore and C.T. Smith (eds.) *Latin America: Geographical Perspectives*, 2nd edition. London: Methuen.

CROUCH, L. and de JANVRY, A. 1980. The class basis of agricultural growth. *Food Policy*, 5, 1, 3–13.

CROW, B. and THOMAS, A. 1985. *Third World Atlas*. Milton Keynes: Open University Press.

CUDDY, M., 1981. European agricultural policy: the regional dimension. *Built Environment*, 7, 200–10.

CUMINGS, B. 1984. The origins and development of the Northeast Asian political economy: industrial sectors, product cycles and political consequences. *International Organization*, 38, 1–40.

CUNNINGHAM, S. 1986. Multinationals and restructuring in Latin America, in C.J. Dixon *et al.* (eds.) *Multinational Corporations and the Third World*. Boulder, Co.: Westview Press.

CURREY, B. and HUGO, G. (eds.) 1984. *Famine as a Geographical Phenomenon*. Dordrecht: D. Reidel.

CURTIN, P. *et al.* 1978. *African History*. Boston: Little, Brown.

CYERT, R.M. and MOWERY, D.C. (eds.) 1987. *Technology and Employment. Innovation and Growth in the US Economy*. Washington DC: National Academy Press.

DAMESICK, P. 1986. Service industries, employment and regional development in Britain. *Transactions, Institute of British Geographers*, 11, 212–26.

DANIELS, G. and GOW, I. 1983. The European Community and Japan. In J. Lodge (ed.), *The European Community*, London: Frances Pinter, 225–35.

DANIELS, P. 1982. *Service Industries: Growth and Location*. Cambridge: Cambridge University Press.

—— 1985. Producer services and the postindustrial economy. In R. Martin and B. Rowthorne (eds.) *The Geography of Deindustrialization*. London: Macmillan.

—— 1985b. *Service Industries: A Geographical Appraisal*. London: Methuen.

DANKBARR, B. 1984. Maturity and relocation in the car industry. *Development and Change*, 15, 223–50.

DAVIS, P. (ed.), 1987. *Public–Private Partnerships: Improving Urban Life*. Philadelphia: American Academy of Political Science.

DE JANVRY, A. 1984. The role of land reform in economic development: policies and politics. In C.K. Eicher and J.M. Staatz (eds.) *Agricultural Development in the Third World*. Baltimore: Johns Hopkins University Press.

DELACROIX, J. 1977. The export of raw materials and economic growth: a cross-national study. *American Sociological Review*, 42, 795–808.

DENISON, E.F. 1979. Explanations of declining productivity. *Survey of Current Business*, 59, 1–24.

DE SMIDT, M. 1983. Regional locational cycles and the stages of locating foreign manufacturing plants: the case of the Netherlands. *Tijdschrift voor Economische en Sociale Geografie*, 74, 2–11.

DEUTSCH, K. 1978. *Analysis of International Relations* (2nd edition). Englewood Cliffs, NJ: Prentice-Hall.

DE VRIES, J. 1976. *Economy of Europe in an Age of Crisis 1600–1750*. Cambridge: Cambridge University Press.

DE VROEY, M. 1984. A regulation approach interpretation of contemporary crisis. *Capital and Class*, 23, 45–66.

DEWAR, D. *et al.* 1986. Industrial decentralization policy in South Africa: rhetoric and practice. *Urban Studies*, 23, 363–76.

DEWDNEY, J. 1976. *The USSR*. Folkestone: Dawson.

DICKEN, P. 1980. Foreign direct investment in European manufacturing industry: the changing position of the UK as a host country. *Geoforum*, 11, 289–313.

—— 1986. *Global Shift*. London: Harper & Row.

—— and LLOYD, P.E. 1980. Patterns and processes of change in the spatial distribution of foreign-controlled manufacturing employment in the UK, 1963–1975. *Environment & Planning A*, 12, 1405–26.

DINHAM, B. and HINES, C. 1983. *Agribusiness in Africa*. London: Earth Resources Research.

DIXON, C.J., DRAKAKIS-SMITH, P. and WATTS. H.D. (eds.) 1986. *Multinational Corporations in the Third World*. Beckenham: Croom Helm.

DOBB, M. 1963. *Studies in the Development of Capitalism*. London: Routledge & Kegan Paul.

DODGSHON, R.A. 1987. *The European Past: Social Evolution and Spatial Order.* London: Macmillan.

DOREL, G. 1985. *Agriculture et grandes entreprises aux Etats-Unis.* Paris: Economica.

DORNBUSCH, R. and FISCHER, S. 1985. The world debt problem: origins and prospects. *Journal of Development Planning*, 16, 57–82.

DOYLE, M.W. 1986. *Empires.* Ithaca, NY: Cornell University Press.

DOZ, Y., 1987. International industries: fragmentation versus globalization. In B.R. Guile and H. Brooks (eds.), *Technology and Global Industry.* Washington, DC: National Academy Press, 96–118.

DREWETT, R. and ROSSI, A. 1981. General urbanization trends in Western Europe. In Klaasen, L.H., Molle, W.T.M. and Paelinck, J.H.P. (eds.), *Dynamics of Urban Development.* Aldershot: Gower, 119–36.

DREWNOWSKI, J. 1974. *On Measuring and Planning the Quality of Life.* The Hague: Mouton.

—— 1986. The level of civilization: a new field for the application of social indicators, *Social Indicators Research* 18, 339–47.

D'SOUZA, F. and SHOHAM, J. 1985. The spread of famine in Africa: avoiding the worst, *Third World Quarterly*, 7, 515–31.

DUBY, G. 1968. *Rural Economy and Country Life in the Medieval West.* Columbia: University of South Carolina Press.

—— 1974. *The Early Growth of the European Economy: Warriors and Peasants from the Seventh to the Twelfth Century.* London: Weidenfeld & Nicolson.

DUIGNAN, P. and GANN, L.H. 1985. *The United States and Africa: A History.* Cambridge: Cambridge University Press.

DUNCAN, O.D. and LIEBERSON, S. 1959. Ethnic segregation and assimilation. *American Journal of Sociology*, 64, 364–74.

DUNCAN, K. and RUTLEDGE, I. 1977. Introduction: Patterns of agrarian capitalism in Latin America. In K. Duncan and I. Rutledge (eds.) *Land and Labour in Latin America.* Cambridge: Cambridge University Press.

DUNFORD, M. and PERRONS, D. 1983. *The Arena of Capital.* London: Macmillan.

DUNN, E.S. 1954. *The Location of Agricultural Production.* Gainesville: University of Florida Press.

—— 1980. *The Development of the US Urban System*, Vol. 1, *Concepts, Structures, Regional Shifts.* Baltimore: Johns Hopkins University Press.

—— 1983. *The Development of the US Urban System*, Vol. 2, *Industrial Shifts, Implications.* Baltimore: Johns Hopkins University Press.

DUNNING, J.H. 1981. *International Production and the Multinational Enterprise.* Hemel Hempstead: Allen & Unwin.

—— 1983. Changes in the level and structure of international production: the last one hundred years. In M. Casson (ed.) *The Growth of International Business.* London: Allen & Unwin.

—— and NORMAN, G. 1987. The location choice of offices of international companies. *Environment and Planning A*, 19, 613–31.

—— and PEARCE, R.D. 1985. *The World's Largest Industrial Enterprises 1962–1983.* New York: St Martin's.

DURHAM, K.F. 1977. Expansion of agricultural settlement in the Peruvian rainforest: the role of the market and the role of the state. Paper presented at the 1977 meeting of the Latin American Studies Association, Houston, Texas, 2–5 November.

EARLE, P. (ed.) 1974. *Essays in European History 1500–1800.* Princeton: Princeton University Press.

EAST, W.G. 1966. *An Historical Geography of Europe.* London: Methuen.

ECONOMIST (27 June, 1987) The rag trade: on the road from Mandalay, 67–8.

EDQUIST, C. 1985. *Capitalism, Socialism, and Technology: A Comparative Study of Cuba and Jamaica.* London: Zed Books.

EDWARDS, C. 1985. *The Fragmented World: Competing Perspectives on Trade, Money and Crisis*. London: Methuen.

EDWARDS, R.C., REICH, M. and GORDON, D. (eds.) 1975. *Labor Market Segmentation*, Lexington, MA: Lexington Books.

EICHER, C.K. 1984. Facing up to Africa's food crisis. In C.K. Eicher and J.M. Staatz (eds.) *Agricultural Development in the Third World*. Baltimore: Johns Hopkins University Press.

EISOLD, E. 1984. Young women workers in export industries: the case of the semiconductor industry in South East Asia. Working Paper, ILO World Employment Programme, ILO, Geneva.

EL-AGRAA, A.M. (ed.), 1985. *The Economics of the European Community*, 2nd edition. Oxford: Philip Allan.

EMMANUEL, A. 1972. *Unequal Exchange: A Study of the Imperialism of Trade*. London: New Left Books.

ENGLISH, C.W. 1983. When workers take over the plant. *US News and World Report*, (18 April), 89–90.

ERLANDSSON, U. 1979. Contact potentials in the European system of cities. In H. Folmer and J. Oosterhaven (eds.), *Spatial Inequalities in Regional Development*, The Hague: Martinus Nijhoff, 93–116.

ERNST, D. 1982. *The Global Race in Microelectronics: Innovation and Corporate Strategies in a Period of Crisis*. Frankfurt: Campus.

ESMAN, M.J. 1977. Scottish nationalism, North Sea oil, and the British response, in M.J. Esman (ed.), *Ethnic Conflict in the Western World*. Ithaca NY: Cornell University Press.

ESTALL, R.C. 1983. The decentralization of manufacturing industry: recent American experience in perspective. *Geoforum*, 14, 133–47.

EVANS, D. and ALIZADEH, P. 1984. Trade, industrialization and the visible hand, in R. Kaplinsky (ed.) *Third World Industrialisation in the 1980s: Open Economies in a Closing World*. London: Cass.

EVANS, P. 1979. *Dependent Development: The Alliance of Multinational, State, and Local Capitalism in Brazil*. Princeton NJ: Princeton University Press.

—— 1987. Dependency and the state in recent Korean development: some comparisons with Latin American NICs, in K-D. Kim (ed.) *Dependency Issues in Korean Development: Comparative Perspectives*. Seoul: Seoul National University Press.

—— and TIMBERLAKE, M. 1980. Dependence, inequality and growth in less developed countries. *American Sociological Review*, 45, 531–52.

EVENSON, R.E. 1984. Benefits and obstacles in developing appropriate agricultural technology. In C.K. Eicher and J.M. Staatz (eds.) *Agricultural Development in the Third World*. Baltimore: Johns Hopkins University Press.

EWERS, H.J. and WETTMANN, R.W. 1980. Innovation-oriented regional policy. *Regional Studies*, 14, 161–79.

FAINSTEIN, N. and FAINSTEIN, S. 1978. Federal policy and spatial inequality. In G. Sternleib and J.W. Hughes (eds.) *Revitalizing the Northeast*. New Brunswick: Rutgers University, Center for Urban Policy Research.

FAIRBANK, J.K. REISCHAUER, E.O. and CRAIG, A.M. 1973. *East Asia: Tradition and Transformation*. Boston: Houghton-Mifflin.

FALLENBUCHL, Z. 1975. The development of the less-developed regions in Poland, 1950, 1970. In A.F. Burghardt (ed.) *Development Regions in the Soviet Union, Eastern Europe and Canada*. New York: Praeger, 14–42.

FEDER, E. 1978. *Strawberry Imperialism*. Mexico City: Editorial Campesina.

FELDMAN, M.A. 1983. Biotechnology and local economic growth: the American pattern. *Built Environment*, 9, 40–50.

FETTER, R.A. 1924. The economic law of market areas. *Quarterly Journal of Economics*, 39, 520–9.

FIALA, R. and KAMENS, D. 1986. Urban growth and the world polity in the nineteenth and twentieth centuries: a research agenda. *Studies in Comparative International Development*, 21, 23–35.

FIELEKE, N.S. 1981. Challenge and response in the automobile industry. *New England Economic Review*, July/August, 37–48.

—— 1986. The decline of the oil cartel. *New England Economic Review*, July/August: 32–41.

FIRN, J. 1975. External control and regional development. *Environment & Planning A*, 7, 393–415.

FISHER, J.S. 1981. Structural adjustments in the Southern manufacturing sector. *Professional Geographer*, 33, 466–74.

FISHLOW, A. 1972. Brazilian size distribution of income. *American Economic Review*, 62, 391–402.

FLANNERY, K.V. 1969. Origin and ecological effects of early domestication. In P.J. Ucko and G.W. Dimbleby (eds.), *The Domestication and Exploitation of Plants and Animals*. London: Duckworth.

FLYNN, N. and TAYLOR, A.P. 1986. Inside the rust belt: an analysis of the decline of the West Midlands economy. *Environment and Planning A*, 18, 865–900.

FORBES, D. 1986. Spatial aspects of Third World multinational corporations' direct investment in Indonesia. In M. Taylor and N. Thrift (eds.) *Multinationals and the Restructuring of the World Economy*. Beckenham: Croom Helm.

—— and THRIFT, N. 1987. International impacts on the urbanization process in the Asian region: a review. In R.J. Fuchs *et al.* (eds.) *Urbanization and Urban Policies in Pacific Asia*. Boulder, CO: Westview Press.

FOTHERGILL, S. and GUDGIN, G. 1983. Trends in regional manufacturing employment: the main influences. In J.B. Goddard and A.G. Champion (eds.) *The Urban and Regional Transformation of Britain*. London: Methuen, 27–50.

FOX, R.G. *et al.* 1981. Ethnic nationalism and the welfare state, in C.F. Keyes (ed.) *Ethnic Change*. Seattle: University of Washington Press.

FRANK, A.G. 1967. *Capitalism and Underdevelopment in Latin America*. New York: Monthly Review Press.

—— 1977. Long live transideological enterprise! The socialist economies in the capitalist division of labour. *Review*, 1, 91–140.

FRANKE, W. 1967. *China and the West: The Cultural Encounter, 13th to 20th Centuries*. Oxford: Basil Blackwell.

FRANKMAN, M.T. 1974. Sectoral policy preferences of the Peruvian government, 1946–1968. *Journal of Latin American Studies*, 6, 289–300.

FRANKO, L.F. 1978. Multinationals: the end of US dominance. *Harvard Business Review*, 56, 111–23.

FREEMAN, D.B. 1973. *International trade, migration and capital flows*. Research Paper No. 146, Dept. of Geography, University of Chicago.

FREEMAN, R.B. 1980. The evolution of the American Labor Market, 1948–80. In M. Feldstein (ed.) *The American Economy in Transition*. Chicago: University of Chicago Press, 349–96.

FRIEDMAN, E. 1979. Maoist conceptualizations of the capitalist world-system, in T.K. Hopkins and I. Wallerstein (eds.) *Processes of the World-System*. Beverly Hills, CA: Sage.

FRIEDMANN, J. 1956. Locational aspects of economic development. *Land Economics*, 32, 213–27.

—— 1961. Integration of the social system: an approach to the study of economic growth. *Diogenes*, 33, 75–97.

—— 1986. The world city hypothesis. *Development and Change*, 17, 69–83.

—— and WEAVER, C. 1979. *Territory and Function*. Berkeley: University of California Press.

FRÖBEL, F., HEINRICHS, J. and KREYE, D. 1977. *Die neue Internationale Arbeitsteilung*. Reinbeck: Rowohlt.
—— 1980. *The New International Division of Labor*. Cambridge: Cambridge University Press.
FRYER, D.W. 1987. The political geography of international lending by private banks. *Transactions, Institute of British Geographers*, 12, 413–432.
FUCHS, R.J. and DEMKO, G.J. 1979. Geographic inequality under socialism. *Annals, Association of American Geographers*, 69, 304–19.
—— and PERNIA, E.M. 1987. External economic forces and national spatial development: Japanese direct investment in Pacific Asia, in R.J. Fuchs *et al.* (eds.) *Urbanization and Urban Policies in Pacific Asia*. Boulder, CO: Westview Press.
GAFFKIN, F. and NICKSON, P. 1984. *Jobs, Crisis and the Multinationals: Deindustrialization in the West Midlands*. Birmingham: Russell Press.
GALBRAITH, J.K. 1977. *The Affluent Society*. Boston: Houghton Mifflin.
GANN, L.H. and DUIGNAN, P. 1978. *The Rulers of British Africa, 1870–1914*. Stanford, CA: Stanford University Press.
GEERTZ, C. 1973. *The Interpretation of Cultures*. New York: Basic Books.
GELLNER, E. 1964. *Thought and Change*. London: Weidenfeld & Nicolson.
GERSCHENKRON, A. 1970. *Europe in the Russian Mirror* Cambridge: Cambridge University Press.
—— 1986. *Economic Backwardness in Historical Perspective* Cambridge, MA: Harvard University Press.
GERSHUNY, J.I. and MILES, I.D. 1983. *The New Service Economy: The Transformation of Employment in Industrial Societies*. New York: Praeger.
GERTLER, M.S. 1986. Discontinuities it regional development. *Society and Space*, 4, 71–84.
GIDDENS, A. 1981. *A Contemporary Critique of Historical Materialism*. London: Macmillan.
GIFFORD, P. and LOUIS, W.R. (eds.) 1971. *France and Britain in Africa: Imperial Rivalry and Colonial Rule*. New Haven, CT: Yale University Press.
GINSBERG, R.H., 1983. The European Community and the United States of America. In J. Lodge (ed.) *The European Community*. London: Frances Pinter 183–96.
GINSBURG, N. 1968. On the Chinese perception of world order, in T. Tsou (ed.) *China in Crisis*: Vol II, *China's Policies in Asia and America's Alternatives*. Chicago: University of Chicago Press.
—— OSBORN, J. and BLANK, G. 1986. Geographic perspectives on the Wealth of Nations, University of Chicago, Department of Geography.
GINZBERG, E. *et al.*, 1986. *Technology and Employment: Concepts and Clarifications*. Boulder: Westview Press.
GLAMANN, K. 1974. European Trade, 1500–1700. In C.M. Cipolla (ed.) *The Fontana Economic History of Europe: Sixteenth and Seventeenth Centuries*. London: Fontana, 427–526.
GODDARD, J.B. and CHAMPION, A.G. 1983. *The Urban and Regional Transformation of Britain*. London: Methuen.
—— and GILLESPIE, A. E. 1987. Advanced telecommunications and regional economic development. In B. Robson (ed.) *Managing the City*. Totowa, NJ: Barnes & Noble.
GOLAY, F.H., 1977. The potential for regionalism. In Pauker, F.H. Golay and C.H. Enloe (eds.), *Diversity and Development in Southeast Asia*. New York: McGraw-Hill, pp. 105–20.
GOLDBERG, M. 1987. *The Chinese Connection: Getting Plugged in to the Pacific Rim Real Estate, Trade and Capital Markets*. Vancouver: University of British Columbia Press.

GOLDSBROUGH, D. 1985. Foreign direct investment in developing countries: trends, policy issues, and prospects. *Finance and Development*, 22, 31–4.

GOMES, C. and PÉREZ, A. 1979. The process of modernization in Latin American agriculture. *CEPAL Review*, 8, 55–74.

GORDON, D.M. 1979. *The Working Poor: Towards a State Agenda*. Washington, DC: The Council of State Planning Agencies.

—— 1984. Capitalist development and the history of American cities. In W.K. Tabb and L. Sawers (eds.) *Marxism and the Metropolis* (2nd edition). New York: Oxford University Press, pp. 21–53.

GORE, C. 1984. *Regions in Question: Space, Development Theory and Regional Policy*. London: Methuen.

GOTTMANN, J. 1980. Confronting Centre and Periphery. In Gottman, J. (ed.), *Centre and Periphery*. London: Sage, 309–54.

GOUDIE, A. 1981. *The Human Impact: Man's Role in Environmental Change*. Oxford: Blackwell.

GRAHAM, J., GIBSON, K., HORVATH., R., and SHAKOW, D.M. 1988 Restructuring in US manufacturing: The decline of monopoly capitalism, *Annals, Association of American Geographers*, 78, 473–90.

GRANBERG, A.G. and SUSLOV, V.I. 1976. Use of Republic and regional inter-sectoral balances in the analysis of territorial proportions of the national economy of the USSR. In Granberg, A.G. (ed.), *Spatial National Economic Models*. Novosibirsk: USSR Academy of Sciences.

GREENHUT, M.L. 1956. *Plant Location in Theory and Practice: the Economics of Space*. Chapel Hill, NC: University of North Carolina Press.

GREENWOOD, D. 1977. Continuity in change: Spanish Basque ethnicity as a social process. In M.J. Esman (ed.) *Ethnic Conflict in the Western World*. Ithaca, NY: Cornell University Press.

GREGORY, D. 1978. *Ideology, Science and Human Geography*. London: Hutchinson.

—— 1987. *Areal Differentiation and Postmodern Human Geography*. Mimeo. Department of Geography, University of Cambridge.

GRIFFIN, K. 1974. *The Political Economy of Agrarian Change*. Cambridge, Mass.: Harvard University Press.

GRIFFITH-JONES, S. 1980. The growth of multinational banking, the Euro-currency markets and their effects on developing countries. *Journal of Development Studies*, 16, 96–109.

—— and RODRIGUES, E. 1984. Private international finance and industrialization in LDCs, in R. Kaplinsky (ed.) *Third World Industrialization in the 1980s: Open Economies in a Closed World*. London: Cass.

GRIGG, D.B. 1975. *The Agricultural Regions of the World*. Cambridge: Cambridge University Press.

—— 1982. Counting the hungry: world patterns of undernutrition, *Tijdshrfit voor Economische en Sociale Geografie*, 73, pp. 66–79.

—— 1985a. *The World Food Problem*. Oxford: Blackwell.

—— 1985b. World patterns of agricultural productivity. *Tijdshrift voor Economische en Sociale Geografie*, 76, 253–60.

GRILLO, R.D. 1980. Introduction. In R.D. Grillo (ed.) '"Nation" and "State" in Europe:' Anthropological Perspectives*. London: Academic Press, 1–30.

GRIMWADE, N. 1988. *New Patterns of International Trade*. Beckenham: Croom Helm.

GRINDLE, M.S. 1986. *State and Countryside: Development Policy and Agrarian Politics in Latin America*. Baltimore: Johns Hopkins University Press.

GROSSMAN, G. 1974. The industrialization of the Soviet Union. In Cipolla, C.M. (ed.), *The Fontana Economic History of Europe*, Vol IV. London: Fontana.

GRUCHMAN, B. and KASINSKI, Z. 1978. Measurement of real progress at the local level: Report on the country case study in Poland. In United Nations Research Institute for Social Development, *Measurement and Analysis of Progress at the Local Level*. Geneva: UNRISD.

GRUNWALD, J. and FLAMM, K. 1985. *The Global Factory*. Washington, DC Brookings Institution.

GUESS, G. 1986. *The politics of US Development Aid*. Beckenham: Croom Helm.

GUGLER, J. 1980. A minimum of urbanism and a maximum of ruralism: the Cuban experience. *International Journal of Urban and Regional Research*, 4, 516–36.

—— and FLANAGAN, W.G. 1978. *Urbanization and Social Change in West Africa*. Cambridge: Cambridge University Press.

GUILE, B.R. and BROOKS, H. (eds.) 1987. *Technology and Global Industry*. Washington DC: National Academy Press.

GUTMAN, P. and ARKWRIGHT, F. 1981. Tripartite industrial co-operation between East, West and South. In F.E.I. Hamilton and G.J.R. Linge (eds.) *Spatial Analysis, Industry and the Industrial Environment, Vol 2, International Industrial Systems*. New York: Wiley, 185–214.

HAAS, E.B. and SCHMITTER, P.C. 1964. Economics and differential patterns of political integration. *International Organization*, 28, 705-57.

HAGEY, M.J. and MALECKl, E. 1986. Linkages in high technology industries: A Florida case study. *Environment and Planning A*, 18, 1477–98.

HAGGETT, P. 1966. *Locational Analysis in Human Geography*. London: Edward Arnold.

—— 1983. *Geography: A Modern Synthesis*, 3rd edition. London: Harper & Row.

HALL, C. 1984. Regional inequalities in well-being in Costa Rica, *Geographical Review*, 74, 48–62.

HALL, J.A. 1985. *Powers and Liberties: The Causes and Consequences of the Rise of the West*. London: Penguin.

HALL, P. 1981. The geography of the 5th Kondratieff cycle. *New Society*, 55, 535–7.

—— BREHENY, M,. McQUAID, R, and HART, D. 1987. *Western Sunrise. The Genesis and Growth of Britain's High-Tech Corridor*. London: Allen & Unwin.

—— MARKUSEN, A.R. OSBORN, R. and WACHSMAN, B. 1983. The American computer software industry: economic development prospects. *Built Environment*, 9, 29–39.

HALL, T.D. 1986. Incorporation in the world-system: Toward a Critique. *American Sociological Review*, 51, 390–402.

HALLETT, E.C., 1981. Economic convergence and divergence in the European Community: a survey of the evidence. In M. Hodges and W. Wallace (eds.) *Economic Divergence in the European Community*. London: Allen & Unwin, 16–31.

HAMILTON, A. 1986. *The Financial Revolution*. Harmondsworth: Penguin.

HAMILTON, C. 1983. Capitalist industrialisation in the four little tigers of East Asia. In P. Limqueco and B. McFarlane (eds.) *Neo-Marxist Theories of Development*. Beckenham: Croom Helm.

HAMILTON, F.E.I. 1978. Multinational enterprise and the European Economic Community. In F.E.I. Hamilton (ed.) *Industrial Change: International Experience and Public Policy*. London: Longman, 24–41.

—— 1984. Industrial restructuring: an international problem. *Geoforum*, 15, 349–64.

—— and LINGE, G.J.R. 1983. Regional economies and industrial systems. In F.E.I. Hamilton and G.J.R. Linge (eds.), *Spatial Analysis, Industry, and the Industrial Environment*, Volume 3. Chichester: Wiley, 1–39.

HANSEN, N. 1981. Mexico's border industry and the international division of labor. *Annals of Regional Science*, 15, 1–12.

HANSSON, K. 1952. A general theory of the system of multilateral trade. *American Economic Review*, 42, 59–88.

HARDACH, G.H. 1973. *Der erste Weltkreig, 1914–1918*. Munich: Verlag.

HARDOY, J.E. and SATTERTHWAITE, D. (eds.) 1986. *Small and intermediate urban centers: their role in regional and national development in the Third World*. Boulder, CO: Westview Press.

HAREN, C.C. and HOLLING, R.W. 1979. Industrial development in nonmetropolitan America: a locational perspective. In R.E. Lonsdale and H.L. Seyler (eds.) *Nonmetropolitan Industrialization*. New York: Wiley, pp. 111–24.

HARPER, R. 1987. A functional classification of management centers in the US. *Urban Geography*, 8, 540–49.

HARRIS, C.D. 1982. The urban and industrial transformation of Japan, *Geographical Review*, 72, 50–89.

HARRIS, N. 1979. *The Mandate of Heaven: Marx and Mao in Modern China*. London: Quartet.

—— 1986. *The End of the Third World: Newly Industrializing Countries and the Decline of an Ideology*. London: I.B. Tauris.

HART, K. 1982. *The Political Economy of Agriculture in West Africa*. Cambridge: Cambridge University Press.

HARVEY, D.W. 1982. *The Limits to Capital*. Chicago: University of Chicago Press.

—— 1985. The Geopolitics of Capitalism. In D. Gregory and J. Urry (eds.) *Social Relations and Spatial Structures*. New York: St Martin's Press, 128–163.

—— 1987. The geographical and geopolitical consequences of the transition from Fordist to flexible accumulation. Paper presented to Rutgers University conference on *America's New Economic Geography*, Washington, DC.

HARVEY, R. 1987. Brazil: Unstoppable. *Economist*, 25 April, survey.

HASAN, P and RAO, D.C. 1979. *Korea: Policy Issueas for Long-term Development*. Washington DC: World Bank.

HAUG, P. 1986. High technology multinationals and Silicon Glen. *Regional Studies*, 20, 103–16.

HAWES, G.A. 1982. Southeast Asian agribusiness: the new international division of labor. *Bulletin of Concerned Asian Scholars*, 14, 20–9.

HAYAMI, Y. 1984. Assessment of the Green Revolution. In C.K. Eicher and J.M. Staatz (eds.) *Agricultural Development in the Third World*. Baltimore: Johns Hopkins University Press.

HEKMAN, J.S. 1980. The future of high technology industry in New England: a case study of computers. *New England Economic Review*, 5–17.

HENDERSON, J. 1987. Semiconductors, Scotland and the international division of labour. *Urban Studies*, 24, 389–408.

—— CASTELLS, M. (eds.) 1987. *Global Restructuring and Territorial Development*. Newbury Park, CA: Sage. Research Paper 220.

HEPWORTH, M. 1986. The geography of technological change in the information economy. *Regional Studies*, 20, 407–24.

HERSHEY, R.D. 1988. Small manufacturers lead revival. *New York Times*, 11 February, D1, D5.

HEWITT, A. and STEVENS, C. 1981. The second home conversation, In C. Stevens (ed.) *EEC and the Third World: A Survey. 1*. London: Hodder & Stoughton, 30–59.

HEWITT DE ALCANTARA, C. 1976. *Modernizing Mexican Agriculture: Socioeconomic Implications of Technological Change, 1940–70*. Geneva: UNRISD.

HICKS, D.A. and GLICKMAN, N.J. (eds.) 1983. *Transition to the 21st Century*. Greenwich, CT: JAI Press.

HICKS, J.R. 1959. *Essays in World Economics*. Oxford: Oxford University Press.

HILHORST, J.G.M. and KLATTER, M. (eds.) 1984. *Social Development in the Third World: Level of Living Indicators and Social Planning*. London: Croom Helm.

HILL, P. 1986. *Development Economics on Trial: The Anthropological Case for the Prosecution*. Cambridge: Cambridge University Press.

HILL, R.C. 1987. Global factory and company town: the changing division of labor in the international auto industry. In J. Henderson and M. Castells (eds.) *Global Restructuring and Territorial Development*. Newbury Park, CA: Sage, 18–37.

HIRSCHMAN, A.O. 1958. *The Strategy of Economic Development*. New Haven: Yale University Press.

HOBSBAWN, E.J. 1968. *Industry and Empire*. New York: Pantheon.

HODGSON, G. 1984. *The Democratic Economy: A New Look at Planning, Markets, and Power*. London: Penguin.

HOFFMAN, K. and RUSH, R. 1983. *Microelectronics and Clothing: The Impact of Technical Change in a Global Industry*. Geneva: International Labour Organization.

HOGGART, K. 1981. Social needs, political representation and federal outlays in the East North Central United States of America. *Environment and Planning A*, 13, 531–46.

HOLLAND, S. 1976. Meso-economics, multinational capital and regional inequality. In R. Lee and P. Ogden (eds.) *Economy and Society in the EEC: Spatial Perspectives*. Farnborough: Saxon House, 38–62.

—— 1980. *UnCommon Market*. London: Macmillan.

HOOVER, E.M. 1948. *The Location of Economic Activity*. New York: McGraw-Hill.

HOPKINS, A.G. 1973. *An Economic History of West Africa*. London: Longman.

HOPKINS, M. 1983. Employment trends in developing countries, 1960–1980 and beyond. *International Labour Review*, 122. 461–78.

HOSAN, P. and ROO, D.C. (eds.) 1979. Korea, Baltimore: Johns Hopkins University Press.

HOSSAIN, M. 1982. Agrarian Reform in Asia – A review of recent experiences in selected countries, in S. Jones *et al.* (eds.) *Rural Poverty and Agrarian Reform*. New Delhi: Allied.

HOWLAND, M. 1988. Plant closures and worker displacement, *Journal of Planning Literature*, 3, 3–21.

HSU, R.C. 1982. Agricultural financial policies in China, 1949–80. *Asian Survey*, 22, 638–58.

HUDDLESTON, B., MERRY F., RAIKES, P., and STEVENS, C., 1982. The EEC and Third World food and agriculture. In C. Stevens (ed.) *EEC and the Third World: A Survey 2*. London: Hodder & Stoughton, 15–46.

HUDSON, R. 1983. Regional labour reserves and industrialization in the EEC. *Area*, 15, 223–30.

HUGHES, H. and WAELBROEK, J. 1981. Can developing country exports keep growing in the 1980s? *The World Economy*, 4, 127–48.

HUMPHREY, J. 1984. Labor in the Brazilian motor vehicle industry, in R. Kronish and K.S. Mercle (eds.) *The Political Economy of the Latin American Motor Vehicle Industry*. Cambridge, Mass.: MIT Press.

HYMER, S.H. 1975. The multinational corporation and the law of uneven development. In H. Radice (ed.) *International Firms and Modern Imperialism*. London: Penguin.

ILBERY, B. 1985. *Agricultural Geography*. Oxford: Clarendon Press.

INDEPENDENT COMMISSION ON INTERNATIONAL DEVELOPMENT ISSUES (BRANDT REPORT) 1980. *North–South: a Programme for Survival*. London: Pan Books.

—— (BRANDT II) 1983. *Common Crisis. North–South Cooperation for World Recovery*. London: Pan Books.

ISARD, W. 1956. *Location and Space-Economy*. Cambridge: MIT Press.

—— 1975. *Introduction to Regional Science*. Englewood Cliffs, NJ: Prentice-Hall.

JACKSON, J.S. 1968. *Planters and Speculators: Chinese and European Enterprise in Malaya*. Kuala Lumpur: University of Malaya Press.

JACKSON, R.H. 1986. Conclusion. In P. Duignan arid R.H. Jackson (eds.) *Politics and Government in African States, 1960–1985*. London: Croom Helm.

JACOBS, J. 1969. *The Economy of Cities*. New York: Random House.

—— 1984. Cities and the wealth of nations. *The Atlantic Monthly*, March, 41–66.

JENKINS, R.O. 1987. *Transnational Corporations and the Latin American Automobile Industry*. Pittsburgh: University of Pittsburgh Press.

—— 1988. *Transnational Corporations and Uneven Development: The Internationalization of Capital and the Third World*. London: Methuen.

JOEKES, S.P. 1987. *Women in the World Economy*. New York: Oxford University Press.

JOHNSON, A.W. and EARLE, T. 1987. *The Evolution of Human Societies: From Foraging Group to Agrarian State*. Stanford, CA: Stanford University Press.

JOHNSON, C. 1982. *MITI and the Japanese Miracle*. Stanford, CA: Stanford University Press.

JOHNSTON, R.J. 1976. *The World Trade System: Some Enquiries into its Spatial Structure*. New York: St Martin's Press.

—— 1980a. *City and Society*. Harmondsworth: Penguin.

—— 1980b. *The Geography of Federal Spending in the USA*. Chichester: Wiley.

—— 1982. *The American Urban System*. New York: St Martins Press

—— 1984. The world is our oyster. *Transactions, Institute of British Geographers*, 9, 443–59.

—— 1986. The state, the region, and the division of labor, in A.J. Scott and M. Storper (eds.) *Production, Work, Territory: The Geographical Anatomy of Industrial Capitalism*. Boston: Allen & Unwin.

JONES, D. and ANDERSON, M. 1983. Competition in the world auto industry: implications for production location. Unpublished paper, University of Sussex, England.

JONES, E.L. 1981. *The European Miracle*. Cambridge: Cambridge University Press.

JONES, S. 1982. Introduction, in S. Jones *et al*. (eds.) *Rural Poverty and Agrarian Reform*. New Delhi: Allied.

—— *et al*. (eds.) 1982. *Rural Poverty and Agrarian Reform*. New Delhi: Allied.

JOSHI, P.C. 1982. Poverty, land hunger and emerging class conflicts in rural India. In S. Jones *et al*. (eds.) *Rural Poverty and Agrarian Reform*. New Delhi: Allied.

JUDD, D.R. and READY, R.L. 1986. Entrepreneurial cities and the new policies of economic development. In G.E. Peterson and C.W. Lewis (eds.) *Reagan and the Cities*. Washington, DC: Urban Institute Press, 209–248.

KAFKALAS, G. 1987. State and capital as agents of spatial integration in the world-economy. *Society and Space*, 5, 303–18.

KALDOR, M. 1978. *The Disintegrating West*. London: Allen Lane.

KALE, S.R. and LONSDALE, R.E. 1979. Factors encouraging and discouraging plant location in nonmetropolitan areas. In R.E. Lonsdale and H.R. Seyler (eds.) *Nonmetropolitan Industrialization*. New York: Wiley, 47–56.

KAPLINSKY, R. 1984a. The international context for industrialisation in the coming decade. In R. Kaplinsky (ed.) *Third World Industrialisation in the 1980s : Open Economics in a Closing World*. London: Cass.

—— 1984b. *Automation: The Technology and Society*. London: Longman.

KARASKA, G: 1975. Perspectives on the less developed regions in Poland. In A.F. Burghardt (ed.) *Development Regions in the Soviet Union, Eastern Europe and Canada*. New York: Praeger, 43–64.

KATOUZIAN, H. 1983. Shi'ism and Islamic economics: Sadr and Bani Sadr, in N.R. Keddie (ed.) *Religion and Politics in Iran: Shi'ism from Quietism to Revolution*. New Haven, CT: Yale University Press.

KEDOURIE, E. 1960. *Nationalism*. London: Hutchinson.

KEEBLE, D. 1978. Industrial decline in the inner city and conurbations. *Transactions, Institute of British Geographers*, 3, 101–14.

—— OWENS, P.L. and THOMPSON, C. 1982. Regional accessibility and economic potential in the European Community. *Regional Studies*, 16, 419–31.

—— 1983. The urban–rural manufacturing shift in the European Community. *Urban Studies*, 20, 405–18.

KEINATH, W.F. 1985. The spatial component of the post-industrial society. *Economic Geography*, 61, 223–40.

KEITH, R.G. 1977. *Haciendas and Plantations in Latin American History*. New York: Holmes & Meier.

KEMP, T. 1978. *Historical Patterns of Industrialization*. London: Longman.

KEMPER, N.J. and DE SMIDT, M. 1980. Foreign manufacturing establishments in the Netherlands. *Tijdschrift voor Economische en Sociale Geografie*, 71, 21–40.

KEOHANE, R.O. 1984. *After Hegemony*. Princeton: Princeton University Press.

KILJUNEN, M.L. 1980. Regional disparities and policy in the EEC. In D. Seers and C. Vaitsos (eds.) *Integration and Unequal Development*. London: Macmillan, 199–222.

KIM, S.S. 1979. *China, the United Nations, and World Order*. Princeton, NJ: Princeton University Press.

KIM, Y-S. 1984. A geographical study of social well-being in S. Korea, Kyung Hee Study in Geography No. 6, Dept of Geography, Kyung Hee University, Seoul.

KINDLEBERGER, C.P. 1978. *Manias, Panics, and Crashes: a History of Financial Crises*. New York: Harper & Row.

—— 1981. Dominance and leadership in the international economy. *International Studies Quarterly*, 25, 252–71.

KING, R. 1982. Southern Europe: dependency or development? *Geography*, 67, 221–34.

KIRBY, A. 1979. *The Inner City: Causes and Effects*. Newcastle: RPA Books.

—— 1982. *The Politics of Location*. London: Methuen.

KIRCHNER, J. 1983. Supercomputing seen key to economic success. *Computerworld*, 3 October, 8.

KLEIN, L. 1981. The European Community's regional policy. *Built Environment*, 7, 182–9.

KNIGHT, D.B. 1982. Identity and territory: geographical perspectives on nationalism and regionalism. *Annals, Association of American Geographers*, 72, 514–31.

KNOX, P.L. 1982. Living in the United Kingdom. In R.J. Johnston and J.C. Doornkamp (eds.) *The Changing Geography of the United Kingdom*. London: Methuen, 291–308.

—— 1984. *The Geography of Western Europe: A Socio–Economic Survey*. Beckenham: Croom Helm.

—— and KIRBY, A. 1984. Public provision and the quality of life. In A. Kirby and J. Short (eds.) *Britain Now: A Contemporary Human Geography*. London: Macmillan, 82–96.

—— et al. 1988. *The United States: A Contemporary Human Geography*. London: Longman.

KOESTER, U. and BALE, M. 1984. The CAP of the European Community: a blessing or a curse for developing countries? Washington, DC: World Bank.

KOJIMA, R. 1982. China's new agricultural policy. *The Developing Countries*, 20, 390-413.

KONDRATIEFF, N. 1984. *The Long-Wave Cycle*. New York: Richardson & Snyder.

KOPYTOFF, I. 1987. *The African Frontier: The Reproduction of Traditional African Societies*. Bloomington, IN: Indiana University Press.

KORNHAUSER, D. 1982. *Japan: Geographical Background to Urban and Industrial Development*. London: Longman, 2nd edition.

KOROPECKYJ, I.S. 1975. National income of the Soviet Union republics in 1970: revision and some applications. In Z.M. Fallenbuchl (ed.) *Economic Development in the Soviet Union and Eastern Europe*. New York: Praeger, 287–331.
—— 1977. Regional development in postwar Poland. *Soviet Studies*, 29, 108–27.
KREBS, G. 1982. Regional inequalities during the process of national economic development: a critical approach. *Geoforum*, 13(2), 71–81.
KRUEGER, A. 1978. Alternative trade strategies and employment in developing countries. *American Economic Review*, 68, 523–36.
—— 1986. Aid in the development process. *World Bank Research Observer*, 1, 57–78.
KRUMME, G. 1981. Making it abroad: the evolution of Volkswagen's North American production plans. In F.E.I. Hamilton and G.J.R. Linge (eds.) *Spatial Analysis, Industry and the Industrial Environment*, Volume 2. Chichester: Wiley, 329–56.
KUHN, H.W. and R.E. KUENNE. 1962. An efficient algorithm for the numerical solution of the generalized Weber problem in spatial economics. *Papers and Proceedings of the Regional Science Association*, 8, 21–33.
LABOVITZ, I.M. 1978. Federal expenditures and revenues in states. *Intergovernmental Perspective*, 44, 16–23.
LANDSBERGER, H.A. (ed.) 1969. *Latin American Peasant Movements*. Ithaca, NY: Cornell University Press.
LANGLEY, L.D. 1983. *The Banana Wars: An Inner History of American Empire, 1900–1934*. Lexington, KY: University Press of Kentucky.
LANGTON, J. 1984. The industrial revolution and the regional geography of England. *Transactions, Institute of British Geographers*, 9, 145–67.
LARDY, N.R. 1984. Prices, markets, and the Chinese peasant, in C.K. Eicher and J.M. Staatz (eds.) *Agricultural Development in the Third World*. Baltimore: Johns Hopkins University Press.
LASH, S. and URRY, J. 1987. *The End of Organized Capitalism*. Cambridge: Polity Press.
LATHAM, A.J.H. 1978. *The International Economy and the Undeveloped World, 1865–1914*. Beckenham: Croom Helm.
—— 1981. *The Depression and the Developing World, 1914–1939*. Beckenham: Croom Helm.
LAUE, T.H. von, 1960. The state and the economy. In Black, C.E. (ed.), *The Transformation of Russian Society*. Princeton: Princeton University Press.
LAVROV, S.B. and SDASYNK, G.V. 1982. The growth pole concept and the regional planning experience of developing countries. *Development Dialogue* 3, 15–27.
LAW, C.M. 1983. The defense sector in British regional development. *Geoforum*, 14, 169–84.
—— 1985. The geography of industrial rationalization: The British motor car assembly industry 1972–1982. *Geography*, 70, 1–12.
LEE, R. 1976. Integration, spatial structure and the capitalist mode of production. In R. Lee and P. Ogden (eds.) *Economy and Society in the EEC*. Farnborough: Saxon House, 11–37.
LELE, U. 1984. Rural Africa: modernization, equity, and long-term development. In C.K. Eicher and J.M. Staatz (eds.) *Agricultural Development in the Third World*. Baltimore: Johns Hopkins University Press.
LENG, L.Y. 1983. Economic aspects of supranationalism: the case of ASEAN. *Political Geography Quarterly*, 2, 21–30.
LESSARD, D.R. and WILLIAMSON, J. 1987. *Capital Flight and Third World Debt*. Washington DC: Institute for International Economics.
LESSER, A. 1961. Social fields and the evolution of society. *Southwestern Journal of Anthropology*, 17, 40–8.
LEUNG, C.K. and CHIN, S.S.K. (eds.) 1983. *China in Readjustment*. Hong Kong: Center of Asian Studies, University of Hong Kong.

LEVER, H. and HUHNE, C. 1987. *Debt and Danger: The World Financial Crisis*. London: Penguin.

LEVINSON, C. 1980. *Vodka Cola*. Horsham: Biblios.

LEWIS, P. 1988. Third World funds: wrong-way flow. *New York Times*, 11 February, Dl, D9.

LEWIS, W.A. 1952. World production, prices and trade 1860–1960. *Manchester School*, 20, 105–38.

—— 1955. *The Theory of Economic Growth*. London: Allen & Unwin.

—— 1978a. *The evolution of the international economic order*. Princeton: Princeton University Press.

—— 1978b. *Growth and Fluctuations, 1870–1913*. London: Allen & Unwin.

LIGHT, I. 1983. *Cities in World Perspective*. New York: Macmillan.

LIM, H-C. and YANG, J. 1987. The state, local capitalists, and multinationals: the changing nature of a triple alliance in Korea. In K-D. Kim (ed.) *Dependency Issues in Korean Development: Comparative Perspectives*. Seoul: Seoul National University Press.

LIN, Y-S. 1979. *The Crisis of Chinese Consciousness: Radical Antitraditionalism in the May Fourth Era*. Madison, WI: University of Wisconsin Press.

LINGE, G.J.R. and HAMILTON, F.E.B. 1981. International industrial systems. In G.J.R. Linge and F.E.I. Hamilton (eds.) *Spatial Analysis, Industry and the Industrial Environment*. Chichester: Wiley, 1–117.

LIPIETZ, A. 1980. Inter-regional polarisation and the tertiarisation of space. *Papers of the Regional Science Association*, 44, 3–17.

—— 1986. New tendencies in the international division of labor: regimes of accumulation and modes of regulation. In A.J. Scott and M. Storper (eds.) *Production, Work, Territory: The Geographical Anatomy of Industrial Capitalism*. Boston: Allen & Unwin.

—— 1987. *Mirages and Miracles: The Crises of Global Fordism*. London: Verso.

LITTLE, I. 1982. *Economic Development: Theory, Policy, and International Relations*. New York: Basic Books.

LLOYD, P.E. and DICKEN, P. 1972. *Location in Space: A Theoretical Approach to Economic Geography*. London: Harper & Row.

—— and REEVE, D. 1982. Northwest England 1971–1977: a study in industrial decline and economic restructuring. *Regional Studies*, 16, 345–60.

LO, F-C. and SALIH, K. 1978. *Growth Pole Strategy and Regional Development Policy: Asian Experiences and Alternative Approaches*. Oxford: Pergamon.

LOCATELLI, R.L. 1985. *Industrializacao, Crescimento e Empregno: Uma Avaliacao da Experiencia Brasileira*. Rio de Janeiro: IPEA/INPES.

LOCKWOOD, W.W. 1954. *The Economic Development of Japan: Growth and Structural Change, 1868–1938*. Princeton: Princeton University Press.

LODGE, J. 1982. *The European Community and New Zealand*. London: Frances Pinter.

LONSDALE, J. 1985. The European scramble and conquest in African history. *The Cambridge History of Africa*, Vol. 6, Ch. 12.

LÖSCH, A. 1943. *Die raumliche Ordnung der Wirtschaft: eine Untersuchung uber Standort, Wirtschaftgebiete und internationalen Handel*. Jena: Fischer.

—— 1954. *The Economics of Location*. (trans. W.H. Woglom) New Haven: Yale University Press.

LOUP, J. 1983. *Can the Third World Survive?* Baltimore: Johns Hopkins University Press.

LOVE, J. 1983. Concentration, diversification and earnings instability: some evidence on developing countries' exports of manufactures and primary products. *World Development*, 11, 111–23.

LOW, D.A. 1973. *Lion Rampant: Essays in the Study of British Imperialism*. London: Cass.

LUCKINGHAM, B. 1982. *The Urban Southwest*. El Paso: Texas Western Press.

MACLAUGHLIN, J.G. and J.A. AGNEW 1986. Hegemony and the regional question: the political geography of regional industrial policy in Northern Ireland 1945–1972. *Annals of the Association of American Geographers*, 76, 247–61.

MABOGUNJE, A.L. 1986. The geography of aid. Geographical Paper No.90, University of Reading.

McCONNELL, J.E. 1980. Foreign direct investment in the Unites States. *Annals, Association of American Geographers*, 70, 259–70.

—— 1983. The international location of manufacturing investments: recent behavior of foreign-owned corporations in the US. In F.E.I. Hamilton and G.J.R. Linge (eds.) *Spatial Analysis, Industry and the Industrial Environment, Volume 3*. Chichester: Wiley.

—— 1986. Geography of international trade. *Progress in Human Geography*, 10, 471–83.

McDERMOTT, P.J. 1979. Multinational manufacturing firms and regional development: external control in the Scottish electronics industry. *Scottish Journal of Political Economy*, 26, 287–306.

McGRANAHAN, D.V. et al. 1970. *Content and Measurement of Socio-Economic Development: An Empirical Engineering*, Geneva: UNRISD.

McMICHAEL, P. 1984. *Settlers and the Agrarian Question: Capitalism in Colonial Australia*. Cambridge: Cambridge University Press.

McMICHEAL, P. et al., 1974. Imperialism and the contradictions of development. *New Left Review*, 85, 83–104.

McNABB, R. 1980. Segmented labour markets, female employment and poverty in Wales. In G. Ress and T.L. Rees (eds.) *Poverty and Social Inequality in Wales*. London: Croom Helm. 156–67.

McPHAIL, T.L. 1986. *Electronic Colonialism*, 2nd Edition. Newbury Park, CA.: Sage.

MADDEN, C.H. 1956. Some indicators of stability in the growth of cities in the United States. *Economic Development and Cultural Change*, 4, 225–45.

MADDISON, A. 1982. *Phases of Capitalist Development*, New York: Oxford University Press.

MAGAZINER, I. and HOUT, T. 1980. *Japanese Industrial Policy*. London: Policy Studies Institute.

MALASSIS, L. 1975. *Agriculture and the Development Process*. Paris. UNESCO.

MALECKI, E. 1979a. Locational trends in R and D by large US corporations, 1965–1977. *Economic Geography*, 55, 308–23.

—— 1979b. Agglomeration and intra-firm linkage in R and D location in the United States. *Tijdschift voor Economische en Sociale Geografie*, 70, 322–32.

—— 1980. Corporate organization of R and D and the location of technological activities. *Regional Studies*, 14, 219–34.

—— 1984a. Military spending and the US defence industry: regional patterns of military contracts and subcontracts. *Environment & Planning A*, 16, 31–44.

—— 1984b. High technology and local economic development. *Journal of the American Planning Association*, 262–9.

—— 1986. Technological imperatives and modern corporate strategy. In A. J. Scott and M. Storper (eds.) *Production, Work, Territory: The Geographical Anatomy of Industrial Capitalism*. Boston: Allen & Unwin, 67–79.

MANDEL, E. 1975. *Late Capitalism*. London: New Left Books.

—— 1981. The laws of motion of the Soviet economy. *Review of Radical Political Economics*, 13, 35–9.

MANNERS, G. 1971. *The Geography of Energy*. London: Hutchinson.

MANSFIELD, E. 1982. Technology and productivity in the United States. In M. Feldstein (ed.) *The American Economy in Transition*, Chicago: University of Chicago Press, 563–9.

MARKS, S. and RATHBONE, R.(eds.). 1982. *Industrialization and Social Change in South Africa*. London: Longman.

MARKUSEN, A.R. 1983. High-tech jobs, markets and economic development prospects. *Built Environment*, 9, 18–28.

—— 1984. Defence spending and the geography of high-tech industries. Paper given to Policy Forum, Virginia Tech, Alexandria Center.

—— 1985. *Profit cycles, Oligopoly and Regional Development*. Cambridge, Mass.: MIT Press.

—— 1986a. Neither ore, nor coal nor markets: a policy-oriented view of steel sites in the United States. *Regional Studies*, 20, 449–62.

—— 1986b. Defence spending: a successful industrial policy? *International Journal of Urban and Regional Research*, 10, 105–22.

—— HALL, P. and GLASMEIER, A. 1986. *High Tech America*. Boston: Allen & Unwin.

MARSHALL, M. 1987. *Long Waves of Regional Development*. New York: St Martin's Press.

MARTIN, R. L. 1986. Thatcherism and Britain's industrial landscape. In R. L. Martin and B. Rowthorn (eds.), *The Geography of De-industrialisation* London: Macmillan.

—— and HODGE, J.S.C. 1983. The reconstruction of Britain regional policy, 2: Towards a new agenda, *Government and Policy*, 1, 317–40.

—— and B. ROWTHORN (eds.) 1986. *The Geography of De-Industrialisation*. London: Macmillan.

MASSAD, C. 1985. Debt: an overview. *Journal of Development Planning*, 16, 3–24.

MASSEY, D. 1974. Is a 'behavioral' theory really an alternative? In D. Massey and W.I. Morrison (eds.) *Industrial Location: Alternative Frameworks*. London: Centre for Environmental Studies, Paper No. 15.

—— 1984. *Spatial Divisions of Labour*. London; Methuen.

—— and MEEGAN, R. 1978. Industrial restructuring versus the cities. *Urban Studies*, 15, 273–86.

—— 1982. *The Anatomy of Job Loss*. London: Methuen.

MATTERA, P. 1985. *Off the Books: The Rise of the Underground Economy*. New York: St Martin's Press.

MAYFIELD, R.C. 1967. Central-Place hierarchy in northern India. In W.L. Garrison and D.F. Marble (eds.) *Quantitative Geography, Part I*. Evanston: Northwestern University Press.

MEADOWS, D.H., MEADOWS, D.L. and ANDERS, J. 1972. *The Limits to Growth*. London: Earth Island.

MEIER, G.M. and BALDWIN, R.E. 1957. *Economic Development: Theory, History, Policy*. New York: Wiley.

MELLOR, R.E.H. 1982. *The Soviet Union and its Geographical Problems* London: Macmillan. 2nd edition.

MENSCH, G. 1983. *Stalemate in Technology: Innovations Overcome the Depression*. Cambridge: Ballinger.

MENZEL, U. and SENGHAAS, D. 1987. NICs defined: a proposal for indicators evaluating threshold countries, in K-D. Kim (ed.) *Dependency Issues in Korean Development: Comparative Perspectives* Seoul: Seoul National University Press.

MERICLE, K.S. 1984. The political economy of the Brazilian motor vehicle industry. In K. Kronish and K.S. Mericle (eds.) *The Political Economy of the Latin American Motor Vehicle Industry*. Cambridge, Mass.: MIT Press.

METCALF, D. 1969. *The Economics of Agriculture*. London: Penguin.

MEYER, D.R. 1983. Emergence of the American manufacturing belt: an interpretation. *Journal of Historical Geography*, 9, 145–74.

MEYER, J.W. 1982. Political structure and the world-economy. *Contemporary Sociology*, 11, 263–6.

MINTZ, S. 1985. *Sweetness and Power: The Place of Sugar in Modern History*. New York: Viking.

MIRO, C.A. and RODRIGUES, D. 1982. Capitalism and population in Latin American agriculture. *CEPAL Review*. 16, 51–71.

MISHALANI, P., ROBERT, A., STEVENS, C. and WEESTON, A. 1981. The pyramid of privilege. In Stevens, C. (ed.) *EEC and the Third World: A Survey, 1*. London; Hodder & Stoughton, 60–82.

MOLLE, W. and PAELINCK, J. 1979. Regional policy. In P. Coffey (ed.) *Economic Policies of the Common Market*. London: Macmillan, 146–77.

MOLOTCH, H. and LOGAN, J.R. 1985. Urban dependencies. New forms of use and exchange in US cities. *Urban Affairs Quarterly*, 21, 143–69.

MOMMSEN, W.J.1980. *Theories of Imperialism*. New York: Random House

MORELLO, T. 1983. Sweatshops in the sun? *Far Eastern Economic Review*, 15 September, 88–9.

MORGAN, D. 1979. *Merchants of Grain*. London: Penguin.

—— 1980. *Merchants of Grain*. New York: Penguin.

MORISHIMA, M. 1982. *Why has Japan Succeeded?* Cambridge: Cambridge University Press.

MORRIS, M.D. 1980. *Measuring the Condition of the World's Poor*. New York: Pergamon.

MOSES, L.N. 1958. Location and the theory of production, *Quarterly Journal of Economics*, 72, 259–72.

MOSS, M. 1986. Telecommunications and the future of cities. *Land Development Studies*, 3, 33–44.

MOTTURA, G. and PUGLIESE,E. 1980. Capitalism in agriculture and capitalistic agriculture. In F. Buttel and H. Newby (eds.) *The Rural Sociology of Advanced Societies*. London: Croom Helm, 171–200.

MOUDOUD, E. 1986. *The Rise and Fall of the Growth Pole Approach*. Discussion Paper No. 89, Department of Geography, Syracuse University.

MURATA, K. 1980. *An Industrial Geography of Japan*. London: Bell & Hyman.

MURPHEY, R. 1980. *The Fading of the Maoist Vision*. London: Methuen.

MYRDAL, G. 1957. *Economic Theory and Underdeveloped Regions*. London: Duckworth.

NAIRN, A. 1981. Guatemala. *Multinational Monitor*, 2, 12–14.

NAIRN, T. 1977. Super-Power or failure? In T. Nairn (ed.) *Atlantic Europe?* Amsterdam: Transnational Institute, 68–77.

NAKANE, C. 1970. *Japanese Society*. London: Weidenfeld & Nicolson.

NELSON, K. 1986. Labor demand, labor supply and the suburbanization of low-wage office work. In A. J. Scott and M. Storper (eds.) *Production, Work, Territory: The Geographical Anatomy of Industrial Capitalism*. Boston: Allen & Unwin, 149–71.

NEUMAN, S.G. 1984. International stratification and third world military industries. *International Organization*, 38, 167–98.

NEWBY, H. 1980. Rural sociology, *Current Sociology*, 28, 1–141.

NOER, A. 1985. The agglomeration of manufacturing industries in Indonesia's largest cities, with a special focus on foreign and domestic manufacturing investments. Unpublished PhD dissertation, Social Science Program, Syracuse University.

NOGUES, J. et al. 1985. The extent of non-tariff barriers to industrial countries' imports. Washington, DC: World Bank, Development Research Department, Discussion Paper No. Dr.D 115.

NOLAN, P. 1983. De-collectivisation of agriculture in China, 1979–82: a long-term perspective. *Cambridge Journal of Economics*, 7, 381–403.

NORTH, D.C. 1955. Location theory and regional economic growth. *Journal of Political Economy*, 69, 319–40.

—— and THOMAS, R.P. 1973. *The Rise of the Western World: A New Economic History*. Cambridge: Cambridge University Press.

NORTON, R.D. and REES, J. 1979. The product cycle and the spatial decentralization of American manufacturing. *Regional Studies*, 13, 141–51.

NOYELLE, T.J. 1983. The implications of industry restructuring for spatial organization in the United States. In F. Moulaert and P.W. Salinas (eds.) *Regional Analysis and the New International Division of Labor*. The Hague: Kluwer Nijhoff. 113–34.

—— 1987. *Beyond Industrial Dualism. Market and Job Segmentation in the New Economy*. Boulder, CO: Westview Press.

—— and STANBACK, T.M. Jr. 1981. *The Economic Transformation of American Cities*. New York: Conservation of Human Resources.

NUTTER, G.W. 1978. *The Growth of Government in the West*. Washington, DC: American Enterprise Institute.

NYE, J.S. 1970. Comparing common markets: a revised neo-functionalist model. *International Organization*, 24, 796–835.

O'CONNOR, A.M 1978. *The Geography of Tropical African Development: A Study of Spatial Patterns of Economic Change Since Independence*. Oxford: Pergamon (2nd Edition).

Ó hUALLACHÁIN, B. 1987. Regional and technological implications of the recent buildings in American defense spending. *Annals of the Association of American Geographers*, 77, 208–23.

O'KEEFE, P. (ed.) 1983. *Regional Restructuring under Advanced Capitalism*. Beckenham: CroomHelm.

O'LOUGHLIN, J. 1986. World power competition and local conflicts in the third world. In R.J. Johnston and P.J. Taylor (eds.) *A World in Crisis? Geographical Perspectives*. Oxford: Blackwell.

O'RIORDAN, T. 1976. *Environmentalism*, London: Pion.

OAKEY, R. 1984. *High-Technology; Small Firms: Innovation and Regional Development in Britain and the US*. London: Frances Pinter.

ODELL, P.R. 1986. Draining the world of energy. In R.J. Johnston and P.J. Taylor (eds.) *A World in Crisis? Geographical Perspectives*. Oxford: Blackwell, 68–88.

OECD 1979. *The Impact of the NICs on Production and Trade in Manufactures*. Paris: OECD.

OECD 1981. *The Welfare State in Crisis*. Paris: OECD.

OECD 1983. *Industry in Transition*. Paris: OECD.

OECD 1984. *External Debt of Developing Countries*. Paris: OECD.

ORWELL, G. 1962. *The Road to Wigan Pier*. Harmondsworth: Penguin; first published by Victor Gollancz, 1937.

OVERTON, J. 1987. The colonial state and spatial differentiation: Kenya, 1895–1920, *Journal of Historical Geography*. 13, 267–82.

OWEN, N. 1983. *Economies of Scale, Competitiveness and Trade Patterns Within the European Community*. Oxford: Clarendon Press.

PARBONI, R. 1981. *The Dollar and Its Rivals*. London: Verso.

PARKER, G. 1974. The emergence of modern finance in Europe, 1500–1700. In C.M. Cipolla (ed.) *The Fontana Economic History of Europe: The Sixteenth and Seventeenth Centuries*. London: Fontana, 527–89.

PAYER, C. 1974. *The Debt Trap*. Harmondsworth: Penguin.

PEARCE, A. 1979. *Seeds of Plenty, Seeds of Want*. London: Oxford University Press.

PEARSE, A. 1975. *The Latin American Peasant*. London: Cass.

PECK, F.W. and TOWNSEND, A.R. 1985. Spatial redeployment through plant closure and redundancy by foreign companies in the UK 1976–1981. In M.J.Taylor and N.J. Thrift (eds.) *Multinationals and the Restructuring of the World Economy*. Beckenham: Croom Helm.

PEET, R. 1969. The spatial expansion of commercial agriculture in the nineteenth century: a von Thünen interpretation. *Economic Geography*, 45, 283–301.

—— 1972. Influences of the British market on agriculture and related economic development in Europe before 1860. *Transactions, Institute of British Geographers*, 56, 1–20.

—— - 1980. The transition from feudalism to capitalism. In R. Peet (ed.) *An Introduction to Marxist theories of Underdevelopment*. Research School of Pacific Studies, Department of Human Geography, Publication HG/14. Canberra: Australian National University, 51–74.

—— 1983. Relations of production and the relocation of US manufacturing industry since 1960. *Economic Geography*, 59, 112–43.

—— 1987. Industrial devolution, underconsumption and the third world debt crisis. *World Development*, 15, 777–88.

PENOUIL, M. and PETRELLA, R. 1982. *The Location of Growing Industries in Europe*. Vienna: European Coordination Center for Research and Documentation in Social Sciences.

PERKINS, D. and YUSUF, S. 1984. *Rural Development in China*. Baltimore: Johns Hopkins University Press.

PERLOFF, H. and L. WINGO. 1961. Natural resource endowment and economic growth. In J. Spengler (ed.) *Natural Resources and Economic Growth*. Washington DC: Resources for the Future.

PERROUX, F. 1955. Note sur la notion de pôle de croissance. In I. Livingstone (ed.) 1979. *Development Economics and Policy: Selected Readings*. London: Allen & Unwin.

—— 1961. La firme motrice dans la région et la région motrice. *Théorie et Politique de la Expansion Régionale*. Liège, Belgium: Université de Liège.

—— (eds.) 1977. *The Rise of the Sunbelt Cities*. Beverly Hills, CA: Sage Publications.

PERRY, D.C. and WATKINS, A.J. 1981. Contemporary dimensions of uneven urban development in the USA. In M. Harloe (ed.) *City, Class and Capital*, London: Edward Arnold, 115–42.

PETRAS, J. 1984. Toward a theory of industrial development in the third world. *Journal of Contemporary Asia*, 14, 182–203.

PFISTER, U.P. and SUTER, C. 1987. International financial relations as part of the world system. *International Studies Quarterly*, 31, 239–72.

PINDER, D.A. 1978. Guiding economic development in the EEC: the approach of the European Investment Bank, *Geography*, 63, 88–97.

PINDER, J. 1983. *Regional Economic Development and Policy: Theory and Practice in the European Community*. London: Allen & Unwin.

—— 1986. The political economy of integration in Europe: policies and institutions in East and West. *Journal of Common Market Studies*, 25, 1–14.

PIORE, M. and SABEL, C. 1984. *The Second Industrial Divide*. New York: Basic Books.

PIRENNE, H. 1937. *Economic and Social History of Medieval Europe*. London: Macmillan.

PLETSCH, C.E. 1981. The three worlds, or the division of social scientific labor, circa 1950–1975, *Comparative Studies in Society and History*, 23, 565–90.

POLANYI, K. 1957. The place of economies in societies. In, K. Polanyi *et al.* (eds.), *Trade and Market in the Early Empires*. Glencoe, Ill: Free Press.

POLLARD, S. 1981. *Peaceful Conquest. The Industrialization of Europe, 1760–1970*. Oxford: Oxford University Press.

POULANTZAS, N. 1978. *State, Power and Socialism*. London: New Left Books.

POUNDS, N.J.G. 1974. *An Economic History of Medieval Europe.* London: Longman.

PRED, A.R. 1967. *Behavior and Location.* Lund: Gleerup.

—— 1974. *Major Job-Providing Organizations and Systems of Cities.* Association of American Geographers, Resources Papers for College Geography, 27. Washington, DC: Association of American Geographers.

—— 1977. *City-systems In Advanced Economies.* London: Hutchison.

—— 1980. *Urban Growth and City-Systems in the United States, 1840–1860.* London: Hutchinson.

PROBST, A. Ye 1977. Territorial production complexes. *Soviet Geography,* 18, 195–203.

PRYCE, R. (ed.) 1986. *Dynamics of European Union.* Beckenham: Croom Helm.

PUYANA DE PALACIOS, A. 1982. *Economic Integration Among Unequal Partners: The Case of the Andean Group.* New York: Pergamon.

RADA, J. 1983. Technology and the north–south division of labor. In R. Kaplinsky (ed.) *Comparative Advantage in an Automating World.* Brighton: Institute of Development Studies, Bulletin, 13, 2.

RADA, J. 1984. *International Division of Labour and Technology.* Geneva: ILO.

RANGER, T.O. 1976. From Humanism to the Science of Man: Colonialism in Africa and the understanding of alien societies, *Transactions of the Royal Historical Society,* 26, 115–41.

—— 1984. The invention of tradition in colonial Africa. In E. Hobsbawn and T.O. Ranger (eds.) *The Invention of Tradition.* Cambridge: Cambridge University Press.

RAU, W. and RONCEK, D.W. 1987. Industrialization and world inequality: the transformation of the division of labor in 59 nations, 1960–1981. *American Sociological Review,* 52, 359–69.

RAVENHILL, J. 1986. Africa's continuing crises: the elusiveness of development. In J. Ravenhill (ed.) *Africa in Economic Crisis.* New York: Columbia University Press.

RAY, C.F. 1977. The 'real' price rise of primary commodities. *National Institute Economic Review,* 22, 13–28.

REES, J. 1981. The impact of defense spending on regional industrial change in the US. In G.W. Hoffman (ed.) *Federalism and Regional Development.* Austin: University of Texas Press, 193–222.

—— 1983a. Regional economic decentralization processes in the United States and their policy implications. In D.A. Hicks and N.J. Glickman (eds.) *Transition to the 21st Century: Prospects and Policies for Economic and Urban-Regional Transformation.* Greenwich: JAI Press, 241–78.

—— 1983b. Government policy and industrial location. In J. House (ed.) *United States Public Policy,* Oxford University Press, London, 213–62.

—— (ed.) 1986. *Technology, Regions and Policy.* Totowa, NJ: Rowman & Littlefield.

—— 1987. Review of A. Markusen, *Profit Cycles, Oligopoly and Regional Development. Urban Geography,* 8, 171–3.

REISCHAUER, R. 1981. The economy and the federal budget in the 1980s: implications for the state and local sector. In R. Bahl (ed.) *Urban Government Finance: Emerging Trends, Urban Affairs Annual Reviews,* Vol 20. Beverly Hills: Sage, 13–38.

REITSMA, H.A. and KLEINPENNING, J.M.G. 1985. *The Third World in Perspective.* Totowa, NJ: Rowman & Allanheld.

REPS, J.W. 1965. *The Making of Urban America.* Princeton NJ: Princeton University Press.

REYNOLDS, R. 1961. *Europe Emerges: Transition Toward an Industrial Worldwide Society.* Madison: University of Wisconsin Press.

RICHARDSON, H.S. 1973. Theory of the distribution of city sizes: review and prospects. *Regional Studies,* 7, 239–51.

ROKKAN, S. 1980. Territories, centres and peripheries. In Gottmann, J. (ed.), *Centre and Periphery*. London: Sage, 163–204.
—— and URWIN, D. 1983. *Economy, Territory, Identity: Politics of West European Peripheries*. London: Sage.
RONDINELLI, D.A. 1983. Dynamics of growth of secondary cities in developing countries. *Geographical Review*, 73, 42–57.
ROSENBERG, E.S. 1982. *Spreading the American Dream: American Economic and Cultural Expansion, 1890–1945*. New York: Hill & Wang.
ROSS, R. 1982. Regional illusion, capitalist reality. *Democracy*, 2, 93–9.
ROSTOW, W.W. 1978. *The World Economy*. London: Macmillan.
ROTBERG, R. *et al*. 1983. *Imperialism, Colonialism, and Hunger: East and Central Africa*. Lexington, Mass.: Lexington Books.
ROTHCHILD, D. and GYIMAH-BOADI, E. 1986. Ghana's economic decline and development strategies. In J. Ravenhill (ed.) *Africa in Economic Crisis*. New York: Columbia University Press.
RUDOLPH, L.I. and RUDOLPH, S.H. 1987. *In Pursuit of Lakshmi: The Political Economy of the Indian State*. Chicago: University of Chicago Press.
RUTT, S. 1986. The Soviet concept of the territorial production complex and regional development. *Town Planning Review*, 57, 425–39.
SABEL, C.F. 1982. *Work and Politics: The Division of Labor in Industry*. New York: Cambridge University Press.
SAMUELSON, P. 1964. *Economics*. New York: McGraw Hill.
SANDBACH, F. 1980. *Environment, Ideology, and Policy*. Oxford: Blackwell.
SANDERS, R. 1987. Towards a geography of informal activity. *Socio-Economic Planning Sciences*, 21, 229–37.
SANTIAGO, C.E. 1987. The impact of foreign direct investment on employment structure and employment generation. *World Development*, 15, 317–28.
SANTOS, M. 1979. *The Shared Space*. London: Methuen.
SAUER, C. 1952. *Agricultural origins and dispersals*. New York: American Geographical Society.
SAUL, S.B. 1960. *Studies in British Overseas Trade, 1870–1914*. Liverpool: Liverpool University Press.
SAWERS, L. and TABB, W.K. (eds.) 1984. *Sunbelt/Snowbelt*. New York: Oxford University Press.
SAXENIAN, A. 1983a. The genesis of Silicon Valley. *Built Environment*, 9, 7–17.
—— 1983b. The urban contradictions of Silicon Valley. *International Journal of Urban and Regional Research*, 7, 237–62.
SAYER, R.A. 1982. Explanation in economic geography: abstraction versus generalization. *Progress in Human Geography*, 6, 68–88.
—— 1985. Industry and space: a sympathetic critique of radical research. *Society and Space*, 3, 3–29.
SCHAMA, S. 1987. *The Embarrassment of Riches: An Interpretation of Dutch Culture in the Golden Age*. New York: Knopf.
SCHEJTMAN, A. 1982. Land reform and entrepreneurial structure in rural Mexico. In S. Jones *et al*. (eds.) *Rural Poverty and Agrarian Reform*. New Delhi: Allied.
SCHIFFER, J. 1981. The changing post-war pattern of development: the accumulated wisdom of Samir Amin. *World Development*, 9, 515–37.
SCHILLER, A.R. and SCHILLER, H. 1982. Who can own what America knows? *The Nation*, 17, April, 461–3.
SCHLEBECKER, J.T. 1960. The world metropolis and the history of American agriculture. *Journal of Economic History*, 20, 187–208.
SCHMIDT, M.G. 1983. The welfare state and the economy in periods of economic crisis: a comparative study of 23 OECD nations. *European Journal of Political Research*, 11, 1–26.

400 Adjusting to a New Global Economy

SCHMITZ, H. 1984. Industrialisation strategies it less developed countries: some lessons of historical experience. In R. Kaplinsky (ed.) *Third World Industrialization in the 1980s: Open Economies in a Closing World*. London: Cass.

SCHOENBERGER, E. 1987. Competition, competitive strategy and industrial change: the case of electronic components. *Economic Geography*, 63, 112–34

—— 1988. From Fordism to flexible accumulation: technology, competitive strategies and international location, *Society and Space*, 6,245–62.

SCHROEDER, G.E. 1973. Regional differences in incomes and levels in living in the USSR. In V.N. Bandera and Z.L. Melnyk (eds.) *The Soviet Economy in Regional Perspective*. New York: Praeger, 167–95.

SCOTT, A.J. 1982. Production system dynamics and metropolitan development. *Annals of the Association of American Geographers*, 72, 185–200.

—— 1986. High technology industry and economic development: the rise of the Orange County industrial complex, 1955–1984. *Urban Geography*, 7, 3–45.

—— 1987. The semi-conductor industry in Southeast Asia: organization, location, and the international division of labour. *Regional Studies*, 21, 143–60.

—— and M. STORPER (eds.) 1986. *Production, Work, Territory: The Geographical Anatomy of Industrial Capitalism*. Boston: Allen & Unwin.

—— and M. STORPER 1987. High technology industry and economic development: a theoretical critique and reconstruction. *International Social Science Review*, 12, 35–47.

SEERS, D. 1979. The periphery of Europe. In Seers, D., Schafer, B. and Kilijunen, M.I. (eds.), *Underdeveloped Europe*. Hassocks: Harvester Press, 3–34.

SEIBEL, H.D. and DAMACHI, U.G. 1982. *Self-Management in Yugoslavia and the Developing World*. New York: St Martin's Press.

SEIBER, M.J. 1982. *International Borrowing by Developing Countries*. New York: Pergamon.

SEN, A. 1981a. Public action and the quality of life in developing countries. *Oxford Bulletin of Economics and Statistics*, 43. 111–23.

—— 1981b. *Poverty and Famines: An Essay on Entitlement and Deprivation*. Oxford: Clarendon Press of Oxford University Press.

SENDER, J. and SMITH, S. 1986. *The Development of Capitalism in Africa*. London: Methuen.

SHORT, J. 1981. Defense spending in UK regions. *Regional Studies*, 15, 101–10.

SHUNZAN, Y. 1987. Urban policies and urban housing programs in China. In R.J. Fuchs *et al.* (eds.) *Urbanization and Urban Policies in Pacific Asia*. Boulder, CO: Westview Press.

SIRBU, M.A. Jr., TREITEL, R., YORSZ, W. and ROBERTYS. E.B. 1976. *The Formation of a Technology-Oriented Complex*. Cambridge, Mass: MIT Center for Policy Alternatives.

SIVARD, R.L. 1982. *World Military and Social Expenditures 1982*. Washington, DC: World Priorities.

SIVARD, R.L. 1986. *World Military and Social Expenditures 1986*. Washington, DC: World Priorities.

SKINNER, G.W. 1964–65. Marketing and social structure in rural China. *Journal of Asian Studies*, 24, 3–34, 195–228, 363–99.

SKOCPOL, T. 1976. France, Russia, China: a structural theory of social revolution. *Comparative Studies in Society and History*, 18, 181–96.

SLATER, D. 1975. Underdevelopment and spatial inequality: approaches to the problem of regional planning in the Third World. *Progress in Planning*, 4, 111–24.

SMITH, D.M. 1979. *Where the Grass is Greener*. Harmondsworth: Penguin.

SMITH, I.J. 1979. The effects of external takeover and manufacturing employment change in the Northern region, 1963–1973. *Regional Studies*, 13, 421–37.

SMITH, R.H.T. (ed.) 1978. *Market-Place Trade-Periodic Markets, Hawkers, and*

Traders in Africa, Asia and Latin America. Vancouver, BC: Centre for Transportation Studies, University of British Columbia.

SMITH, T. 1979. The underdevelopment of development literature: the case of dependency theory. *World Politics.* 31, 247–88.

—— 1981. *The Pattern of Imperialism: The United States, Great Britain, and the Late-Industrializing World Since 1815.* Cambridge: Cambridge University Press.

SNYDER, D.E. 1962. Commercial passenger linkages and the metropolitan nodality of Montevideo. *Economic Geography,* 38, 95–112.

SOBELL, V. 1984. *The Red Market: Industrial Cooperation and Specialization in Comecon.* Aldershot: Gower.

SOKOLOVSKY, J. 1985. Logic, space, and time: the boundaries of the capitalist world-economy. In M. Timberlake (ed.) *Urbanization in the World-Economy.* New York: Academic Press.

SPENCE, J. 1980. *To Change China: Western Advisers in China 1620–1960.* London: Penguin.

SPRAOS, J. 1980. The statistical debate on the net barter terms of trade between primary commodities and manufactures, *Economic Journal,* 90, 107–28.

—— 1983. *Inequalising Trade?* Oxford: Clarendon Press of Oxford University Press.

STAATZ, J.M. and EICHER, C.K. 1984. Agricultural development ideas in historical perspective. In C.K. Eicher and J.M. Staatz (eds.) *Agricultural Development in the Third World.* Baltimore: Johns Hopkins University Press.

STANBACK, T.M. Jr. and NOYELLE, T.J. 1982. *Cities in Transition,* Totowa, NJ: Allanheld, Osmun.

STEED, G.P.F. and DE GENOVA, D. 1983. Ottawa's technology-oriented complex. *Canadian Geographer,* 27, 263–78.

STEIN, A.A. 1984. The hegemon's dilemma: Great Britain, the United States, and the international economic order. *International Organization,* 38, 355–86.

STEPHENS, J.D. and HOLLY, B.P. 1980. The Changing Patterns of Industrial Corporate Control in the Metropolitan United States. In Brunn, S.D. and Wheeler, J.O. (eds.) *The American Metropolitan System,* London: Edward Arnold, 161–80.

STOKES, E. 1959. *The English Utilitarians and India.* London: Oxford University Press.

STOKES, R. and JAFFEE, D. 1982. The export of raw materials and economic growth. *American Sociological Review,* 47, 402–6.

STONE, C. 1988. Drugs from the Third World. *World Press Review,* January, 64.

STORPER, M. 1985. Oligopoly and the product-cycle: essentialism in economic geography. *Economic Geography,* 61, 260–82.

—— 1987a. The new industrial geography. *Urban Geography,* 8, 585–98.

—— 1987b. Big structures, small events and large processes in economic geography. *Environment and Planning A,* 19, 1111–23.

—— and CHRISTOPHERSON, S. 1987. Flexible specialization and regional industrial agglomerations: the case of the US: motion picture industry. *Annals of the Association of American Geographers,* 77, 104–17.

—— and WALKER, R.A. 1984. The spatial division of labor: labor and the location of industries. In L. Sawers and W. Tabb (eds.) *Sunbelt/Snowbelt: Urban Development and Regional Restructuring.* New York: Oxford University Press.

STRANGE, S. 1986. *Casino Capitalism.* Oxford: Blackwell.

STREETEN, P. 1968. A poor nation's guide to getting aid. *New Society,* 18, 154–6.

STUCKEY, B. 1987. The division of labor and the dynamic of the world economy. In H. Muegge and W. B. Stöhr (eds.) *International Economic Restructuring and the Regional Community.* Aldershot: Avebury, 13–29.

SUHARTONO, F.X. 1987. Growth Centers in the Context of Indonesia's Urban and Regional Development Problems. Unpublished manuscript, Social Science Program, Syracuse University.

SUTCLIFFE, R.B. 1971. *Industry and Underdevelopment*. London: Addison-Wesley.
—— 1984. Industry and Underdevelopment re-examined. In R. Kaplinsky (ed.) *Third World Industrialization in the 1980s: Open Economies in a Closing World*. London: Cass.
SWEEZY, P.M. 1957. *The Theory of Capitalist Development*. New York: Modern Reader Paperbacks.
—— 1980. *Post-Revolutionary Society*. New York: Monthly Review Press.
SWINDELL, K. 1979. Labour migration in underdeveloped countries: the case of sub-Saharan Africa. *Progress in Human Geography*, 3, 239–59.
—— 1985. *Farm Labour*. Cambridge: Cambridge University Press.
SZCZEPANIK, E. 1969. The size and efficiency of agricultural investment in selected developing countries. *FAO, Monthly Bulletin of Agricultural Economics and Statistics*, December, 2.
SZYMANSKI, A. 1979. *Is the Red Flag Flying? The Political Economy of the Soviet Union in the World Today*. London: Zed Press.
SZYMANSKI, R. and J.A. AGNEW. 1981. *Order and Skepticism: Human Geography and the Dialectic of Science*. Washington DC: Association of American Geographers.
TAAFFE, E.J., Morrill, R.L and Gould, P. 1963. Transport expansion in underdeveloped countries, *Geographical Review*, 53, 503–29.
TARRANT, J. 1985. A review of international food trade. *Progress in Human Geography*, 9, 235–54.
TAUSSIG, M. 1978. Peasant economies and the development of capitalist agriculture in the Cauca Valley, Colombia. *Latin American Perspectives*, 18, 62–91.
TAYLOR, M.J. 1986. The product-cycle model: a critique. *Environment and Planning A*, 18, 751–61.
—— and THRIFT, N.J. 1981. Some geographical implications of foreign investment in the periphery. *Tijdschrift voor Economische en Sociale Geografie*, 72, 194–213.
—— and N. J. THRIFT. 1983. Business organisation, segmentation and location. *Regional Studies*, 17, pp. 445–65.
—— and N.J. THRIFT 1985. *Multinationals and the Restructuring of the World Economy*. Beckenham: Croom Helm.
TAYLOR, P.J. 1985. *Political Geography: World-Economy, Nation-State and Locality*. London: Longman.
TEECE, D. 1980. Economies of scope and scope of enterprise, *Journal of Economic Behavior and Organization*, 1, 223–48.
TENG, S-Y. and FAIRBANK, J. 1979. *China's Response to the West: A Documentary Survey, 1839–1923*. Cambridge, Mass.: Harvard University Press.
THOMAS, H. and LOGAN, C. 1982. *Mondragon: An Economic Analysis*. London: Allen & Unwin.
THOMAS, V. 1987. Differences in income and poverty within Brazil. *World Development*, 15, 263–73.
THOMPSON REPORT, 1973. *Report on the Regional Problem in the Enlarged Community*. Brussels: Commission of the European Communities.
THRIFT, N.J. 1986. The geography of international economic disorder. In R.J. Johnston and P.J.Taylor (eds.) *A World in Crisis? Geographical Perspectives*. Oxford: Blackwell.
—— 1987. The fixers. The urban geography of international commercial capital. In J. Henderson and M. Castells (eds.) *Global Restructuring and Territorial Development*. Newbury Park. CA: Sage, 203–33.
—— and LEYSHON, A. 1988. The gambling propensity: banks, developing country debt exposures, and the new international financial system. *Geoforum*, 19, 55–69.
TILLY, C. (ed.) 1975. *The Formation of National States in Western Europe*. Princeton, NJ: Princeton University Press.
—— 1986. Space for capital, space for states. *Theory and Society*, 15, 301–9.

TIMBERLAKE, M. and LUNDAY, J. 1985. Labor force structure in the zones of the World-Economy, 1950–1970. In M.. Timberlake (ed.), *Urbanization in the World-Economy*. Orlando: Academic Press, 325–49.

TIMMER, C.P and FALCON, W.P. 1975. The political economy of rice production and trade in Asia. In L.G. Reynolds (ed.) *Agriculture in Development Theory*. New Haven: Yale University Press.

TIVEY,L. (ed.) 1981. *The Nation State*. London: Robertson.

TODARO, M.P. 1977. *Economics for a Developing World. An Introduction to Principles, Problems and Policies for Development*. London: Longman.

TOSH, J. 1980. The cash crop revolution in Africa: an agricultural reappraisal. *African Affairs*, 79, 79–94.

TOWNSEND, A. 1983. *The Impact of Recession on Industry*: Employment and the Regions, 1976–1981. Beckenham: Croom Helm.

—— 1986. Spatial aspects of the growth of part-time employment in Britain. *Regional Studies*, 20, 313–30.

TOYE, J. 1987. *Dilemmas of Development: Reflections on the Counter-Revolution in Development Theory and Practice*. Oxford: Basil Blackwell.

TUNSTALL,J. 1986. *Communications Deregulation*. Oxford: Basil Blackwell.

TUONG, H.D. and YEATS, A.J. 1981. Market disruption, the new protectionism, and developing countries: a note on empirical evidence from the US. *The Developing Economies*, 19, 107–18.

TURITS, R. 1987. Trade, debt, and the Cuban economy. *World Development*, 15, 163–80.

TURNOCK, D. 1984. Postwar studies on the human geography of Eastern Europe. *Progress in Human Geography*, 8. 315–46.

—— 1988. *The Human Geography of Eastern Europe*. Beckenham: Croom Helm.

TURTON, A. 1982. Poverty reform, and class struggle in rural Thailand. In S. Jones *et al.* (eds.) *Rural Poverty and Agrarian Reform*. New Delhi: Allied.

TYLECOTE, A.B. and LONSDALE-BROWN, M.L. 1982. State socialism and development. In Friedmann, E. (ed.), *Ascent and Decline in the World-system*. Beverly Hills: Sage, 111–23.

TYLER, W.G. 1976. Manufactured exports and employment creation in developing countries: some empirical evidence. *Economic Development and Cultural Change*, 24, 355–73.

—— 1981. Growth and export expansion in developing countries: some empirical evidence. *Journal of Development Economics*, 9, 121–30.

—— 1986. Stabilization, external adjustment, and recession in Brazil: perspectives on the mid-1980s. *Studies in Comparative International Development*, 21, 5–33.

TYSON, L.D. 1980. *The Yugoslav Economic System and Its Performance in the 1970s*. Berkeley, CA: University of California, Institute of International Studies.

UCHITELLE, L. 1987. Corporate profitability rising, reversing 15-year downturn. *New York Times*, 30, November, 1 D11.

ULLMAN, E.L. 1956. The role of transportation and the bases of interaction. In W. Thomas (ed.) *Man's Role in Changing the Face of the Earth*. Chicago: University of Chicago Press.

ULLMAN, E.L. 1960. Geographic theory and underdeveloped areas. In N. Ginsburg (ed.) *Essays on Geography and Economic Development*. Chicago: University of Chicago Department of Geography Research Paper No. 62.

UNIDO. 1980. *World Industry Since 1960: Progress and Prospects*. New York: United Nations Industrial Development Organization.

—— 1981. *A Statistical Review of the World Industrial Situation, 1980*. Vienna: United Nations Industrial Development Organization.

—— 1985. *Industry in the 1980s*. New York: United Nations Industrial Development Organization.

UNITED KINGDOM SELECT COMMITTEE ON THE EUROPEAN COMMUNI-
TIES, 1980. *Policies for Rural Areas in the European Community*, 27th Report,
Session 1979/80, London: HMSO.
UN CENTER ON TRANSNATIONAL CORPORATIONS 1983. *Transnational Cor-
porations in World Development; Third Study*. New York: United Nations.
UNITED NATIONS 1984. *Land, Food, and People*. Rome: FAO.
URRY, J. 1984. Capitalist restructuring, recomposition and the regions. In T. Bradley
and P. Lowe (eds.) *Locality and Rurality; Economy and Society in Rural Regions*.
Norwich: Geo Books.
—— 1985. Social relations, space, and time. In D. Gregory and J. Urry (eds.) *Social
Relations and Spatial Structures*. London: Macmillan.
US Department of Housing and Urban Development 1982. *The President's National
Urban Policy* Report, 1982. Washington, DC: US Government Printing Office.
VAN ONSELEN, C. 1982. *Studies in the Social and Economic History of the
Witwatersrand, 1886-1914*. New York: Longman.
VAPNARSKY, C.A. 1969. On rank-size distributions of cities: an ecological approach.
Economic Development and Cultural Change, 17, 584-95.
VERNON, R. 1977. *Storm over the Multinationals*. Cambridge: Harvard University
Press.
VERREYDT, E. and WAELBROECK, J. 1982. European Community protection
against manufactured imports from developing countries. Washington, DC: World
Bank.
VINING, D.R. 1982. On A Catastrophe Model of Regional Dynamics. *Annals of the
Association of American Geographers*, 72, 554-5.
VOGEL, E. 1980. *Japan as Number 1: Lessons for America*. New York: Harper &
Row.
WACHTEL, H.M. 1987. Currency without a country: the global funny money game.
The Nation, 245 (26 December), 784-90.
WAINWRIGHT, H. 1978. Women and the division of labour. In P. Abrams (ed.)
Work, Urbanism and Inequality. London: Weidenfeld & Nicolson.
WALKER, R.A. 1978. The transformation of urban structure in the nineteenth cen-
tury and the beginnings of urbanization. In K.R. Cox (ed.) *Urbanization and Con-
flict in Market Societies*. Chicago: Maaroufa.
WALLERSTEIN, I. 1974. *The Modern World-System: Capitalist Agriculture and the
Origins of the European World-Economy in the Sixteenth Century*. New York:
Academic Press.
—— 1979a. *The Capitalist World-Economy* Cambridge: Cambridge University Press.
—— 1979b. Underdevelopment and Phase-B: effect of the seventeenth century stagna-
tion on core and periphery of the European world-economy. In W. Woldfrank (ed.)
The World-System of Capitalism: Past and Present. Beverly Hills: Sage, 73-84.
—— 1980. *The Modern World-System II: Mercantilism and the consolidation of the
World-Economy 1600-1750*. London: Academic Press.
—— I. 1984 *The Politics of the World-Economy*. Cambridge: Cambridge University
Press.
—— et al. 1979. Cyclical rhythms and secular trends of the capitalist world-ecomomy
Review, 2,483-500.
WARD, M.F. 1982. Political economy, industrial location and the European motor
car industry in the postwar period. *Regional Studies*, 16, 443-53.
WARDWELL, J. 1980. Toward a theory of urban-rural migration in the developed
world. In D. Brown and J. Wardwell (eds.) *New Directions in Urban-Rural Migra-
tion*. New York: Academic Press.
WARMAN, A. 1980. '*We Come to Object*': The Peasants of Morelos and the National
State. Baltimore: Johns Hopkins University Press.
WARNOCK, J.W. 1987. *The Politics of Hunger*. London: Methuen.

WARREN, B. 1980. *Imperialism: Pioneer of Capitalism*. London: Verso.

WASLYENKO, M. 1981. The location of firms: the role of taxes and fiscal incentives. In R. Bahl (ed.) *Urban Government Finance: Emerging Trends*, Urban Affairs Annual Reviews, 20, Beverly Hills: Sage, 185–90.

WATTS, D. 1980. *The large industrial enterprise: spatial perspectives*. Beckenham: Croom Helm.

WATTS, H.D. 1981. *The branch-plant economy: A study of external control*. London: Longman.

WATTS, M. 1983. *Silent Violence: Food, Famine and Peasantry in Northern Nigeria*. Berkeley: University of California Press.

WEBER, A. 1929. *Theory of the Location of Industries*. Chicago: University of Chicago Press.

WESTPHAL, L. 1978. The Republic of Korea's experience with export-led industrial development. *World Development*, 6, 43–57.

WHEATLEY, P. 1971. *Pivot of the four quarters*. Chicago: Aldine Press.

WHEELER, J.O. 1986. Corporate spatial links with financial institutions: the rôle of the metropolitan hierarchy. *Annals, Association of American Geographers*, 76, 262–74.

WHITE, G. 1987. Cuban planning in the mid-1980s: centralization, decentralization, and participation. *World Development*. 15, 153–61.

WILLETS, W. 1964. The maritime adventures of the great eunuch Ho. In C. Jack-Hinton (ed.) *Papers on early South-East Asian History*. Singapore: Journal of South-East Asian History, 25–42.

WILLIAMS, C.H. (ed.) 1982. *National Separatism*. Cardiff: University of Wales Press.

—— 1986. The question of national congruence. In R.J. Johnston and P.J. Taylor (eds.) *A World in Crisis? Geographical Perspectives*. Oxford: Basil Blackwell.

WILLIAMS, G., 1981. *Third-World Political Organizations*. Montclair, NJ: Allanheld, Osmun.

WILLIAMS, R.G. 1986. *Export Agriculture and the Crisis in Central America*. Chapel Hill, NC: University of North Carolina Press.

WILLIAMS, S.W. 1986. Arming the Third World: the role of the multinational corporation. In C.J. Dixon *et al.* (eds.), *Multinational Corporations and the Third World*. Boulder, CO: Westview Press.

WILLIAMS, W.A. 1981. Radicals and regionalism, *Democracy*, 1 (4), 87–98.

WILLIAMSON, J. and BOTTRILL, A. 1971. The impact of customs union on trade in manufactures. *Oxford Economic Papers*. November, 323–51.

WILLIAMSON, J.G. 1965. Regional inequality and the process of national development: a description of the patterns. *Economic Development and Cultural Change*, 13, 3–45.

WILLIS, R. 1984. Farming in New Zealand and the EEC. *New Zealand Geographer*, 2–11.

WITTFOGEL, K.A. 1957. *Oriental Despotism: A Comparative Study of Total Power*. New Haven: Yale University Press.

WOHLENBERG. E.H. 1976. Public assistance effectiveness by states. *Annals, Association of American Geographers*, 66, 440–50.

WOLF, E.R. 1968. *Peasant Wars of the Twentieth Century*. New York: Harper & Row.

—— 1982. *Europe and the People without History*. Berkeley: University of California Press.

WOLPERT, J. 1964. The decision process in a spatial context. *Annals of the Association of American Geographers*, 54: 537–58.

WOOLLEY, L. 1963. The urbanisation of society. In J. Hawkes and L. Woolley (eds.) *History of Mankind*, Vol. 1 *Prehistory and the beginnings of civilisation*. Paris: UNESCO, chapter 3.

WONG, K.Y. 1987. China's special economic zone experiment: an appraisal. *Geografiska Annaler, Series B*, 69, 27–40.

WORLD BANK. 1979. World trade and output of manufactures. Staff Working Paper, January.

WORLD BANK. 1982, 1983, 1984, 1986b, 1987. *World Development Report*. Washington, DC: World Bank.

WORLD BANK 1985. *China*. Baltimore: Johns Hopkins University Press.

WORLD BANK 1986a. *Poverty and Hunger*. World Bank Policy Study. Washington, DC: World Bank.

WORLD RESOURCES INSTITUTE 1986. *World Resources 1986*. New York: Basic Books.

WORTMAN, S. and CUMMINGS, R.W. 1978. *To Feed This World*. Baltimore: Johns Hopkins University Press.

YANOWITCH, M. 1977. *Social and Economic Inequality in the Soviet Union*. London: Martin Robertson.

YAPA, L. 1979. Ecopolitical economy of the Green Revolution. *Professional Geographer*, 31, 371–6.

YATES, R. L. 1959. *Forty Years of Foreign Trade*. London: Allen & Unwin.

YOFFIE, D.B. 1983. *Power and Protectionism: Strategies of the Newly Industrializing Countries*. New York: Columbia University Press.

YUILL, D., ALLEN, K., and HULL, C. 1980. *Regional Policy in the European Community: the role of regional incentives*. Beckenham: Croom Helm.

ZIMBALIST, A. 1987. Cuban industrial growth, 1965–84. *World Development*, 15, 83–93.

ZIMBALIST, A. and ECKSTEIN, S. 1987. Patterns of Cuban development: the first twenty years. *World Development*, 15, 5–22.

Index